SERIOUS PLAY

UNIVERSITY SEMINARS

LEONARD HASTINGS SCHOFF MEMORIAL LECTURES

The University Seminars at Columbia University sponsor an annual series of lectures, with the support of the Leonard Hastings Schoff and Suzanne Levick Schoff Memorial Fund. A member of the Columbia faculty is invited to deliver before a general audience three lectures on a topic of his or her choosing. Columbia University Press publishes the lectures.

David Cannadine, *The Rise and Fall of Class in Britain* 1993

Charles Larmore, *The Romantic Legacy* 1994

Saskia Sassen, *Sovereignty Transformed: States and the New Transnational Actors* 1995

Robert Pollack, *The Faith of Biology and the Biology of Faith: Order, Meaning, and Free Will in Modern Medical Science* 2000

Ira Katznelson, *Desolation and Enlightenment: Political Knowledge After the Holocaust, Totalitarianism, and Total War* 2003

Lisa Anderson, *Pursuing Truth, Exercising Power: Social Science and Public Policy in the Twenty-first Century* 2003

Partha Chatterjee, *The Politics of the Governed: Reflections on Popular Politics in Most of the World* 2004

David Rosand, *The Invention of Painting in America* 2004

George Rupp, *Globalization Challenged: Conviction, Conflict, Community* 2007

Lesley A. Sharp, *Bodies, Commodities, and Technologies* 2007

SERIOUS PLAY

DESIRE AND AUTHORITY

IN THE POETRY OF

OVID, CHAUCER, AND ARIOSTO

ROBERT W. HANNING

Columbia University Press ♔ New York

COLUMBIA UNIVERSITY PRESS

PUBLISHERS SINCE 1893

NEW YORK   CHICHESTER, WEST SUSSEX

Library of Congress Cataloging-in-Publication Data

Hanning, Robert W.

Serious play : desire and authority in the poetry of Ovid, Chaucer, and Ariosto / Robert W. Hanning.

p. cm.—(Leonard Hastings Schoff memorial lectures)

Includes bibliographical references and index.

ISBN 978-0-231-15210-5 (cloth : acid-free paper)—ISBN 978-0-231-52639-5 (e-book)

1. Comic, The, in literature.   2. Desire in literature.   3. Authority in literature.   4. Ovid, 43 B.C.–17 or 18 A.D.—Criticism and interpretation. 5. Chaucer, Geoffrey, d. 1400—Criticism and interpretation.   6. Ariosto, Lodovico, 1474–1533—Criticism and interpretation.   I. Title.   II. Series.

PN56.C66H36 2010

809'.917—dc22

2010003740

Columbia University Press books are printed on permanent and durable acid-free paper.

This book is printed on paper with recycled content.

Printed in the United States of America

c 10 9 8 7 6 5 4 3 2 1

References to Internet Web sites (URLs) were accurate at the time of writing. Neither the author nor Columbia University Press is responsible for URLs that may have expired or changed since the manuscript was prepared.

CONTENTS

PREFACE AND ACKNOWLEDGMENTS

My mother, may she rest in peace, was guided through her long life by an impressive collection of aphorisms; among her favorites was "an open confession is good for the soul." Since I have always tried to be an obedient son, I will begin this volume with a confession, an explanation, and then a few heartfelt statements of gratitude. I confess, then, that I never expected to give the lectures on which these chapters are based at the point in my life, and academic career, when I did. But having been invited to deliver the thirteenth annual Leonard Hastings Schoff Lectures at Columbia University in October 2005, I decided, not without considerable trepidation, to share with an educated general audience my admiration and affection for three European poets whom I have come to know and love through decades of teaching them to undergraduates and graduates, primarily at Columbia University but also en passant at Yale, Princeton, Johns Hopkins, and at the Bread Loaf School of English of Middlebury College and Lincoln College, Oxford. Specifically, I proposed to consider some of the cultural anxieties that underlie, and social or political crises that activate, the comic poetry of Augustan Rome's Publius Ovidius Naso, fourteenth-century London's Geoffrey Chaucer, and early-sixteenth-century Ferrara's Ludovico Ariosto. Ovid's career in Rome coincided with the triumph of centralized imperial power, in the person of Augustus, over the institutions of the Roman republic. Chaucer composed most of his major poetry in the politically fraught and ultimately catastrophic reign of Richard II, deposed in 1399 and subsequently murdered. Ariosto was a courtier and sometime public servant of the Este dynasty, despotic rulers of a small, northern Italian city-state, the independence of which was perpetually threatened by the larger, more powerful political entities that surrounded it. The duchy of Ferrara only survived because the Este sold their services as mercenaries to the highest bidder—in the process entering into cynical and constantly shifting alliances with their grander neighbors—during a period when Italy was under constant occupation by the armies of the several European states fighting for hegemony over all or parts of the Italian peninsula.

As I have taught, so have I learned, and these chapters are dedicated to all the students who have shared my enjoyment and expanded my understanding of Ovid, Chaucer, and Ariosto, but especially to the participants in my graduate seminar on these poets—my first attempt at treating them all and exclusively in one course—in the fall 2004 semester in Columbia's Department of English and Comparative Literature. Without the insights and enthusiasm of my students, my Schoff Lectures could never have been delivered, which is not to say that they are in any way responsible for errors and infelicities in the revised versions that follow.

The same disclaimer applies to the contribution and support of two dear friends: first, my longtime colleague David Rosand, Meyer Schapiro Professor of Art History at Columbia, with whom I taught many times an undergraduate seminar on myths of love in the art and literature of the Renaissance, in which Ovid and Ariosto are featured players. In the spring of 2005, in chatting with David about this and that, I made the fatal mistake of mentioning that as a result of the wonderful time I had had with the students in that graduate seminar on (with apologies to messrs Pavarotti, Domingo, and Carreras) The Three Poets, I was thinking of attempting, some time in the distant future, a little monograph on them: nothing particularly scholarly, more in the nature of an appreciation (that old-fashioned term!). Scarcely were the words out of my mouth when David was on his way to (or on the phone with) Prof. Robert Belknap, the director of Columbia's University Seminar Program (the immediate sponsor of the Schoff Lectures), nominating me for the next installment in a series to which he (Prof. Rosand) had made such a distinguished contribution a few years earlier. The rest, as they say, is history—a history for which I pronounce myself deeply indebted to the University Seminars, to Prof. Belknap, and to his assistant, Ms. Alison Garforth—as I suddenly had to face the daunting prospect of actually trying to make sense of these three great comic poets in only a few months, and for what I would have to call their (and my) ideal audience. You must believe, O ideal audience (now metamorphosed into what I hope will be an ideal, or at least tolerant, readership), that I pronounced Prof. Rosand's name in conjunction with short, until recently unprintable locutions more than once during the intervening period of gestation as I struggled to discharge the obligation placed on me by his act of friendship, by my prospective listeners, and above all by those exemplary bards. Now, however, all is written—and revised for publication—for better or for worse, so all is forgiven. Seriously, thank you, David, for all you have done for me and been to me over these many years.

I also owe a profound debt of gratitude to Professor Joseph Solodow of Southern Connecticut State University, a brilliant classical scholar and literary critic and a steadfast friend, with whom in years past it was also my pleasure to teach at Columbia and whose exemplary writings about Ovid have long since played a major role in the development of my understanding and embrace of that poet. He has corrected many errors of understanding and translation, and has offered invaluable comments on various parts of the manuscript.

Two colleagues, Profs. Joan Ferrante—dearest, oldest friend and coconspirator!—and Paul Strohm kindly consented to provide introductory remarks to the Chaucer and Ariosto lectures, for which many thanks. And thanks as well to the members of the unofficial group of New York area medievalists, the "New York Meds"—beginning its twenty-first year as I write this—to which I presented an early version of the Ovid lecture; their helpful criticism on this and many other occasions been an unfailing source of encouragement and friendship.

Thanks to Alice Newton, administrator of the Columbia University Seminars, for support and assistance when I badly needed it; to Philip Leventhal and Michael Haskell, my editors at Columbia University Press; and to the two anonymous readers of the manuscript, whose suggestions I appreciated (and mostly followed).

As always, a special word of thanks is owed my wife, Professor Barbara Russano Hanning, of the City College of New York and the Ph.D. program in Music of the City University of New York, who has done yeoman service as, among many other things, my comic muse for the last forty-six-plus years and who has suggested many improvements in the diction of both text and (in the case of Ovid) translations; and to our daughter Biagina, who was deprived of her, and my, Saturday morning softball game for many a week because of these lectures. (Gina, blame Prof. Rosand.)

Finally, a comment on my translation policy, which may prove startling to some of my readers. For Chaucer, I have offered no ongoing translation, only some glossing of words or phrases; his English is close enough to ours that

I would not deny my readers the peculiar pleasure of enjoying his poetry as he wrote it. For Ariosto, I have followed the safer course of providing (with occasional modifications) the standard English translation by Guido Waldman, admirable in its accuracy and fluency, though (alas!) in prose. My main innovation involves Ovid. On the basis of my understanding (articulated early in the chapter on his amatory poetry) that the social and sexual milieux of Ovid's Rome were in many ways similar to those of today's New York City—in both cases, the milieux in question represent only a tiny slice of a very large metropolitan pie—I have attempted to translate the passages I quote into a version of colloquial New York speech, often rendering the Latin quite freely but seeking throughout to be faithful to how I believe Ovid would have responded to partner (and sexual satisfaction) seeking, dating, and entering into, or escaping from, relationships as practiced in twenty-first-century Gotham. The results may not please everyone—especially classicists?—and are in any case bound to be ephemeral, as language conventions and fads change frequently. But since the same can be said of most literary criticism (including these lectures-turned-chapters), there is perhaps an appropriateness (if not always a success) to my efforts.

RWH

INTRODUCTION

We live in times that are favorable to laughter.

—Stéphane Guillon, French satirist

You cannot be memorably funny without at some point raising topics which the rich, the powerful, and the complacent would prefer to see left alone.

—George Orwell

For as long as I can remember, I have been strongly attracted to good comic writing. This is partly because I really do believe that a daily dose of laughter is beneficial to one's mental (and perhaps physical) health and partly because I find much human behavior (beginning with my own) and much institutional policy (beginning with that of the institution that employed me for forty-five years) quite ridiculous, in ways that prompt either howls of laughter or tears of despair. Given my already stated commitment to the former, I'm drawn to the kind of commentary on people and institutions that provides me with my minimum daily requirement. But it's also the case that I am fascinated by the ways in which the best comic writers offer both amusement at and sympathy for the human condition: not a simple task, nor one deserving of the patronization that such writers have all too frequently suffered at the hands of the high priests of high seriousness.

The following chapters offer appreciations of three premodern comic poets— Publius Ovidius Naso of Augustan Rome, Geoffrey Chaucer of late-medieval London, and Ludovico Ariosto of the high-Renaissance Italian court of the

Este dukes of Ferrara—specifically, appreciations of how these privileged individuals, writing basically for elite audiences, make comedy out of two very
dangerous topics, *desire* and *authority*. I want to stress the word "appreciations"
because it signifies that my desired target for this book is the educated, general
reader of reasonably wide, indeed, catholic tastes. This is not a scholarly work;
however, its form and methods should not be taken as in any way a critique of
the myriad scholarly investigations that my chosen texts have attracted, and
from which the understanding of them has profited, over the last century and
beyond. I am the profoundly grateful beneficiary of scholarship on and criticism of Ovid, Chaucer, and Ariosto, and I have tried to indicate specific instances of indebtedness in my notes and bibliography. But my research for the
following chapters has, by design, not been exhaustive. My goal is not to alert
my readers to the current state of Ovidian, Chaucerian, or Ariostan scholarship
but rather to explain, as clearly and persuasively—but also as entertainingly—as
I can, why I find these great comic writers not only fun to read but also challenging to think about (and with) and ultimately deeply instructive on personal, social, and political issues, both of their times and places and of our own.
My fondest hope is that as a result of reading these essays of appreciation and
elucidation, the reader will be tempted to discover for him- or herself the pleasures of firsthand acquaintance with their subjects.

A few words about how I arrived at my choice of topics seem in order. In the
fall 2004 semester, I offered my final solo seminar after forty years of teaching
in Columbia University's Graduate Program in English and Comparative Literature. Believing that although *"aller Anfang ist schwer,"* every ending should
be fun, I decided to make my last hurrah a last guffaw as well, by proposing a
seminar in appreciation of my three favorite comic poets, whom I had taught
many times before but never as an ensemble. To my pleasant surprise, sixteen
students signed up for the seminar, which, thanks to them, became one of my
most exciting and satisfying teaching experiences.

From our discussions emerged two concerns central to all three poets: desire,
with its capacity to make the men and women in its grasp behave selfishly, desperately, and, above all, foolishly; and authority—be it political, social, religious, or cultural—the wielders and defenders of which all too frequently open
themselves to ridicule by their tyranny, vanity, hypocrisy, or downright inepti-
tude. Ovid, Chaucer, and Ariosto share a need to speak comic truth to power,
challenging or mocking the claims of both political and literary authority even
as they recognize their dependence on both. Now nibbling, now gnawing at the
hands that feed them, these virtuosi of deflation and disrespect are also abundantly aware of the dangerous game they are playing vis-à-vis the most powerful

members of their respective audiences, patrons and rulers who can reward but also (as Ovid, especially, was to experience) punish. For what defines the world of these comic writers is the fact of so much authority gathered in so few people, not diffused by universal suffrage or by the mass media (and, now, the Internet). To my students, as to me, the resultant high-wire act, in which fantasies of comic audacity seem often to court real rebuke and even disaster, is a central part of the achievement and ongoing attractiveness of these three great poets.

In the spirit of that seminar, then, my goal in the following chapters is a deeper, more satisfying intuition of how such poets go about constructing a world that simultaneously amuses, enlightens, and disturbs us—an exceptional achievement for which Renaissance theorists had a name: *serio ludere*, serious play.

T he challenges posed to the comic poet by the topics of desire and authority are in fact quite divergent. (Since my three poets are men, I'll use the masculine pronoun in generalizing about premodern comic poetry; in the modern era, women novelists and, more recently, women stand-up comedians have successfully overthrown the male hegemony over funny business.) His basic problems in dealing with *desire* are conceptual and technical: what does he want to say about this most universal, most problematic, most exalted, and most easily mocked component of the human affective experience, and how can he say it in a way that is both amusing and, at some level, recognizably truthful? The major challenge is to avoid appearing to stand somewhere outside and above the human condition, looking down from an elevated location on the perplexing, often painful experience of love and lust with an air of superiority, scorn, or judgment. This is the perspective of satire, not of comedy: a perspective that often deploys the tropes and commonplaces of misogyny, misogamy, even misanthropy as shafts of savage indignation launched against an all too easy target, viz., the silly words and sillier deeds of besotted lovers. By contrast, the comic writer must engage desire empathetically, betraying affection for and identification with those caught up in its toils, even as he communicates a lively sense of how ridiculous, how irresistibly funny, the whole business is, as desire bends us out of shape, makes us prey to self-delusion, even makes us sick. He can appropriate the discourses of misogyny and misogamy, but never unironically, always with a wink to the audience that says, in effect, that frustration, hurt feelings, or insecurity may make such formulations attractive as emotional safety valves, but they're not to be confused with the truth—whatever *that* may be.

On the other hand, the peril posed by authority to the premodern comic poet, in particular—one who writes or performs in a milieu dominated politically by emperor, king, or despotic prince and culturally by established "classics" and the achievements of illustrious predecessors—is pragmatic: in training his comic sights on authoritative figures and concepts, how much can he get away with without risking his status, his safety, even his life? How can he laugh at cultural authority without being branded as a philistine or someone with no respect for established excellence, or at political authority, its foibles and follies, its inconsistencies and hypocrisies, its overreaching and underachieving, without feeling its wrath? Can a comic poet ever count on the continued tolerance of even the most permissive patron or prince when his predilection for parody and relish for ridicule focus on the powerful one's personal quirks, ideological imperatives, or announced policies?[1]

It seems to me that the achievement of great comic poets is in fact closely related to their well-honed capacity for outrageousness. To be successfully funny they have to take risks: bringing to the surface in witty, virtuosic language the contradictions and self-aggrandizement lurking beneath the ringing pronouncements and espoused credos of their political leaders; pouncing on the inconsistencies and ridiculing the pieties of the religious, economic, social, and cultural systems to which their audiences subscribe; and (to universalize their appeal and stand the test of time) submitting to hilarious and embarrassing scrutiny the desire-driven routines, transactions, and interpersonal interactions in which all of us engage—that rhizome of strategies for surviving and thriving in which we invest time, energy, pride, and ego.

Such poetry aims to amuse but also to enlighten. Ovid jokingly literalizes the truth-telling aspiration of the comic poet when he "reports" the response of an incredulous young Roman male ("aliquis iuven[is]") to reading the *Amores*: "quo ab indice doctus / composuit casus iste poeta meos [what bigmouth spilled the beans to that poet about *my* love life]?" (*Amores* 2.1.9–10). In fact, however, truth telling can also rebound on its maker in the form of censure or worse. To be really effective, the premodern comic poet had to skate on thin ice: if the ice held, he reaped the rewards of enjoyment and appreciation from his well-placed audience, plus support and advancement from official patrons or other powerful well-wishers; if it cracked, he could find himself in some very cold water indeed.

Of the poets under consideration in the following chapters, Ovid most clearly takes aim at contemporary ideological programs, in their often hypocritical relationship to actual patterns of behavior.[2] Ovid is also the comic poet of lifestyles, whose poetry is, to borrow A. O. Scott's description (in the *New York Times*) of politically oriented late-night television comedy, "wired into every fluctuation of the zeitgeist"—or at least into major fluctuations in the zeitgeist of Augustan Rome, including its culture's many gaps between ideology and practice. Nonetheless, the aim of the *Amores* and *Ars amatoria* is less "calibrated to flatter the moral and intellectual self-regard of [its] audience" (to quote Scott again) than it is to amuse them by offering a comic mirror of their erotic behavior, its foibles and inconsistencies, and thereby—who knows?—perhaps to encourage insights that might undermine their "self-regard" as members of a powerful, modern elite enjoying the pleasures afforded by life in the world's capital city.[3]

Chaucer's comic poetry centers more on his narratorial persona's outsider status, combining frequently expressed inadequacy or perplexity with respect to desire, intimidation in the face of illustrious literary forbears (ancient or recent), and defensiveness in response to the disrespect, patronization, or outright antipathy he experiences, or anticipates, from those in his audience (be they kings, bossy innkeepers, or skeptical lovers) who declare (or might declare) their authority to judge him and his writings. Richard Firth Green and other Chaucerian critics see in this strategy of negative self-presentation a risible mimesis of the poet's position vis-à-vis the court, the Crown, and the nobility to whom he turned for patronage and advancement; one could also argue that it plays out, at the metaphoric level of personal inferiority, the situation of the language (English) in which he addresses a court audience accustomed to seeking entertainment in French texts. The perils and self-exculpatory gestures of the translator and "lewed compilatour" (i.e., uneducated collector of material authored by others) are as much staples of the Chaucerian repertory as are the repeated statements of being "unlikely" or unschooled in matters of the heart.[4]

At least later in his poetic career, Chaucer's major audience was probably not the court per se, but rather a London cohort of literate clerks, lawyers, royal household knights, and government bureaucrats: a fairly new stratum that existed in a complex economic, social, and political relationship to more established structures of power and rank. Hence, even as the poet's enactment of inferiority—especially in the Prologue to the *Legend of Good Women* (about which I will have a good deal to say)—reflected his recognition of his delicate relationship to King Richard II and his court during the 1380s (a decade that featured Richard's quarrels with some of his most powerful subjects and Chaucer's consequent vulnerability as the king's appointee to the Controllership of Customs for the Port of London), that self-denigrating posture could also serve a separate function as a comic mirror for his London circle, recording or prompting that group's wry meditations on the tension between its importance to the state and its near-invisibility in traditional "estates" thinking.[5]

Perhaps the most ingenious form taken by a comic mirror is that found in Ariosto's *Orlando Furioso*, where the poet invents several narratorial surrogates, among them the sycophantic courtier and the passion-addled lover of a "cruel" (that is, sexually unresponsive) mistress. Through these figures (the latter based in part on the Ovidian narrator-lover of the *Amores*, as well as on the frustrated protagonists of the Petrarchan lyric and its many Renaissance imitators), the comic writer becomes a full participant in the world at which he is laughing. But then, at the exact midpoint of the *Furioso*, Ariosto has his amorous narrator claim that he is experiencing a lucid interval ("lucido intervallo"), during which he can see clearly the damage that desire inflicts on him and all other lovers. That lucid interval—of uncertain duration and origin—can stand as a metaphor for the insight of the comic writer that enables him to hold up the mirror of ridicule and complaint—not the satirist's savage scorn—to the world of which he is an inhabitant, the crazy game in which, though an astute spectator, he's also a player. Moreover, in what might be called an externalized lucid interval a few cantos later, the poet has no less exalted a personage than one of the four authors of the Christian Gospels—those repositories of divine truth—explain to a knight, while on a visit to the Moon (!), that poets who celebrate the exploits of heroes and the virtues of rulers, thus supporting both cultural and political authority (as the Ariostan courtier-narrator repeatedly does), are in fact notorious liars!

In the chapters that follow, then, I will attempt to characterize the themes of desire and authority as crises that function with cultural specificity to the moment in which, and audience for which, the poets wrote; as indices of the human condition conceived of, rightly or wrongly, as universal and timeless; and as literal or metaphorical representations of the difficult situation of the poet and his muse or vocation vis-à-vis the social and political powers on which his success, livelihood, and even personal safety depend. Responding with laughter to such a taxonomy of troubles might at first seem inappropriate, but I'm sure it's just the response Ovid, Chaucer, and Ariosto would have wanted, and indeed worked hard to provoke.

A NOTE ON TEXTUAL REFERENCES

Ovid: Quotations from and references to the *Amores* give the book number followed by the number of the poem within that book, then the line number(s) within the poem, e.g., *Amores* 1.6.9–16. Quotations from and references to the *Ars amatoria*, *Metamorphoses*, and *Tristia* give the book number followed by the line number(s) within that book, e.g., *Ars* 2.305–10. Quotations from and references to the *Remedia amoris* and *Medicamina faciei* give only line number(s), as these works are not subdivided.

Chaucer: Quotations from and references to *The Book of the Duchess*, *The Parlement of Foules*, *Anelida and Arcite*, *The House of Fame*, and *The Legend of Good Women* give the line numbers of these poems. (*The House of Fame* is divided into books, and the *Legend* into Prologue and separate tales, but in both cases the line numbering is consecutive.) Quotations from and references to *Troilus and Criseyde* give the book number followed by the line number(s) within that book, e.g., *TC* 2.1–49. Quotations from and references to the General Prologue and tales of *The Canterbury Tales* follow the system adopted in the standard edition (*The Riverside Chaucer*, 3rd ed.), which is based on the order and grouping of tales and their interconnecting links found in the so-called Ellesmere manuscript (written within a few years of Chaucer's death); for each tale the number of its group is followed by its line number(s), e.g., *CT* 1.26–35.

Ariosto: Quotations from the *Orlando Furioso* follow the third (final) edition of the poem published by Ariosto, which has forty-six books, or cantos. Each canto is divided into eight-line stanzas (octaves, *ottave*). It's customary, in quoting from or referring to the poem, to give the canto number followed by the octave number and the line number(s) within the octave, e.g., *OF* 1.7.1–6.

NOTES

1. Prof. Robert Provine, on *The Leonard Lopate Show*, radio program, WNYC, New York, 16 November 2007, "Please Explain: Laughter," pointed out that Plato worries about comedy in the *Republic*, while Eco's *Name of the Rose* plays with the idea that comedy is subversive of the fear of God (and therefore of God's authority and, by extension, the authority of the institutional Church, as God's presumed mouthpiece, to control behavior in God's name).

2. Cf. twenty-first-century media comedy directed at the G. W. Bush administration and its war hawks who never served in the armed forces and may well have cheated to avoid doing so.

3. See A. O. Scott, "Falling-Down Funny," *New York Times Magazine*, 12 November 2006, 22–24.

4. See Richard Firth Green, "The Familia Regis and the Familia Cupidinis," in *English Court Culture in the Later Middle Ages*, ed. V. J. Scattergood and J. W. Sherborne (New York: St. Martin's, 1983), 87–108. Green sums up the issue thus, in *Poets and Princepleasers: Literature and the English Court in the Late Middle Ages* (Toronto: University of Toronto Press, 1980), 112: "Chaucer's self-depreciation . . . , for all its playful irony, reflects a quite genuine change that had come about in the

relationship between the poet and his audience with the passing of the relatively independent status of the professional minstrel."

Chaucer refers to himself as "but a lewd compilatour of the labour of olde astrologiens" in the Preface to his *Treatise on the Astrolabe* (a navigational instrument) (*Riverside Chaucer*, gen. ed. Larry Benson [Boston: Houghton Mifflin, 1987], 662). For a discussion of this phrase and the concept behind it see A. J. Minnis, *Medieval Theory of Authorship* (London: Scolar, 1984), 190–210.

5. On the doctrine or, more precisely, the rhetorical construct, of the three estates of society—those who pray (the clergy), those who fight (knights and other professional soldiers), those who labor (traditionally, the peasantry)—see Georges Duby, *The Three Orders: Feudal Society Imagined*, trans. Arthur Goldhammer (Chicago: University of Chicago Press, 1980). For a sermon on the three estates preached in Chaucer's London, 1387, see Ione Kemp Knight, ed., *Wimbledon's Sermon: Redde rationem villicationis tue* [Render an account of your stewardship], *a Middle English Sermon of the Fourteenth Century* (Pittsburgh, Penn.: Duquesne University Press, 1967). On Chaucer's audience, see this volume chapter 2, note 2.

SERIOUS PLAY

1

OVID'S AMATORY POETRY

ROME IN A COMIC MIRROR

The amatory poetry of Publius Ovidius Naso consists of three books of *Amores* (elegies mostly about love and lovers) and two pseudo-textbooks: the *Ars amatoria* (an expert's guide in skillful loving) and the *Remedia amoris* (how to fall out of love or a guide for the unhappily hooked). In its pseudo-autobiographical account of episodes in the amorous life of a poet-lover,[1] who by turns relishes the heights and laments the depths to which his passions transport him, the *Amores* hews to but also virtuosically expands the conventions of elegiac love poetry developed, during the latter years of the first century B.C.E., by Ovid's older contemporaries, Gallus, Propertius, and Tibullus. By contrast, the *Ars amatoria* offers its prescriptions for satisfying erotic desire (supposedly without succumbing to passion's complexities and humiliations) to male and female neophytes through the mediation of a self-appointed professor of love, the *magister* or *praeceptor amoris*, who bases his expertise, more or less, on the very experiences he had as the protagonist of the *Amores*, now pedantically elevated to pedagogical (and frequently self-deconstructing) exemplarity as strategies of deceitful ingratiation in deed and, especially, word. Central to this proposed exercise in picking up, making out, and getting in is the *magister*'s embrace, for himself and his students, of a program of urbane self-fashioning that improves on nature by means of artful but low-keyed grooming and deportment and is on calculated display in the public spaces and at the public activities and amusements of Augustan Rome. The *magister* calls this skill set "*cultus*"; today's urbanites—especially those resident in cities such as New York, the Rome of the twenty-first century—may recognize its practitioners as Ovidian (and therefore somewhat tongue-in-cheek) versions of cool, with-it metrosexuals.

As Vergil is the poet par excellence of the Roman Empire, so Ovid is the quintessential poet of the *urbs*, the city of Rome as a cosmopolitan center: a depot of the wealth (and talent) of empire and (at least to judge from Ovid's admittedly exaggerated representation of it) a place where people of leisure (both native-born and immigrant) pursue their needs and agendas with a certain characteristic urban style, seeking advantage and pleasure, especially sexual pleasure, through strategies of self-construction and deception. Ovid's poetry balances a genuine affection for this *urbs* with a constant, ironically inflected amusement at the snobbery, assumptions of sexual entitlement, and self-aggrandizing (not to say, self-delusory) antics of its urbane, sophisticated denizens. The effect of his combination of amatory discourses and personae, with its mélange of conquests and failures, its bouillabaisse of anticipation, anxiety, frustration, and disappointment, is to create a comically distorted image, by turns sympathetic and risible, of some of the erotic fantasies, expectations, and practices (including letdowns) current among young members of Ovid's socioeconomically elite Roman audience: a funhouse mirror allowing part of his audience, at least, to see a version of itself in what we might call truthful distortion, while providing amusement for older, supposedly wiser members of that same audience.

Like many of today's comic performers, such as stand-up comedians and late-night talk-show hosts, Ovid found inspiration for his wit in the complexities and frustrations of human relationships and also in the inevitable gaps between institutional ideals and ideologies, on the one hand, and the foibles, follies, and hypocrisies of social and political reality, on the other. In his comic writings—and in many parts of his less overtly or completely comic poems, such as the *Heroides* and the *Metamorphoses*—he communicates a profound understanding of the disappointment and impotence (literal and metaphorical) that result from hopes dashed, aspirations thwarted, and self-esteem mocked in our encounters with ultimately unmanageable desire—the varieties and complexities of which resist control and deliver pain as often as pleasure—and with the forces of external authority that threaten personal autonomy and the pursuit of happiness. All of which is to say that the Ovidian comic mirror also reflects important truths—told, to be sure, with comic obliquity—about people (metonymically, lovers and poets), their needs, and the settings in which they pursue those needs.

Hence, intertwined with its explorations of the pitfalls and pratfalls of desire, Ovid's amatory poetry offers seriocomic meditations on authority, which it confronts, directly and obliquely, from two perspectives, at once objecting to the tyranny and mocking the futility of attempts to impose limits on personal freedom—and especially on the quest for satisfaction of personal desires—by means of draconian laws, appeals to traditional values, and even the re-creation of Rome's urban topography in the image of the *princeps*, Augustus—all in service to the ideology of empire. Roman elegiac poetry, of which the *Amores* are arguably the supreme example, focused on personal experiences of desire and grief; it exalted leisure and the leisurely pastimes—including lovemaking—collectively described by the Latin term *otium*, over the active life of self-advancement and contribution to the common good, designated in Latin by *otium*'s antonym, *negotium*. Elegiac protagonists usually opted for genteel poverty instead of pushy, uncouth wealth, for making love instead of war, and for chasing other peoples' wives or concubines instead of being married with children, in accord with the laws rewarding marriage and punishing adultery imposed on Rome's citizens by imperial authority. The cultural cheek of all of Ovid's amatory poetry—*Ars* and *Remedia* as well as *Amores*—enacts disrespect for authority, even the self-proclaimed authority of the *magister amoris*, but also ruefully recognizes the often irresistible power—of Caesar, of Cupid (the latter perhaps a stand-in for the former)—arrayed against its imaginings of pleasure and freedom. How fitting, if unfortunate, that the poet ended his life in exile from Rome imposed on him by the emperor whose supreme authority Ovid laughed at, feared, and completely understood.

A s was the case with many other Roman men of letters of his and later eras, Ovid was not a native of the city that inspired his comic genius and was the scene of his fall from imperial grace. Born in 43 B.C.E. in Sulmona, about ninety miles southeast of Rome in what is now the Abruzzi, Ovid was the younger of two sons of a family of established equestrian rank, that is, the class below the senatorial. He came to Rome as a young man after studies in Sulmona and Athens and continued his rhetorical education in Rome. (About twenty years after Ovid's death in 18 C.E., Seneca the Elder, in the preface to his retrospective collection of exercises practiced in Roman schools of rhetoric [*Controversiae* 2.2.12], noted that Ovid didn't much care for logical argumentation as a student, preferring instead the freer form of persuasive rhetoric that would eventually form the basis for the pleading letters of the *Heroides*.)

The poet himself tells us, in an autobiographical poem written in exile, that his father sought to discourage him from a literary career, warning that even Homer had died poor (*Tristia* 4.10.21–22). It was advice that Ovid tried yet

failed to follow, but he did in effect memorialize it in a passage of the *Ars ama-*
toria where the *magister amoris* tells his male students that since the desirable
women of Rome are all gold diggers—and Rome is full of available *nouveaux*
riches, profiteers from the extended period of civil wars—they aren't much impressed by suitors who try to offer as gifts poems (such as Ovid's, presumably).
If Homer himself came without a more tangible (not to say fungible) gift, he'd
quickly be shown the door:

> Quid tibi praecipiam teneros quoque mittere versus?
>   Ei mihi, non multum carmen honoris habet.
> Carmina laudantur, sed munera magna petuntur. . . .
> Ipse licet venias Musis comitatus, Homere,
>   Si nihil attuleris, ibis, Homere, foras.

(Should I also advise you to send tender poems as gifts? It's a shame, but
poetry doesn't rank very high in that department. Sure, your poems will
be praised, but it's gifts with big price tags that are in demand. . . . If you,
yourself, Homer, should show up with the Muses as your entourage, but
you have nothing high-end to offer, then, Homer, it's right back out the
door for you!)   (*Ars* 2.273–75, 279–80)

Ovid's publication of the *Amores* at about age twenty established his reputation; during the next two decades he consolidated it, probably revising the
elegy collection and composing the *Ars amatoria*, the *Remedia amoris*, and the
Heroides, a collection of letters on amorous themes supposedly written by heroines (and in a few cases heroes) of classical legend.[2] As a result of the popularity of these works, which Ovid read aloud to gatherings drawn from Rome's
small elite that patronized and enjoyed the arts,[3] the poet became famous and
reasonably well off.

He was wedded three times; only the third marriage proved lasting and
happy, surmounting even the aggravated circumstances of his exile, in which his
wife did not accompany him. That exile came at the height of his success, in the
year 8 of our era, when Ovid ran afoul of the only true source of unbridled political authority in his world: Octavianus Augustus, the grandnephew and adopted son of Julius Caesar who, since his triumph over Antony and Cleopatra in
the battle of Actium (31 B.C.E.), which ended a long and disastrous period of
civil war engulfing not just the Italian peninsula but the entire eastern Mediterranean, reigned as absolute ruler, or *princeps*, over the Roman empire, however

much he contrived for some years to occlude that absoluteness. Suddenly, and
for reasons still not fully understood, Augustus banished—or, more precisely,
relegated—Ovid for life to Tomi, an outpost on the Black Sea (in present-day
Romania) at the very edge of the Roman Empire. ("*Relegatio* was milder than the
exilium of the late republic in that the poet's property was not confiscated and his
civic rights were not taken from him, but it was harsher, in Ovid's case, in that he
was ordered to stay in one designated locality".)[4]

The imperial capital city that Ovid was forced to leave far behind, and for
his return to which he apparently never ceased to hope and agitate (albeit
unsuccessfully), was, as I have already mentioned, the ultimate destination of
wealth and immigrants from all over the empire; here is how one recent histo-
rian of Rome describes it:

> As the capital of the western world, Rome was the brain and stomach of
> a vast organism, the Roman empire. The city consumed large amounts of
> grain which the provinces furnished as tribute, and in return Rome guar-
> anteed peace and security for the subject peoples. . . . The population of
> the capital . . . probably exceeded a half million permanent residents. . . .
> Perhaps a third of the inhabitants of imperial Rome were slaves, and
> many of the free population were descended from slaves. . . . Many pro-
> vincials moved to the capital of their own volition. . . . In many respects,
> imperial Rome was New York on the Tiber, . . . a vast melting pot of many
> ethnic groups. . . . Augustus tried to slow the alien tide and limited the
> freeing of slaves, but his efforts were in vain.[5]

As the spoils of both imperial conquest and commerce poured into Rome, the
urbs especially attracted speculators and *novi homines* (new men) who were not
members of Rome's traditional (and tiny) wealthy elite—some were even freed
slaves—but had profited in various ways during the period of instability marked
by civil war and the resulting proscriptions and confiscations, by the assassination of Julius Caesar, and by the subsequent wars for control of the empire that
ended at Actium.[6]

The new imperial court was a center of intrigue and high living, and wealthy
Romans threw themselves into a life of luxury and little restraint, responding
not only to the resources made available to them by Roman conquests but also
to the loosening, during the period of civil war and mass immigration, of

authority over manners and morals traditionally exercised by noble families and lineages.[7] In its depictions of strategies of seduction and counterbalancing moments of erotic frustration and desperation, Ovid's amatory poetry reflects the undoubtedly widespread quest for personal, sexual satisfaction in a metropolitan center full of attractive strangers: sex and the *urbs*, if you will.[8]

But while the old and new rich of Rome lived the high life and patrons such as Maecenas and Messalla (perhaps Ovid's patron) held dinner parties for their array of clients or encouraged and supported poets such as Vergil, Horace, and Ovid, the vast majority of Romans lived in squalor. To quote Thomas Africa once again:

> Although Augustus bragged that he had found Rome a town of brick and made it a city of marble [Suetonius, "Augustus," 28.3], his boast could literally apply to only a few temples and public buildings. . . . Imperial Rome was not just a collection of public buildings and monuments— it was also a city of homes, most of them shabby. Though handsome villas graced the suburbs and many mansions lay within the city itself, Rome was essentially a great slum, congested, foul-smelling, and noisy. . . . Unable to expand horizontally, Rome swelled upward and became a city of tenements. . . . Jerry-built by unscrupulous contractors, the tenements were enormous firetraps, and the city was often swept by disastrous fires. So crowded were the streets that vehicular traffic was forbidden in the city during daylight hours. . . . At night the city was plunged in darkness and the side streets became a jungle of crime.

The best that could be said for the lives of the vast majority of Romans was that "the inhabitants were clean and bathed with more regularity than any people in European history. The Roman baths were a triumph of hygiene and sane living, compared to which the Middle Ages were a thousand-year stench."[9]

There are no tenements in the Rome of Ovid's amatory poetry; given his social status and that of his audience, this is not surprising.[10] But he couldn't be unaware of—to paraphrase Jacob Riis's famous characterization of the teeming Lower East Side of Manhattan in the late nineteenth and early twentieth centuries—how the other half lived—or, in this case, much more than half. That this is so, at least one oblique reference makes clear: a comic boast by the protagonist, in *Amores* 1.6, to the obdurate doorman barring his access to his *puella* (girl). Emboldened by his passion, he says, he has braved the formerly terrifying night, only to face now the threat of a rejection far worse than any mugging:

At quondam noctem simulacraque vana timebam;
  mirabar, tenebris quisquis iturus erat.
risit, ut audirem, tenera cum matre Cupido
  et leviter "fies tu quoque fortis" ait.
nec mora, venit amor—non umbras nocte volantis,
  non timeo strictas in mea fata manus.
te nimium lentum timeo, tibi blandior uni;
  tu, me quo possis perdere, fulmen habes.

(Once upon a time, I was afraid of the night with its imagined threats;
I was amazed that anyone would dare go out in the dark. Then I heard
Cupid chuckle, and his sweet mother, too, and he announced, "You, too,
are about to become brave." Love came without delay, and now I don't
fear the shadows that fly about at night, nor [imaginary] fists clenched to
do me in [with a blow]. You alone terrify me by being so immovable; I
cringe before you alone. You have the only lightning bolt that can finish
me off.)   (1.6.9–16)

In any case, what we find in Ovid's amatory poetry is not documentary realism but a complex, seriously playful response to a partly observed, partly fantasized *urbs* of wealth and elegance. The emperor's perspective on the capital city
of his empire would, I think, have been quite different. As he contemplated it
from the Palatine, he would have perceived threats to his rule from three quarters: the members of the great oligarchical families that had dominated the
now destroyed Republic, who had not been his supporters during the period of
civil strife and now resented his power over them; the masses, poor and disen-
franchised, who could easily be incited by famine or general discontent to riots
damaging to his authority and to social and political stability; and the liber-
tinism of the cultural elite, both old and new, whose readiness to engage in
adulterous affairs, lack of interest in marriage and childrearing, and general
hedonism ill accorded with *pietas*, or respect, toward traditional Roman values
newly (and officially) espoused by Augustus, and furthermore signalled a will-
ingness to avoid the responsibility of producing a new generation of army offi-
cers and civil servants, needed to govern a far-flung empire.

The emperor's response to these threats took appropriate forms: to pacify
the traditional, pro-Republican oligarchy, Augustus clothed his absolute authority in the rhetoric and institutions of a revived Republic (see Crook, "Augustus"); to satisfy the Roman masses, he distributed free grain to 200,000,
and, as the other component of his famous "bread and circuses" policy, he

established new games and holidays for the enjoyment of all (see Suetonius, "Augustus," 43, in *Lives*)—including free public games ninety-three days each year—thereby dissipating plebeian discontent. As Africa says, "In the excitement of the circus and the fast pace of urban life, the Roman masses could forget their poverty as long as the grain dole was forthcoming" (*Rome of the Caesars*, 17). Against relaxed sexual and marital mores his initiatives were emphatic: on the one hand, he offered rewards to women who bore a large number of children and instituted penalties for those who had not married or had children by a certain age; on the other, the *lex Julia de adulteriis coercendis* of 18 B.C.E. established a permanent court to enforce strict punishments for female adultery and male *stuprum* (i.e., adultery or fornication by a Roman man, at least of upper class, with any "respectable" woman—a category, according to the most stringent recent scholarly interpretation, that excluded only prostitutes and their pimps [*lenae*]). The *lex Julia* also set sharp limits on the nature and extent of the traditionally sanctioned, purely intrafamilial punishments for a woman's sexual transgression, as, for example, the right of husband or father to kill with impunity a wife or daughter caught *in flagrante delicto* with her lover. The actual success and extent of this legislation, which is only known to us from much later commentaries by Roman legists, is a matter of debate among classical scholars, but its intent—to control male and, especially, female sexuality and limit the chances for illegitimate children—is clear enough.[11]

Finally, in his new role as first citizen of a supposedly rejuvenated Republic presiding over a world empire, Augustus undertook building campaigns that resulted in new temples, monuments, and fora (see Suetonius, "Augustus," 29), testaments in gold and marble to Roman power but also carefully inscribed with words and images that celebrated (and thus constructed) the de facto emperor's role as Rome's protector and parent: the *pater patriae*, the possessor on a universal scale of the absolute authority claimed by the *paterfamilias* in the traditional noble Roman family (Crook, "Augustus," 133). When book 8 of Vergil's *Aeneid*—that bittersweet, often minor-key hymn to imperial Rome and its leader—describes Aeneas's embassy to Evander, king of the Arcadians, whose village stood on the future site of Rome, it offers several passages contrasting, implicitly or explicitly, the primitive dwellings and shrines observed by the Trojan leader with the glorious edifices destined to be built in those very places under the Augustan aegis.

It is, I believe, in the context of all this Augustan activity designed to shore up and glorify the empire and its de facto ruler that we must place Ovid's amatory poetry if we are to understand the nature and extent of its challenges to Augustus's authority. Even if these challenges did not directly result in the poet's ban-

ishment, they may have mined a rich vein of resentment at imperial policies felt
by members of his elite audience. For instance, there was surely some resistance
within that audience to Augustan hegemony; furthermore, if we are to believe
Suetonius's description, in his *Life of Augustus*, of the emperor's amorous propen-
sities ("Augustus," 69, 71), there would have been discontent at the hypocrisy involved in the imperial insistence on sexual restraint and constancy and, vis-à-vis
court luxury, at the programmatic exaltation of traditional Roman virtues—
hard work, simple living, devotion to the good of the state, and piety toward the
gods—as salutary alternatives to the supposed decadence and irresponsibility of
contemporary Roman life and its urbane pursuits.[12] The comic mirror that Ovid
holds up to his city's sophisticated seekers of erotic pleasure, even as it invites
laughter at the excesses and delusions of their quests, reflects the tension between *princeps* and conservative opinion, on one side, and "modern" relaxation of
limits and mores, on the other, by placing under negative scrutiny ideologies that
value the past over the present, public duty and self-sacrifice over private self-
fulfillment, and making war or money over making love.

I'll have more to say later in this chapter about the presence of Augustus,
represented directly or obliquely, in the amatory poetry. The unavoidable reality of imperial power and authority lurks behind Ovid's fanciful depiction, in
many passages of both the *Amores* and the *Ars amatoria*, of a capricious, relent-
less, irresistible god of love. Conversely, the limits of that power, in the face of
personal desires, find subversive embodiment in the *magister amoris*, whose attempts to impose the restraint of *ratio* (system) on the passionate force (*impetus*) of desire repeatedly collapse—his authority, in this context, mocked by the
power of that same "fierce boy" (*saevus puer*), Cupid.

O vid's amatory verse is written in elegiac couplets: usually closed couplets
with a hexameter first line and a pentameter second. According to traditions well established by Ovid's time, such elegiac verse was reserved for
lighter or more personal subjects—such as expressions of love or sorrow—while
weightier subjects—for example, history- or tradition-based epics—were to be
expressed in poetry written exclusively in hexameters. According to a hierarchy
of genres within Roman poetics, poems on the public matters—war, heroism,
tragic myths and legends—that constituted a society's identity-defining inheritance of shared stories and values were assumed to be superior in estimation and
worth to the celebration or exploration of private emotions and experiences
(however generically expressed). From this hierarchy of form and matter followed a set of conventions designed to buttress and, as it were, naturalize it.

For example, and most important, the opposition between elegy and more "responsible" genres is frequently assimilated to the dichotomy, which I've already mentioned, between lives of *otium* and *negotium*, the former term signifying idleness, leisure, repose, and (by implication) sloth; the latter, business, occupation, employment, but also household supervision and public affairs—in sum, all the praiseworthy, indeed "masculine" pursuits of the privileged Roman man, by avoidance of which the elegiac love poet and his alter ego protagonist lay themselves open to the further imputation of effeminacy.[13]

During the remarkably brief generative period of Roman elegy—little more than a quarter century—its exponents, including Gallus (whose poetry is lost), Propertius, Tibullus, and Ovid, expressed their resistance to the hierarchy of genres and verse forms and justified their poetic enterprise through a variety of strategies. One of these, deployed to excellent comic effect in the opening elegy of each book of Ovid's *Amores*, is the *recusatio*, a declaration of unwillingness or inability to compose poetry in a genre deemed more worthy or dignified than erotic elegy (cf., for non-Ovidian examples, Propertius, *Elegies*, 2.1, 3.9). More directly, the elegists registered dissent from the Augustan imperial agenda, with its stress on the extension, protection, and administration of a far-flung empire and its moral legislation intended to impose state control over marriage, childrearing, and sexuality. They opposed to this agenda a (mostly fictive) private sphere of desire, praising *otium* and, in effect, thumbing their noses at authoritative canons of respectability—to the amusement, acclaim, and at times, we must assume, disapproval of their elite audiences and powerful patrons. As Gian Biagio Conte puts it, "Elegy inherits, from Catullus chiefly, the sense of moral rebellion, the taste for *otium*, for a life remote from civic and political engagement and disposed instead to cultivate private sentiments and to make them the object of poetic activity."[14]

Ovid was the latest and greatest of the elegists. His boastful but entirely accurate comment says it all: "Tantum se nobis elegi debere fatentur, / Quantum Vergilio nobile debet epos [Elegy acknowledges that it owes as much to me as noble epic does to Vergil]" (*Remedia*, 395–96). His irreverence, comic force, wit, and wordplay extended the impact of the elegy, and he then expanded its generic boundaries in several directions.[15] He created comic textbooks parodying poems, such as Vergil's *Georgics*, that present themselves as guides to a particular human skill or practice: in one of these, the poet instructs women in the art of creating and applying cosmetics (the apparently unfinished *Medicamina faciei*); in others, he rewrites the supposedly autobiographical confessions, boasts, and complaints of the love elegy into a system for finding love (or at least sex) in contemporaneous Rome (*Ars amatoria*), but also for escaping from a love affair gone bad (*Remedia amoris*). The *Heroides* is a collection of supposed letters written by heroines of myth and legend, complaining of their treatment by men (Ovid later added pairs of letters exchanged between legendary heroes and heroines), while the *Fasti* offers a seriocomic commentary on the calendar of Roman feast days. Finally, Ovid returned to the elegiac form in his years of exile, composing the *Tristia*, poems centering on and lamenting his relegation, and the *Ex Ponto*, letters to friends and important Romans, pleading his case (unsuccessfully) for a return to Rome.

Did Ovid's poetry contribute to his relegation? His defense in *Tristia*, book 2, addressed to Augustus, suggests that both *carmen*—"song," in this case, the *Ars amatoria*—and *error*—accidentally (like mythic Actaeon) seeing something he should not have—did him in; the elegy is, however, suspiciously jokey in some of its self-exculpatory moves, so that its sincerity is hard to measure. (See the end of this chapter for a brief comment on book 2 of *Tristia*.) There is, however, a passage in *Remedia amoris* in which Ovid hints at self-censorship owing to the fact that "Nuper enim nostros quidam carpsere libellos, / Quorum censura Musa proterva mea est [For recently some [would-be] critics have been slandering my poems, censuring my Muse as a shameless one]" (*Remedia*, 361–62). Attributing such attacks to envy, and claiming to pay no heed to them "dum toto canter in orbe [as long as my songs are sung everywhere]" (363), the poet nonetheless defends himself by appealing to the very generic conventions at which he elsewhere (and, indeed, perhaps here, too) pokes affectionate fun: he advises the putative critic, "At tu, quicumque es, quem nostra licentia laedit, / Si sapis, ad numeros exige quidque suos [But as for you, whoever you are, whom my [supposed] licentiousness offends, if you were really smart you would recognize the link between my subjects and their verse form]" (371–72). Just as tragedy and epic have their own meters and subject matters, so "Blanda pharetratos Elegia cantet Amores, / Et levis arbitrio ludat amica suo [charming Elegy should sing of Cupid-driven loves, and, in love herself, should be gently playful in exactly the way she chooses]" (379–80). Generic decorum, a foundational concept of Roman literary theory, provides the ultimate justification for Ovid's kind of poetry: not Homer's Achilles or Andromache but the famous courtesan Thais finds an appropriate residence within elegiac poetry: "Thais in arte mea est; lascivia libera nostra est; / Nil mihi cum vitta [the hair band worn by respectable matrons and only them, according to Roman sumptuary laws]; Thais in arte mea est [my poetry is all about Thais; our wantonness is right out in the open. Long skirts and high necklines are definitely not my territory; with me, it's all about Thais]" (385–86). The bookended circularity of this couplet perhaps deliberately reflects the circularity of its argument: I'm writing about the things you are supposed to write about in elegy, and I'm writing in elegy so I can write about those things. That the poet predicts greater triumphs (393–94) might only have further annoyed Augustus (were it he behind Ovid's recognition of disapproving readers).

In this chapter, as already indicated, I'll deal only with the explicitly amatory poetry—*Amores, Ars, Remedia*—plus some analysis of the fragmentary poetic treatise on cosmetics, *Medicamina faciei*, an important example of Ovid's treatment of a central theme of his poetry, namely, the crucial role of *cultus* (self-cultivation, self-construction) in achieving success, especially in one's dealings with the opposite sex (for Ovid, unlike other elegists, adopts a resolutely heterosexual posture in his amatory poetry) (Habinek, "Invention of Sexuality," 31–38). I'll conclude with some final generalizations and a brief analysis of book 2 of *Tristia*.

AMORES: ALWAYS HOPELESS BUT NEVER SERIOUS

The last two lines of Robert Frost's sonnet "The Oven Bird" say of its title creature, "The question that he frames in all but words / Is what to make of a diminished thing." Using words and wit, Ovid imprints the opening of the *Amores* with a double mark of diminution—more precisely of challenged wholeness or integrity—suggesting, I'll argue, that his poetic intention and execution have not emerged unscathed from confronting crises of desire and authority.[16]

First comes *Epigramma ipsius*, the poet's own preliminary comment:

Qui modo Nasonis fueramus quinque libelli,
     tres sumus; hoc illi praetulit auctor opus.
ut iam nulla tibi nos sit legisse voluptas,
     at levior demptis poena duobus erit.

(We who were once Naso's five books [of poems] are now only three; our author preferred this version to that other one. So now, if you take no pleasure in having read us, at least your pain will be reduced by two cutouts).

And then, as the first elegy opens:

Arma gravi numero violentaque bella parabam
     edere, materia conveniente modis.
par erat inferior versus—risisse Cupido
     dicitur atque unum surripuisse pedem.

(I was all set to write about arms and violent wars, in weighty verses yet, with form fitted to contents. The second line matched the first—[but] Cupid, they tell me, laughed as he snuck off with one foot [from the *inferior versus*, the second line].)   (1.1.1–4)

I am not arguing that this reiterated image of truncation, which sends up both the low reputation of the elegy in the hierarchy of genres and the convention of generic decorum (here form determines content, rather than vice versa), identifies the *Amores* as a work memorializing defeat or despair. On the contrary, this is a collection of poems of comic force and impact, full of virtuosity and bravado, rich in wordplay, much of it sexually suggestive, and it boasts undoubted moments of triumph: 1.5, for instance, records the narrator's aggressively successful sexual encounter with his *puella*, Corinna; the opening poem of book 2 exalts the power of humble elegy to secure, more successfully than culturally prestigious epic, its singer's entry into the beloved's bedchamber; and 2.12 opens with a raucous paean of triumph over all the obstacles placed between the narrator and his constant enjoyment of Corinna.

Nonetheless, much of the comedy of the *Amores* derives from its protagonist's all too frequent frustrations and indignities as he seeks to obey the exigencies of his desire, alternately priding himself on being able to get the better of Eros and admitting his complete victimization by the god (and by the *puella*, not always Corinna, who is his erotic quarry); as in most comedy, our laughter is provoked by the exposure of plans foiled, promises broken, boasts shown to be hollow and overreaching, and claims of success premature, exaggerated, incapable of achievement, or downright delusional. Underlying the poet-lover protagonist's hopes and expectations—and occasional erotic triumphs—is a sense of how fragile and fleeting they are and how subject he and they are to the limits placed on them by the vagaries of desire and the many counterposing faces of authority. In sum, beneath the comic surface of the *Amores* is a fear—or suspicion or awareness—of futility, deriving from the presentation of the narrator as a poet all too prone to the irresistible dictates of erotic desire.

Hence, whenever I consider the achievement of the *Amores* and seek to define the nature of Ovidian comedy vis-à-vis its Roman polar opposite, Vergilian *gravitas*, I'm reminded of the old joke that purports to capture the essential difference between Germany's earnest efficiency and Austria's cheerful disorganization: in Berlin (as, e.g., in the *Aeneid*), the dictum goes, things are always serious but never hopeless, while in Vienna (or, *mutatis mutandis*, in the *Amores*) things are always hopeless but never serious.

The narrator-protagonist's plight is well summed up in *Amores* 2.4, the burden of which is that he is attracted to every good-looking Roman girl ("quas tota quisquam probet urbe puellas") he sees; he begins his catalogue of all the types who excite him with this rueful confession:

> Non ego mendosos ausim defendere mores
> falsaque pro vitiis arma movere meis.
> Confiteor—siquid prodest delicta fateri;
> in mea nunc demens crimina fassus eo.
> Odi, nec possum, cupiens, non esse quod odi;
> heu, quam quae studeas ponere ferre grave est!
> Nam desunt vires ad me mihi iusque regendum;
> auferor ut rapida concita puppis aqua.
> Non est certa meos quae forma invitet amores—
> centum sunt causae, cur ego semper amem.

(I haven't got the nerve to defend my faulty morals, or to put on false armor to protect my vices. I confess—if it does me any good to confess my sins; and having confessed, I'm going crazy over those faults of mine. I hate [myself], but no matter how much I want to, I can't stop being what I hate. Oh, God, how hard it is to keep hauling that baggage you're trying to get rid of! For I lack the strength and the superego to control myself; I'm carried away like a boat caught in heavy seas. There's no one kind of beauty that alone turns me on; there are a hundred reasons why I'm always falling in love.)   (2.4.1–10)

(One cannot but recall the song, "When I'm not near the girl I love, I love the girl I'm near," from the Broadway musical, *Finian's Rainbow* [1947], or the Crosby, Stills and Nash analogue, "Love the One You're With.")

Although the Ovidian persona in the *Amores* appears rarely to be in control of his life as either poet *or* lover, this posture affords comic cover for focused commentary on (and at the expense of) both poetic traditions and the cultural climate of Augustan Rome. Habinek (in "Invention of Sexuality") argues that one important component of that climate is the lack of a code of values and standards imposed and shared by a hereditary political (and thus cultural) elite; such a code, formerly maintained by the Senatorial class for its collective social as well as political benefit, was a casualty of the upheavals caused by the civil wars that doomed the Republic, brought newly rich and powerful groups to Rome, and, with Octavian's victory, ushered in the Principate. With many of its traditional social bonds frayed or burst, along with the mores that expressed and strengthened them, Rome became a "world city" full of atomized individuals seeking pleasure and influence by any means possible—a situation that also bred new kinds of frustration, atomization, and alienation, some of which, viewed from a comic, erotic perspective, Ovid dramatizes in the *Amores* under the implied rubric (I would argue) of "always hopeless, never serious."

I n the opening elegy of the *Amores*, in lines already quoted (1–4) the poet-narrator boldly announces an epic subject of potentially Vergilian scope (its opening word, "*arma*," echoing that of the *Aeneid*) and in exact accord with decorum of meter and genre ("materia conveniente modis"). But both the content and form suffer almost immediate deflation, by the god's intervention (3) in stealing a foot from the second line, making it a pentameter and the first two lines an elegiac couplet, quite unsuited to the announced theme of war. There are actually three jokes here at the poet's expense: merely out of a malicious sense of fun (*risisse*), a god can override his professed poetic goal; he isn't in sufficient control of his situation to know exactly what happened to him ("risisse Cupido / dicitur"); and in any case, his intention to compose an epic in its proper meter subverts itself even before Cupid can: the "inferior versus" (2) proclaiming "materia conveniente modis," far from being "par," is already a pentameter!

The outraged poet charges the *saev[us] puer* with meddling where he has no right to and in effect violating divine as well as poetic decorum: "Pieridum vates, non tua turba sumus [we're the Muses' poets, not part of your mob]" (6), he contends; what would happen to the world if Venus and Minerva, Ceres and Diana, or Apollo and Mars exchanged the attributes that define their powers and spheres of influence? Anger quickly gives way to apprehension: is Cupid making a massive power grab, seeking to expand his already great empire, and have Apollo and the poets he patronizes hence lost their autonomy? "An, quod ubique, tuum est? . . . / vix etiam Phoebo iam lyra tuta sua est? [So, is everything everywhere yours? Is even Apollo barely sure his lyre is safe [from you]?]" (15–16).[17] These lines contain both humor at the expense of the self-proclaimed, supposedly exalted (but easily compromised) status of poets and, I would argue, an oblique comment on the consequences of Augustus's seizure of absolute power, however disguised by him as the renovation of the Roman Republic.

The poet's complaint that, thanks to Cupidian intervention, "cum bene surrexit versu nova pagina primo, / attenuat nervos proximus ille meos [sure, the first line on this new page rose up well, but then that second one, its force weakened, just fell flat]" (17–18), alludes ironically to the traditional charge of effeminacy leveled against love poets and their verse by partisans of a more austere, heroic poetic art: the elegiac couplet, however erect [*surrexit*] in its first line, flops in its second.[18] Then, by confessing that he has no "materia . . . numeris levioribus apta [subject appropriate for this lighter verse]" (19), that is, no object of sexual desire, masculine or feminine, "aut puer aut longas compta puella comas [neither a boy nor a girl with beautiful, long hair]" (20), about whom he might write in elegiac couplets, the poet creates a fateful opening for Cupid: willfully misreading a complaint about his indecorous interference as a plea for his erotic assistance, the god chooses an arrow from his quiver and impales the poet with it, in two lines of Ovidian word painting that brilliantly capture the effort involved in a small boy's stretching taut a big bow and finally letting fly its shaft: "lunavitque genu sinuosum fortiter arcum / 'quod' que 'canas, vates, accipe' dixit 'opus!' [so he bent his curved bow way back against his knee, and said, 'Okay . . . poet . . . take . . . *this* as something for you to sing about']" (23–24): on *opus* the arrow is let fly, and all but simultaneously thuds into the heart of its target (cf. *Amores II*, 28).[19]

What's left for the stricken poet is admission of his painful defeat—"Me miserum! . . . / uror, et in vacuo pectore regnat Amor [*Oy, veh!* I'm burning up; Love has set up shop in my once vacant heart]" (25–26)—a farewell to the now forsaken epic subject and meter: "ferrea cum vestris bella valete modis [goodbye, clanking battle poems]!" (28); and an instruction to his Muse henceforth to compose "per undenos . . . pedes" (30), the eleven metrical feet of the elegiac couplet.

In Ovid's hands, the *recusatio* becomes a comic dystopia of poetic inspiration, a testament to the hopelessness of trying to compose on a noble, elevated theme when the god of love (whose tyrannical authority recalls that of the *princeps*) has other plans for you. (It's a sad chronicle of poetic emasculation: that stolen foot sounds suspiciously like a euphemism for another kind of truncation.) But not satisfied to send up in this way the notion that love poetry results from passion rather than calculation (or, to use the poet's own terms in the *Remedia amoris* [10], *impetus* rather than *ratio*), Ovid also directs his wit at the conventional hierarchy of genres, in effect inverting the process whereby the choice of topic dictates the choice of meter: only after having stolen a poetic foot from the bard's would-be epic verse does Cupid justify (or, in poetic terms, make decorous) this sneaky theft by invading and occupying his victim's hitherto loveless heart (*vacuum pectus*), like some ambitious Roman general. I know of no more original and amusing account of the beginning of either a love affair or a collection of love poems, but beneath the deliciously impartial irreverence of its verse, *Amores* I.I betrays a profound understanding of, and sympathy for, those whose lives are disrupted and priorities intemperately reordered by the (always) unexpected onset of erotic desire or by the irresistible demands of state power.

The comic spectacle of lost control in *Amores* 1.1 is refracted in a variety of ways throughout the collection. The first elegy of book 2 restates the poet's inability to devote himself to more serious subject matter, but this time it is the vagaries, rather than the onset, of love that upsets his plans and elegy's power, rather than Cupid's, that is on display. *Amores* 2.1 begins boastfully, the poet offering ironic tribute to his own fame as an elegist in a marvelously epigrammatic pentameter: "Ille ego nequitiae Naso poeta meae [I'm that (very) Ovid (you've heard about), the poet of my own worthlessness/idleness/wantonness]" (2.1.2; the noun *"nequitia"* can carry all these meanings, thus conveying, as it mocks, the connection of the elegy with lack of public value, with *otium*, and with sexual indulgence). But, he continues, once I undertook a mythical epic, the war of the earthly giants against the Olympian gods, and just as I was about to have Jupiter hurl defensive thunderbolts at his enemies, "Clausit amica fores!" (2.1.15–17)

Through the brilliant comic stroke of these last three, wholly unexpected words—my girlfriend slammed the door (on me)—the poem signals a sudden crisis in the poet's personal situation and, simultaneously, a drastic but unavoidable alteration of his poetic agenda, described with comic urgency and superlative Ovidian wit:

> ego cum Iove fulmen omisi;
> excidit ingenio Iuppiter ipse meo.
> Iuppiter, ignoscas! nil me tua tela iuvabant;
> clausa tuo maius ianua fulmen habet.

(I put aside the lightning and Jupiter with it; Jupiter himself fell [i.e., like a lightning bolt] out of my thoughts. Sorry, Jupe! Your big guns are no use to me; that closed door was a louder thunderclap than [any of] yours.)   (2.1.17–20)

Elegy alone, not epic, will soften the hard-hearted door ("mollierunt duras lenia verba fores," [2.1.22]); hence there's nothing for it but to say, "heroum clara valete / nomina; non apta est gratia vestra mihi [Farewell, famous roll call of heroes; your help is not what I need now]!" (2.1.35–36)

Lurking behind this playful statement of *epos interruptum* and the hopelessness of resisting love's generic imperative may be a more serious Ovidian meditation on the relative importance of personal and sociohistorical values (represented, respectively, by elegiac and epic/mythological poetry) in the life of the polity: there comes a time, *Amores* 2.1 hints, when individual needs and desires cannot (or can no longer) be subordinated to the demands or edicts of the state, the *res publica*. Seen in this light, the poem could be construed as expressing muted resistance to Roman imperialism or to Augustus's attempts to exert his regulatory authority over the sexual and marital lives of his most important subjects.

As with issues of poetic vocation, so in representations of love and its crises Ovid often exploits hopelessness for comic effect in the *Amores*. The *amica's* closed door is perhaps the *Amores'* central symbol, or evocation, of the intersection between crises of desire and authority. In 1.6, an example of the *paraclausithyron*—an elegiac subgenre depicting the excluded lover's complaint at (and to) the portals of his *amica's* house—the narrator's pleas that the door be opened and threats to break it down gain comic force from its obvious status as a metonymic displacement of the opening that is the real object of his desire; when he asks the *ianitor* (a servant, and thus a representative, of the paterfamilial authority that stands athwart the narrator's desire) to open the door just enough for him to slip in sideways, since "longus amor tales corpus tenuavit in usus / aptaque subducto pondere membra dedit [my long [bondage to] love has slimmed me down to do things like this, / making my *membra* suitable by taking away the flab]" (1.6.5–6), the humor of his request arises from both the bizarre, implied image of skewed (lateral?) sexual intercourse ("*membra*" can refer generally to the body, or specifically to the penis; Adams, *The Latin Sexual Vocabulary*, 46) and the literalization of the lyric commonplace that unrequited love makes a suitor waste away.

The obviously phallic reference I've noted in *Amores* 1.1's imagery of the poet's lines rising and then unexpectedly falling can also be read as an indirect expression of insecurity about sexual, not just poetic, potency. This fear is realized in *Amores* 3.7, a long lament for an occasion on which, despite being bedded with a beautiful and eager young woman, "illius ad tactum Pylius iuvenescere possit [at whose touch even Nestor could have been rejuvenated]" (3.7.41), he cannot perform. "Truncus iners iacui [I lay there like a dead tree trunk]" (3.7.15), he confesses, adding, "a, pudet annorum: quo me iuvenemque virumque? / nec iuvenem nec me sensit amica virum [at my age this is shameful! What good is being young and male? To my *amica* I was neither young nor male!]" (3.7.19–20).

In 1.4 the poet anticipates yet another kind of anguish, this one prompted by the prospect of attending a public banquet at which not only his *amica* but her *vir* (husband? keeper?) will be present, rendering impossible open affection between the lovers. The body of the poem recounts the strategies and pleas, addressed to the beloved, by which the poet-lover attempts to deny, or at least mitigate, the obvious hopelessness of his situation; the ingenuity and complexity of these efforts generate pathetic comedy because of their obviously foreordained futility, a futility already acknowledged in his first suggestion: "Ante veni, quam vir," he proposes, only to add, "nec quid, si veneris ante, / possit agi video; sed tamen ante veni [Come to the banquet before your man; I don't see what we can accomplish if you do come first, but come anyway]" (13–14). By a fearful symmetry, what he wants to happen after the end of the banquet displays the same trajectory of a strategy urged, followed closely by the admission of its ineffectuality:

Cum surges abitura domum, surgemus et omnes,
   in medium turbae fac memor agmen eas.
Agmine me invenies aut invenieris in illo:
   quidquid ibi poteris tangere, tange, mei.
Me miserum! Monui, paucas quod prosit in horas;
   separor a domina nocte iubente mea.

(When you get up with all the rest of us to go home, remember to go with the flow in the middle of the crowd. In all that movement, you look for me or I'll find you; and whatever part of me you can touch, do so. Dammit! all my schemes can only buy us a few short hours; I'm going to be separated from my lady-love because night wants it that way.)

(1.4.55–60)

Then, as the banquet unfolds, a litany of coded signs for the lovers to exchange—"excipe furtivas et refer ipsa notas" (1.4.18)—including raised eyebrows, words written in wine on the banquet table, cheeks touched, rings twisted on fingers, and earlobes tugged—grows ever funnier in its desperate exfoliation (1.4.19–26). Even the poet's dire threat to make a scene if she submits to her *vir*'s hateful embrace—"oscula si dederis, fiam manifestus amator / et dicam 'mea sunt!' [if you grant him kisses, I'll reveal myself as your lover and insist, 'those kisses are mine!']" (1.4.39–40)—quickly subsides into mute acquiescence and dread: "Haec tamen adspiciam, sed quae bene pallia celant, / illa mihi caeci causa timoris erunt [So I'll see [the kisses], but whatever [caresses] your garments hide will really stoke my blind fears]" (1.4.41–42). The trouble is, he admits, he has in his day done so many things "quae pallia celant" that "exemplique metu torqueor, ecce, mei [I'm tortured by fear of my own exploits [in lovemaking]"]" (1.4.46)—a line that gains comic force by postponing to its very end the source of the tormenting example: himself!

Powerlessly contemplating the sexual liberties the *vir* will take with the *amica* behind closed doors that night, the poet begs his beloved to yield only grudgingly and without pleasure; and then, with an unexpected turn, a final couplet offers profound, albeit humorous, insight into how we deal with the hopelessness of thwarted, jealous desire: "Sed quaecumque tamen noctem fortuna sequetur, / cras mihi constanti voce dedisse nega [But nonetheless, whatever may happen tonight, tomorrow deny to me in an unwavering voice that you gave in [to him]!]" (1.4.69–70) In other words, I can't deal with the truth; just tell me what I want to hear. Of course, such a plea condemns its maker to perpetual uncertainty about whether or not his *amica* is telling him the truth.

The ending of *Amores* 1.4 introduces us to two features of Ovid's comic technique that appear elsewhere in the *Amores*: the poet-lover's preference for lies over truths and the shift or twist in perspective that takes the reader (or listener, in one of Ovid's first Roman audiences) by surprise and, through its witty manipulation of expectations, offers insights into human responses to the shocks of existence.

The startling shift in perspective operates both within and between the collection's constituent poems. *Amores* 1.10 begins as a denunciation of a woman he has hitherto loved: "Cur sim mutatis, quaeris? quia munera poscis [Why have I changed like this, you ask? because you asked for presents]" (1.10.11). The poet, in high dudgeon, rails against women who demand something in return for granting sexual favors—"quae Venus ex aequo ventura est grata duobus, / altera cur illam vendit et alter emit [why should sex, which is supposed to be equally good for both partners, be sold by one and bought by the other]?" (1.10.33–34)—supporting his case with examples drawn from nature and mythology. But no sooner has he warned women against the evil consequences of their greed—"parcite, formosae, pretium pro nocte pacisci; / non habet eventus sordida praeda bonos [don't you dare, just because you're hot, charge for a night of lovemaking; sleazy extortion doesn't make for happy endings]" (1.10.47–48)—than his argument takes a wrenching, entirely unexpected turn: it's quite all right to ask for presents from rich suitors! ("Nec tamen indignum est a divite praemia posci; / munera poscenti quod dare possit, habet [There's nothing wrong in asking a rich guy to give in return for what he gets; he has the wherewithal to pay the bill]" [1.10.53–54]). As for poorer folk, let them offer what they can; "est quoque carminibus meritas celebrare puellas / dos mea [and to sing the praises, in my songs, of girls who deserve it is what *I* have to offer]" (59–60). Via this shrewd enjambment, the poem abandons its original theme and briefly becomes a praise of the poet whose songs can immortalize their subjects—a traditional claim here lightly ridiculed as a rather crass, self-aggrandizing intrusion into a poem that seemed headed in a very different direction. Ovid concludes with a final, dizzying twist by declaring that what bothers the poet is not giving, but only being asked, and expected, to give. "Quod nego poscenti," the last line explains, "desine velle, dabo [What I won't give if you ask, if you don't ask, I'll give]!" (64) In other words, I'll pay for sex, but only on my terms; so what this elegy is really all about is who has the power to commodify a relationship—a power men are unwilling to cede to women.

As a poetic corpus, the *Amores* is also replete with instances of whole poems offering radically different perspectives. One instance must suffice: in *Amores* 2.19, the poet angrily instructs the *vir* of his *puella* to place her under heavier guard, if not in his own interest then in that of the lover, so that the latter will want her more (2.19.1–2). Obstacles, he argues, nourish desire, and despite his wry, typically Ovidian recognition that this is a strategy of self-inflicted pain— "ei mihi, ne monitis torquear ipse meis [oh, boy! I hope I'm not done in by my own smart-assed advice]" (2.19.34)—not to say self-induced hopelessness, he persists in it, summing up his situation in an epigram analogous to the last line of 1.10: "Quod sequitur, fugio; quod fugit, ipse sequor [What seeks me out I run away from; what runs away from me, I follow]" (2.19.36). The poet's characterization of the insufficiently protective husband as a pander, "quid mihi ... cum lenone marito [what do I want with a pimp-husband]?" (2.19.57), identifies this elegy as, in part, a comic commentary on the Augustan legislation against adultery that, among its other provisions, held a husband liable to the accusation of pandering if he did not divorce his adulterous wife and refer her case to a special morals court.[20] But that the poem prefers erotic paradox to legal obligation its last line places beyond doubt: it commands the husband, "Me tibi rivalem si iuvat esse, veta!" (2.19.60): if you want me to be your rival, forbid it!

But then, in *Amores* 3.4, the Ovidian surrogate attempts to persuade a *durus vir* that there's no point in his guarding his *puella* too closely, since such restrictions are unnecessary for a good woman, unavailing for a faithless one. Again paradox abounds, in brilliantly sculpted verses: "Quae, quia non liceat, non facit, illa facit [A woman who doesn't do it only because she can't do it, does it]!" (3.4.4) And, with supreme irony, the poet turns the very argument he used in 2.19 to encourage a restrictive regime into an argument in favor of its opposite: "Quidquid servatur cupimus magis, ipsaque furem / cura vocat

[Whatever we can't get at we want all the more; fences attract thieves]"
(3.4.25–26). Then the inevitable twist: after giving all the reasons why a harsh
regimen won't keep its object chaste, the poet accuses the overly protective
husband of being *rusticus*, that is, a country bumpkin who doesn't understand
the mores of Rome, the great *urbs* (more on this key Ovidian putdown in my
discussion of the *Ars amatoria*); if you'll just lift your guard on your *domina*,
he advises, good things will happen to you: "sic poteris iuvenum convivia semper inire/ et, quae non dederis, multa videre domi [that way, you'll always have
a place at the young people's banquets and notice many [gifts] around the
house that you never gave [her]]" (3.4.47–48). This closing couplet contains
allusions to the situations depicted in 1.4 (flirting at the banquet) and 1.10
(accepting presents from rich men in return for sexual favors), thus implying
exactly who will be the "benefactor" of a newly compliant, albeit (from the
perspective of Augustan law) criminal, husband.

To conclude this appreciation of the *Amores*, I'll suggest that Ovid presumably knew he was playing for high stakes in his representation of situations that
refer, or appear to refer, to the person, policies, and authority of Augustus. I've
already noted the subversive allusions to the *princeps*'s moral legislation (the
Lex Julia de adulteriis coercendis) in *Amores* 2.19 and 3.4 and the coded resistance to the imposition of public obligations on personal desires in *Amores* 2.1;
I'll mention one last instance of negative allusion occurring in *Amores* 1.2,
which dramatizes the narrator's realization that he is in love, and thus in bond-
age to Cupid, who rides in an obviously Roman triumph, accompanied by his
victims and his followers while the crowd acclaims him (1.2.23–36). The narrator's description concludes with the observation, "his tu militibus superas
hominesque deosque; / haec tibi si demas commoda, nudus eris [with such warriors as these [including Error and Furor; for their significance with respect to
Ariosto's *Orlando Furioso*, see chapter 3], you conquer both men and gods; if
you lacked this support, you'd be deprived [of your power]]" (1.2.37–38). Beyond the obvious joke that Cupid is already, in Roman iconography, literally
nudus, are we to read these lines as an indirect suggestion that Augustus is a
bullying conqueror who would be exposed (*nudus*) as considerably less than the
great *princeps* were it not for the army whose loyalty he has so assiduously cultivated, in good part by offering them *commoda* (fringe benefits, retirement
bonuses) after the completion of their military service? (Ovid jokes about these
commoda in *Ars amatoria*, 1.131–32.) The implication remains, even though the
poem ends with the narrator asking Cupid not to tyrannize over him since he
has surrendered, urging the god, "adspice cognati felicia Caesaris arma— / qua

vicit, victos protegit ille manu [follow the example of your kinsman Caesar's [i.e., Augustus's], successful campaigns—he protects his defeated enemies with the very hand that beat them]" (1.2.51–52).[21]

Did Augustus read these elegies? Was he amused? Or shocked? Could they have played any role in the exercise of imperial authority that resulted in Ovid's eventual relegation to a Black Sea port? At this distance, we cannot know; we can only chuckle.

THE *ARS AMATORIA* AND *REMEDIA AMORIS*: OVID TAUGHT ME EVERYTHING I KNOW ABOUT LOVE—BUT WAS IT ENOUGH?

Ars amatoria: The Pursuit of Desire in "Modern" Rome—and Whose City Is This, Anyway?

At first sight, there seems no continuity between the poet-lover's many tribulations in the *Amores* and the supremely confident words of the next Ovidian persona, Dr. Ovid, self-promoting professor of erotic affairs (*magister amoris*), that open the *Ars amatoria*: "Siquis in hoc artem populo non novit amandi, / Hoc legat et lecto carmine doctus amet [If there's anyone here who doesn't know the fine art of making love, you'd better read this; as soon as you have, you'll make out like an expert]" (*Ars* 1.1–2). The *Ars* propounds strategies (heavily dependent upon deceit) calculated to get its users into a woman's bed; even its third book, supposedly designed to help women in matters of desire as books 1 and 2 advised men, is a very thinly (and comically) disguised set of "counsels" designed to make women more sexually available to the men who desire them.[22]

As any reader of Ovid's amatory poetry quickly recognizes, however, a good deal of the supposed wisdom contained in and promulgated by the *Ars* recasts, as expert advice, situations experienced by the Ovidian persona as poet-lover in the three books of the *Amores*, and much of the rest constitutes a collection of the already hoary clichés about the relations (especially courtship and sexual) between men and women, as well as gender stereotypes (especially about women's vices), all packaged as a pseudoscientific how-to manual.[23] By means of this material, as I've already suggested, Ovid focuses—with laughter but also, I think, an element of empathy—on the behavior and the fantasies of certain elite segments of Augustan Roman society. Within the fiction of the *Ars*, however, the work is intended for neophytes, and to that end the *magister* casts a wide net for clients: the hucksterish opening lines of the *Ars*, quoted above, promise much to many.

Nonetheless, the magisterial authority is not all-inclusive: in book 2 of the
Ars, bemoaning the influence of the gifts of the wealthy on the hearts of *amicae*
and *puellae*, the *magister* admits,

> Non ego divitibus venio praeceptor amandi:
>   Nil opus est illi, qui dabit, arte mea;
> Secum habet ingenium, qui, cum libet, "accipe" dicit;
>   Cedimus: inventis plus placet ille meis.

(I'm not about to offer love lessons to rich guys; if he can open his wallet,
he has no need for my tricks. He has enough going for him if he can say,
"Here, sweetie, take this." I give way to him; that will please the girls a lot
more than any schemes of mine.)   (*Ars* 2.161–64)

Analogously, in book 3, addressed specifically (and as I've just suggested,
somewhat hypocritically) to women, we are told that women who rank with
the fabled beauties of myth and legend have no need for the *magister*'s wiles:

> Turba docenda venit, pulchrae turpesque puellae:
>   Pluraque sunt semper deteriora bonis.
> Formosae non artis opem praeceptaque quaerunt;
>   Est illis sua dos, forma sine arte potens.

(It's the mob of ordinary women, attractive and unattractive, that comes
to be instructed—and there are always more of the latter than the former. The really beautiful aren't looking for any instructions or routines
from me; they have their own resources: looks more powerful than my
tricks.)   (*Ars* 3.255–58)

The limits of the *magister*'s writ, excluding as it does the rich and the beautiful,
define the borders of Ovid's comic universe: a world in which men and women
imperfectly endowed by nature or fortune eagerly flock to the experience-
schooled expert to learn techniques of self-adornment, self-construction, and
self-presentation that will lead them to sexual satisfaction.

However, this bright façade of amatory expertise cannot completely conceal
a darker reality, wherein the experience of genuine, unfabricated (as opposed
to feigned, staged) desire is repeatedly shown to create crises of uncontrollable
emotion.[24] The opening lines of the *Ars amatoria*, even as they claim that the
narrator's qualifications as a teacher guarantee his pupils their hearts' (and

loins') desire, also suggest that the experience of love on which he bases his expertise—"usus opus movet hoc" (*Ars* 1.29)—is hardly one of unalloyed success (or control). The gap between promise and performance is implicit in the ambiguity surrounding the narrator's chosen title of *magister*. The term is usually (and correctly) translated as "master" (its lineal descendant in English), that is, teacher of others, as is the case at the end of books 2 and 3, where the men and women who have followed the path of Ovidian precepts into someone's bed are instructed to inscribe the spoils of their victories, "Naso magister erat [Ovid taught us everything we know (about love)]." But its original meaning in Latin is the helmsman of a ship, as *Ars* 1.6 makes explicit: "Tiphys in Haemonia puppe magister erat." Like Tiphys, the helmsman of Jason's legendary ship, the Argo, and Automedon, who guided the chariot of Achilles, the *magister* declares himself not simply a teacher of human beings but a tamer of superhuman forces, one who has been appointed by Venus "artificem tenero . . . Amori;/ Tiphys et Automedon dicar Amoris ego [schoolmaster of young Love; I should be called Cupid's Tiphys and Automedon]" (*Ars* 1.7–8). Like a steed resisting the bit or the waves fighting the helmsman's attempt to steer a direct course, *Amor*, thus put to school, will resist his *magister*'s control: "Ille quidem ferus est et qui mihi saepe repugnet [he's pretty fierce, and keeps on resisting me]" (*Ars* 1.9). And the plot accordingly thickens; despite an initial boast that subduing him will be simple—"Sed puer est, aetas mollis et apta regi [But he's only a kid, a little twerp I can easily control]" (*Ars* 1.10)—the description that ensues of the relationship between the "praeceptor Amoris [love's teacher]" (*Ars* 1.17) and his charge becomes increasingly harsh in its imagery, agitated in its tone, and gladiatorial rather than pedagogical in its intent: although a "saevus . . . puer . . ."

> Et mihi cedet Amor, quamvis mea vulneret arcu
> Pectora, iactatas excutiatque faces.
> Quo me fixit Amor, quo me violentius ussit,
> Hoc melior facti vulneris ultor ero.

([He's a] ferocious boy, sure, but Love will give in to me, no matter how much he shoots his arrows into my heart and shakes that torch at me he's always waving around. The more he pierces, the worse he burns me, the better I'll be avenged for every wound he makes.)   (*Ars* 1.18, 21–24)

Aside from making the poem that follows seem more a victim's desperate attempt at vengeance upon his oppressor than an expert's communication of the secrets of his success to a clueless audience, this opening depiction of wrestling with love initiates an ongoing crisis of authority for the *magister*, who claims to be able to teach such self-control but must frequently admit that, as a lover, he has been unable to follow his own rules. For example, after urging a lover to put up with a rival and allow his *amica* to come and go freely, without succumbing to jealousy, the *magister* adds, "Haec ego, confiteor, non sum perfectus in arte; / Quid faciam? Monitis sum minor ipse meis [Listen, I confess I haven't completely mastered this rule myself. What can I do? I'm no match for my own rules]" (*Ars* 2.547–48), a quintessentially Ovidian comment—possibly with the Augustan moral legislation in mind—on the gap between the human inclination to construct regulatory systems and the human inability to adhere to them. Similarly, in a passage in the *Remedia amoris*—that antidote to the *Ars*, mapping for unhappy lovers escape routes from their beds of pain—the *magister* equates himself with the legendary Homeric physician to the Greeks, only to admit that he was a physician who could not heal himself:

> Haeserat in quadam nuper mea cura puella:
>   Conveniens animo non erat illa meo:
> Curabar propriis aeger Podalirius herbis,
>   Et, fateor, medicus turpiter aeger eram.

> (Not long ago, I took a strong interest in a certain girl, but she wasn't exactly thrilled by my advances. A sick Podalirius, I tried a dose of my own medicine, and, I have to tell you, I was one knocked-out love doctor.)
>
> (*Rem* 311–14)

What I've just called the *magister*'s "revenge" against love as an unmanageable passion consists in his promulgating a system of techniques of seduction that, when scrupulously followed, will allow its adherents to find, win, and keep a sexual partner:

> Principio, quod amare velis, reperire labora,
>   Qui nova nunc primum miles in arma venis.
> Proximus huic labor est placitam exorare puellam:
>   Tertius, ut longo tempore duret amor.

> (First of all, you rookies in this new army, get to work finding someone you want to love [note the allusion to love as warfare, a parallel established in detail in *Amores* 1.9]. The next job is to win over the girl that

pleases you; finally, you have to make sure the love affair will last a long
time.)   (*Ars* 1.35–38)

For the *magister*'s pupils, this is to happen through their own initiative and
on their own terms, rather than by their becoming (like the narrator of the
Amores in the first elegy of that collection) Cupid's unexpected and helpless
victims.

Of course, the very fact that the *magister* must subsequently offer what one
might call the countercourse of the *Remedia amoris* suggests that staying free of
passionate relationships and the anguish they can cause is not so easy, and he is
compelled to recognize this danger—that real passion will trump calculated
sexual predation—even as he advises his male neophytes of the many places in
Rome where they can pick up *puellae*:

> Et fora conveniunt (quis credere possit?) amori:
> ... Illo saepe loco capitur consultus Amori,
>   Quique aliis cavit, non cavet ipse sibi:
> ... Hunc Venus e templis, quae sunt confinia, ridet:
>   Qui modo patronus, nunc cupit esse cliens.

(Even the law courts—who could believe it?—are great places for finding
love; often the lawyer becomes love's victim there. He's supposed to protect others, but he can't protect himself. From her nearby temple, Venus
has a good laugh: the big lawyer now needs his own lawyer to plead his
case.)   (*Ars* 1.79, 83–84, 87–88)

And again, of making your move at a gladiatorial show in the Forum:

> Illa saepe puer Veneris pugnavit harena,
>   Et qui spectavit vulnera, vulnus habet.
> Dum loquitur tangitque manum poscitque libellum
>   Et quaerit posito pignore, vincat uter,
> Saucius ingemuit telumque volatile sensit,
>   Et pars spectati muneris ipse fuit.

(Often enough Venus's boy fights on that sand, so the guy watching the
battle becomes a casualty himself: while he's chatting and brushing her
hand, and asking for a look at the program, and checking to see who's

winning after he's placed his bet, he suddenly feels the winged dart and
has to groan with the pain—and now he's part of the show he thought he
was just watching.)   (*Ars* 1.165–70)

T he quest for the object of desire should begin within an apparently cir-
cumscribed period of freedom (from Cupid's attacks? from Augustan
political or marital responsibilities?): "Dum licet, et loris passim potes ire
solutis,/ Elige cui dicas, 'tu mihi sola places' [While it's still possible to be out
and about, and not on some short leash, pick up a chick you can tell, 'You're my
one and only']" (*Ars* 1.41–42). This last line implies not only freedom of choice
but also access to a rhetoric of desire that functions as an instrument of pursuit, not as an expression of feelings. The following, image-laden lines make
clear the predatory nature of this pursuit :

Haec tibi non tenues veniet delapsa per auras;
    Quaerenda est oculis apta puella tuis.
Scit bene venator, cervis ubi retia tendat,
    Scit bene, qua frendens valle moretur aper;
Aucupibus noti frutices; qui sustinet hamos,
    Novit quae multo pisce natentur aquae:
Tu quoque, materiam longo qui quaeris amori,
    Ante frequens quo sit disce puella loco.

(She won't just appear to you out of thin air; it's up to you to lay eyes on
the right girl. The hunter knows very well where to spread his nets for
the stag, knows the valley where the wild boar hides out, gnashing
his teeth; the right bushes are familiar to the fowler, and to the fisherman
the streams best stocked with fish. So if you're looking for the raw material for a long love affair, you'd better learn first where such a girl will
hang out.)   (*Ars* 1.43–50)

The hypothetical male disciple of the *magister* is then led, step by supposedly
authoritative step, through two books of instructions. Book 1, for example, after
explaining where to pick up girls in Rome, ticks off the stages of wooing, or, in
the continuing image of predation, trapping them like birds: "capies, tu modo
tende plagas [you'll catch them, you only need to spread your nets]" (*Ars* 1.270).
Enlist the aid of the *puella's* maidservant (and perhaps seduce her as well [*Ars*
1.351–98]); send pleading and flattering letters, models of insincere eloquence

(*Ars* 1.437–86); and follow up at ostensibly fortuitous public encounters by communicating discreetly, in words and signs, your admiration and desire (*Ars* 1.487–504). A brief excursus (*Ars* 1.505–24) reviews the dos and don'ts of personal appearance (keep your toga clean and your sandals buckled; don't curl your hair or scrape it off your legs), in preparation for the climactic campaign: invited to a dinner party with your *puella* and her *vir*, feign drunkenness (the real thing breeds quarrelsomeness), so that you can speak your desires without being blamed; communicate in words and signs; cozy up to the *vir* ("Tuta frequensque via est, per amici fallere nomen [It's so safe to do you see it all the time: friendship as scam]" [*Ars* 1.585]); and when the dinner crowd gets up to leave, seize the occasion to get close to the *puella* and make your direct, albeit deceitful, pitch: "Est tibi agendus amans, imitandaque vulnera verbis [Now's the time to play the wounded lover—that's the line to use]" (*Ars* 1.611). The stage is set for conquest, so deploy all your strategies: coax, cry, steal kisses, use force (*Ars* 1.673), or just ask (*Ars* 1.711), or perhaps make a strategic withdrawal (*Ars* 1.717–18) and even pretend you only want to be friends (*Ars* 1.720–22). If all else fails, the pale, thin, sleepless look may just work: "Ut voto potiare tuo, miserabilis esto, / Ut qui te videat, dicere possit 'amas' [To get what you want, look a wreck; that way, anyone who sees you will have to say, 'You must be in love']" (*Ars* 1.737–38). The book concludes with the *magister*'s warning not to trust the intentions of friends and his admission that women, far from being all alike, come in an enormous variety of types—"sunt diversa puellis / Pectora"—who, accordingly, cannot all be wooed/hunted in the same way (*Ars* 1.763–66).

For the actual reader, then or now, of the *Ars amatoria*, the point, of course, is not to profit from the *magister*'s suspect, self-contradictory strategies for seduction—go ahead and rape her, that's what they all want; no, just ask for sex, they all want to be asked; or, wait, try backing off because "quod refugit, multae cupiunt [many chicks go for the guy who plays hard to get]" (*Ars* 1.717)—but rather to enjoy Ovid's brilliant strategies for creating a parodic mirror of Roman sexual attitudes and fantasies, a mirror in which can also be seen both more universal crises attendant upon human desire and quite specific tensions occasioned by the attempted imposition of Augustan authority and ideology (including the opportunistic revival of "traditional Republican values") on elite Roman society—especially its erotic practices—and on the very face of the *urbs* itself. In what follows, I will call attention to some central elements of Ovidian comic creativity in the *Ars*; there are far too many such for any inclusive scrutiny here. My favorites include the place and significance of mirrors, literal and metaphorical; the central importance of the concept of *cultus* (and its binary opposite, *rusticus*) for Ovid's depiction of self-construction as a major facet of modern Roman gender and erotic relationships; eloquence (verbal and nonverbal) and the rhetorical theory of decorum as keys to dealing with the variety of erotic objects and situations recognized by the *magister amoris*, an experiential copiousness that compromises the supposedly systematic nature of the *magister's* program for finding, and making, love; Ovid's bathetic uses of mythology as part of the *magister's paideia*; the actual structure of the *Ars amatoria* (and, for that matter, the *Remedia amoris*), which is less a progressive sequence of stages in the hunt for sexual gratification, leading inexorably to the couch of consummation, than a series of comic episodes or routines in which stated principles or goals are subverted, trivialized, or ridiculed (this category is to a great extent a general application of the particular dynamic of the *magister's* use of mythology); and some of the ways in which Ovid mocks or at least questions Augustan programs and authority in the *Ars amatoria*, even while recognizing the force of that authority.

In characterizing the *Ars amatoria* as a comic mirror, I've taken my cue from the multiple attestations within the poem to the importance of mirrors (and mirroring) within its imagined world of sexual pursuit and gender relations. Furthermore, the part of Ovid's poetic oeuvre under discussion here exhibits mirrorlike tendencies, suggesting the poet's attachment to both that artifact's reflecting function and its peculiar characteristic of reversing the image it reflects. The *Amores* contains situations involving the pursuit of desire that are then reversed, like mirror images, in later elegies and then, as I've noted, restated as advice given to his charges by the *magister amoris* in the *Ars amatoria*. For example, as we've seen, *Amores* 1.4 dramatizes a dinner party at which the lover's *puella* appears with the man to whom she is attached; the frantically jealous lover gives instructions to the *puella* on how to interact surreptitiously with him behind her man's back, especially by means of signs: "Me specta nutusque meos vultumque loquacem; / excipe furtivas et refer ipsa notas [Glance at me; keep an eye out for my nods and telltale grimaces. Catch and send back my secret signs]" (1.4.17–18). *Amores* 2.5 offers a specular inversion: now the lover has come to a dinner party with his *puella* and catches her making the same kind of hidden signs to another man, including writing words of love on the table using wine for ink ("conscriptaque vino / mensa, nec in digitis littera nulla fuit [the table [was] scribbled on in wine: no shortage of messages inscribed by your fingers]" [2.5.17–18]). Then, in the first book of the *Ars amatoria*, the young man is told how to woo the girl of his choice at a dinner party, using coded language and gestures and the pretense of drunkenness:

Hic tibi multa licet sermone latentia tecto
  Dicere, quae dici sentiat illa sibi;
Blanditiasque leves tenui perscribere vino,
  Ut dominam in mensa se legat illa tuam.

(Now you can get away with saying things, thinly disguised in ambiguous words, that she'll be able to figure out are meant for her; you can even
write some vaguely flattering things on the table in wine, letting her read
there that she's your baby)   (*Ars* 1.569–72)

When in book 3 of the *Ars* the *magister* undertakes, as he claims, to teach
women how to attract and hold men, thus reversing the agenda of books 1 and
2, he proposes many of the same strategies, but inverted: for example, in *Ars* 1
the man is taught, via the predatory imagery already noted, where to look for
unattached girls in Rome; in *Ars* 3 the *puellae* are instructed where to go to be
seen by men—to the same places, of course, and with the same metaphors:

Casus ubique valet; semper tibi pendeat hamus:
  Quo minime credas gurgite, piscis erit.
Saepe canes frustra nemorosis montibus errant,
  Inque plagam nullo cervus agente venit.

(Good luck can happen anywhere; always have your hook baited. Where
you least think you'll need it, here comes the fish. Even while the hunting
dogs are wandering around the rugged forest finding no prey, the stag
can fall into the hunter's trap on its own.)   (*Ars* 3. 425–28)

Ars 1.437–38 explains how to write a flattering letter to a *puella*; *Ars* 3.469–
70 teaches a woman how to interpret and respond to a man's flattering letter.
Ars 1.619–20 instructs men in the importance of flattery; *Ars* 1.631, in the efficacy of false promises, in *viva voce* wooing; *Ars* 3.475–76 instructs *puellae*
in handling such strategies and countering male deceit with female—"Iudice
me fraus est concessa repellere fraudem [in my opinion, you're allowed to use
fraud to head off fraud]" (*Ars* 3.491)—even as *Ars* 1.643–44 claims to men that
since women mostly cheat, it's all right to cheat back: "Fallite fallentes [cheat
the cheaters]" (*Ars* 1.645). In the domain of desire, deception forever encounters its reflection in the mirror of gender relations. The *Remedia amoris* offers
a final specular reversal: advice on how to achieve a satisfactory relationship is
inverted to provide information on how to get over a failed relationship (more

on this below), for example, in wooing a *puella*, find euphemisms to minimize
her physical or behavioral blemishes (*Ars* 2); in escaping the emotional effects
of a love affair gone sour, find ways to exaggerate in your mind those same
physical or behavioral blemishes (*Remedia*).

Except for the straightforward imitation of *Amores* in *Ars*, all these mirrorings communicate the same message: there's more than one way to look at experience; different perspectives give different results. Seneca the Elder tells the
(probably apocryphal) story (*Controversiae* 2.2.12) that one of Ovid's three favorite lines in his own poetry (in fact, the first among them) was "semibovemque
virum et semivirumque bovem [the halfbull man and halfman bull]" (*Ars* 2.24),
a description of the Minotaur born from Pasiphae's unholy love for a bull. Each
half of this line is a reverse image of the other, with the result that the same
information is presented in two very different ways, each with a distinct resonance about the relationship between the bestial and the human—not just
in the Minotaur but in all of us. Such a perspective implicitly controverts a
univocal view of history and human experience, thus challenging Augustan
orthodoxy's one, official way to view recent Roman history. The Ovidian mirror reveals oppositions and alternatives. One human experience yields many
different forms of expression, understanding, and (self-interested) interpretation. (Ovid offers a prime instance of varying responses to the same experience
when he describes how the Sabine women reacted to being kidnapped, while
watching a theatrical performance, by Roman soldiers who wanted them as wives:
"Nam timor unus erat, facies non una timoris [there was unity of fear, but variety in showing it]" [*Ars* 1.121]. I'll return to the implications of this Ovidian ac-
knowledgment of and fascination with variety in a later section.

In classical Rome, as elsewhere in time and space, mirrors were associated
primarily with women, and Ovid conforms to this generalization in several,
though not all, of the places where literal mirrors appear in the *Ars amatoria*,
serving two opposing purposes depending on the circumstances in which they
appear: either to tell (or show) the truth, for better or for worse, or to assist in
routines of self-adornment designed in part to conceal the truth.

Early in book 1, having catalogued for his male charges venues all over Rome
where they can find skirts worth chasing, the *magister* now incites them to hot
pursuit by assuring them that women are creatures of unquenchable desires,
and thus easily won:

> Prima tuae menti veniat fiducia, cunctas
>   Posse capi. . . .
> Haec quoque, quam poteris credere nolle, volet.

(First of all, take my word for it, every woman is catchable; even the one
you can't believe wants it, wants it.)   (*Ars* 1.269–70, 274)

Indeed, it's only convention that keeps the woman from making the first move
instead of the man: "Conveniat maribus, nequam nos ante rogemus, / Femina
iam partes victa rogantis agat [If it weren't a convention that we men should ask
first, the already smitten woman would gladly play that role]" (*Ars* 1.277–78).
To support his contention, the *magister* turns to the mythological tale of Pasiphae, King Minos's queen, who fell in love with a white bull and could not rest
until she coupled with him:

> Ipsa novas frondes et prata tenerrima tauro
> > Fertur inadsueta subsecuisse manu.
> It comes armentis, nec ituram cura moratur
> > Coniugis, et Minos a bove victus erat.
> Quo tibi, Pasiphaë, pretiosas sumere vestes?
> > Ille tuus nullas sentit adulter opes.
> Quid tibi cum speculo, montana armenta petenti?
> > Quid totiens positas fingis, inepta, comas?
> *Crede tamen speculo quod te negat esse iuvencam.*

(It's said that with her very own hands—hands unaccustomed to such
chores—she gathered young leaves and tender grass for her bull. She goes
to the fields with the herd, not stopping to think about her husband, and
so Minos is bull-dozed. What's the point, Pasiphae, of wearing your best
gown out there? That four-footed adulterer of yours isn't impressed by
such a show. What good will a mirror do, as you head for the herd in the
hills? Why do you keep checking your hairdo with it, silly? Instead, look
again, and *believe that mirror when it tells you you're no cow.*)[25]
                                        (*Ars* 1. 299–307; emphasis added)

This passage, which continues with Pasiphae's jealous slaughtering of cows
she sees as rivals and culminates in her being, if one may so put it, pacified in
her desires (and becoming pregnant with the dreaded minotaur) by hiding,
properly positioned, within a wooden cow created for her by Daedalus, is
vintage Ovid in its crescendo of rhetorical questions and final admonition to
the long dead, and in any case imaginary, taurophile. But what gives it its special comic flavor is the introduction of the mirror into the myth. According to
the *magister*, the sex-crazed Pasiphae makes two specular (and spectacular)

mistakes. The first is bringing her mirror with her out into the field with the herds, in order to make sure by consulting it that her *pretiosas vestas* and her *positas comas* are in good order. Such primping would make sense if the lover she sought to seduce were a stylish (or, to use the term central to my next section, *cultus*) young Roman, but is completely lost on a bull, a creature lacking any appreciation of human artifice. The second error is even worse: the queen is so intent on using her mirror as an aid to elegant self-embellishment that she neglects to consult it to be reminded who she is (and isn't): "believe the mirror that testifies you're no heifer!" This, one of my favorite Ovidian lines, combines the comedy of the ridiculous—of course Pasiphae knows she's not a cow—with a serious insight to which the presence of the mirror points: we can be so carried away by our desires—erotic or otherwise—as to lose our grip on our actual situation in life, which, if seriously confronted, would make clear to us the impracticality or self-destructiveness of those desires. A Pasiphae blind to the message of her mirror is a Pasiphae living, as we would say, in denial.

The truth-telling mirror has a reprise in book 3 of the *Ars amatoria*, in a passage where the *magister*, in instructing women in the behavior that attracts men, underscores the mortal enmity of extreme emotion to cultivated beauty:

> Pertinet ad faciem rabidos compescere mores:
>   Candida pax homines, trux decet ira feras.
> Ora tument ira: nigrescunt sanguine venae:
> . . . Vos quoque si media speculum spectetis in ira,
>   Cognoscat faciem vix satis ulla suam.

> (Part of beauty's job is to curb foul moods. An even temper works best with people; leave rage to wild beasts. Anger distorts your features and makes your veins pop out. If you could look in the mirror when you're furious, girls, I don't think even one of you would recognize herself.)
>
> (*Ars* 3.501–3, 507–8)

Here the mirror's task is *not* to show you who you are in a general sense, but who you are (and should not be) at a particular moment.

By contrast, the mirror as an instrument of self-construction, helping a woman decide not who she is but who, through effective self-adornment, she might become, appears early in book 3 when the *magister* counsels his female charges on strategies of calculation:

Vos quoque nec caris aures onerate lapillis,
   Quos legit in viridi decolor Indus aqua,
Nec prodite graves insuto vestibus auro,
   Per quas nos petitis, saepe fugatis, opes.
Munditiis capimur: non sint sine lege capilli:
. . . Nec genus ornatus unum est: quod quamque decebit
Eligat, et speculum consulate ante suum.

(Also, don't make your ears sag with precious rocks, the kind swarthy
Indians collect from green waters, nor should you stagger in weighed down
by a gold-encrusted gown. In trying to attract us by showing off your
wealth, you're only turning us off. Be elegant and neat—that grabs us;
don't walk around with your hair a mess. There's no one, all-purpose way
to look good; each girl should go with what works for her, and start out
by consulting her mirror.)   (*Ars* 3.129–33, 135–36)

The mirror is not simply a reflecting surface to show the *puella* what she
looks like but an instrument of self-construction, an important adjunct in
the process of making the calculations and choices that are personal, not
generic.

The *Ars amatoria* doesn't fully exempt men from engagement with mirrors,
but the results recall Narcissus more than Pasiphae: in keeping with gender
stereotypes the poem implies comic disapproval of the male viewer taking so
much pleasure in his skillful self-adornment that it skews his judgment of how
women will respond to him. Assuring his female acolytes in book 3 that it's
easy to deceive men into thinking you love them, the *magister* says, "praecipue
si cultus erit speculoque placebit, / Posse suo tangi credet amore deas [espe-
cially if he's stylish and will be pleased by what he sees in the mirror, he will
believe that goddesses could fall in love with him]" (*Ars* 3.681–82). Here, in-
flated self-esteem transforms the mirror from a truth-telling counselor to a
flattering sycophant.

On the other hand, when Apollo appears to the *magister* in book 2 of the *Ars*,
with a message that each man chasing a woman should be aware of and flaunt
the angles from which he looks best and the things he does best (*Ars* 2.493–510;
more on this wonderful passage when I turn to Ovid's dealing with mythology),
the mirror, though not explicitly mentioned, will obviously help decide the first
of these categories. Finally, there's the specular moment in the *Ars amatoria* that
presents a reflecting surface not made of glass or metal but of flesh and blood. In

advising men in book 1, the *magister* suggests proper behavior toward the *puella* they have chosen as the object of their advances if they encounter her at a theater (where men and women sat separately, unlike the games, where they were not segregated):

> Plaudas, aliquam mimo saltante puellam:
>   Et faveas illi, quisquis agatur amans.
> Cum surgit, surges; donec sedet illa, sedebis.

(Applaud when an actor dances the role of a woman, and root for the lover in the play. Get up when she does; she sits down, you sit down.)

(*Ars* 1.501–03)

By imitating the choices and movements of the proposed beloved, the lover in effect constructs himself as her mirror! If she looks at him, she will see her own behavior in his.

Again, we see Ovid's own comic mirror at work: the image of the young man bobbing up and down and otherwise mimicking the woman he seeks to bed is more than faintly ridiculous, but it reminds us of all the ways in which we efface our own choices and even personality to obtain attention or favor from those who have what we want—possibly those who have power over us. The lover mimicking his beloved at the theater may not have seemed very different to Ovid from the courtier conforming himself to the desires of Augustus or the client groveling (literally or figuratively) before the wealthy patron.[26]

Elsewhere, the *magister* literalizes the metaphor of self-abasement embedded in this passage when he tells his pupil not to hesitate to hold his *puella*'s mirror for her—presumably so that she has both hands free to fix her hair or repair her makeup—even though that task was usually performed by a slave (*Ars* 2.215–16). Indeed, for a Roman woman of a certain elegance the most important function of a mirror on a day-to-day basis was as an aid in the application of cosmetics to her face. The reiterated presence of the mirror in the *Ars amatoria* thus provides an excellent point of entrance into a consideration of Ovid's preoccupation in his amatory poetry with the concept of *cultus*, or urbane sophistication, of which cosmetics are an emblem as well as a literal manifestation.

Behind Ovidian *cultus* lay a Roman tradition of *urbanitas*, signifying the ensemble of qualities—refined speech and manners, personal charm, equanimity in dealing with life's challenges—that distinguished the deportment of the *urbanus* (citizen of Rome) from the (stereotypically) boorish and uncivilized speech, appearance, and behavior supposedly characteristic of rustics, but also, as the empire expanded, of the provincials who were pouring into Rome from the rest of the Italian peninsula and the newly conquered territories.[27] By Cicero's time [mid-first century B.C.E.], the term *rusticitas* had been coined in certain culturally conservative circles to comprehend and stigmatize these negative qualities. Concurrently, however, Cicero and other self-appointed arbiters of taste and deportment also began to criticize as "hyperurbane" what seemed to them overly precious forms of pronunciation, dress—oiled hair a particular culprit here—and behavior among Romans. The animus directed at the hyperurbane (*perurbani*) also implied a critique of the perceived (and real) influence of Greek culture on upper-class Roman education and life, which struck many traditionalists as decadent and thus deeply threatening to hallowed Roman virtues and institutions, all distinguished, they believed, by robust simplicity.

Ovid rarely uses the terms *urbanus* or *urbanitas*, prefering the term *cultus*. He also innovated by shifting the emphasis of urbane behavior from qualities of a more socially beneficial nature to skills—self-adornment, polished behavior, flattery—honed to gain personal advantage, especially in sexual matters. (Cf. p. 22, on *Amores* 3.4: the husband who isn't *rusticus* will let others woo his wife for the social and economic benefits accruing thereby.) Hence, for example, while appearing to concur in the rejection by Cicero and others of an overly refined male appearance and deportment—

> Sed tibi nec ferro placeat torquere capillos,
> Nec tua mordaci pumice crura teras.
> Ista iube faciant, quorum Cybeleïa mater
> Concinitur Phrygiis exululata modis.
> Forma viros neglecta decet . . .

> (But no curling your hair with a curling iron, or shaving your legs with pumice stone. That's fine for the types who spend their time howling at the moon as followers of Cybele; a casual chic works better for real men.)
>
> (*Ars* 1.505–9)

—the Ovidian *magister amoris* does so on the basis of vanity's hindering the successful quest for heterosexual satisfaction, not because it offends traditional Roman sensibilities. Addressing his female clientele in book 3 of the *Ars*, in a prime example of Ovidian parody of "respectable" attitudes toward male *perurbanitas*, the *magister* equates such self-fashioning with duplicity and effeminacy:

> Sed vitate viros cultum formamque professos,
>   Quique suas ponunt in statione comas.
> Quae vobis dicunt, dixerunt mille puellis:
>   Errat et in nulla sede moratur amor.
> Femina quid faciat, cum sit vir levior ipsa,
>   Forsitan et plures possit habere viros?

(But avoid men who are always pushing their elegance and good looks, always making sure their hair is just so. Their line to you they've already tried out on a thousand other girls. Love like theirs is always on the move, never stays long in one place. What's the hope for a woman when a man is prettier than she is, and may even have more boyfriends than she does?)   (*Ars* 3.433–38)

Such men, with their fine clothes (*Ars* 3.445) and many-ringed fingers (446), are not to be trusted; "Forsitan ex horum numero *cultissimus* ille / Fur sit [the most elegant of them all may turn out to be a thief]" (*Ars* 3.447–48, emphasis added), "*cultissimus*" here to be equated, I think, with *perurbanus*.[28]

Two passages in Ovid's poetry establish an etiology for *cultus* and elucidate some of the cultural resonances that underlie the term's status as both a central element in his comic mirror of urbane Rome and a major instrument of his challenge to Augustan authority and ideology. That the most basic context for *cultus* is agricultural—the cultivation of the earth—the opening lines of Ovid's fragmentary treatise, *Medicamina faciei*, or face cosmetics, make clear, even as they establish their didactic goal of improving or preserving a woman's natural looks:

> Discite quae faciem commendet cura, puellae,
>   Et quo sit vobis forma tuenda modo.
> Cultus humum sterilem Cerealia pendere iussit
>   Munera, mordaces interiere rubi.
> Cultus et in pomis sucos emendat acerbos,
>   Fissaque adoptivas accipit arbor opes.
> Culta placent.

(Girls! Learn the routines that will improve your looks, and preserve them as well. Cultivation makes once-sterile ground yield a bounty of grain, while getting rid of all the choking weeds. It also makes fruits sweeter and juicier, and grafts fruit trees to make newer, better varieties. The products of cultivation give greater pleasure.)   (*Medicamina*, 1–7)

In other words, *cultus* signifies intervention in nature's processes, in order to improve the quantity and quality of nourishment; as such, it was central to ancient Mediterranean civilization's success and expansion. Bread and wine, the most characteristic products of that civilization, are the results of a twofold process of cultivation: grow better food, then transform it from its natural to its manufactured state.

As *cultus* moves from the realm of agriculture to that of human shelter and comfort, the pleasure it gives arises less from bounty than from adornment, and its success requires both new skills and far-flung sources of raw materials, such as had been made available to Rome through imperial conquest and aggressive commerce:[29]

> Auro sublimia tecta linuntur,
>   Nigra sub imposito marmore terra latet:
> Vellera saepe eadem Tyrio medicantur aëno:
>   Sectile deliciis India praebet ebur.

(Tall buildings are covered with gold, and the ground is completely obscured by their marble foundations. Woolen cloth is repeatedly dipped into the dying vats; imported Indian ivory is carved into delightful little *tchotchkes*.)   (*Medicamina*, 7–10)

The summit of *cultus*, at least in this treatise, is the care of the body and improvement of its appearance. Achieving this summit, *Medicamina faciei* makes clear, involves the exploitation of all the resources of empire for ingredients that, when laboriously blended by the slaves who are another fruit of Roman world conquest, become beauty creams, body scrubs, and facial and hair colorings. But before offering recipes for several such obviously expensive concoctions, Ovid further defines human *cultus* in terms of the desires that drive it, contrasting such desires to those of an earlier, simpler rural life that lacked the aesthetic appreciation that validates self-adornment:

> Forsitan antiquae Tatio sub rege Sabinae
>   Maluerint, quam se, rura paterna coli:
> Cum matrona, premens altum rubicunda sedile,

Assiduum duro pollice nebat opus,
Ipsaque claudebat quos filia paverat agnos,
   Ipsa dabat virgas caesaque ligna foco.
At vestrae matres teneras peperere puellas.
   Vultis inaurata corpora veste tegi,
Vultis odoratos positu variare capillos,
   Conspicuam gemmis vultis habere manum:
Induitis collo lapides oriente petitos,
   Et quantos onus est aure tulisse duos.
Nec tamen indignum: sit vobis cura placendi,
   Cum comptos habeant saecula nostra viros.

(Maybe those ancient Sabine girls, back in the time of old King Tatius,
would rather have tended the family farm than tending to their own faces;
in those days the ruddy-hued woman of the house, plumped down on her
high stool, applied her calloused hands diligently to her spinning, and
then by herself penned up the lambs that her daughter had taken out to
pasture, and then by herself gathered the twigs, chopped the logs, and
threw them on the hearth fire. But you girls are a whole different—and
more refined—generation. You want to drape your bods in gold lamé
gowns; you want new hairdos, newly perfumed, regularly; you want to
show off rings with big rocks on your fingers, and adorn your neck with
precious stones imported from the East—stones so heavy that your ear
couldn't support two in an earring. There's nothing wrong with all that:
you're only dressing up to attract today's men, who are themselves pretty
dressed up.)   (*Medicamina*, 11–24)

These lines transform the relationship between agricultural and urban *cultus*
from one that is evolutionary or analogical to one of binary opposition; they
accomplish this by inserting Roman history into the discussion. The picture that
the poem offers of the Sabines, neighbors and rivals of the earliest Romans and
always exemplars of old-time virtue, administers a verbal poke in the eye to
those among the Roman elite and intelligentsia who supported Augustus's ideological traditionalism, looking back, as I've already noted, on the (idealized)
early days of Rome as a virtuous Golden Age.[30] Ovid's more extended evocation
of the Sabines, and of the Romans of Romulus's day who stole their daughters in
order to have children by them, comes early in the *Ars amatoria* (cf. *Aeneid*
8.635–37 for a brief, nonparodic evocation of this story), in a vividly realized passage of great comic force that treats all the participants in this famous early

triumph of Roman expansionism as uncouth hicks and the theater where the
Rape of the Sabine Women took place as a primitive site of hillbilly entertainment, in contrast to the elegant stages of Augustan Rome:

Tunc neque marmoreo pendebant vela theatro,
    Nec fuerant liquido pulpita rubra croco;
Illic quas tulerant nemorosa Palatia, frondes
    Simpliciter positae, scena sine arte fuit;
In gradibus sedit populus de caespite factis,
    Qualibet hirsutas fronde tegente comas.

(No beautiful awnings hung over marble theaters in those days, nor were
the stages sprayed with pleasing fragrances; instead, some leafy branches
were brought in from the wooded Palatine hill nearby and scattered
around the otherwise bare stage. The audience sat on risers made of blocks
of turf, their shaggy hair decorated by the occasional stray leaf.)

(*Ars* 1.103–08)

To find a statement of the admiration for an idealized Roman past that
Ovid here sends up, and of corresponding disapproval for a present perceived
as decadent, we need look no further than the preface to the monumental history of Rome composed by his contemporary and fellow immigrant to the *urbs*,
Livy. "I am aware," he writes,

that most readers will take less pleasure in my account of how Rome began and in her early history; they will wish to hurry on to more modern
times and to read of the period, already a long one, in which the might of
an imperial people is beginning to work its own ruin. . . . I invite the
reader's attention to the much more serious consideration of the kind of
lives our ancestors lived, of who were the men, and what the means both
in politics and war by which Rome's power was first acquired and subsequently expanded; I would then have him trace the process of our moral
decline, to watch, first, the sinking of the foundations of morality as the
old teaching was allowed to lapse, then the rapidly increasing disintegra-
tion, then the final collapse of the whole edifice, and the dark dawning of
our modern day when we can neither endure our vices nor face the remedies needed to cure them. . . . I hope my passion for Rome's past has not
impaired my judgment; for I do honestly believe that no country has ever
been greater or purer than ours or richer in good citizens and noble

deeds; none has been free for so many generations from the vices of avarice and luxury; nowhere have thrift and plain living been for so long held
in such esteem. Indeed, poverty, with us, went hand in hand with content-
ment. Of late years wealth has made us greedy, and self-indulgence has
brought us, through every form of sensual excess, to be, if I may so put it,
in love with death both individual and collective. But bitter comments of
this sort are not likely to find favor, even when they have to be made.

                                          (*The Early History*, 17–18)

Livy's complaint about wealth and self-indulgence could well have been
aimed at the adornment of *teneras puellas* described in the lines I have just
quoted from the *Medicamina faciei* (11–24), a kind of comic hymn to the excesses of modern *cultus* as well as a further implicit recognition of its connection to the material rewards of imperial conquest. As for the *comptos viros*
whom today's *puellae* must seek to please, they have now become as concerned
with self-adornment as their women folk: "Feminea vestri poliuntur lege mariti, / Et vix ad cultus nupta, quod addat, habet [Your husbands have been taking a page out of your style magazines: a bride can hardly find anything to
outdo them]" (*Medicamina*, 25–26). Here Ovid alludes to the supposed effeminacy of the hyperelegant *perurbani*, contemned by Cicero, as I've mentioned,
and, for example, by Seneca the Elder:

> Look at our young men: they are lazy, their intellects sleep; no-one can
> stay awake to take pains over a single honest pursuit. Sleep, torpor and a
> perseverance in evil that is more shameful than either have seized hold
> of their minds. Libidinous delight in song and dance transfixes these
> effeminates. Braiding the hair, refining the voice till it is as caressing as
> a woman's, competing in bodily softness with women, beautifying them-
> selves with filthy fineries—this is the pattern our youths set themselves.
>
> (*Controversiae* 1. Pref. 8).

Even without subscribing to Livy's idealizing antiquarianism, we can perhaps understand his annoyance, or Seneca's, at a society or social group that
exalts *cultus*. Since *cultus* is basically all about the ornamentation and embellishment of nature, and since the urban/urbane version of *cultus*, unlike its
rural analogue or antecedent, doesn't make for better food or drink, it's easy to
dismiss the life that centers on the cultivation of self, physically and behavior-
ally, as superficial (i.e., concerned only with surfaces) or to condemn it as a
waste of time, a distraction from more serious issues, a squandering of valu-

able resources, and a source of social discontent and division. Also, if particular behaviors and the use of cosmetics are the marks of wealth and power, it's easy to counterfeit wealth and power by using cosmetics and so on, thus upending the sign system of the social hierarchy. Fear of such socially subversive signification in fact underlies the repeated recourse to sumptuary laws and anticosmetic polemics throughout European history.[31]

In the face of, and tacitly recognizing, such reservations about the Roman lifestyles of the rich and famous, Ovid's amatory poetry makes its most comprehensive statement about and commitment to *cultus* in *Ars amatoria* 3.101–28, a passage that traverses with characteristic Ovidian surefootedness a dazzling series of rhetorical transformations to arrive at a final ringing statement of the *magister*'s (and, one cannot but believe, to a certain extent his creator's) self-congratulation for living in a Rome where personal cultivation or, as we might say, elegant self-construction, holds sway as ideal and practice. As a comic endorsement of satisfaction at one's placement in time and space it remained unchallenged until W. S. Gilbert had his chorus exalt Ralph Rackstraw, the young hero of *HMS Pinafore*, for having had the good sense to be born an Englishman rather than a Russian, a Prussian, or (God forbid) an Italian.

The opening words of this passage, "Ordior a cultu" (I begin with *cultus*), could be the motto of all Ovid's amatory poetry. As in *Medicamina faciei*, the *magister* begins with examples of nature improved by cultivation—cultivated grapes yield better wine; cultivated (i.e., well manured and properly rotated) soil produces more robust crops—and moves by analogy from the earth to the body, where the situation at once becomes more complicated. Beauty, a gift of the god ("dei munus" [*Ars* 3.103]), is given to few; for the rest of women, it can be achieved, like better crops, by *cura*, the personal care that parallels the cultivation of the earth. Furthermore (and here the division between naturally beautiful women and those not so graced breaks down), even natural beauty fades if it is uncared for ("facies neglecta peribit, / Idaliae similis sit licet illa deae [beauty, even the most Venus-like, will vanish if it's neglected]" [*Ars* 3.106–7]). An excellent face needs tending to, even as does a naturally fertile plot of land; where the latter needs its mulch and manure, the former needs its cosmetics. The analogy (though not articulated) is precise; it justifies women's use of cosmetics as a legitimate extension of cultivation: from the food one eats to the body it nourishes. But it is also not quite satisfactory: there is an unavoidable strain of comedy in the implicit comparison of a face to a field and cosmetics to mulch and manure. Furthermore, the warning that *facies neglecta peribit* cannot but remind any reader (but especially, in Ovid's culture as in ours, any female reader) of the inevitably transitory nature of beauty, thus imparting to cosmetic intervention a note, however faint, of desperation and futility. A field can be renewed and bear new crops; a face can only age.

(This may be the place to say that I think Ovid would have been fascinated by the twenty-first-century *cultus* of plastic surgery, tummy tucks, botox and collagen injections, and other such interventions with nature in order to keep an old body looking young [if sometimes rather too tightly wound]. Even as he chuckled at their excesses [constant comic fodder on today's talk shows and situation comedies], he would recognize the imperatives that lead people in New York, Los Angeles, and other centers of high-octane *cultus* to deploy this latest version of cosmetic *skill* [another meaning of Latin *ars*] in order to compete with younger or more naturally attractive rivals for jobs or sexual partners and to hold at bay, however temporarily, time and its henchperson, the tell-tale mirror. [Contemplating the aging process, the narrator of *Medicamina faciei* warns, "Tempus erit, quo vos speculum vidisse pigebit, / et veniet rugis altera causa dolor [The time will come when it will really hurt to look in the mirror [cf. Pasiphae!]; your sadness will only add more wrinkles to the ones already there]" (47–48).] Besides, how could someone named Naso [nose] not appreciate the ironic potential of the nose job, especially since, as we've seen, he offers a comic etiology for his writing elegiac couplets by describing how Cupid in effect bobbed a foot from what was intended to be a hexameter line, appropriate for deployment in a grander genre than love poetry.)

As in the *Medicamina faciei*, Ovid subtly redefines his argument in binary rather than analogical terms: in the old days, women had no need to cultivate their bodies because their men wouldn't appreciate the effort; Hector and Ajax were too busy fighting and killing to notice whether or not their wives were wearing rouge or had applied eye shadow:

> Si fuit Andromache tunicas induta valentes,
>   Quid mirum? duri militis uxor erat.
> Scilicet Aiaci coniunx ornata venires,
>   Cui tegumen septem terga fuere boum?

(If Andromache dressed in clothes that looked almost like armor, so what? She was, after all, the wife of a rugged soldier. And would you get all dolled up if you lived with Ajax, whose idea of a good suit was seven ox hides?)   (*Ars* 3.109–12)

This comment, with typical Ovidian slyness, cuts several ways. It gleefully subverts the epic genre—in the rigid hierarchy of genres of Roman literary theory, far above the love lyric in dignity and importance—by suggesting that its heroes were uncultivated slobs; it takes an indirect jab at contemporary soldiers, in Roman elegiac poetry a traditional rival of poets for the love of beautiful women; and, of course, it alludes to the already noted predilection of men as well as women for high fashion and careful self-cultivation in Augustan Rome, to the horror of all who found in such behavior clear evidence of Roman decline.

Furthermore, by asking his audience to adopt, however briefly and amusedly, a new perspective on the warrior heroes of classical legend, Ovid obliquely suggests the possibility, and the importance, of looking at familiar things in new ways, such flexibility of viewpoint and response constituting an important part of a survival kit for life in a multiethnic metropolis, then as now.

Having shifted his ground from the analogy between cultivation of the earth and the face to a justification of female *cultus* via a contrast between yesterday's simplicity and today's elegance, the *magister amoris* now shifts it again, appropriating for his use the topos of Roman past versus Roman present that received canonic (though differently intended) status in book 8 of Vergil's *Aeneid* (cf. *Aeneid* 8.97–100, 337–58). The topos affects to praise Roman continuity while glorying in Augustus's *renovatio urbis*, but Ovid manipulates it just enough (*Ars* 3.113–20) to give it new bite, reconstructing the past as unpleasantly primitive—the senate house had a roof of wattles; the Palatine, site of a temple to Apollo and Augustus's own palace, was a cattle pasture—and to remind us that Augustus has fabricated a golden present in true imperial style, by conquering other nations and exploiting their resources ("Nunc aurea Roma est, / Et domiti magnas possidet orbis opes [Now Rome is golden, possessing as it does the great wealth of a tamed world-empire]" [*Ars* 3.113–14]). Given the elegiac poets' frequently expressed distaste for war and war profiteering, this is not necessarily a celebratory comment.[32]

Finally, the peroration: the *magister* abandons his role as tutor of women in the care and augmentation of their beauty and proclaims his own allegiance to the present (or, more precisely, his self-congratulatory relief at not having been born sooner) and to a specifically modern and urban *cultus* that accords with his values. In the process he blithely dismisses both the cult of a glorious Roman past and the rapacity of a contemporary, exploitative imperial materialism:

> Prisca iuvent alios: ego me nunc denique natum
>   Gratulor: haec aetas moribus apta meis.
> Non quia nunc terrae lentum subducitur aurum,
>   Lectaque diverso litore concha venit:

Nec quia decrescunt effosso marmore montes,
    Nec quia caeruleae mole fugantur aquae:
Sed *quia cultus adest,* nec nostros mansit in annos
    Rusticitas, priscis illa superstes avis.

(Let other people celebrate the good old days; I, on the other hand, celebrate the fact that I was born now, not then—this is the age that I belong
in: not because we're prying all that gold out of the earth, or bringing to
Rome shells gathered on far-off shores; not because we're leveling mountains to get their marble, or pushing back the sea to make room for our
coastal mansions; *no!* it's because now—finally—we've got *style,* and the
uncouth Rome of our grandfathers is nowhere in sight these days.)[33]

                                       (*Ars* 3.121–28; emphasis added)

What began as *cultus* expressed in the rustic terminology of agri- and viticul-
tures ends, here as in the *Medicamina faciei,* as an opposition between elegant
modernity and a now surmounted, ancestral *simplicitas rudis* and *rusticitas.*

The basic strategy of Ovid's amatory poetry makes *cultus* a central component of its protagonists' quest to satisfy erotic desire. This poetic decision in
effect doubles the audacity of the *Amores, Ars amatoria,* and *Remedia amoris*
vis-à-vis traditional Roman conservatism, which looked askance at modern
elegance and (especially in its Stoic component) regarded desire as foolish,
indeed, a kind of madness or enslavement to passion and therefore a waste of
time or, worse, a distraction from duty. Ovid, on the other hand, was intrigued,
amused, and attracted, as well as appalled, by the essential role of such artifice
in the identification and pursuit of objects of desire—specifically, at least for
the poet, heterosexual desire—in the modern *urbs.*

Cultus behavior takes many forms in the *Ars amatoria.* For example, in
counseling women in book 3, the *magister amoris* advises them to adopt strategies of dress and behavior that parallel and extend the function of facial cosmetics by helping them hide or neutralize their individual shortcomings:

    Occule mendas,
    Quaque potes vitium corporis abde tui.
Si brevis es, sedeas, ne stans videare sedere:
    Inque tuo iaceas quantulacumque toro;
Hic quoque, ne possit fieri mensura cubantis,
    Iniecta lateant fac tibi veste pedes.

Quae nimium gracilis, pleno velamina filo
    Sumat, et ex umeris laxus amictus eat. . . .
Exiguo signet gestu, quodcumque loquetur,
    Cui digiti pingues et scaber unguis erit.
Cui gravis oris odor numquam ieiuna loquatur,
    Et semper spatio distet ab ore viri.

(Hide your flaws, and as much as you can disguise your body's failings: if you're short, stay seated, so that you don't look as though you're sitting down even when you're standing up; just lie back on your couch, and, so that no one can see exactly how small you really are, hide your feet by throwing a robe over them. Too thin? Be sure to choose heavy fabrics, and let your clothes hang loosely from your shoulders. Fat fingers or chewed-on nails? Only small gestures when you speak, please. Bad breath? Better not speak before you've eaten, and even then keep your distance from your date's face.) (*Ars* 3.261–68, 275–78)

Even laughing (*Ars* 3.281) and weeping (*Ars* 3.291) can be subjected to control, as women learn, in effect, to apply cosmetics to their emotions.

The challenge, for women and for men, is to keep *rusticitas*, in the sense of *un*controlled emotions and behavior, at bay, as well as the opposite extreme, self-construction that fails by its obviousness: "Sed sit, ut in multis, modus hic quoque: rusticus alter / Motus, concesso mollior alter erit [So, as is often the case, here too you mustn't overdo it; sure, you want to avoid behaving like a hick, but you also don't want to come on as obnoxiously smooth]" (*Ars* 3.305–6).

This latter caveat makes it clear that if *cultus* (and the *ars* behind it) is to be effective in the pursuit of desire, it must disguise itself. As the *magister* puts it, "si latet, ars prodest [atfulness works best when it conceals itself]" (*Ars* 2.313), and in support of that maxim he counsels his female charges against revealing their cosmetic secrets: "Non tamen expositas mensa deprendat amator/ Pyxidas: ars faciem dissimulata iuvat [but don't let your love find all your cosmetics lying in the open on your dresser; your best face is best put on with skill that isn't obvious]" (*Ars* 3.209–10). Noting that the application of beautifying products can be a messy affair and the separate ingredients sometimes noxious, he generalizes, "Ista dabunt formam, sed erunt deformia visu: / Multaque, dum fiunt, turpia, facta placent [These products will make you beautiful, but the process itself is not a pretty sight; a lot of things are ugly in the doing but delightful when they're all done]" (*Ars* 3.217–18). One cannot but wonder whether the poet, or some of his readers, might not understand this last line as an oblique reference to the long period of warfare and widespread misery that ended in the triumph of Augustus, now celebrated throughout Rome on monuments placed there by the victor.

Ovidian erotic *cultus* turns out to be an exercise in self-construction that must constantly attune itself to ever-changing circumstances. The strategies of the *cultus* lover reflect an aptitude or talent (*ingenium* in Ovid's Latin); taken together they constitute an *ars*, or skill, that aims at the management of self and other in every possible situation. As the *magister* puts it, "Quo non ars penetrat [where can't you find skill at work]"? (*Ars* 3.291).[34] One should even cultivate faults, if faults become fashionable; refering to an apparently upper-class fad for lisping (rediscovered centuries later by the English nobilitiy), the *magister* says of *cultae puellae*, "In vitio decor est: quaerunt male reddere verba; / Discunt posse minus, quam potuere, loqui [Even defects can be charming, when cultured chicks deliberately abuse the language, having learned to be able to be 'unable' to speak it properly]" (*Ars* 3. 295–96; the second line is a typically playful and ironic Ovidian paradox).

One especially important instance of skill at work involves responses to the role of chance in life, and a fortiori in wooing. The *magister* makes it clear that there are moments when the noncultivated body is attractive, when chance delivers beauty by accident: of the terrified Sabine women carried off for forced marriages: "Et potuit multas ipse decere timor [Fear made a lot of them more attractive]" (*Ars* 1.126); of Ariadne, frantic in her abandonment by Theseus on Naxos: "Clamabat, flebatque simul, sed utrumque decebat; / Non facta est lacrimis turpior illa suis [She wept and howled at the same time, looking better than ever; her tears did nothing to ruin her beauty]" (*Ars* 1.533–34); of Andromeda tied to a rock for the sea-monster to devour her but saved by Perseus, who falls in love with her: "Quid minus Andromedae fuerat sperare revinctae / Quam lacrimas ulli posse placere suas [What could Andromeda possibly have considered less likely than that her tears could turn somebody on]?" (*Ars* 3.429–30); and—Chaucer's Wife of Bath take note!—"Funere saepe viri vir quaeritur; ire solutis / Crinibus et fletus non tenuisse decet [Sometimes a funeral for one husband is the best place to look for another; mussed up hair and uncontrollable sobbing can be powerful aphrodisiacs]" (*Ars* 3.431–32; cf. *Canterbury Tales* 3.593–99.). How does the practitioner of *cultus* respond to this phenomenon? By counterfeiting "chance," of course:

> Et neglecta decet multas coma; saepe iacere
>   Hesternam credas; illa repexa modo est.
> Ars casum simulat . . .

(A lot of girls look even better when their hair seems uncombed; it looks untouched since yesterday, but in fact it's just been fixed. Skill pretends to be chance.)   (*Ars* 3.153–55)

Just as the *magister amoris* warns his female clients against letting their cosmetic routines be observed *in medias res* by present or prospective lovers, so he issues similar cautions concerning the deployment of persuasive language, a specifically (and analogous) male form of amatory *cultus*. Refering to the rhetorical training that formed a central part of the education of young men of good birth, the *magister* urges its relevance to the composition of love letters but warns against letting it become obvious:

> Disce bonas artes, moneo, Romana iuventus,
>   Non tantum trepidos ut tueare reos;
> Quam populus iudexque gravis lectusque senatus,
>   Tam dabit eloquio victa puella manus.
> Sed lateant vires, nec sis in fronte disertus;
>   Effugiant voces verba molesta tuae.
> Quis, nisi mentis inops, tenerae declamat amicae? . . .
> Sit tibi credibilis sermo consuetaque verba,
>   Blanda tamen, praesens ut videare loqui.

(Young Romans, I advise you to learn the noble arts of rhetoric—and not just so that you can be of service to fearful defendants in lawsuits. The girl you want will go down to defeat before eloquence just as much as the people, a stern judge, or the whole elected senate would. But keep all that skill secret; don't come across as too expert, and don't let big words creep into your letters begging for her love. Who but an idiot would make pompous speeches to his little sweetie? Just say believable things in normal, but persuasive, language so that you seem to be right there, speaking to her.)
                                                          (*Ars* 1.459–65, 467–68)

Hiding the effort and calculation that go into one's supposedly sincere appeals for sexual reward is the verbal parallel to hiding the effort and calculation that go into a woman's cosmetic improvement of her face. Rhetoric is verbal cosmetics; cosmetics can be called facial rhetoric. Just don't get caught putting on the paint. "Tantum, ne pateas verbis simulator in illis, / Effice, nec vultu destrue dicta tuo [But for God's sake, don't let her see that you're making it all up as you go along, and don't let your looks contradict all your fine phrases]" (*Ars* 2.311–12).

Not deceit itself—be it with the colors of makeup or the colors of rhetoric— but its revelation brings shame.[35] At the very end of book 3, when two lovers have finally ended up in one bed and the ultimate satisfaction of desire is at hand, passion again creates a final problem, this time by its uncontrollable absence in the female partner: the *magister* insists that both partners should enjoy climax together (an unusual attitude in Ovid's civilization)[36] but adds, "Tu quoque, cui veneris sensum natura negavit, / Dulcia mendaci gaudia finge sono [As for you, whom nature has left numb in the erogenous zones, you'd better fake an orgasm with all the right sounds]" (*Ars* 3.797–98) (Meg Ryan's famous restaurant scene of venereal fakery in the movie *When Harry Met Sally* would, we may confidently assume, have earned two enthusiastic thumbs up from the *magister*, and probably from his creator as well). He cautions further, "Tantum, cum finges, ne sis manifesta, caveto: / Effice per motum luminaque ipsa fidem [Only, when you fake it, make sure it's not obvious; convince him by your writhing body and rolling eyes]" (*Ars* 3.801–2). (This situation cannot but remind the reader of Ovid's amatory verse of the plight of the male protagonist of *Amores* 3.7, whose inopportune impotence cannot be so easily disguised.)

The necessary commitment to deception, which extends to almost all acts of self-construction, constitutes a crisis that hovers over both male and female quests to attract and keep a lover; the *Ars amatoria* simultaneously celebrates such deception as the heart (and art) of *cultus* and makes clear the risk of exposure and rejection that always threatens to disarm the snares and traps of the *magister's* sexual hunting party.[37]

Ovid's game with respect to the eloquence of seduction is to bring into comic juxtaposition two different verbal situations and suggest that they are analogous. At one level there is the would-be seducer's time-honored recourse to a supposedly sincere, actually fraudulent language to get into a woman's bed; at another there is the perpetual worry by Greek and Roman moralists about the power of rhetoric to convince its listeners of what is false, that is, about the gap between language as a means of persuasion and language as a vehicle of truth or teacher of virtue. (Indeed, the *magister* makes it clear, among his many mirrorings of books 1 and 2 of the *Ars* in book 3, that women can deploy seductive eloquence—both verbal and in signs such as sighs and tears—as well as men: "Efficite," he advises his female disciples, "(et facile est) ut nos credamus amari; / Prona venit cupidis in sua vota fides [Make it happen that we think we're really loved; it's easy, because when you've been bitten by the love bug, you want to believe such things]" [3.673–74]. The last half of 673 is a parody of a famous Vergilian line, *Eclogues* 10.69, "amor omnia vincit, et nos cedamus amori [love conquers all, so we should surrender to love].")

The strategies of the *cultus* lover, adjusted as they must be to the variety of both the prey they seek to ensnare and the situations in which the chase is mounted, reveal that the *Ars* engages in an elaborate textual assimilation of erotic pursuits to the rhetorical strategies taught in the schools of Rome to young men of privileged status, based on the principle of decorum: the adjustment of what one says and how one says it to the circumstances in which one finds oneself and to one's estimation of the character, interests, and intelligence of one's audience.[38] The implicit equation of sexual conquest to legal or political success, with persuasive eloquence as the common denominator of these activities and key to their successful prosecution, constitutes both an amused confirmation of the importance of verbal facility—flattery, prevarication, and so on—in erotic activities and, perhaps, a more tart commentary on the lessened stature of rhetoric in the public sphere (given the evisceration of republican traditions of senatorial debate by the power gathered in the hands of one man, the *princeps*), forcing its practitioners to readdress their skills (appropriately disguised as the sincere utterances of heartsick lovers) to the private sphere of sexual (as opposed to political) desire.

I've already quoted the *magister*'s warning against using the rhetoric of the law court or school competition to attempt to win the acquiescence of a *puella*. In a more positive light, he recommends the tactic of flattery, to be varied according to the circumstances (that is, the physical attributes and cosmetic or sartorial choices) of its object:

> Sive erit in Tyriis, Tyrios laudabis amictus:
> > Sive erit in Cois, Coa decere puta.
> Aurata est? ipso tibi sit pretiosior auro;
> > Gausapa si sumpsit, gausapa sumpta proba.
> Astiterit tunicata, "moves incendia" clama,
> > Sed timida, caveat frigora, voce roga.
> Conpositum discrimen erit, discrimina lauda:
> > Torserit igne comam, torte capille, place.
> Brachia saltantis, vocem mirare canentis,
> > Et, quod desierit, verba querentis habe.

(If she's partial to Tyrian colors, praise those Tyrian rags; to Coan, then say you prefer those. Does she accessorize in gold? Then she's more precious to you than gold itself. If she affects rough woolen sweaters, approve of them; and if she shows up wearing a slinky, thin little dress, declare to her, "You're setting me on fire!" but then, very timidly, say that you're afraid she'll catch cold in it. Is her hair very precisely parted? Compliment her on that; if she's used hot curlers, be delighted with those tight curls. Marvel at the moves of a good dancer, the voice of one who likes to sing—and complain a little when she decides to stop.)

(*Ars* 2.297–306)

Such instability of persons and circumstances in the world of the *Ars amatoria* provides a constant challenge to both the would-be lover (or seducer) and his self-appointed expert guide to affairs of the heart. The underlying seriocomic message of the amatory poetry—addressed, to be sure, to a male audience—is that by recourse to a particularly human skill we deal with the variety of life's experience, adapting ourselves to the circumstances in which we find ourselves.

It is this capacity for infinitely flexible, self-aggrandizing behavior—for example, the ability of a man to adjust his flattery to glamorize the shortcomings and faults of any woman he meets, while concealing that it is flattery—that turns out to be the hallmark of the *cultus vir* (and, indeed, the *culta puella*) of the *Ars amatoria*. It is a gift that, in turn, fatally compromises the authority of the *magister amoris*, the secret of whose system for finding, winning, and keeping a lover turns out to be . . . *there is no system*: you have to make it up as you go along; just don't reveal that that's what you're doing. He lets the cat out of the bag at the end of book 1:

Finiturus eram, sed sunt diversa puellis
   Pectora: mille animos excipe mille modis.
Nec tellus eadem parit omnia; vitibus illa
   Convenit, haec oleis; hac bene farra virent.
Pectoribus mores tot sunt, quot in ore figurae;
   Qui sapit, innumeris moribus aptus erit,
Utque leves Proteus modo se tenuabit in undas,
   Nunc leo, nunc arbor, nunc erit hirtus aper.
Hi iaculo pisces, illi capiuntur ab hamis:
   Hos cava contento retia fune trahunt.
Nec tibi conveniet cunctos modus unus ad annos:
   Longius insidias cerva videbit anus.

(I was about to conclude—but, oh yes, I have to add that womens' hearts and minds are very diverse, so that you'll need a thousand different techniques for a thousand different attitudes. You can't get every kind of harvest from the same plot of land; grapes, olives, grains—each needs its own kind of soil. There are as many different temperaments as there are faces, so the smart guy is the one who can adapt to an incredible variety of situations, the way Proteus—Mr. Change himself—could turn himself into gentle waves, or a lion, a tree, even a bristly boar. After all, some people go spearfishing, while others use hooks, and still others haul them in by the netful. Nor, by the way, is it "one size fits all" in making out where age is concerned: an old doe has learned to keep her distance from snares like the ones you're setting.) (*Ars* 1.755–66)

That this crucial advice is presented as an afterthought—"Finiturus eram sed" and so on—is, I think, an Ovidian joke: the *praeceptor amoris* has, in effect, attempted unsuccessfully to forget it, despite its obvious importance, because it torpedoes his claim to have a single system (*ratio*) for controlling desire (*impetus*) and enjoying sex without suffering. A system whose first commandment is, be ready for anything and adapt your responses accordingly—"Qui sapit, innumeris moribus aptus erit" (*Ars* 1.760)—can hardly be called a system at all; the fact of infinite variety in men, women, and their interactions definitively elevates individual initiative and maneuverability over magisterial authority. At the same time, the fact that all this decorous (in the rhetorical sense of the term) behavior, through all its permutations, has the same goal in view—the bedroom in which books 2 and 3 of the *Ars amatoria* conclude—reminds us of how relevant to seductive eloquence is Ovid's description in book 2 of the art of that master storyteller (and lover), Ulysses: "Ille referre aliter saepe solebat idem [He had a knack for retelling the same story in a lot of different ways]" (*Ars* 2.128).

I've just quoted one passage illustrative of such rhetorical decorum (*Ars* 2.297–306); an earlier quotation (*Ars* 3.261–80) had the *magister* cataloguing the many different ways women can dress and behave to hide their defects, and there we are reminded of all the forms taken by nonverbal signification and communication in the world of human interaction, forms also subject to constant vetting for their appropriateness in pursuing the quest for sexual satisfaction. (As the *magister* puts it elsewhere, "Saepe tacens vocem verbaque vultus habet [The face, however silent, often has a voice and words of its own]" [*Ars* 1.574].) There's also a decorum of signs at the games:

At cum pompa frequens caelestibus ibit eburnis,
    Tu Veneri dominae plaude favente manu;

Utque fit, in gremium pulvis si forte puellae
   Deciderit, digitis excutiendus erit:
Etsi nullus erit pulvis, tamen excute nullum:
   Quaelibet officio causa sit apta tuo. . . .
Parva leves capiunt animos: fuit utile multis
   Pulvinum facili composuisse manu.
Profuit et tenui ventos movisse tabella,
   Et cava sub tenerum scamna dedisse pedem.

(But when those regular processions, the ones with the ivory statues
of the gods, go by, be sure to give Lady Venus the biggest hand; and if it
should happen that a piece of dust falls on the chick's lap, brush it off with
your hand or, if there is no dust . . . brush it off anyway. Almost anything
can provide a good excuse to show that you're at her service. Little things
can impress featherbrains: many a guy has gotten good mileage out of re-
arranging a seat cushion, and it also sometimes works to get the hot air
moving around her with a fan, or to prop up her little feet on a stool.)

(*Ars* 1.147–52, 159–62)

Timing can be a crucial component of successful eloquence, by signs or
words. In the early stages of courtship, when a man is trying to pick up a complete stranger in a public place, there's a decorum of speech: "Hic tibi quaeratur
socii sermonis origo, / Et moveant primos publica verba sonos [What you need
is an opening for some friendly chat, but nothing that seems too intimate and
private right away]" (*Ars* 1.143–44)—pick-up lines are notoriously tricky to get
right. At a horse race, "Cuius equi veniant, facito, studiose, requiras: / Nec mora,
quisquis erit, cui favet illa, fave [Be sure to find out by asking her which horses
are coming to the starting gate, and don't lose any time in saying you're betting
on her favorite]" (1.145–46). But at a military triumph, when a Roman general
reenters the city leading captive enemy chieftains and acknowledging the raucous approval of the crowd, expertise (indifferently real or feigned), not accommodation, is appropriate:

Atque aliqua ex illis cum regum nomina quaeret,
   Quae loca, qui montes, quaeve ferantur aquae,
Omnia responde, nec tantum siqua rogabit;
   Et quae nescieris, ut bene nota refer. . . .
Ille vel ille, duces; et erunt quae nomina dicas,
   Si poteris, vere, si minus, apta tamen.

(And if some girl in that crowd should ask you the names of the captive kings, or what places, mountains, and rivers are represented in the victory procession, tell her everything—even if she doesn't ask you. And as for what you don't know—as far as *she* knows, you know it well. "That one and that one there, they're the leaders"; and you'll reel off their names—their real names, if you can; if not, just make some up that sound right.)

(Ars 1.219–22, 227–28)

Finally, at a later stage of the pursuit, adaptation of communication to circumstance becomes a complicated, virtuosic game:

> Interea, sive illa toro resupina feretur,
>   Lecticam dominae dissimulanter adi,
> Neve aliquis verbis odiosas offerat auris,
>   Qua potes ambiguis callidus abde notis . . . .
> [In the theater,] illam respicias, illam mirere licebit:
>   Multa supercilio, multa loquare notis.

(If she's being carried along, reclining on her cushions, sidle up to her litter as if by accident, and in case there are some hostile ears open nearby, skilfully couch your love chat in double meanings and euphemisms. In the theater, it's okay to look her over with obvious admiration; you can say a lot with your eyebrows and your gestures.)

(Ars 1.487–90, 499–500)

One feature of Roman rhetorical training was the ability to interpret facts or situations in such a way as to extract from them meanings, however counterintuitive or farfetched, that served the forensic (legal) or deliberative (political) aim of the speaker. This interpretive tactic was called a *color*.[39] Ovid was clearly attracted to and amused by the application of colors, and the main area in which he practiced this rhetorical trick, with comic inventiveness, was in his appropriation of classical myths and legends, both Greek and Roman. He was, in short, a superb exploiter of these characters and stories, imposing on them delightfully outrageous meanings to support whatever point he wished at the moment to make about his *praecepta amoris*—in some cases to illustrate the happy outcome of following his advice for achieving sexual satisfaction (or, conversely, on ending no longer desired amorous liaisons), in others suggesting how much better off the heroes and heroines of myth and legend would

have been had they been able to profit from his counsels—but also subverting
their culturally iconic status by trivializing them, equating them with the pick-up
schemes and erotic crises of Ovid's Roman contemporaries.

For example, according to the *magister*, self-knowledge plays a foundational
role in the performance of *cultus*, but it is a self-knowledge that parodies rather
than conforming to the Socratic understanding of that famous byword of the
Delphic oracle. Ovid flaunts his subversion of this major philosophical tradition by intruding a superbly bathetic Apollonian epiphany into a discusssion
of how to calm down your *puella* after she catches you making love to another
woman (viz., make love to her: "Oscula da flenti, Veneris da gaudia flenti, / Pax
erit [Kiss those weeping eyes, make love to the weeper—peace will follow]"
[*Ars* 2.459–60]):

> Haec ego cum canerem, subito manifestus Apollo. . . .
>   . . . vates ille videndus adit.
> Is mihi 'Lascivi' dixit 'praeceptor Amoris,
>   Duc, age, discipulos ad mea templa tuos,
> Est ubi diversum fama celebrata per orbem
>   Littera, cognosci quae sibi quemque iubet.
> Qui sibi notus erit, solus sapienter amabit,
>   Atque opus ad vires exiget omne suas.'

(Just as I was writing this, who should appear but Apollo, definitely a
poet worth watching. He said to me, "Head ref in the game of love, come
on! Bring your students to my temple, where the inscription, famous all
over the world, advises all comers to know themselves. Only the man who
knows himself will really be smart in matters of love, and get the job done
using all his resources.")   (*Ars* 2.493, 496–502)

The descent from these elevated sentiments is hilariously abrupt and precipitous:

> 'Cui faciem natura dedit, spectetur ab illa;
>   Cui color est, umero saepe patente cubet:
> Qui sermone placet, taciturna silentia vitet:
>   Qui canet arte, canat; qui bibit arte, bibat.'

(If nature gave him good looks, let him make sure they're always on view;
if he's got a great tan, let him always lie down bare-chested. If he has a

pleasing voice, he shouldn't stay silent for long; does he sing skilfully? Let
him sing; drinks with style? Down the hatch!)   (*Ars* 2.503–6)

Self-knowledge, in other words, is purely material and strategic, part of a campaign to impress (in this case) the woman (or women) with whom you want to
score by showcasing the qualities that will make you most attractive to the opposite sex. To be avoided, in this version of Apollonian wisdom, is not ignorance or some moral failing but ostentation, showing off, trying too hard, having a social tin ear—in the terminology of the great Renaissance courtier and
theorist of courtiership, Castiglione, lacking *sprezzatura*; in more contemporary jargon, not being cool: "Sed neque declament medio sermone diserti, /
Nec sua non sanus scripta poeta legat [But don't let any of them start bloviating
in the middle of a conversation, or some crackpot poet break into verse—his
own]" (*Ars* 2.507–8).[40]

Ovid's comic technique here is obviously one of outrageous trivialization,
turning the message of the Delphic oracle, and of its greatest classical exponent, Socrates (as mediated by Plato), into fashion and dating advice. At the
same time, however, this appropriation of a philosophical tradition slyly suggests that knowledge, and how we cultivate it, is no elevated and disinterested
pursuit of wisdom; rather, it is driven, like all our actions, by desire. Other
uses of the mythological canon by the *magister amoris* are analogously irreverent, even if they claim to be exemplary rather than epiphanic. *Ars* 1.525–64, a
brilliantly ecphrastic account of the discovery of the abandoned Ariadne on
the island of Naxos by the god Dionysus/Bacchus, who ravishes her, makes
her his bride, and promises her immortality as a heavenly constellation, becomes, for the *magister*, an occasion for warning that, if you're trying to attract
(with a view to seducing) an attached woman at a banquet, pretending to be
drunk—Bacchus, of course, the god of wine—is a better strategy than actually being drunk. Early in book 2, the story of the escape of Daedalus and Icarus
from King Minos (for whom Daedalus had constructed the labyrinth imprison-
ing the Minotaur) supposedly clarifies the *magister*'s self-appointed task: "Non
potuit Minos hominis conpescere pinnas; / Ipse deum volucrem detinuisse paro
[Minos couldn't ground the winged man; I, on the other hand, am trying to restrain a winged god]" (*Ars* 2.97–98), but the far-fetched parallel/contrast—
winged man/winged god—seems less revealing than the implicit warning—to
which the *magister* seems oblivious—that, just as Icarus's enthusiasm for flight
defeats his father's cautionary counsel, so the *impetus* of desire must finally over-
match the *ratio* that the *magister* undertakes to impose upon it.[41]

To adduce one further example, in a passage immediately before the Apollonian epiphany I just mentioned, Ovid introduces a parodic, dystopian origin myth in which primitive humans, brutal and asocial, accidentally discover how to make love, with the result that "blanda truces animos fertur mollisse voluptas [enticing pleasure, they say, softened harsh souls]" (*Ars* 2.477); the *magister* introduces this myth to provide an antecedent for, and to justify, making love to your *amica* in order to calm her down after she has discovered that you have been cheating on her. Such eccentric excursions into mythology constitute a distorted, funhouse reflection of the serious recourse of Roman authors—Cicero, Vergil, et al.—to the canon or archive of myths in order to enlist the cultural cachet of this body of traditional story and lore in support of moral, political, and ideological agendas.

O vid's bathetic appropriations of canonic myths and legends is a special adaptation of the predilection for comic deconstruction on view throughout the *Ars amatoria*, a technique that endows parts of the text with the air of a stand-up comedian's performance, where an initial air of serious discussion gives way to progressively sillier or more grotesque utterances, jokes, and parodic stereotypes, from which no situation, institution, or person—including the comedian him- or herself—emerges unscathed. One instance of this deconstruction must stand for many; it occurs early in book 2, the announced purpose of which is to how to convert a one-night stand into a lasting relationship.

The passage begins at line 99 with an attack by the *magister* on any resort to the charms and potions of folk magic to prolong a sexual relationship. (I'll have more to say about this Ovidian aversion in my discussion of the *Remedia amoris*.) Renouncing all such profanities, he offers a high-minded alternative: "Sit procul omne nefas; ut ameris, amabilis esto: / Quod tibi non facies solave forma dabit [Stay away from all that godforsaken nonsense; if you want to be loved, be lovable—something neither a gorgeous face nor a great body will give you]" (*Ars* 2.107–8). The next sixty-eight lines will thoroughly undercut such sententious moralizing.

The *magister* drapes his earnest thesis with garlands of practical advice and popular wisdom: if you really want to keep your *domina*, and not be abandoned by her, "ingenii dotes corporis adde bonis [add cultivation of the mind to the cult of the body]" (*Ars* 2.112); beauty inevitably fades with time (2.113–18), so add to the perishable gifts of your body gifts of mind that will endure to the grave (2.119–20). From this high plateau we move down a bit to specifics: cultivate the *ingenuas artes* (liberal arts), learn Greek and Latin well. Here the *magister* adduces an *exemplum virtutis*: Ulysses, who made up for what he lacked in beauty by his eloquence ("non formosus erat, sed erat facundus" [2.123]). At which point, warning flags go up: eloquence, as we've abundantly seen in book 1, is less a virtue of the mind than a strategy for seduction; furthermore, the *magister* proceeds to offer an instance that hardly seems to support his recommendation of *facunditas* as a way of prolonging a love affair: he introduces a seaside conversation between Calypso and Ulysses, the point of which turns out to be that the goddess's own eloquence—she argues enthymematically, from the fact that incoming waves have washed away Ulysses's diagram in the sand of his nighttime raid on the Trojan camp (*Iliad* 10), that he himself will be destroyed if he commits himself to the treacherous sea—fails to keep the Greek hero from abandoning her (*Ars* 2.129–42).

Seeming to refocus his own argument ("Ergo age" [*Ars* 2.143], the rough equivalent of "but seriously, folks,"), the *magister* returns to his theme that treacherous beauty ("falla[x] . . . figur[a]") is not to be trusted, counterposing not eloquence but "dextera indulgentia [strategic tolerance]" (*Ars* 2.145), by which he means, it turns out, being amicable rather than combative with one's beloved. This binary provides the opening for some hoary but also culturally pointed, comic stereotypes: don't quarrel with your *amica*, the *magister* warns; leave that to husbands and wives, since that's all they do, anyway—especially wives: "Hoc decet uxores; dos est uxoria lites [That's okay for wives; quarrels are their dowry]" (*Ars* 2.155). Since you're not being brought together by the law (in marriage) but by love, be nice to her so that she'll be glad to see you (*Ars* 2.157–60). Besides obviously tapping into a well-established vein of misogamy, these lines have an anti-imperial sting in their tail. By suggesting that quarrels and ill-will define marriage, they in effect undercut Augustan initiatives encouraging well-to-do Romans to marry and rear families, out of *pietas* toward the empire, and offer instead a clear endorsement of the kind of hanky-panky celebrated in the *Ars*, though (officially) frowned on in imperial legislation.

But what's this: in a passage I mentioned at the beginning of my consideration of the *Ars amatoria*, the *magister* now declares that his advice is not intended for the rich, who can get what they want by giving :

Non ego divitibus venio praeceptor amandi:
　Nil opus est illi, qui dabit, arte mea;
Secum habet ingenium, qui, cum libet, "accipe" dicit;
　Cedimus: inventis plus placet ille meis.

(I'm not setting up to be the love professor to the rich; opening my book does nothing for the guy who can open his wallet instead. Whoever can say, whenever he wants, "Here: take this," has plenty of love smarts; trust me, he'll do better that way than with any of my schemes.)

(*Ars* 2.161–64)

The double-edged implication is that the rich can't be bothered to be nice to their *amicae* and they get away with it because the only thing that matters to women is getting lots of gifts. Here, as elsewhere in the amatory verse (cf. *Amores* 1.8, *Ars* 1.399–436), Ovid makes fun of the misogynist conviction (still current in some circles) that "diamonds are a girl's best friend." By contrast with those who can buy a woman's affections—Ovid's audience would probably recognize a swipe at the *novi homines* who brought their war profits to Rome during and after the civil wars—the *magister* declares himself the poet of the poor: "Pauperibus vates ego sum, quia pauper amavi; / Cum dare non possem munera, verba dabam [I'm the poor man's bard because it was as a poor man that I looked for love: when I couldn't give gifts, I gave words]" (*Ars* 2.165–66). This, too, is an old joke: "*dare verba*" in Ovid's Latin means "to lie"; hence, the command, "*amabilis esto*" if you wish to keep your beloved, turns out to be a euphemism for the same deceitful eloquence earlier so important in winning her.

One move remains to complete this Ovidian deconstruction of moralizing authority and its advice for making love endure. Not only must the poor lover rely on using kind words to retain his *amica*, he can't even object when she treats him badly: "Pauper amet caute: timeat maledicere pauper,/ Multaque divitibus non patienda ferat [No resources? You'd better be a cautious lover, afraid to raise your voice in anger at your girlfriend; the poor guy has to put up with a lot that a Wall Street type wouldn't stand for]" (*Ars* 2.167–68)—so it turns out that even outside marriage women are scolds (yet another miogynistic cliché)! Magisterial advice now collapses into pathetic confession: once, he admits—in *Amores* 1.7, to be precise—my anger led me to muss my *domina*'s hair; not only did this cost me an extended banishment from her bed, but I had to pay for the *tunica* she claimed I tore, though I don't think I did, before she'd let me back in: ("Nec puto, nec sensi tunicam laniasse; sed ipsa / Dixerat, et pretio est illa redempta meo" [*Ars* 2.171–72])—the golddigger theme sounded again. The precipitous descent from the sententious heights of "beauty fades, so make your love last by gifts of mind and character," down a slippery slope of well-tested comic themes bumps to a halt with one final cliché, insulting to the *magister*'s self-esteem (and subversive of his bona fides as an expert): "At vos, si sapitis, vestri peccata magistri / Effugite, et culpae damna timete meae [So you, if you're smart, avoid your teacher's mistakes, and don't get stung the way he was]" (*Ars* 2.173–74). That is, I'm the teacher; do as I say, not as I do.

Book 1 of the *Ars amatoria* abounds in misogynistic and misogamist commonplaces such as those just instantiated. All women want to be wooed; the woman's sexual appetite is stronger and less governable than the man's (*Ars* 1.279–82); all women are gold diggers (*Ars* 1.399–400); women are all deceivers by nature—"Non mihi, sacrilegas meretricum ut persequar artes, / Cum totidem linguis sint satis ora decem [Ten mouths, each with its own wagging tongue, still wouldn't be enough for me to put on the record all the unconscionable tricks of those sluts]" (*Ars* 1.435–36)—so it is acceptable to deceive them in return: "fallite fallentes [trick the tricksters]" (*Ars* 1.645). All women are vain and believe they are desirable and thus are more easily fooled by flattery (*Ars* 1.613–14); you can use physical force to have your way with a woman because, with her, "no" really means "yes"; and not to act in this situation reflects the lover's *rusticitas*, not his *pudor* (decency) (*Ars* 1.669–78).

In embracing truisms that strike modern readers (quite accurately) as prime expressions of traditional Mediterranean sexism, the *magister amoris* indirectly (and against his will) testifies to the power of *eros* to undercut, or expose as useless, the system of seduction techniques he is propounding. As the circumstance-oriented exhortations of a trained orator (which, of course, Ovid was), such accusations implicitly acknowledge, by transference and projection, the often uncontrollable power of desire over men (not, as claimed, over women) and— even worse for the *magister*—they reflect his fear that, when most needed, the persuasive skills he seeks to inculcate in his male pupils will fail them. This fear stands revealed in his plea to women (*Ars* 1.617–18)—oddly placed in book 1, which otherwise reflects a male point of view—to be accommodating to men whose protestations of desire are obviously phony, as they may come in time to believe their own lies. In other words, this guy is too lousy a rhetorician to convince you with his lies, but he's dumb enough to convince himself!

Whatever Ovid thought about women—and his ancestral culture, as I've just noted, was, and remains to this day, rich in traditions expressing, through the medium of clichés about women's greed, lustfulness, and chronic infidelity, male fears of female power and ability—we cannot safely equate the *magister*'s outbursts with those of his author. These are rhetorical ploys by which the *magister* hopes to encourage his troops and thus earn their accolades for his pedagogical skills. Behind his creation, the poet invites his readers to laugh— however tasteless such laughter may seem today—at the self-contradictory

arguments and stereotypical characterizations by which men seek to justify
their domination (or at least attempted domination) of women.

O vid's most extended commentary on the *Ars amatoria* is also the most
problematic. It constitutes the second book of the *Tristia*, written in exile,
and is addresed to Augustus, pleading for if not the end of his exile then at least
persmission to move to an outpost of empire less unforgivingly rugged—and, we
might add, less lacking in *cultus*—than Tomis. Ovid assures the *princeps* that if
the latter had actually had the time to read the *Ars*—which of course he hadn't
because running an empire left no time for literary trivia—he would have discovered that it was an entertaining fiction bearing no resemblance to the poet's
own, respectable life (*Tristia* 2.220–40),[42] and that it was carefully labeled as a
text never intended for the eyes of Roman matrons (*Tristia* 2.275–76; cf. *Ars*
1.31–34). Furthermore, Greek and Roman literature abound in erotic and adulterous elements that have not been singled out for condemnation (*Tristia* 2.371–
408); indeed, Ovid is writing in an elegiac tradition full of poems about wives
fooling husbands (*Tristia* 2.445–70), while popular plays (mimes), such as those
Augustus has seen, indeed patronized, have as part of their conventions adultery and young men carrying on affairs (*Tristia* 2.497–517).

Ovid argues, in other words, that Augustus is swimming against a longstanding cultural tide in refusing to recognize that *eros* (passion), with all its
problems and complications, is a crucial dimension of human experience, celebrated, anatomized, and bemoaned in poetry of all kinds, times, and places.
Placed within this broad context, a comic poem ("*liber iocosa*" [*Tristia* 2.422])
such as the *Ars amatoria* would only seem salacious to those whose minds were
already perverted (*Tristia* 2.275–79, 301–2, 307–8)—hardly a propitiatory appeal to the emperor!

This virtuoso performance—which bears some relation, *avant la lettre*, to
Freud's famous joke about the broken pot—is not necessarily to be taken seriously. It's an extended exercise in deliberative rhetoric, ostensibly designed to
reverse Augustus's decree of relegation, and traverses all possible avenues of
persuasion, including a supposedly sincere reprise of that elegiac standby, the
recusatio (*Tristia* 2.313–38, including a surely tongue-in-cheek reference to *Amores*
2.1 [333–34]), and such heavy doses of self-pity and flattery that it also registers
as an extended exercise in (to paraphrase one of New York's favorite euphemis-
tic occupations) lament and grovel.[43]

Nor are classicists convinced that the defense of the *Ars* that makes up the
greater part of the book even speaks to the reason for the poet's banishment.

Ovid says that two sins have ruined him, *carmen* and *error* (*Tristia* 2.207), but that he must remain silent concerning the latter lest he reopen imperial wounds by bringing the damaging past to light. But "altera pars superest, qua turpi carmine factus / arguor obsceni doctor adulterii [that leaves the charge of having composed a disgusting poem that makes me a tutor of filthy adultery]" (*Tristia* 2.211–12). Earlier, comparing himself to Acteon, punished for unwittingly discovering Diana naked at her bath, he asks rhetorically, "Cur aliquid vidi? Cur noxia lumina feci? / Cur imprudenti cognita culpa mihi? [Why did I even see something like that? Why did I make criminals of my eyes? How could I be such a jerk, to let myself know anything about such a crime?]" (*Tristia* 2.103–4) It may well be that Ovid's involvement, voluntarily or not, in a sexual intrigue, or a pattern of same, by Augustus's granddaughter Julia was the real occasion for his banishment in 8 C.E., and the publication, some years before, of the *Ars* (by this time widely known and hailed among Rome's literate elite) was a face-saving excuse by the Emperor to get a talkative witness to a family scandal out of town fast and permanently.

Be that as it may, Ovid's multifold justification of his amorous poetry, even if of dubious sincerity, can give us clues to what is going on in and behind the poet's seriocomic vision. But what his apologia, full of praise for Augustus's wisdom, virtue, and benevolence, does not address is the implicit challenge, in the largest sense, that his amatory poetry, and especially the *Ars amatoria*, offers to Augustan policy, ideology, and propaganda.[44] Perhaps Ovid's most substantial, and certainly his most obvious, engagement of imperial authority lies in the *Ars amatoria*'s challenge to Augustus's program of imposing on Rome, through his massive building campaigns, his own constructed image as the city's, and the empire's, divinely sanctioned, benevolent ruler and protector. Through its depictions and appropriations of Roman civic topography, the *Ars amatoria* challenges the authority of the emperor over the City of Rome, its public spaces, and their propagandistic significance. In books 1 and 3 of the *Ars*, the adepts of the *magister amoris* use newly renovated Augustan sites as places to pick up and be picked up, as theaters of self-construction leading to sexual self-aggrandizement. All the places mentioned in book 1 where the *magister* advises young Roman men to search for lovable, or at least beddable, women were constructed or reconstructed by Augustus, or associated with his family.[45] Even an (imagined) imperial triumph, celebrating the return of Augustus's grandson, Gaius Caesar, from a successful engagement against enemies beyond the borders of the empire (*Ars* 1.213–28), becomes, as we've seen (pages 54–55), an occasion for a pick-up artist to construct himself as an expert on imperial geography by identifying (whether accurately or inaccurately; it makes no difference)

the conquered rivers or mountains borne along in allegorical pageants, to impress (with a view to later seducing) the girl standing next to him, when, watching the parade go by, she asks for that information.

So while the public spaces of Rome serve as the visible signs—the embodiment in marble and gold—of the empire's claim on the personal loyalties and
activities of its subjects, they function concurrently as the settings of quests for
a purely personal satisfaction that has nothing to do with public and imperial
policy. Rome, the *magister* assures his male charges, offers no end of prey, to be
sought in a variety of habitats: "Tot tibi tamque dabit formosas Roma puellas,
/ 'Haec habet,' ut dicas, 'quicquid in orbe fuit' [Rome will offer you so many, so
gorgeous girls that you'll have to say, 'All the beauty in the world is right here']"
(*Ars* 1.55–56). The world's pulchritude, like its resources and products, has
ended up in imperial Rome. The trick is to seize the occasion, to act in a manner that turns the particular space and occasion into a wooing opportunity.[46]

By its representation, however exaggerated and ironic, of Augustus's temples, theaters, arenas, and circuses as the playgrounds of Venus, Cupid, and
their sectaries of both sexes, Ovid's amatory poetry pointedly if obliquely asks,
who controls, and to what end, the space that is Rome? What forces should
direct and harness the energies of the city? Will they be personal or corporate?
Directed toward pleasure and self-fulfillment (with all its dangers and foibles) or
service to larger and not necessarily sympathetic ideals and obligations? Which,
finally, possesses the more important authority over the city: its builders and
official guardians, who preside over its ideological significance, or its users, who
experience it as the stage on which they play out their lives?

The *Ars amatoria* is, in sum, a comic commentary on what happens when
Roman power, education, and wealth (especially new wealth) intersect with
human desire in a new "world city" (Habinek's term)—formed by the phenom-
ena of imperial conquest and commerce—in which the older bonds of family,
clan, and class no longer have their former sway over public and private life, and
hedonism, prompted by new wealth and influence, seeks to use the resources of
the city to fuel a self-consciously stylish, modern quest for self-gratification even
as a newly centralized state (ruled by the *princeps*) seeks to control personal
behavior—especially erotic behavior—so that it serves the larger needs and
goals of that state. The resultant civic and social tensions, focused in part on
gender relationships pursued now for sexual pleasure rather than, as in the
past, for social status or interfamilial alliance, animate the *Ars amatoria*. Crises
of desire and authority (the latter displaced from the person and policies of the
princeps to the more overtly dubious realm of the *magister*'s uneasy synthesis of
experiential pessimism and programmatic optimism) render the poetic struc-

ture unstable and obliquely suggest a similar instability in the larger structures of imperial rule. What the *Ars* finally leaves us with is an image of verbal and behavioral strategies constantly shifting and improvising to cope with protean human experience; in other words, the very negation of Augustan and imperial permanence hymned by Vergil in the *Aeneid*.[47]

Remedia amoris: When Your Relationship Goes South; Or, What Happens When You Play It Backward

In just about the entire Western poetic discourse of love, from antiquity to the present, the greatest crises attendant upon erotic involvement result from unreturned, asymmetrical, impeded, or suddenly rejected desire. In the *Amores*, Ovid treats some of these situations as instances of or occasions for moment-to-moment crisis management: strategies of coded conspiracy (1.4), attempted persuasion (1.3, 1.6, 2.2, etc.), willed self-delusion (1.4), and so forth—strategies, I've suggested, that expose, from a comic perspective, the hopelessness so often a camp follower of those engaged in campaigns fought under Cupid's banner. By contrast, the comic conceit generating the *Remedia amoris* is that expertise on falling in love and expertise on falling out of love (when necessary) can flow with equal facility from the mouth (and pen) of the same expert. As the *magister amoris* assures his erstwhile (male) follower: "Tu mihi, qui, quod amas, aegre dediscis amare, / Nec potes, et velles posse, docendus eris [But you who must now learn to unlove what you love, who want to do this but can't—you'll be taught how by me]" (*Rem* 297–98). The *magister*'s advice is supposedly for both sexes—"Sed quaecumque viris, vobis quoque dicta, puellae, / Credite: diversis partibus arma damus [Whatever I say to men, girls, you must believe that I'm saying to you as well; we'll supply arms impartially to each side in this war]" (*Rem* 49–50)—but its dominant paradigm is of a man escaping a cruel woman.

As the *Ars amatoria* excludes the rich and the beautiful from its audience, so the *Remedia* declares the strong-willed exempt from its teachings:

> Optimus ille sui vindex, laedentia pectus
>   Vincula qui rupit, dedoluitque semel.
> Sed cui tantum animi est, illum mirabor et ipse,
>   Et dicam, "monitis non eget iste meis."

(The guy who really can call himself a free man is the one who cuts himself loose from a self-destructive relationship and then makes a clean

break from grieving about it. If anybody really is that strong, even I will
be impressed, and I'll admit, "This guy has no need for my advice.")

(*Rem* 293–96)

This exception made, the *magister* minces no words in boasting of his new
accomplishment:

Me duce damnosas, homines, conpescite curas,
  Rectaque cum sociis me duce navis eat.
Naso legendus erat tum, cum didicistis amare:
  Idem nunc vobis Naso legendus erit.

(Follow my advice, men, and control those crippling emotions; follow my
advice, and get them, and your life, back on an even keel. It was Naso you
needed to read when you were learning how to be a good lover; it's that
very same Naso you need so badly to read right now.)   (*Rem* 69–72)

The image of the straight-sailing ship (70) looks back to the beginning of the
Ars, where the *magister* declares himself to be love's helmsman, conquering by
his experience-born skills the rough seas of passion (a claim, as we've seen, frequently contradicted by the *magister*'s description of love's irresistible power).
But whereas in the *Ars* there is a double, somewhat self-contradictory understanding of what the *magister* is in fact teaching—self-control or control of others for the sake of one's pleasure—here in the *Remedia* self-control—what we
might call steering clear of passion—is precisely and entirely the issue.

Me duce . . . me duce; Naso legendus erat . . . Naso legendus erit. The situations
are opposed—learning how to love, learning how not to love (or, more precisely,
to "un-love")—but the repetitions that balance and, in effect, frame these lines
suggest a closed system in which countervailing forces coexist within the
sublime equilibrium of the *magister*'s controlling vision. Or, as he puts it
elsewhere,

Ad mea, decepti iuvenes, praecepta venite,
  Quos suus ex omni parte fefellit amor.
Discite sanari, per quem didicistis amare:
  Una manus vobis vulnus opemque feret.

(All you young men taken for a ride and then left high and dry by love,
come check out my system: the same teacher who taught you how to love

will now teach you how to stop the bleeding from a broken heart; the
hand that wounds can also heal.)   (*Rem* 41–44)

Nor is this the extent of his boastfulness about what we might call his ambi-
dextrous (ambisextrous?) delivery of erotic counseling. Claiming that attention
to his *magisterium* would have changed the course of mythology—and of history itself—by teaching frustrated lovers how to squelch their unlawful or unrequited passions, he insists:

> Vixisset Phyllis, si me foret usa magistro,
>   Et per quod novies, saepius isset iter;
> Nec moriens Dido summa vidisset ab arce
>   Dardanias vento vela dedisse rates; . . .
> Da mihi Pasiphaën, iam tauri ponet amorem: . . .
> Crede Parim nobis, Helenen Menelaus habebit,
>   Nec manibus Danais Pergama victa cadent.

(If she'd followed my advice, Phyllis would have lived, and taken the path
she did more than just nine times; when Dido, from her vantage point
atop her castle, saw the Trojan ships setting out from her harbor under
full sail, she wouldn't have regarded it as a death sentence. Send me
Pasiphae as a student, and that's the end of her love for a bull. Entrust
Paris to me, Menelaus keeps Helen, and the Trojan War never happens;
end of story.)[48]   (*Rem* 55–58, 63, 65–66)

Of course, the *magister*'s disciples will recall equally outrageous claims of opposite valence, uttered in the *Ars amatoria*, about mythic heroines whose tragic
abandonment by treacherous males could have been averted had they available
to them the magister's advice on how to attract men:

> Quantum in te, Theseu, volucres Ariadna marinas
>   Pavit, in ignoto sola relicta loco! . . .
> Et famam pietatis habet, tamen hospes et ensem
>   Praebuit et causam mortis, Elissa, tuae.
> Quid vos perdiderit, dicam? Nescistis amare:
>   Defuit ars vobis; arte perennat amor.

(Thanks to you, Theseus, Ariadne is quaking with fear of circling sea
birds, abandoned on an uncharted island. As for you, Dido, your guest

was famous for his morals, but all he did was leave you with a sword and a cause to use it on yourself. What did you women in? Shall I tell you? It was because you didn't know how to be compelling lovers. You lacked the tricks of the trade that make love last.)   (*Ars* 3.35–36, 39–42)

This opening comic move of the *Remedia* shares the stage with another: as a counterpoint to his boasting, the *magister* has some explaining to do to the god of love, who feels outraged or threatened (or both), depending on how one interprets the tone of the *Remedia*'s opening lines: "Legerat huius Amor titulum nomenque libelli: / 'Bella mihi, video, bella parantur' ait [Love saw the title page of this book; 'Uh, oh,' he said, 'someone's getting ready to make war on me']" (*Rem* 1–2). Insisting that he remains Love's poet, and follower—"ego semper amavi, / Et si, quid faciam, nunc quoque, quaeris, amo [I've always been a lover, and if you ask what I think I'm doing now, I'm still a lover]" (*Rem* 7–8)—and that "nec nova praeteritum Musa retexit opus [nor is this new poem an exposé of the last one]" (*Rem* 12), the Ovidian alter ego justifies his latest poetic effort as a rescue operation: "At siquis male fert indignae regna puellae, / Ne pereat, nostrae sentiat artis opem [But if any guy lies crushed under the heel of an unworthy girlfriend, if he's not to die [from such treatment], he'll need all the help he can get from my expertise]" (*Rem* 15–16). Furthermore, he adds opportunistically, in saving lovers from self-destruction, he's also saving Cupid from the ugly reputation of a murderer: "Qui, nisi desierit, misero periturus amore est, / Desinat; et nulli funeris auctor eris [As for the poor slob who'll die from an unhappy love affair unless he gets out of it, let him get out, and then you won't be responsible for the funeral]" (*Rem* 21–22). Of course, with very few exceptions the convention that disappointed lovers will kill themselves—or be murdered by love—is just that, a (literary) convention, especially of classical myth. The following lines, in arguing that Cupid, as a child, should (in effect) make love, not war, leaving the business of death to his stepfather, Mars, continue to play with conventions: they present themselves as an espousal of divine decorum, but are actually a send-up of generic decorum:

Et puer es, nec te quicquam nisi ludere oportet; . . .
Vitricus et gladiis et acuta dimicet hasta; . . .
Tu cole maternas, tuto quibus utimur, artes. . . .
Effice nocturna frangatur ianua rixa,
   Et tegat ornatas multa corona fores:
Fac coeant furtim iuvenes timidaeque puellae,
   Verbaque dent cauto qualibet arte viro:

Et modo blanditias rigido, modo iurgia posti
  Dicat et exclusus flebile cantet amans.
His lacrimis contentus eris sine crimine mortis;
  Non tua fax avidos digna subire rogos.

(After all, you're just a kid; playing should be the only thing you care
about. Leave the weapons of mass destruction to your stepfather, and
you practice your mother's skills, which are safe to use. Let the front door
be damaged in nightly fights and the doorway be covered with bouquets
left by many lovers; arrange secret meetings between young men and their
fearful married girlfriends; and let them make up any kind of story they
can to fool the suspicious husband. Let the lover, shut out from his mistress's house, sing sad songs and use now flattery, now argument to get
past that tightly closed door. You'll be happy enough with all the resulting
tears, without being responsible for anyone's demise; your torch should
never go near a voracious funeral pyre.)

(Rem 23, 27, 29, 31–38)

In other words, the repertory of the elegiac poets is Cupid's domain; he will
escape capital blame if he is satisfied with the deceptions, lies, quarrels, and laments of urbane young lovers (iuvenes timidaeque puellae)—that is, if he confines
his campaigns to the landscape of desire fabricated by those poets, within which
it's indecorous to let lovers die, and avoids the terminal pathos of many of Ovid's
own Heroides, to say nothing of the tragic guilt of Vergil's Dido. In sum, Ovid
uses the conceit of his magister's self-exculpating lecture to a paranoid Cupid in
order to poke fun once again (as in Amores 1.1, 2.1, and 3.1), but from a different
perspective, at the poetic traditions that defined the topics and the boundaries
of elegiac poetry. And the god, thus lectured and persuaded, permits the magister to go forward with the latter's "art of un-loving," in a line that, by its structure, ironically recalls Amores 1.1.24, in which the same god launches the arrow
that will introduce the poet to the pains of love and thus to the routines and
conventions of elegiac poetry: "Haec ego: movit Amor gemmatas aureus alas, /
Et mihi. 'propositum perfice' dixit 'opus' [When I had finished, Love, bling and
all, shook his gem-encrusted wings and said to me, 'Okay, go ahead and finish
what you've started']" (Rem 39–40).

The passages I have juxtaposed that contrast the respective claims of the Remedia amoris and Ars amatoria to supposed efficacy in relieving the distress of
mythological heroines are more than just delightful examples of Ovidian comic
hyperbole. Taken together, they illustrate one of two intertwined techniques

that constitute Ovid's larger poetic strategy in composing the *Remedia*. Each of these techniques should possess contemporary resonance for a twenty-first-century reader. On the one hand, we can recognize in the *Remedia* a distinctive, pseudo-therapeutic regimen of recovery: Professor Naso's twelve-step program, a sequence of psychological and behavioral strategies designed to lessen and eventually unravel completely an erotic entanglement that has gone bad; a guide to freeing oneself from an unrewarding and potentially self-destructive dependency (albeit one that resulted from following rules laid down by the *magister amoris*); but a guide that also incorporates warnings on the many dangers of and occasions for backsliding.

On the other hand, supporting (or perhaps comically subverting) this display of medico-psychological mastery is a rhetorical campaign that provides an exemplary parallel (mutatis mutandis) to the late-twentieth-century joke that asks what you would get if you were to play a record of country music songs backward and answers that you would get back your dog, your house, your sweetheart, and your sanity. Which is to say, Ovid also presents the *Remedia* as a systematic reversal of the advice proferred in the *Ars*—in effect, a virtuosic parody of the *disputatio ad utramque partem* (argument taking both sides of a debated question) as practiced (indeed, honed to perfection) in the Roman rhetorical schools—such that the *Ars* "played backward" yields the *Remedia* and, of course, vice versa. The presence of the selfsame Dido on both lists of mythological or legendary lovers just mentioned (Phyllis also figures in lines I have not quoted from the *Ars*)—those who would have done better had they possessed the *Ars* and those who could have saved themselves a lot of heartache had they read the *Remedia*—underscores this strategy of reversed eloquence. Cupid sums it up best when he addresses the *magister* as "O qui sollicitos modo das, modo demis amores [You who first give, then take away, *agita*-inducing desires]" (*Rem* 557). And the *magister* himself, counseling recovering lovers, "teneros ne tange poetas," confesses, "summoveo dotes impius ipse meas [don't even think about reading love poets (I'm shooting myself in the foot by placing my own work out of bounds)]" (*Rem* 757–58; the reference is presumably to *Ars* 2.273–74, where he considers the possibility of sending "teneros . . . versus" ["sweet verses"] to "doctae puellae." ["well-read girls"]).

Although it's fairly easy to distinguish these two elements of the *Remedia* in the abstract, keeping them separate in reading (or interpreting) the text is much more complicated since the distinction is in fact artificial and ex post facto. Nonetheless, I'll begin with a few remarks on the poem as an addict-rehabilitation system and look somewhat more closely at an extended passage that deals with the dangers of backsliding; then I'll devote the larger part of my discussion to Ovid's fairly systematic reversal (or inversion) in the *Remedia* of advice given in the *Ars* since this is where he devotes most of his energy in creating a comic rebuttal to his handbook for aspiring lovers.

I am hardly the first reader of the *Remedia amoris* to note the similarities between its approach to the problem of breaking off an obsessive but unhappy erotic relationship and modern programs of rehabilitation for those addicted to tobacco, alcohol, or narcotics. In fact, the latest edition and translation of the text in the widely used Loeb Classical Library labels its three major sections, "Therapy After Separation," "Therapy in Her Presence," and "Causes of Recidivism." But I believe it's important to keep in mind that the *magister's* system for breaking the hold of desire on one's existence grapples with the same problem that haunts his system for winning or keeping an object of desire: the sheer variety of human characteristics and situations, necessitating, for at least the possibility of success, a pragmatic, frequently shifting strategy rather than the consistent application of a single, one-size-fits-all set of rules. In other words, one thing that doesn't change from *Ars amatoria* to the *Remedia amoris* is the key role played by *suitability* (the analogue, I've suggested, to *decorum* in rhetorical practice) in any response to situations or crises of desire and to the people who generate them. As the *magister* puts it, "Nam quoniam variant animi, variabimus artes; / Mille mali species, mille salutis erunt [Now since temperaments vary so much, we'll vary our treatments; for a thousand types of illness, we'll offer a thousand cures]" (*Rem* 525–26). Recalling the ending of *Ars* book 1 is inescapable: "sunt diversa puellis / pectora: mille animos excipe mille modis" (*Ars* 1.755–56; see this chapter, pages 52–53).

From its beginning, then, the rehabilitation project for the erotically addicted must incorporate flexibility, as opposed to consistency, of response. In his opening round of strategies for extinguishing desire, the *magister* first espouses a policy of nipping desire in the bud:

Dum licet, et modici tangunt praecordia motus,
   Si piget, in primo limine siste pedem.
Opprime, dum nova sunt, subiti mala semina morbi,
   Et tuus incipiens ire resistat equus.

(While you still can, while you're only experiencing mild desires, if they make you uncomfortable, then freeze on the very first step of the ladder of love. Suppress, while they're still new, those first symptoms of love; hold your horses right at the starting gate.)   (*Rem* 79–82)

If "*equus*" is here a colloquial euphemism for the penis, it adds spice to the meta-phor,[49] but a few lines later he admits this advice may not be universally appli-cable and adjusts it, advising caution and delay where prompt and decisive ac-tion would be futile in the face of a desire neither incipient nor fading but rather at its fullest intensity:

> Si tamen auxilii perierunt tempora primi,
>   Et vetus in capto pectore sedit amor,
> Maius opus superest. . . .
> Qui modo nascentes properabam pellere morbos,
>   Admoveo tardam nunc tibi lentus opem.
> Aut nova, si possis, sedare incendia temptes,
>   Aut ubi per vires procubuere suas:
> Dum furor in cursu est, currenti cede furori;
>   Difficiles aditus impetus omnis habet.

(But if it's way past the time for first aid because an old love is in complete control of your heart, this is going to be a much bigger job. I was in a hurry to expel your infection in its early stages, but now, coming in as a relief pitcher late in the game, I have to move much more slowly. You try to stamp out the fire either when it's new or when its strength has pretty much given out; while it's raging, however, give way before its heat because it's difficult to come to grips with the sheer force of it.)

(*Rem* 107–9, 115–20)

The admission in this last line in effect attaches a debunking asterisk to the absoluteness of the *magister*'s claim, at the beginning of the *Remedia*, that he has created a foolproof regimen of control over passion: "Et quod nunc *ratio* est, *impetus* ante fuit" (*Rem* 10; emphasis added); if in fact you can't control *impetus*, he now counsels, you must learn to outwait it: "Temporis ars medicina fere est [Be patient, patient; it's like medicine]" (*Rem* 131). Similarly, after counseling feigned indifference—you may even come to believe it!—to the woman from whom you wish to, but because of erotic obsession cannot, break away (*Rem* 491–522), the *magister* abruptly changes field, advising instead, "Desine luctari . . . ; / Explenda est sitis ista tibi, quo perditus ardes [Stop fighting it; instead, try to quench that burning thirst that you can't see relief from]" (*Rem* 531, 533), that is, give in to your desire, but overdo it: "Taedia quaere mali: faciunt et taedia finem [Aim for the disgust that comes from overindulgence; that disgust will set you free]" (*Rem* 539).

At yet another point, the *magister* is even forced to acknowledge that, like the ungovernable force of passion, so the variety of erotic situations in which his charges may find themselves could undercut the authority of his teachings. While urging a disgruntled lover, after lovemaking, to search the naked body of his *amica* for blemishes and faults, he adds, "Sed quoniam totidem mores totidemque figurae, / Non sunt iudiciis omnia danda meis [But since there's so much variety when it comes to bodies, don't be entirely ruled by my strategies]" (*Rem* 425–26); that is, you may look for blemishes and be excited instead by what you see. But his most insightful and self-subverting comment on this subject seems to be, "exemplo quemque docente suo [each one learns from his own example]" (*Rem* 684), in which case, the would-be ender of his addiction might well ask, who needs a loquacious teacher to smother him (or her?) in endless strategies and aphorisms?.

A quick survey of some of those strategies and recommendations should serve to confirm Ovid's anticipation (albeit from a comic perspective) of modern rehabilitative schemes. The avoidance of occasions that accommodate or encourage addictive behavior is crucial; in the case of desire, the *magister* insists, leisure is the danger, engaging in useful activity the antidote:

> Fac monitis fugias otia prima meis.
> Haec, ut ames, faciunt. . . .
> Otia si tollas, periere Cupidinis arcus; . . .
> Cedit amor rebus: res age, tutus eris.

> (My first rule is, avoid free time, which opens you to desire. Keeping busy breaks Cupid's bow. Love retreats from a full schedule; get to work and you'll be spared.)   (*Rem* 136–37, 139, 144)

Aside from the commonsensical quality of this advice—submitting oneself to demanding routines and tasks distracts one's attention from otherwise insistent, ultimately irresistible cravings—it incorporates yet another Ovidian joke at the expense of the Roman generic theory and decorum to which I've referred in connection with traditional (conservative) complaints about the elegiac poets' espousal of a private ethos of love and leisure (*otium*) in defiance of Roman values of public activity (*negotium*) and responsibility. Take away *otia*, the magister contends (cf. that joke about playing a country music song backward!), and Cupid's bow is broken, that is, love fades, your addiction ends, you get your self-possession back. Otherwise, he warns, love will fill the empty spaces of an idle life: "Sic venit ille puer, sic puer ille manet [Here comes that boy [i.e., Cupid], and here he'll stay]" (*Rem* 168).

The first concrete step ("prima tempora" [*Rem* 234]) in the *magister*'s program of busyness—he also refers to it as "artis . . . ianua nostrae [the gateway to my system]" (*Rem* 233)—is putting physical distance between yourself and the causes of your addiction. For the Roman lover, that means fleeing urban leisure and the desire it breeds and immersing himself in the myriad routines of country life (*Rem* 169–212). But this geographical version of going cold turkey will not be easy to initiate or to endure, the *magister* admits: "Dura aliquis praecepta vocet mea; dura fatemur / Esse [Some will call my rules harsh; harsh is exactly what they are; I admit it]" (*Rem* 225–26). And Ovid has him paint an amusing but psychologically penetrating picture of the addicted lover's ingenuity at finding ways to put off or curtail his salvific exile:

> Flebis, et occurret desertae nomen amicae,
>   Stabit et in media pes tibi saepe via. . . .
> Nec pluvias opta, nec te peregrina morentur
>   Sabbata, nec damnis Allia nota suis.
>   . . . nec, maneas ut prope, finge moras:
> Tempora nec numera, nec crebro respice Romam,
>   Sed fuge . . .

(You'll cry, and the name of your abandoned mistress will echo inside you; often you'll drag your feet in the middle of the journey. But don't hope for a rain delay or use holidays—or, for that matter, anniversaries of national defeats—as an excuse to suspend your trip. Don't make up reasons for delay so that you can stay close to home. Don't count the days that you'll be gone or keep looking back toward Rome—just get out of there!)   (*Rem* 215–16, 219–20, 222–24)

The emphatic, finger-shaking anaphoras ("nec . . . nec . . . nec") of the *magister*'s admonition parody the stern lecture of a parent to a child ingeniously manufacturing excuses for not taking a bitter but necessary medicine—the parallel is in fact suggested by the *magister* himself: "Saepe bibi sucos, quamvis invitus, amaros / Aeger [Often when I've been sick, I've had to take bitter medicines, however unwillingly]" (*Rem* 227–28)—as he insists that only complete and long absence (and thus abstinence) will defeat persistent, persevering desire:

> Quod nisi firmata properaris mente reverti,
>   Inferet arma tibi saeva rebellis Amor.

Quidquid et afueris, avidus sitiensque redibis,
  Et spatium damno cesserit omne tuo.

(If you come running back with anything less than rock-solid willpower,
Love the insurgent will immediately renew his vicious attacks. Never
mind that you took a leave of absence; you've come back still hungering
and thirsting for love, and all your travels will have done you no good.)

(*Rem* 245–48)

If, however, flight from Rome, and the object of desire, be impossible, the
magister has at the ready a considerable repertory of strategies designed to
turn proximity to that object into something other than a disaster. Since some
of these strategies involve the precise, even verbally precise, reversal of advice
designed to help the would-be lover achieve the relationship from which, disenchanted, he is now seeking desperately to escape, I will mention only a few,
and those briefly, saving them for fuller treatment in the next section; basically, they involve the willed metamorphosis of the once (and, in effect, still)
beloved into an object of hatred and revulsion. "Saepe refer tecum sceleratae
facta puellae, / Et pone ante oculos omnia damna tuos [Think often of all the
things that terrible woman has done to you, and let your mind dwell on all
your grievances]" (*Rem* 299–300), the *magister* advises. Or do what I did when
miserable because rejected by an uninterested *puella*: "Profuit adsidue vitiis
insistere amicae, / Idque mihi factum saepe salubre fuit [It helped to keep
coming back to my mistress's faults; that usually made me feel better]" (*Rem*
315–16); the therapies' resemblance to adolescent sulks will not have been lost
on Ovid's sophisticated Roman audiences, with the difference that these are
strategic—and therefore forced, rather than sincerely felt—complaints, con-
demnations of demon rum by one who secretly would love a glassful at that
moment: "'Quam mala,' dicebam, 'nostrae sunt crura puellae!' / Nec tamen, ut
vere confiteamur, erant ['God! My girl's legs are really ugly,' I'd say to myself—
which, to tell you the truth, they weren't at all]" (*Rem* 317–18). It will also help,
continues the *magister*, to persuade your mistress to make a fool of herself in
front of you (on the face of it, an unlikely prospect): "Quin etiam, quacumque
caret tua femina dote,/ Hanc moveat, blandis usque precare sonis [Why not
try this: plead with your woman to do something that she doesn't do well]"
(*Rem* 331–32), be it singing *sine voce* (having no voice), conversing in *barbara
sermone* (Latin as a second language), or laughing so as to expose crooked
teeth (*Rem* 333, 335, 339, respectively; see this chapter, pages 82–83, for the
precise quotation).

Rising to a dubious didactic summit, the *magister* advises the disciple trapped in a debilitating love affair to seek a cure—by taking another mistress! (Addicted to gin? Try knocking down a bottle of rum every day, as well.) The comic intent of this counsel is first telegraphed by Ovid via his surrogate's implicitly misogynistic aside, hinting at female sexual voracity: "Hortor et, ut pariter binas habeatis amicas / (Fortior est, plures siquis habere potest [Here's my advice: take two mistresses at the same time—although I admit you have to be pretty damned strong to take on more than one])" (*Rem* 441–42); carried away by this bright idea, the *magister* offers instances drawn from classical mythology—always a favorite Ovidian comic resource—to support it: Paris's love for Helen after Oenone; Tereus's for Philomela after Procne, and other examples of skewed, self-serving interpretation (Paris and Tereus were two-timing ravishers, not jilted lovers) that Ovid deploys in parodic imitation of the "colors" used by professional rhetoricians to impose helpful meanings on or draw favorable conclusions from the "facts" proposed for debate in the mock-forensic *Controversiae* of the schools of rhetoric in imperial Rome. Rejecting further corroborating testimony—"Quid moror exemplis, quorum me turba fatigat," he huffs—the magister makes his categorical pronouncement: "Successore novo vincitur omnis amor [Why should I take the time to give examples, the sheer number of which exhausts me. Every old love is wiped out by a new one]" (*Rem* 461–62).

Ovid now brings this mythological stew to a comic boil, turning his revisionary sights on nothing less than Homer's *Iliad*. Modestly disavowing credit for formulating *nova iura* (new laws), the *magister* adduces as his great precedent the behavior of Agamemnon in the *Iliad*: having had to restore his concubine Chryseis to her father, the seer Calchas, Agamemnon, in order to repair his damaged pride and status, claims Achilles' concubine, a political transaction the *magister* wilfully misinterprets as an erotic one: "Dixit, et hanc habuit solacia magna prioris, / Et posita est cura cura repulsa nova [He spoke, and his new bedmate more than made up for the loss of her predecessor; in other words, the new love drove out the old]" (*Rem* 483–84). The conclusion the *magister* draws from this butchering of the crucial opening move of ancient Europe's premier epic combines blatant misprision with outrageous self-puffery in one of the truly great Ovidian comic climaxes:

Ergo adsume novas auctore Agamemnone flammas,
    Ut tuus in bivio distineatur amor.
Quaeris, ubi invenias? artes tu perlege nostras:
    Plena puellarum iam tibi navis erit.

(Therefore, with Agamemnon as your model, start a new fire in your heart, so that you can leave your old love behind in the dust. Where will you find this new love, you ask? By reading my *Ars amatoria*, of course; do that, and your love boat will soon have a full female passenger list.)

(*Rem* 485–88)

Ovid gives one more therapeutic counsel, this one not mediated by the Great Books (Homer's, or the *magister*'s own) but more personal in origin, a message to the author directly from Cupid—or else just something he dreamed up: "Is mihi sic dixit (dubito, verusne Cupido, / An somnus fuerit: sed puto, somnus erat) [He said these things to me; I'm not sure if it was Cupid himself, or only a dream, but it probably was a dream]" (*Rem* 555–56; the anticlimactic deflation is a characteristically Ovidian comic touch). If you want to stop loving, the god/dream tells him, just concentrate on all your other problems—we all have plenty of them: "Ad mala quisque animum referat sua, ponet amorem; / . . . Et quis non causas mille doloris habet? [Whoever turns his attention to his troubles will quickly forget about love. . . . And who doesn't have a thousand things to make him unhappy?]" (*Rem* 559, 572).

Despite his plethora of recommendations, however, the *magister* must admit that escape from erotic addiction is not easily accomplished. Among the most verisimilar passages in Ovid's presentation of the *Remedia* as a rehabilitational tract are those that warn its supposed target audience about the difficulty of breaking ingrained erotic habits and the consequent danger of relapses on the road to the complete conquest of one's obsession with a cruel or unresponsive object of desire. Some of these warnings are as obvious to us as to the poet's first audiences, for example, "Quisquis amas, loca sola nocent, loca sola caveto! [Whoever you are, lover, places where you're alone are dangerous; avoid them!]" (*Rem* 579). Without company to distract him, the addict will focus on what he craves but must avoid: "Tristis eris, si solus eris, dominaeque relictae / Ante oculos facies stabit, ut ipsa, tuos" (*Rem* 583–84 [You'll be sad if you're alone, and at that moment the face of the lover you gave up will come up in your mind, as if she were really there]), the delusion of an erotic delirium. Likewise, "Scripta cave relegas blandae servata puellae: / Constantes animos scripta relecta movent [It's a big mistake to read old letters you've saved from your old sweetheart; re-reading love letters weakens even the strongest resolve]" (*Rem* 717–18); "Et loca saepe nocent; fugito loca conscia vestri / Concubitus; causas illa doloris habent [Places often make problems; stay away from places where you've made love with her, as they can really put you in a funk]" (*Rem* 725–26)—in other words, no erotic tourism allowed. Other counsels seem to abort themselves in the telling, as when the recovering lover is advised to pay surprise visits that catch the amica *inerma* (unarmed), that is, without the seductive accoutrements of cosmetics and jewelry: "Infelix vitiis excidet illa suis [The poor thing will be done in by her own imperfections]," the *magister* crows, only to append yet another self-correction: "Non tamen huic nimium praecepto credere tutum est: / Fallit enim multos forma sine arte decens [But it's not safe to trust this particular advice too much; a female body that looks good without adornment has done in many a lover]" (*Rem* 348–50).

Quintessentially Ovidian, in its fusion of comic commentary and penetrating psychological insight, is the extended passage at *Remedia* 609–68, which, even as it piles on sententious or amusing metaphors and analogies, manifests real understanding of the perils encountered by those seeking to defeat an addiction.

As the passage begins, the *magister* describes how his precepts—"quidquid mea Musa iubebat [whatever my Muse dictated]" (*Rem* 609)—once steered a young disciple toward a safe haven—"Inque suae portu paene salutis erat [he was almost safely into port]" (*Rem* 610)—until the supposedly recovering erotoholic fell off the wagon, finding himself among other addicts—"Reccidit, ut cupidos inter devenit amantes [He backslid, as soon as he fell in with some passionate lovers]" (*Rem* 611)—thereby reexposing himself to the arrows Cupid had been shooting at victims such as him since the opening elegy of the *Amores*—"Et, quae condiderat, tela resumpsit Amor [giving Love the chance to take his arrows out of storage]" (*Rem* 612)—or, in the *magister*'s alternative (if implicit) explanation, he became accidentally reinfected by eye contact with lovers:

> Siquis amas, nec vis, facito contagia vites;
>   Haec etiam pecori saepe nocere solent.
> Dum spectant laesos oculi, laeduntur et ipsi,
>   Multaque corporibus transitione nocent.

> (If you're an unwilling lover, avoid situations as contagious to you as the diseases that are always affecting sheep. There are plenty of contagious diseases that threaten people, and if you look at sick people, you can become sick yourself.)   (*Rem* 613–16)

The images of Love unpacking, for immediate redeployment, his mothballed armor, of desire as a contagious disease, and of lovers as sickened sheep elicit smiles, but the notion that the *iuvenis* who had progressed to the final stages of the *magister*'s recovery program can so easily relapse upon falling into the bad company of *cupidos amantes* reflects a truth to which any recovering alcoholic, finding him or herself in a situation where everyone else is drinking, might testify.

The love addict's desire for a fix will be inflamed by proximity: "Proximus a tectis ignis defenditur aegre; / Utile finitimis abstinuisse locis [It's hard to protect your house from a fire that starts next door; it's better to stay away from fire hazards]" (*Rem* 625–26). Indeed, "alter, si possis, orbis habendus erit [if you can, you ought to live in another world altogether]" (*Rem* 630). Seeing the former beloved has often proved fatal to the *magister*'s regimen of rehabilitation:

> vicinia laesit:
> Occursum dominae non tulit ille suae.
> Vulnus in antiquum rediit male firma cicatrix,
> Successumque artes non habuere meae.

(Being too close sabotaged the recovering lover; he couldn't deal with running into his former mistress. The scar on the old wound hadn't fully healed, so it opened again, in the process dooming all my good advice to failure.)   (*Rem* 621–24)

Nor is she alone to be avoided; "nec veniat servus, nec flens ancillula fictum / Suppliciter dominae nomine dicat 'ave!' [don't let her servant come, or her hand-maid, who will cry crocodile tears and bring pleading greetings from her mistress]" (*Rem* 639–40). Even proclaiming the end of love can be a trap, as Ovid puts it in a characteristcally witty paradox: "et malim taceas quam te desisse loquaris: / Qui nimium multis 'non amo' dicat, amat [and I'd rather have you shut up than brag about having stopped loving her; whoever keeps saying, to anybody who'll listen, 'I'm over it' . . . isn't over it]" (*Rem* 647–48). Neither going cold turkey nor relying on present hatred to suppress past love meets the *magister*'s approval:

> Sed meliore fide paulatim extinguitur ignis
>   Quam subito; lente desine, tutus eris . . . .
> Non curare sat est: odio qui finit amorem,
>   Aut amat, aut aegre desinit esse miser.

(But a fire is more effectively extinguished little by little, rather than suddenly; so withdraw slowly, and you'll be safe. And it's enough to be indifferent to her; if your love ends in hatred, either you're still in love, or you're going to be miserable for a long time.)

(*Rem* 649–50, 657–58)

With this latter caveat in mind, he recalls a situation where a furious husband, preparing a legal action—the Roman equivalent of a nasty divorce—against his wife, angrily summoned her to come out of the litter in which she was being carried to court and, when she appeared, "visa coniuge mutus erat.... / Venit in amplexus, atque 'ita vincis' ait [seeing his wife, he was dumbstruck; he threw himself into her arms, saying, 'You win']" (*Rem* 666, 668).

I could go on at much greater length recounting the bits and shards of advice. But I will conclude with one that leads well into a consideration of the *Remedia* as a systematic, comic reversal, or bouleversement, of the *Ars*. In the course of advising the recovering lover not to risk backsliding by asking anyone (especially her servants) how your former beloved is faring, the magister urges, "Perfer! Erit lucro lingua retenta tuo [Get with the program! It'll be better for you to keep your mouth shut]" (642): silence, not eloquent speech—the mainstay, we recall, of the *Ars*—is the prescription for success.

There are many more screamingly obvious reversals of *Ars amatoria* in the *Remedia amoris*. With respect to the *thalamus* (bedroom) where the lovers come to consummate their erotic relationship, the *magister* in *Ars* book 2 counsels mutual pleasure giving leading to a shared, simultaneous climax (*Ars* 2.725–28; cf. 3.794); in the *Remedia* he advises the unhappy lover to spend time just beforehand with a prostitute, in order to dull the edge of passion: "Quamlibet invenias, in qua tua prima voluptas / Desinat: a prima proxima segnis erit [Pick up somebody or other for a preliminary quickie, thanks to which you'll be pretty pooped out for the main event]" (*Rem* 403–4). In the *Ars*, he advises women to choose a method and posture of lovemaking that is most flattering to them (*Ars* 3. 771–86) and not to let too much light into the room while in the act, adding michievously (and not a little misogynistically), "Aptius in vestro corpore multa latent [It's best that large parts of your body stay in the shadows]" (*Ars* 3.808). In the *Remedia*, his counsel becomes:

Et pudet, et dicam: venerem quoque iunge figura,
    Qua minime iungi quamque decere putas.

Nec labor efficere est: rarae sibi vera fatentur,
   Et nihil est, quod se dedecuisse putent.
Tunc etiam iubeo totas aperire fenestras,
   Turpiaque admisso membra notare die.

(It's ugly, but I'll say it anyway: make love in whatever contorted positions are most difficult and least flattering. That's not hard to do: women
rarely tell themselves the truth, so they tend to think that nothing, no
posture, can be unbecoming to them. I'll add that you should throw the
windows wide open, allowing the daylight to expose the parts she should
hide.)   (Rem 407–12)

This not only inverts his advice to women but suggests that they have not followed it if they think they look good from any angle.

In the *Ars amatoria*, men and women on the make are urged to frequent the
theaters, the men to seek out beauty, the women to expose theirs to male gaze;
in the *Remedia*, the theaters are to be avoided (*Rem* 751), as are the colonnades
where women stroll, which men are told to frequent in the *Ars* (*Rem* 621; cf. *Ars*
1.67–74). When, as I've noted, the *magister* claims he could have saved Pasiphae
from her cruel fate (*Rem* 63; see this chapter, page 67), he does more than reverse his teaching; he contradicts it: in *Ars* 1.295–307, Pasiphae, we recall, functions as an exemplar of women's insatiable and elemental lust, unteachable by
her mirror, never mind by the *magister*!

Whereas, in *Ars*, part of the secret to holding on to your *puella* is what one
might call decorous flattery, that is, deploying language that ameliorates her
particular blemishes—"Nominibus mollire licet mala [to mitigate failings by
renaming them]," as the *magister* puts it (*Ars* 2.657), and "lateat vitium proximi-
tate boni [hide that fault behind the nearest virtue]" (*Ars* 2.662)—in the *Remedia* the opposite strategy—exaggerating such faults—is called for. In the *Ars*:

       fusca vocetur,
   Nigrior Illyrica cui pice sanguis erit:
Si straba, sit Veneri similis: si rava, Minervae:
   Sit gracilis, macie quae male viva sua est;
Dic habilem, quaecumque brevis, quae turgida, plenam . . .

(If she's darker than Illyrian pitch, just call her "dusky"; squint-eyed?
why, just like Venus in that statue. If she has a scratchy voice, compare it

to Minerva's; if her body is life-threateningly anorexic, call her "slim." Practically a midget? "Compact" will do, as will "zaftig" if she's balloonlike.)   (*Ars* 2.657–61)

In the *Remedia*:

> Turgida, si plena est, si fusca est, nigra vocetur:
>   In gracili macies crimen habere potest.
> Et poterit dici petulans, quae rustica non est:
>   Et poterit dici rustica, siqua proba est.

(Call her "blimp" if she's full-bodied, "black" if she's dusky; you can stigmatize a slender girl by calling her emaciated, and one who's urbane by saying she's stuck up. And, if she's honest, then call her a naïve hick.)

(*Rem* 327–30)

The pursuit of such strategies points obliquely to a larger truth: "Et mala sunt vicina bonis" (*Rem* 323), which in this context might best be translated, "There's not much distance between defects and virtues," implying, I think, that the crucial distinguishing element lies not within the object of scrutiny itself but rather in the feelings of desire or distaste (even forced, feigned distaste) toward that object held by its observer.

Perhaps even more striking is the inversion, in the *Remedia*, of the *magister*'s advice to his female adepts in book 3 of the *Ars amatoria* about how they can dress and behave in such a way as to disguise their natural defects or shortcomings (*Ars* 3.261–68, 275–80, quoted in this chapter, pages 46–47). Now in rebuttal, as it were, in the *Remedia* he counsels men seeking liberation from a woman to encourage her *dis*advantageous self presentation:

> quacumque caret tua femina dote,
>   Hanc moveat, blandis usque precare sonis.
> Exige uti cantet, siqua est sine voce puella:
>   Fac saltet, nescit siqua movere manum.
> Barbara sermone est? Fac tecum multa loquatur;
>   Non didicit chordas tangere? Posce lyram.
> Durius incedit? Fac inambulet; omne papillae
>   Pectus habent? Vitium fascia nulla tegat.
> Si male dentata est, narra, quod rideat, illi.

(Whatever your girl isn't good at, keep asking her to do it until she gives in. Urge her to sing if she has a lousy voice; make her dance for you if she doesn't know the moves. A real Brooklyn accent? Insist that she keep talking. Never learned to play the lyre? Get her one. If she walks awkwardly, take her for long strolls. Is she all boobs? Don't let her wear anything that keeps them from flopping. And if she has lousy teeth, tell jokes to make her laugh.)   (*Rem* 331–39)

Aside from the amusement generated by our recognition of this practice of reversals, Ovid cultivates it as a way of demonstrating that desire is the medium through which we see and judge the world, however inaccurately. Having proposed to his male disciple a strategy of what might be called negative voyeurism—gazing with disenchantment, even disgust, on the woman to whom he has just made love (*Rem* 413–18; cf. this chapter, page 83)—he adds, concerning the faults thus catalogued, "Forsitan haec aliquis (nam sunt quoque) parva vocabit [Maybe someone will call these small matters (because they are!)]" (*Rem* 419). It is perception (in this case, jaundiced postcoital perception), not fact, that counts.

Yet another reversal (or more precisely, inversion) involves the *magister*'s advice that the aggrieved lover court disillusionment by surprising his *amica* in stages of incomplete preparation, that is, before she has fully applied to herself the adornments central to the self-construction of the *culta puella*, so that

> Pyxidas invenies et rerum mille colores,
>   Et fluere in tepidos oesypa lapsa sinus.
> Illa tuas redolent, Phineu, medicamina mensas:
>   Non semel hinc stomacho nausea facta meo est.

(You will find makeup jars and a thousand kinds of rouge, and gooey lanolin creams dripping down into her bosom. Those cosmetics stink like the dung the Harpies shat onto your food, Phineas: they've turned my stomach more than once.)   (*Rem* 353–56)

In *Ars* book 3, the *magister* warned the women he is tutoring,

> Non tamen expositas mensa deprendat amator
>   Pyxidas: ars faciem dissimulata iuvat.

Quem non offendat toto faex inlita vultu,
    Cum fluit in tepidos pandere lapsa sinus?
Oesypa quid redolent?

(But don't let your lover discover your cosmetic jars all set up for action;
your beauty is best served by hiding the skill that goes into it. Who
wouldn't be put off by that junk smeared all over your face, when warm
rivulets of it spread out and drip down into your bosom? How that lanolin cream stinks!)   (*Ars* 3.209–13)

Speaking for throughly enamored men, the *magister* also asks, "Cur mihi
nota tuo causa est candoris in ore? / Claude forem thalami! Quid rude prodis
opus? [Why do I have to know exactly what makes your complexion so lily
white? Close your bedroom door! Why exhibit the work in progress?]" (*Ars*
3.227–28). It should be noted, however, that this passage lays the groundwork
for its use in the *Remedia* by continuing, "Multa viros nescire decet; pars
maxima rerum / Offendat, si non interiora tegas [Men shouldn't know a lot
of things; much of what you do would put them off, if you didn't keep it under wraps]" (*Ars* 3.229–30). The carefully measured, neutrally described cosmetic recipe of *Medicamina* has been reimagined as a messy, even nauseating
process existing in binary opposition to the elegant, seductive finished product. Worse, the *Remedia* suggests, via a memorably paradoxical Ovidian epigram, that just as the *thalamus* hides a *puella's* disgusting beauty secrets, so
the expensive accessories that complement her cosmetics effectively hide a
body that is far less significant, or attractive, than what decorates it: "Aufer-
imur cultu: gemmis auroque teguntur / Omnia; *pars minima est ipsa puella
sui* [We're deceived by elegance; everything is disguised by all that gold and
jewelry. The girl herself is the least part of her]" (*Rem* 343–44, emphasis
added).

As we've seen, Ovid's deployment of the concept of *cultus* is complicated: on
the one hand (in the *Medicamina faciei*), he links rural *cultus*—grafting trees
and so on—to its urban analogues, such as ornamenting buildings and, above
all, ornamenting the body with makeup and wigs; on the other hand, in the *Ars
amatoria*, he touts the embellishment of one's behavior with flattery, artfully
disguised eloquence, and strategic "mirroring" of the *puella's* actions and pref-
erences as a mark of urban (and urbane) *cultus* that, like elaborate cosmetic
routines, sets its practitioners apart from those whose attitudes and actions are
unpolished, uncool—in short, *rusticus*. Now, in *Remedia amoris*, we find the
relative merits of rusticity and urbanity reversed: going to the country and tak-

ing pleasure in grafted trees provides an escape from and antidote to the mis-
fortunes of frustrated city love:

> Venerit insitio; fac ramum ramus adoptet,
>   Stetque peregrinis arbor operta comis.
> Cum semel haec animum coepit mulcere voluptas,
>   Debilibus pinnis inritus exit Amor.

(Grafting time has come; make one branch accept another spliced into it,
so that the tree will be covered in imported leaves. Once the pleasure given
by such things begins to soothe the spirit, Love, now ineffectual, flies away
on crippled wings.)   (*Rem* 195–98)

The role of deception in the pursuit, or abandonment, of desire affords Ovid
the occasion for another change of valence. In all of his amatory verse, deception
plays an important part; it shapes interpersonal relations, especially those built
on desire, perhaps more than any other behavioral strategy. But while deception
in its various forms—from flattery and cosmetic self-enhancement, through systematic disguise of one's less desirable physical features, to outright lies—plays
an important role in a man's pursuit of a *puella* (*Ars* books 1 and 2) or in a woman's
attraction and control of a man (*Ars* book 3), it's seen in quite a different light in
Remedia amoris, a world where desire, now seen as destructive rather than consti-
tutive of one's pleasure, is to be escaped, not embraced. In *Ars* book 1, the *magister*
tells his male pupils that women alone can be deceived without angering the
gods, since women are themselves deceivers and deserve the comeuppance:

> Fraus absit; vacuas caedis habete manus.
> Ludite, si sapitis, solas impune puellas:
>   Hac minus est una fraude tuenda fides.
> Fallite fallentes: ex magna parte profanum
>   Sunt genus; in laqueos quos posuere, cadant.

(No cheating; keep your hands free from violence. If you're wise, deceive
only women—you can get away with that. Be honest with this one exception. Trick the tricksters; they are for the most part a crooked gender,
and they should only fall into their own traps.)   (*Ars* 1.642–46)

By contrast, in *Remedia*, at a key point in the unfolding program of rehabilitation, deceiving onself rather than others becomes a necessary strategy. Of

course, self-deception is a strategy fervently embraced by the *Amores* narrator, when he begs his *puella* to deceive him for his own pleasure (*Amores* 2.11) or peace of mind (*Amores* 1.4), but these are stratagems of desperation to fend off the erotic frustration and hopelessness that, as we've seen, perpetually threaten the protagonist of that work. The *magister* of *Remedia* has a different type of self-deception in mind when he warns, "Donec dediscis amare, / Ipse tibi furtim decipiendus eris [Until you learn how not to love, you must learn to deceive yourself]" (*Rem* 211–12). Elsewhere he proposes a strategy for breaking free of an unwanted lover by first fooling her about your supposed lack of interest in her—

> Quamvis infelix media torreberis Aetna,
>   Frigidior glacie fac videare tuae:
> Et sanum simula, ne, siquid forte dolebis,
>   Sentiat; et ride, cum tibi flendus eris.

(Although you feel as though you're frying in the middle of Aetna's volcano, make yourself seem ice cold to your girl, and pretend to be completely over her. Otherwise, she'd probably sense it if you were suffering, and laugh at your tears.)   (*Rem* 491–94)

—and then yourself: "Quod non es, simula, positosque imitare furores: / Sic facies vere, quod meditatus eris [Pretend to be what you're not, pretend that you're over your anger; if you keep pretending, what you want to happen will really happen]" (*Rem* 497–98). His conclusion: pretence of indifference suitably sustained can become fact: "Intrat amor mentes usu, dediscitur usu: / Qui poterit sanum fingere, sanus erit [Love enters minds over time, as if by accident; over time, it can leave in the same way. Whoever can fake sanity can become sane]" (*Rem* 503–4). This sequence precisely reverses *Ars* 1.611–12, 615–16, where the *magister*, advocating for his male clients, cynically encourages women to give in to obviously phony expressions of love, since whover only wants sex today may (!) offer true love tomorrow (or next year? See this chapter, page 61). Ovid has the *magister* himself refer, with a chuckle we can share, to this earlier advice, even offering a supposed confirmation of it: "Deceptum risi, qui se simularat amare, / In laqueos auceps decideratque suos [I've laughed at someone who fooled himself, pretending to be in love and then falling like a birdcatcher into his own trap]" (*Rem* 501–2).

On the other hand, self-deception can backfire: the *magister* recommends that the unhappily ensnared lover retreat to the countryside, far from Rome, as a kind of detoxification zone, and pursue there pastimes such as deer and boar hunting, bird catching, and fishing (activites, here literalized, that serve in the *Ars* as metaphors for hunting and snaring a *puella*—another kind of reversal. But he also admits:

> Forsitan a laribus patriis exire pigebit:
>   Sed tamen exibis: deinde redire voles;
> Nec te Lar patrius, sed amor revocabit amicae,
>   Praetendens culpae splendida verba tuae.

> (Perhaps it will upset you to leave the ancestral home behind, but you'll go nonetheless. Then you'll want to go back, but it will be your love for your mistress, not desire for that ancestral home, that's luring you, even though you try to cover up your big mistake with bigger words.)
>
> *(Rem* 237–40)

As I noted in my discussion of the *Ars amatoria*, the idiom Ovid uses for lying is *"dare verba,"* to give words. In the passage quoted above from early in the *Remedia*, young lovers practice the deceptions appropriate to elegy, "verbaque d[a]nt cauto qualibet arte viro [and tell the suspicious husband whatever lies they can think up]" (*Rem* 34); again at *Remedia* 95, the *magister,* impressing upon his pupil the importance of breaking off a nascent (and presumably potentially hurtful) romance quickly and, conversely, the dangers of not doing so, warns that "verba dat omnis amor, reperitque alimenta morando [love always lies, and feeds on your delay]." The overt message here is that love deceives; the implicit cultural significance is that instead of reality, you are likely to get only the language of desire detached from genuine feelings. The point is reiterated later in the *Remedia amoris,* when the *magister* cautions against insincere expressions of love, to which vanity makes the besotted lover vulnerable: "Desinimus tarde, quia nos speramus amari: / Dum sibi quisque placet, credula turba sumus [We're always too slow in breaking up because we hope against hope that we're loved. Given this need to think well of ourselves, we lovers are an easily fooled bunch]" (*Rem* 685–86). Conversely, in *Ars* 1.611–14, the success of male deceitful language has already been linked to female self-deception about one's lovableness; to his disciple the *magister* declares,

> Est tibi agendus amans, imitandaque vulnera verbis;
>   Haec tibi quaeratur qualibet arte fides.
> Nec credi labor est: sibi quaeque videtur amanda;
>   Pessima sit, nulli non sua forma placet.

(It's time for you to play the lover, using the language of suffering; you have to make her believe that, by all means necessary. But don't think it's so hard to be believed: every broad thinks she's eminently lovable, however hideous she may be; there isn't one who's not pleased with her own looks.)

His rehabilitative program concluded, the *magister* dismisses the patients (for such they have been) from his clinic with a valedictory prayer: "Di faciant, possis dominae transire relictae / Limina, proposito sufficiantque pedes [God willing, you'll be able to walk right past your former mistress's house; may your feet be up to that task]" (*Rem* 785–86); a closing admonition: "Et poteris; modo velle tene: nunc fortiter ire, / Nunc opus est celeri subdere calcar equo [and you *will* be able to, as long as you stick to your plan. Now for the strong finish: you're in the homestretch—time to dig in those spurs]" (*Rem* 787–88); and a final promise of restoration, tied to letting go of past antipathy toward a rival: "At certe, quamvis odio remanente, saluta; / Oscula cum poteris iam dare, sanus eris [Even if you're still angry, be sure to give him a hearty hello; and when you'll finally be able to give him a hug, and mean it—why, then you'll be completely cured]" (*Rem* 793–94).

POSTSCRIPT

In the *Remedia amoris* as in the *Ars amatoria* (See, e.g, *Ars* 2.99–107), Ovid distinguishes his erotic or antierotic strategies from the use of potions and spells as instruments for initiating, extending, or ending erotic engagements, and he warns his acolytes, "Ergo quisquis opem nostra tibi poscis ab arte, / Deme veneficiis carminibusque fidem [So if you're someone who wants my system to help you, then scrap any allegiance you may have to potions and spells]" (*Rem* 289–90). To explain his antipathy, the *magister* proposes a binary opposition between benign and potentially toxic regimens: "Ista veneficii vetus est via; noster Apollo / Innocuam sacro carmine monstrat opem [That's the old way of sorcerer's poisons; I'm allied to Apollo and embrace the harmless power of inspired poetry]" (*Rem* 251–52). I would interpret this binary differently, however, as yet another case of the *magister*'s modern *cultus*—urbane skills and strategies perceived by insight and honed by experience—flaunting its superiority to traditional (what we would call folk) remedies inherited from a more primitive (*rusticus*) stage of civilization that sought the intervention of supernatural forces in human affairs (including affairs of the heart). Chuckling at such naivete, the *magister* promises,

Me duce non tumulo prodire iubebitur umbra,
  Non anus infami carmine rumpet humum;
Non seges ex aliis alios transibit in agros,
  Nec subito Phoebi pallidus orbis erit.
Ut solet, aequoreas ibit Tiberinus in undas:
  Ut solet, in niveis Luna vehetur equis.
Nulla recantatas deponent pectora curas,
  Nec fugiet vivo sulpure victus amor.

(My system doesn't invoke ghostly spirits to come out of their tombs, nor
require old crones to split open the earth thanks to some profane incan-
tation. Crops won't leap from one field to another, nor will the sun suddenly become pale. The Tiber will flow into the sea as usual, and as usual
the moon will ride the sky in all her brightness. No hearts will have cares
lifted from them by charms, nor will love be chased away by stinking
fumes of sulphur.)   (Rem 253–60)

In addition, Ovid's attentiveness in his amatory poetry—indeed, all his
poetry—to the psychological and emotional complexities of human desire would
inevitably make him dubious of universally efficacious medicinal "cures" for
any and all resultant crises. This skepticism registers in his persona's comment
on the situation of Circe who, having fallen in love with Odysseus/Ulysses, is
unable, despite her famous spells, either to prevent his departure or to suppress
her own passion:

Omnia fecisti, ne callidus hospes abiret:
  Ille dedit certae lintea plena fugae.
Omnia fecisti, ne te ferus ureret ignis:
  Longus in invito pectore sedit amor.

(You did everything you could to keep your shrewd guest from getting
away, but he sped away under full sail. You did everything to keep from
being scorched by the fierce flames of desire, but love still took up residence, a squatter in your unwilling heart.)   (Rem 265–68)

The next couplet sums up the magister's (and, I believe, his creator's) scorn for
seeking such magical antidotes to the human condition: "Vertere tu poteras
homines in mille figuras, / Non poteras animi vertere iura tui [You could

change men into a thousand shapes, but you couldn't change the laws govern-
ing your own soul]" (*Rem* 269–70) As we have seen, the *magister* recognizes
(indeed, is forced to recognize) that the "laws of the soul" accommodate an
enormous variety of people and situations, requiring flexible, protean strategies—
not shape-changing potions—by those who would satisfy (or, in the *Remedia*,
extinguish) desire.

The rivalry, then, seems absolute between two clashing forms of authority
in matters of desire: a supposedly erotic (or antierotic) pharmacopaeia founded
in timeless nature—animal, vegetable, or mineral—and a specifically "modern" and urban/e *magisterium* based on the observation and practice of an infinitely variable human pursuit of (or flight from) desire. Except, of course—a
typically Ovidian comic codicil—for those aphrodisiac vegetables, such as on-
ions or *salax eruca* (salacious arugula—does this account for its recent rise in
popularity in trendy, erotomaniacal New York City?), which the *magister* advises his acolytes to consume (*Ars* 2.422) or avoid (*Rem* 795–802), depending
on the circumstances. The latter passage, coming at the very end of the *Remedia amoris*, makes clear Ovid's parodic intent behind his *magister*'s resort to
diet counselling:

> Ecce, cibos etiam, medicinae fungar ut omni
> > Munere, quos fugias quosque sequare, dabo.
> Daunius, an Libycis bulbus ubi missus ab oris,
> > An veniat Megaris, noxius omnis erit.
> Nec minus erucas aptum vitare salaces,
> > Et quicquid Veneri corpora nostra parat.
> Utilius sumas acuentes lumina rutas,
> > Et quidquid Veneri corpora nostra negat.

> (Look, I'll even tell you which foods to eat and which to avoid, in order to
> fulfill all my medical obligations to you. Onions, whether the Libyan or
> Megaran variety, are all bad for you. It's just as important to avoid aphro-
> disiac arugula, and anything else that gets us up for lovemaking. It's bet-
> ter to eat bitter herbs that sharpen your eyesight, and everything else
> that douses our desire to do it.)   (*Rem* 795–802)

The wonderful miscellaneousness and too-neat, near-echo opposition of "et
quicquid Veneri corpora nostra parat" and "et quidquid Veneri corpora nostra
negat" constitutes not only an implicit dismissal of what we might call garden-

variety strategies of advice to the lovelorn (or love-stuffed), but also the poet's final wink to his audience acknowledging the comic intent of his rhetorical strategy in constructing an *Ars*-backward *Remedia amoris*—a wink reinforced by the nudge within the same passage in the further advice to the escaping lover, "Utilius sumas acuentes lumina rutas," a dietary supplement designed to overcome the proverbial blindness attributed to love, as well, doubtless, to sharpen the recovering erotic addict's perception of the shortcomings (certainly present in abundance, the *magister* has already suggested) in the soon-to-be-former object of desire.

CONCLUSION

Ovid's poetry, a triumph of serious play, takes the measure of the tensions between public and private imperatives, between glorifying a mythical past and fully grasping and enjoying the opportunities for pleasure afforded by an opulent present, between quantitative (or materialistic) and qualitative (or talent-based) pursuits of that pleasure. The result is a comedy that both celebrates and sends up human ingenuity in its struggles against the passions that would defeat it and the economic and political power that would crush it. The comic mirror that Ovid holds up to his adopted city reveals important truths about urban values and behavior and about the inevitable contradictions between political and personal agendas. As we stare into that mirror, past its many depictions of laughable presumption and deceit, misjudgment and folly, stunningly self-interested argumentation and self-inflicted damage, we discover keen and often disturbing insights about the power and limits of authority and, above all, about the strength of our desires and the fragility of the structures by which we seek to control or satisfy them.

This is part of the paradox of Ovid's comic poetry: like that of the other elegists, it not only acknowledges but revels in its inferiority in theme, genre, and dignity to the poets of the classical pantheon and to texts that take war, history, or (in Lucretius's case) the universe itself as their subject. Yet it also manages to suggest that the wit, irony, and sense of incongruity or excess that collaborate in the fabrication of a comic vision of one's personal situation, city, and world are at least as deserving of respect, and at least as likely to tell truths both enjoyable and uncomfortable, as are utterances traditionally held to be culturally significant because of the seriousness of their subject and mien. Such an assumption is at once outrageous, ridiculous, and dangerously attractive, as much to us today as I must assume it was to Ovid's first audiences.[50]

NOTES

The section on the *Amores* contains passages borrowed from or closely paraphrasing my essay "Always Hopeless, Never Serious: Wit and Wordplay in Ovid's Amores," in *Approaches to Teaching the Works of Ovid and the Ovidian Tradition*, ed. Barbara Boyd and Cora Fox (New York: Modern Language Association,
2010), in press (copyright Modern Language Association; used by permission).

1. See Boyd, *Ovid's Literary Loves*, and Ginsberg, "The Idea of Character in Ovid,"
   on this double persona.
2. See Tarrant, "Ovid and Ancient Literary History," 13–14, for a brief chronology
   of Ovid's works, recognizing the uncertainties.
3. See Townend, "Literature and Society."
4. Wheeler, in Ovid, *Tristia, Ex Ponto*, xviii.
5. Africa, *Rome of the Caesars*, 5–6; cf. Crook, "Political History," 104, who describes
   the *Princeps* as reacting against "too much foreign blood in the citizen body and
   too many layabouts!"
6. See Treggiari, "Social Status," esp. 886–87, "The Social Legislation of Augustus
   and the Julio-Claudians."
7. See Wallace-Hadrill, "The Imperial Court," and Treggiari, "Social Status."
8. Habinek, "Invention of Sexuality"; cf. note 10.
9. Africa, *Rome of the Caesars*, 8–9.
10. For Ovid's comic sense of residential hierarchy within this exalted social sphere,
    see *Metamorphoses*, 1.163–64, where Jupiter calls a celestial council to deal with a
    crisis on earth, and the gods move obediently along the Milky Way toward his
    palace, which is flanked by the equally posh dwellings of major deities, while, as
    Humphries felicitously puts it in his translation, "the lesser gods live in a meaner
    section, / An area not reserved, as this one is, / For the illustrious Great Wheels of
    Heaven / (Their Palatine Hill, if I might call it so)" (8).
11. See Gibson's introduction in Ovid, *Ars Amatoria*, 27–35, on the wide reach of the
    law. Habinek, "Invention of Sexuality," following Cohen, sees as the *lex Julia*'s
    main intention the imposition of state power over the family—an invasion of the
    res privata of the *paterfamilias*—as part of the totalitarian program of Augustus,
    and he sees Ovid's amatory poetry as a reflection of and response to this legisla-
    tion that "disembedded sexual behavior from its traditional familial context,
    where it had been regulated by forces of honor and shame, and instead described
    it as a freely chosen activity between legal persons, one subject to scrutiny and
    regulation in the public sphere" (29). His thesis is that since, "during the course
    of the Roman Cultural Revolution, that is the period in which the Roman elites
    came to terms with their status as rulers of an empire, the city of Rome was itself
    transformed from an overgrown Italian town to a world capital," accordingly,
    "during one discrete historical period Rome experienced the swift change and

dislocation of the individual that [Don] Milligan [*Sex-Life* (Boulder: University of Colorado Press, 1993)] and others describe as the permanent condition of modern cities" (26). "The breakdown of traditional ties of loyalty and community, the atomization of the individual, and the rationalization and commodification of human relationships are all features of the world-city, in antiquity as in the modern era" (42), features fundamentally at odds with "a social system in which sex is closely associated with issues of legitimacy, alliances between clans, and male privilege" (27).

Habinek does not consider the possible impact of Ovid's comic perspective on the poet's representations of sexuality, nor does he appear to grant the possibility of irony in the positions taken by the Ovidian narrators. See further McGinn, "Concubinage," and *Prostitution, Sexuality, and the Law*; Treggiari, "Social Status," and *Roman Marriage*; and Wallace-Hadrill, "*Mutatio morum*."

12. See Horace's *Carmen saeculare*, written in response to the Secular Games of 17 B.C.E., organized by Augustus ostensibly in honor the founding of Rome but actually as another way of glorifying himself and his reign. In this poem, Horace specifically lauds Augustus's marriage legislation (17–24); cf. Horace, *Carmina* 4.5.20–24 for a similar praise of the legislation against adultery. In other poems (e.g., *Carmina* 4.15.9–20), he celebrates Augustus's devotion to and revival of the discipline and virtue of the old Republic. According to Crook, "Augustus shared with Cicero the belief in a superior early and middle Republic, whose victories had been based on better morals and solider family virtues, and he strove to re-create that idealized past" ("Augustus," 132,). Treggiari, comments, "The decade after 23 BC saw concentrated legislation in several areas. Augustus himself claimed that his laws re-introduced old standards and set an example to posterity. Like Horace, he harks back to a mythical past" ("Social Status," 886). I remain dubious of the emperor's moral sincerity.

13. See Merriam, *Love and Propaganda*: "Devoting oneself entirely to literary and intellectual pursuits, especially to the exclusion of a political or military career, would seem suspect to many Roman aristocrats, as we learn from Cicero: 'Because of the tranquility of that life, and the pleasure of the knowledge itself, than which nothing is more pleasant to people, more men devoted themselves to this than was beneficial to the republic. And as men with excellent talents gave themselves to the pursuit, because of that great faculty of vacant and free time, more by far than was necessary men affluent in too much free time and abundant talent dedicated themselves to caring and seeking and investigating it'" (6, quoting Cicero's *De oratore* 3, 15, 56–57).

14. Conte, *Latin Literature*, 324. Cf. 334, on Propertius's "rejection of the *mos maiorum* [ancestral values], of the primary values of the *civitas*, in favor of an existence totally dedicated to love (1.6.27–30)." See Merriam, *Love and Propaganda*, 5–11, for a useful, sharply delineated summary of elegist attitudes. "The major Latin

love elegists all lived and worked during the Augustan age and all, to a greater or
lesser extent, resisted the demands of conformity which the age imposed upon
Roman citizens. . . . The forces which the elegists resisted, the pressures toward
military and political careers, were the common forces which had always worked
upon the Roman aristocracy and equestrian class [Ovid's]; but we can also see
their attitudes as more specific to their time. For in their time a new pressure was
added to those of class and family, as Augustus established himself as the cham-
pion of traditional Roman morals, and aspired to a regeneration of such tradition. Such was the reason for the moral legislation, the Julian laws he passed and
attempted to pass, in order to promote marriage and support Roman families.
And it is in this context that the elegists take their stand against convention. . . .
[I]t is clear that the very act of writing love poetry, personal and irresponsible
poetry, can be interpreted as an act of resistance against a regime that encourages
conformity and respectability" (5–6). "Marrying well and establishing large families to serve the *princeps'* Rome into the future would seem to be the last thing
that would appeal to the Latin elegists, for it would demonstrate conformity and
a sense of responsibility. This sense of responsibility was so closely tied as to be
inextricable from the military demands of Roman life, and the love elegists were
united in their opposition to living the soldier's life. . . . The three elegists expressed their resistance to the regime in different ways. . . . Ovid tended to ridicule the leader, and treat the entire regime as a huge and incomprehensible joke"
(10–11). Cf. Davis, *"Praeceptor amoris"*: "I think it fair to say that Ovid consistently
treats Augustan themes, the moral legislation, the building program, military
policy, the promotion of antique values and so on, with a flippancy which suggests
indifference to the emperor's program" (194). Simpson, *Reform and Cultural Revolution*, summarizes elegantly: "All Ovidian love poetry is sensitive to the ways in
which elegy draws on, yet seeks to neutralize, history" (127–28).

15. See Harrison, "Ovid and Genre."

16. Cf. Fyler,*"Omnia vincit amor"*: "The asymmetrical lines of the elegiac couplet suggest a comically hobbled genre. Elegy personified has one foot longer than the
other (*Amores* 3.1.8), and Thalia rides on a lopsided chariot (*Ars* 1.264–65). Indeed, it is likely that the epigraph to the *Amores*, which notes a change from five
libelli to three, is more than a foreword to a revised edition: it confirms, as a struc-
tural analogue, Ovid's self-proclaimed insufficiency" (198).

17. In *Metamorphoses* 5, Cupid enacts just such a "massive power grab" at the insistence of his mother, Venus, who urges him to shoot an arrow at Hades, god of the
underworld, in order to enflame the latter with desire for Proserpina, and thus
establish Love's dominion over the only realm of the universe not yet under his
(and Venus's) control. See *Metamorphoses* 5.360–84. As Venus exhorts her son (in
Humphries's translation): "Take your all-conquering weapons, O my son, . . . /
And let the speeding arrows find the heart / Of the god on whom the final lot be-

stowed / The world below the world. You rule the others, / Even great Jove, you rule the great sea-gods, / And their great monarch. Why should Hell alone / Hold out against us? Let our empire spread!" (365–72).

18. "*Nervus*" was a common euphemism for the male member; see Adams, *The Latin Sexual Vocabulary*, 38.

19. "*Opus*," in addition to its literal meaning, task, was slang in Ovid's Latin for the sex act (Adams, *The Latin Sexual Vocabulary*, 156–57).

20. Treggiari, "Social Status," 890.

21. On this poem see Habinek, "Ovid and Empire," 47–48.

22. Cf. Gibson's introduction in Ovid, *Ars Amatoria*, 20–21, 35–36.

23. On the evolution of a textual culture of "expertise" in the late Republic, replacing the traditional, orally transmitted, control of the Senatorial elite over large areas of public performance and commemoration, see Wallace-Hadrill, "*Mutatio morum*," who stresses Augustus's appropriation of expertise and moral as well as political authority, formerly the collective property of Rome's Senatorial class. See further the section on "The Didactic Tradition and *Ars* 3" in Gibson's introduction to Ovid, *Ars Amatoria*, 7–13.

24. See especially Fyler, "*Omnia vincit amor*," and Leicester, "Ovid Enclosed," on this aspect of Ovid's amatory poetry.

25. Leach relates this episode and many other "georgic" aspects of the *Ars* to Ovid's programmatic parody of the subjects and style of Vergil's *Georgics*, and, through Vergil's poem, of "the great number of didactic (and patriotic?) poems produced under Augustus" ("Georgic Imagery," 154n. 15).

26. Ovid may have been onto something about the important role mimicry plays in successful wooing. An article in the *New York Times* of 12 February 2008 (Benedict Carey, "You Remind Me of Me: Decoding the Subtle Cues That Lead to Human Rapport, Scientists Train Their Focus on Mimicry") reports that "researchers have begun to decode the unspoken, subtle elements that come into play when people click . . . [and] have found that immediate social bonding between strangers is highly dependent on mimicry, a synchronized and usually unconscious give and take of words and gestures that creates a current of goodwill between two people." For students of the *magister*, there will of course be nothing unconscious about the process, and with Ovidian precision, the article notes that "by understanding exactly how this process works, researchers say, people can better catch themselves when falling for an artful pitch [*Remedia amoris?*], and even sharpen their own social skills in ways they may not have tried before [if they haven't read *Ars amatoria*]." Much of the article explores the difference between social mimicry that happens unconsciously and that which reflects a specific agenda: "It is one thing to move like a naturally synchronized swimmer through the pools of everyday conversation without thinking, however. It is another to deliberately employ mimicry to persuade or seduce," whether the aim is commercial or sexual

gain. Some people are intuitive mimics, while others "have developed ways to engage their skills indirectly," that is, for profit of one kind or another. The whole article, and the subject on which it reports, would, I believe, have been catnip for Ovid.

27. See Ramage, *Urbanitas*.

28. See Habinek, "Invention of Sexuality," 31–38, on Ovid's heterosexuality and resistance to feminized maleness.

29. Cf. Habinek, "Ovid and Empire," 50–51; Africa, *Rome of the Caesars*, 19, records anxieties within Rome about its exploitation of rest of empire, and hatred of Rome among the colonies because of it.

30. Connors, "Field and Forum," notes that while *rusticus* and *rusticitas* were pejorative concepts in Roman rhetorical theory—based on the idea that country folk lacked training in oratory and therefore could not speak well, that is, persuasively, in public legal or political fora—a rhetorical style that avoided the extremes of hick-like rusticity and overblown, effeminate theatricality was considered properly cultivated—a metaphor itself drawn from the rural world of agriculture. She explains the apparent paradox by documenting the strong association within elite Roman culture between a simple (that is, idealized) country life and traditional Roman virtues, an association Ovid takes obvious delight in skewering. To describe effective Roman rhetoric as *cultus* thus placed behind a patriotic smokescreen the fact that it owed an enormous debt to the rhetorical practice of the supposedly decadent Greeks. As Connors, puts it, "The fact that rhetorical expertise was imported to Rome from Greece is implicitly played down when the work of rhetoric is figured as the native work of farming. . . . [T]he image [of cultivation] serves to 'naturalize' the artificial acculturation of the élite through imported rhetorical education" (77). Ovid, ever the rhetorician, adapted this trickery to his own needs.

31. On Roman sumptuary laws, see, e.g., Hunt, *Governance of the Consuming Passions*, 19–22.

32. Note the contrasting tone of Vergil's analogous lines, *Aeneid* 8. 347–50, Evander leading Aeneas on a tour of "pre-Rome":

> Hinc ad Tarpeiam sedem et Capitolia ducit,
> aurea nunc, olim silvestribus horrida dumis.
> Iam tum religio pavidos terrebat agrestis
> dira loci, iam tum silvam saxumque tremebant.

> (Hence he leads him to the Tarpeian house, and the Capitol—golden now, once bristling with woodland thickets. Even then the dread sanctity of the region awed the trembling rustics; even then they shuddered at the forest and the rock.)

33. With respect to the latter disavowal, see Ramage, *Urbanitas*, 88: "It's important to notice that as the poet [through his alter ego, the *magister amoris*] speaks he is careful to dissociate himself and his desires completely from the contemporary pursuit of wealth and luxury, for it is too easy to ignore his assertion that he is not interested in gold and all it brings." Cf. the *magister's* scornful comment (*Ars* 2.277–78) about the relative worth of poetry and wealth as gateways to a woman's heart: "Aurea sunt vere nunc saecula: plurimus auro/ Venit honos: auro conciliatur amor [This is really a golden age; many honors, and even love, can be gotten with gold]."

34. Cf. *Ars* 1.113, of the theatrical performance that was the occasion for the rape of the Sabine women: "plausus tunc arte carebant [in those days, applause was artless]." By implication, even applause can be made polished, *cultus*, as it is nowadays.

35. Indeed, deceit, in the form of pretense, can even make lovemaking more exciting: The *magister* advises his female acolytes:

> Quae venit ex tuto, minus est accepta voluptas:
> Ut sis liberior Thaide, finge metus.
> Cum melius foribus possis, admitte finestra,
> Inque tuo vultu signa timentis habe.
> Callida prosiliat dicatque ancilla "perimus!"
> Tu iuvenem trepidum quolibet abde loco.

> (Safe lovemaking doesn't cut it; even if you're as carefree as Paris Hilton, pretend to be terrified. Sure, entering by the front door is easier—but make him climb in through a window, and while he does it, have fear written all over your face. Then let that smart little maid of yours come rushing in, screaming, "We're as good as dead!" and you shove the guy [who's quaking by now] into some hiding place or other.)   (*Ars* 3.603–8)

The similarity of this advice to the plot of hundreds of medieval (and later) comic tales of adultery will not be lost on the reader familiar with them.

36. Habinek, "Invention of Sexuality," 34–37.

37. See, from a somewhat different perspective, Solodow's brilliant analysis of the relationship among deceit, self-fashioning, and the work of the artist ("Ovid's *Ars Amatoria*," 117–25).

38. See Eden, *Hermeneutics*, 17–18, 26–28: "decorum . . . in elocution or style . . . serves to accommodate the particular case" (27–28).

39. See the introduction to Seneca, *Controversiae*: "A 'colour' . . . was a line of approach to the case [the *controversia*, a pseudolegal case containing difficulties and paradoxes to test the rhetorical skills of those who debated them], a method of interpreting the facts that was to the advantage of the speaker" (xviii).

40. On Castiglione, see chapter 3, pages 185, 239–40. Cf. Goffman's theorization of advantageous self-presentation (*The Presentation of Self*). Is the "non sanus . . . poeta" (*Ars* 2.508) Ovid's funhouse-mirror characterization of himself?

41. See Fyler, *Chaucer and Ovid*, 125.

42. See Toohey, "Eros and Eloquence," 205: to Augustus "Ovid insists that there is no necessary relationship between his instruction and 'real life.'" This clever, simultaneous exculpation of both Ovid and Augustus contains as well an implicit ironization by the poet of the traditional *otium-negotium* binary: since Caesar lacked the leisure time to read his poem carefully (or at all), the *Ars* has been improperly blamed, but judgment without full consideration of the facts is a dangerous mark of tyranny, which hides behind its imperial schemes to avoid taking the time to make judgments on one's subjects carefully and accurately. So Ovid in effect redefines *otium*, which, seen in this light, becomes a strategic withdrawal from the activity of the moment in order to make careful and just judgments based on deliberation, not rumor or misinformation.

43. If Ovid could not, in fact, resist making even his relegation an occasion for comic hyperbole, he has had at least one inheritor of this approach. When Carl Reiner and Mel Brooks updated in the year 2000 the comedy sketch of an interview with a 2,000-year-old man that they had originated for television in 1961, Brooks, playing the double millenarian, describes himself as "an avid Ovidian" and recalls the headline in the *Roman Tribune* (a parody of the famously lapidary headlines in the show business newspaper, *Variety*), on the occasion of the poet's relegation by the *Princeps*: "Ovid Ousted; Augustus Disgusted."

44. Solodow puts it well: "[Ovid] often notably subverts central features of Roman political and cultural life, suggesting that they are really important only in so far as they serve the cause of the lover; ultimately, at least in Ovid's playful account, their final reference is to love, and love is therefore more important than they are" ("Ovid's *Ars Amatoria*," 112).

45. Cf. Davis, "*Praeceptor amoris*," 187: "At [*Ars*] 1.67–88, Ovid lists a number of places suitable for finding a girlfriend. Every single location has dynastic associations. . . . No doubt Augustus relished allusions to his monumental achievements in works of poetry, but can we really believe that he appreciated references like this?" In the thirteenth-century French adaptation of the *Ars amatoria*, the adaptor substitutes Parisian for Roman public places where women are to be sought. And in New York City today, in addition to myriad singles bars, there are public places and spaces well known to be sites for making social and sexual connections.

46. Cf. Leach, "Georgic Imagery," 142: "The language and imagery of the poem celebrate the glories of urban civilization through numerous references to Roman artifacts—theatres, temples, cosmetics and gems. All of these objects acquire their highest value from their usefulness to the strategies of love."

47. For more on this, see Davis, "*Praeceptor amoris.*"

48. On Phyllis, cf. *Ars* 3.37–38, and Ovid, *The Art of Love*, trans. Mozley and Goold, 121n. On this comic strategy, by which Ovid trivializes classical culture's canonic myths, cf. Fyler, "*Omnia vincit amor,*" 199.

49. Against this reading, see Adams, *The Latin Sexual Vocabulary*, 34.

50. Cf. Solodow: "Play permits greater complexity [than seriousness *tout court*]: we must take a serious remark in a serious way; but a joking remark may be taken either seriously or not" ("Ovid's *Ars Amatoria*," 110)—which is why barbed humor is so effective as a socio-verbal weapon: it has deniability but also earns respect for its wit from all but (perhaps) its butt. Solodow (110n. 8), quotes Johan Huizinga, *Homo Ludens: A Study of the Play Element in Culture* (1938; repr., Boston, 1955), 45: "The play-concept as such is of a higher order than seriousness. For seriousness seeks to exclude play, whereas play can very well include seriousness."

REFERENCES

Ovid

Amores. Trans. Guy Lee. London: John Murray, 1968.

Amores I: Text and Prolegomena. Ed. J. C. McKeown. Liverpool and Leeds: Cairns, 1987.

Amores II: A Commentary on Book One. Ed. J. C. McKeown. Liverpool and Leeds: Cairns, 1989.

Ars amatoria. Trans. B. P. Moore. Rev. A. D. Melville. In *The Love Poems*, trans. A. D. Melville. Oxford World's Classics. Oxford: Oxford University Press, 1990.

Ars Amatoria, Book 3. Ed. Roy K. Gibson. Cambridge: Cambridge University Press, 2003.

The Art of Love and Other Poems. With a translation by J. H. Mozley. 2nd ed. Rev. G. P. Goold. Loeb Classical Library. Cambridge, Mass.: Harvard University Press; London: Heinemann, 1985.

Heroides, Amores. With a translation by Grant Showerman. Rev. G. P. Goold. Loeb Classical Library. Cambridge, Mass.: Harvard University Press, 1977.

Medicamina faciei. In *The Art of Love and Other Poems*, with a translation by J. H. Mozley, 2nd ed., rev. G. P. Goold, Loeb Classical Library. Cambridge, Mass.: Harvard University Press; London: Heinemann, 1985.

Metamorphoses. Trans. Rolfe Humphries. Bloomington: Indiana University Press, 1955.

Remedia amoris. In *The Art of Love and Other Poems*, with a translation by J. H. Mozley, 2nd ed., rev. G. P. Goold, Loeb Classical Library. Cambridge, Mass.: Harvard University Press; London: Heinemann, 1985.

Tristia, Ex Ponto. With a translation by A. L. Wheeler. Rev. G. P. Goold. Loeb Classical Library. Cambridge, Mass.: Harvard University Press, 1988.

Other Primary Texts

Biondi, Biondo, ed. *Lex Iulia de adulteriis (No. 14); Leges Iulia et Papia Poppaea [de maritandis ordinibus] (No. 28).* Part 3: "Leges populi Romani." In *Acta divi Augusti. Pars prior,* ed. S. Riccobono, 112–28, 166–97. Rome: Reale accademia d'Italia, 1945.

Horace. *Odes and Epodes.* With a translation by C. E. Bennett. Rev. ed. Loeb Classical Library. Cambridge, Mass.: Harvard University Press; London: Heinemann, 1978.

Livy. *The Early History of Rome.* Trans. Aubrey de Selincourt. Baltimore: Penguin, 1960.

Propertius. *Elegies.* Ed. and trans. G. P. Goold. Loeb Classical Library. Cambridge, Mass.: Harvard University Press, 1990.

Seneca the Elder. *Controversiae.* Vol. 1 of *Declamations,* with a translation by M. Winterbottom, 2 vols. Loeb Classical Library. Cambridge, Mass.: Harvard University Press; London: Heinemann, 1974.

Suetonius. *Lives of the Twelve Caesars.* With a translation by J. C. Rolfe. Intro. K. R. Bradley. Rev. ed. 2 vols. Loeb Classical Library. Cambridge, Mass.: Harvard University Press, 1998.

Vergil. *Aeneid.* With a translation by H. Rushton Fairclough. Rev. ed. 2 vols. Loeb Classical Library. Cambridge, Mass.: Harvard University Press; London: Heinemann, 1934.

Secondary Sources

Adams, J. N. *The Latin Sexual Vocabulary.* London: Duckworth, 1982.

Africa, Thomas. *Rome of the Caesars.* New York: John Wiley, 1965.

Bowman, Alan K., Edward Champlin, and Andrew Lintott, eds. *Cambridge Ancient History.* 2nd ed. Vol. 10, *The Augustan Empire.* Cambridge: Cambridge University Press, 1996.

Boyd, Barbara Weiden. *Ovid's Literary Loves: Influence and Innovation in the* Amores. Ann Arbor: University of Michigan Press,1997.

Brunt, P. A. *Italian Man Power, 225 BC–14 AD.* Oxford : Clarendon, 1971.

Cohen, David. "The Augustan Law on Adultery: The Social and Cultural Context." In *The Family in Italy from Antiquity to the Present,* ed. David I. Kertzer and Richard P. Saller, 109–26. New Haven, Conn.: Yale University Press, 1991.

Connors, Catherine. "Field and Forum: Culture and Agriculture in Roman Rhetoric." In *Roman Eloquence: Rhetoric in Society and Literature,* ed. William J. Dominik, 71–89. London: Routledge, 1997.

Conte, Gian Biagio. *Latin Literature: A History.* Trans. Joseph B. Solodow. Rev. Don Fowler and Glenn W. Most. Baltimore, Md.: Johns Hopkins University Press, 1994.

Crook, J. A. "Augustus: Power, Authority, Achievement." In *Cambridge Ancient History*, 2nd ed., ed. Alan K. Bowman, Edward Champlin, and Andrew Lintott, vol. 10, *The Augustan Empire*, 113–46. Cambridge: Cambridge University Press, 1996.

——. "Political History, 30 BC–AD 14." In *Cambridge Ancient History*, 2nd ed., ed. Alan K. Bowman, Edward Champlin, and Andrew Lintott, vol. 10, *The Augustan Empire*, 70–112. Cambridge: Cambridge University Press, 1996.

Davis, P. J. "*Praeceptor amoris*: Ovid's *Ars Amatoria* and the Augustan Idea of Rome." *Ramus* 24, no. 2 (1995): 181–95.

Dominik, William J., ed. *Roman Eloquence: Rhetoric in Society and Literature*. London: Routledge, 1997.

Eden, Kathy. *Hermeneutics and the Rhetorical Tradition*. New Haven, Conn.: Yale University Press, 1997.

Fyler, John M. *Chaucer and Ovid*. New Haven, Conn.: Yale University Press, 1979.

——. "*Omnia vincit amor*: Incongruity and the Limitations of Structure in Ovid's Elegiac Poetry." *The Classical Journal* 66, no. 3 (1971): 196–203.

Ginsberg, Warren. "The Idea of Character in Ovid: The *Amores*." In *The Cast of Character: The Representation of Personality in Ancient and Medieval Literature*, chap. 1. Toronto: University of Toronto Press, 1983.

Goffman, Erwin. *The Presentation of Self in Everyday Life*. Rev. ed. Garden City, N.Y.: Doubleday Anchor, 1959.

Habinek, Thomas. "The Invention of Sexuality in the World-City of Rome." In *The Roman Cultural Revolution*, ed. Habinek and Alessandro Schiesaro, 23–43. Cambridge: Cambridge University Press, 1997.

——. "Ovid and Empire." In *The Cambridge Companion to Ovid*, ed. Philip Hardie, 46–61. Cambridge: Cambridge University Press, 2002.

——. "*Pannonia Domanda est*: The Construction of the Imperial Subject Through Ovid's Poetry from Exile." In *The Politics of Latin Literature: Writing, Identity, and Empire in Ancient Rome*, 151–69. Princeton, N.J.: Princeton University Press, 1998.

Habinek, Thomas, and Alessandro Schiesaro, eds. *The Roman Cultural Revolution*. Cambridge: Cambridge University Press, 1997.

Hardie, Philip, ed. *The Cambridge Companion to Ovid*. Cambridge: Cambridge University Press, 2002.

Harrison, Stephen. "Ovid and Genre: Evolutions of an Elegist." In *The Cambridge Companion to Ovid*, ed. Philip Hardie, 79–94. Cambridge: Cambridge University Press, 2002.

Hunt, Alan. *Governance of the Consuming Passions: A History of Sumptuary Law*. New York: St. Martins, 1996.

Leach, Eleanor Winsor. "Georgic Imagery in the *Ars amatoria*." *TAPA* 95 (1964): 142–54.

Leicester, H. Marshall, Jr. "Ovid Enclosed: The God of Love as *Magister amoris* in the *Roman de la Rose* of Guillaume de Lorris." *Res publica litterarum* 7 (1984): 107–29.

McGinn, T. A. J. "Concubinage and the *Lex Julia* on Adultery." *Transactions of the American Philological Association* 121 (1991): 335–75.

———. *Prostitution, Sexuality, and the Law in Ancient Rome.* Oxford: Oxford University Press, 1998.

Merriam, Carol U. *Love and Propaganda: Augustan Venus and the Latin Love Elegists.* Brussels: Latomus, 2006.

Ramage, Edwin S. *Urbanitas: Ancient Sophistication and Refinement.* University of Cincinnati Classical Studies 3. Norman: University of Oklahoma Press for University of Cincinnati, 1973.

Simpson, James. *Reform and Cultural Revolution.* Vol. 2 of *The Oxford English Literary History, 1350–1547.* Oxford: Oxford University Press, 2002.

Solodow, Joseph B. "Ovid's *Ars Amatoria*: The Lover as Cultural Ideal," *Wiener Studien* 11 (1977): 106–27.

Tarrant, Richard. "Ovid and Ancient Literary History." In *The Cambridge Companion to Ovid*, ed. Philip Hardie, 13–33. Cambridge: Cambridge University Press, 2002.

Toohey, Peter. "Eros and Eloquence: Modes Of Amatory Persuasion in Ovid's *Ars Amatoria*." In *Roman Eloquence: Rhetoric in Society and Literature*, ed. William J. Dominik, 198–211. London: Routledge, 1997.

Townend, Gavin. "Literature and Society." In *Cambridge Ancient History*, 2nd ed., ed. Alan K. Bowman, Edward Champlin, and Andrew Lintott, vol. 10, *The Augustan Empire*, 905–29. Cambridge: Cambridge University Press, 1996.

Treggiari, Susan. *Roman Marriage: Iusti conjuges from the Time of Cicero to the Time of Ulpian.* Oxford: Clarendon, 1991.

———. "Social Status and Social Legislation." In *Cambridge Ancient History*, 2nd ed., ed. Alan K. Bowman, Edward Champlin, and Andrew Lintott, vol. 10, *The Augustan Empire*, 873–904. Cambridge: Cambridge University Press, 1996.

Wallace-Hadrill, Andrew. "The Imperial Court." In *Cambridge Ancient History*, 2nd ed., ed. Alan K. Bowman, Edward Champlin, and Andrew Lintott, vol. 10, *The Augustan Empire*, 283–308. Cambridge: Cambridge University Press, 1996.

———. "*Mutatio morum*: The Idea of a Cultural Revolution." In *The Roman Cultural Revolution*, ed. Thomas Habinek and Alessandro Schiesaro, 3–22. Cambridge: Cambridge University Press, 1997.

CHAUCER:

DEALING WITH THE AUTHORITIES

OR, TWISTING THE NOSE THAT FEEDS YOU

At one point early in what is perhaps Geoffrey Chaucer's first extended narrative poem, *The Book of the Duchess* (*BD*), the narrator describes reading a story in a book that he has picked up to drive the night away during a bout of insomnia that has lasted, he tells us, for eight years and left him pretty much a nervous wreck. The story freely adapts the tale of Ceyx and Alcyone from book II of Ovid's *Metamorphoses*, in which Ceyx is drowned on a sea voyage while Alcyone prays to Juno for his safe return. Upset by her futile entreaties, the goddess sends a messenger to the realm of Morpheus, god of sleep, with instructions to him to bring before Alcyone in her slumber a vision of Ceyx bearing news of his death. After reading the story, the narrator expresses wonder at the idea of gods who could make a person sleep, "for I ne knew never god but oon." He continues,

And in my game I sayde anoon	*at once*
(And yet me lyst ryght evel to pleye)	*I had no desire*
Rather then that y shulde deye	
Thorgh defaute of slepynge thus,	
I wolde yive thilke Morpheus	*give this*
. . . the alderbeste	*very best*
yifte that ever he abod hys lyve.	*that he ever had in his life*
	(*BD* 238–42, 246–47)

That is: a complete, luxurious bedroom set in a chamber newly painted with gold and hung with expensive tapestries. No sooner has he made this extravagant, and obviously impossible, promise than he falls asleep and dreams his own dream—a tribute to the recently dead Blanche, duchess of Lancaster, presumably intended for her husband and Chaucer's sometime patron, John of Gaunt, duke of Lancaster.[1]

I offer the lines I have quoted as a kind of exhibit A because they describe a moment of serious import for the narrator, whose sleeplessness (implicitly the result of his loss, paralleling Alcyone's, of an object of desire) has, by his own admission in lines preceding those quoted above, brought him to a point of moral and emotional paralysis. And yet his response to this crisis is a "game," even though he hardly feels like playing: the game of imagining what would make a suitable, and suitably luxurious, bribe to a god of sleep, if there were one for a Christian to bribe. Furthermore, this serious play works: no sooner has the narrator constructed his extravagant fantasy than "such a lust [desire, wish] anoon me took / To slepe that ryght upon my book/ Y fil aslepe" (BD 273–75)—a statement that suggests, simultaneously, the inspirational, the problem-solving, and the somniferous qualities of a book in which

> were written fables
> That clerkes had in olde tyme,   *scholars*
> And other poetes, put in ryme
> To rede and for to be in minde,
> While men loved the lawe of kynde.   *nature*
>
>   (BD 52–56)

This description constitutes a miniature, irony-tinged description of, and tribute to, a major part of Chaucer's literary heritage: stories inherited from an earlier time, transmitted for both their moral and aesthetic worth—hence the role of learned men ("clerkes") as well as poets in the transmission—and designed not simply to be read for pleasure but to be stored away in the reader's memory as an authoritative repository of truths, including truths about the correct objects of human desire—in this case, the natural law that should govern both emotions and behavior. The neat and economical intertwining of issues of desire and authority in these few lines sets the tone for my examination, in the following pages, of some of the crises of desire and authority confronted, with comic virtuosity, at several moments that I've chosen from among Chaucer' s major writings.

Chaucer was born in London early in the 1340s, the son of a well-to-do London wine merchant who was able to place him by his midteens in at least

part time service to the nobility. This was the beginning of Chaucer's long career under two successive English kings, Edward III and Richard II, as royal
official, diplomat, and civil servant, a series of positions that brought him into
contact with great nobles like John of Gaunt; with the powerful merchant oligarchy that ruled London; and, most to our benefit, with a circle of midlevel
court officials, London literati and members of literate professions whom he
most likely saw as the target audience for his complicated, ironic, and frequently oblique seriocomic poetry.[2] He lived through the tumultuous reign of
Richard II, saw Henry Bolingbroke depose Richard in 1399, becoming Henry
IV, and died in October 1400. His burial in Westminster Abbey appears not to
have been a recognition of his poetic prowess, which only became an article of
literary faith in the decades after his death.[3]

C haucer's poetry suggests that he perceived two major challenges to its success: one was to master, and communicate effectively to his audiences, the
complex relationship between love as a crisis-ridden human experience and love
as a convention-driven literary subject; the other was to deliver a comic truth
about the nature of both literary (or, more broadly, cultural) and political authority: their power, limits, and challenges or dangers to those (like himself)
under their sway. The two interests came into an alignment particularly fruit-
ful for his poetry in the authoritative literary discourses of desire that he inherited from both recent French and Italian poets—his familiarity with Dante,
Petrarch, and Boccaccio was unique among English writers of his day—and
their predecessors of ancient Rome: Vergil, Statius, and especially Ovid. This
latter group achieved an exalted status in medieval education as auctores, a
term connoting not just authorship but also, and more importantly, cultural
authority based on the possession of exemplary moral and philosophical value
as well as aesthetic excellence.[4]

Several of Chaucer's poems contain seriocomic theorizations of the problematic relationship between an authoritative poetic heritage and the "modern" poet's imaginative engagement with human desire. (In Helen Cooper's
lapidary formulation, Chaucer "did not accept auctoritas on trust".)[5] His preferred narratorial persona for such matters is humble and not overly bright;
often he's a non-lover grappling with how to understand, or to write effectively
about, love.[6] The most desperate statement of the obstacles involved comes in
the opening, seven-line stanza of *The Parlement of Foules* (PF), that is, "The
Debate Among the Birds," about which I'll shortly have more to say:

The lyf so short, the craft so long to lerne,
Th'assay so hard, so sharp the conquerynge,
The dredful joye alwey that slit so yerne: *slides away   quickly*
Al this mene I by Love, that my felynge
Astonyeth with his wonderful werkynge   *that so completely*
                                                         dazes my understand-
                                                         ing by its strange ways

So sore, iwis, that whan I on hym thynke
Nat wot I wel wher that I flete or synke.   *I don't even know*
                                                         whether I'm floating
                                                         (*PF* 1–7)

Note how cleverly this stanza intertwines the generic difficulties of the poetic vocation, evoked in the opening line, with its obvious echo of Horace's "ars longa, vita brevis est" (i.e., life's too short to master art's challenges), and the particular challenge of that vocation's favorite subject, "Love," the centrality of which is underscored by the word's placement at the exact midpoint of the stanza.

A much fuller, more comprehensive statement of the pitfalls confronting the would-be love poet occupies the first seven stanzas—in some manuscripts labeled prohemium (Prologue)—of the second book (of five) of Chaucer's greatest complete poem, *Troilus and Criseyde* (TC), identified by its narrator as a "tragedye" (5.1786), but shot through with comic moments, including this apologia for the problems the narrator encounters in attempting to bring an old story to a potentially critical audience of his contemporaries.

The first book of *Troilus and Criseyde* has recounted the sudden love of the Trojan prince Troilus for Criseyde, the widowed daughter of a Trojan priest of Apollo who has defected to the Greek host besieging Troy. The onset of desire immobilizes Troilus until Pandar, his close friend and Criseyde's uncle, arouses him by offering to act as his go-between, a project to which the prince consents as book 1 concludes. There follow forty-nine lines that exemplify the Chaucerian narratorial voice at its most subtle, comic, and provocative:

Owt of thise blake waves for to saylle,
O wynd, o wynd, the weder gynneth clere,
For in this see the boot hath swych travaylle,
Of my connyng, that unneth I it steere.
This see clepe I the tempestous matere
Of disespeir that Troilus was inne;
But now of hope the kalendes bygynne.

O lady myn, that called art Cleo,
Thow be my speed fro this forth, and my Muse,
To ryme wel this book til I have do;
Me nedeth here noon other art to use.
Forwhi to every lovere I me excuse,
That of no sentement I this endite,
But out of Latyn in my tonge it write.

Wherfore I nyl have neither thank ne blame
Of al this werk, but prey yow mekely,
Disblameth me if any word be lame,
For as myn auctor seyde, so sey I.
Ek though I speeke of love unfelyngly,
No wondre is, for it nothyng of newe is;
A blynd man kan nat juggen wel in hewis.

Ye knowe ek that in forme of speche is chaunge
Withinne a thousand yeer, and wordes tho
That hadden pris, now wonder nyce and straunge
Us thynketh hem, and yet thei spake hem so,
And spedde as wel in love as men now do;
Ek for to wynnen love in sondry ages,
In sondry londes, sondry ben usages.

And forthi if it happe in any wyse,
That here be any lovere in this place
That herkneth, as the storie wol devise,
How Troilus com to his lady grace,
And thenketh, 'So nold I nat love purchace,'
Or wondreth on his speche or his doynge,
I noot; but it is me no wonderynge.

For every wight which that to Rome went
Halt nat o path, or alwey o manere;
Ek in som lond were al the game shent,
If that they ferde in love as men don here,
As thus, in opyn doyng or in chere,
In visityng in forme, or seyde hire sawes;
Forthi men seyn, 'Ecch contree hath his lawes.'

Ek scarsly ben ther in this place thre
That have in love seid lik, and don, in al;
For to thi purpos this may liken the,
And the right nought; yet al is seid or schal;
Ek som men grave in tree, som in ston wal,
As it bitit. But syn I have bigonne,
Myn auctor shal I folwen, if I konne.

(*TC* 2.1–49)

The opening stanzas of the prohemium establish a dialectic of involvement and detachment in the narrator's attitude toward his story. He begins with a gesture of emotional engagement by metaphorically assimilating his artistic enterprise to the changing fortunes of his protagonist: he describes "the boot . . . of my connyng" laboring, almost beyond control, on a "see" constituted by "the tempestuous matere / of disespeir that Troilus was inne." Yet he sees his own weather begin to clear as (and because) his protagonist sails out of stormy despair toward a new season of hope. Then, as if sensing potential danger in too close an involvement with his characters, he quickly strikes a more detached pose, defining his goal as the purely technical one, "to ryme wel this book til I have do," and excusing himself to lovers (the poem's imagined audience) as a mere translator by noting "that of no sentement I this endite, / But out of Latyn in my tonge it write." Accordingly, he continues in stanza 3, he can accept no responsibility for faults of diction ("if any word be lame"), since his will be a most exact translation: "as myn auctor seyde, so sey I." As for lack of affect, his ignorance about love excuses him there: "A blynd man kan nat juggen wel in hewis" (with a pun on rhetorical colors, techniques that add bite to declamation).

The reason for all this backpedaling is now revealed: the narrator is worried about the potential for disaffection in some lover who, hearing the poem's representation of Troilus's words and deeds in wooing Criseyde, will judge them negatively on the basis of his own experience—"I wouldn't do it that way!" (2.33). So he adds more sandbags to the levee holding off an expected flood of criticism, adducing both the instability of language over time—words once current now sound silly, but in their day they were effective in wooing (2.22–26)—and the variability of both amorous discourse and behavior, across space ("sondry londes") and time ("sondry ages"). There's more than one way to get to Rome, the narrator counsels, but he then pushes his self-exculpatory argument to an extreme that would seem to deny to a literary text any validity as a general statement about amorous behavior (or any other human behavior, for that matter) in the face of such universal variety (2.43–46; note the parallel between this admission of disabling variety and the Ovidian *magister*'s admission, at end of book I of the *Ars amatoria*, of the variety of women, which necessitates a protean strategy.)

In a final metaphoric move, the argument turns away from the variety of sexual experience to the variety of media in which to record it—"ek som men grave in tree, som in stone wal, as it bitit [happens]"—and this move allows the narrator to dodge the questions he has raised about the limits of language as communication and literature as mimesis, returning meekly to his self-appointed task of translation "out of Latyn in my tonge." Or rather, almost to dodge them because some shred of understanding what a Pandora's box he has opened underlies the conditional clause he appends to the final line of his Prologue: "Myn auctor shal I folwen, *if I konne*" (emphasis added). This confession contrasts with and undermines his earlier insistence, already quoted, that "as myn auctor seyde, so sey I."

This last line requires contextualization. Both the notion of "following" an auctor and the broader significance of "if I konne" occur elsewhere in Chaucer's poetry. The introductory "Invocation" to *Anelida and Arcite*, a short, perhaps incomplete text, announces the narrator's intention

> in Englyssh to endyte   *compose*
> This olde storie, in Latyn which I fynde,
> Of Quene Anelida and fals Arcite
> That elde . . .   *the passage of time*
> Hath nygh devoured out of oure memorie.
>
> (*Anelida*, 9–12, 14),

The "Invocation" concludes with the line, "First folowe I Stace, and after him Corinne" (*Anelida*, 21). The opening lines of the story of Dido in *The Legend of Good Women* (*LGW*)—an anthology of victimized women (about which more later) adapted from Ovid's *Heroides* and other classical sources—echo more precisely the last line of the Prologue to book 2 of *Troilus and Criseyde*:

> Glorye and honour, Virgil Mantoan,   *of Mantua*
> Be to thy name! and I shal, *as I can*,
> Folwe thy lanterne, as thow gost byforn,
> How Eneas to Dido was forsworn.
> In thyn Eneyde and Naso wol I take   *from your   Ovid*
> The tenor, and the grete effectes make.
>
> (*LGW* 924–29; emphasis added)

These three passages allude to but also disguise Chaucer's dealings with and attitude toward the textual foundations upon which he erected his poetic edifice. In the mouth of the Troilus narrator, to "folwen" an auctor suggests translational fidelity limited only by lack of ability. (In this case, however, Chaucer treats his actual auctor—not the fictitious Latin author, "Lollius," mentioned elsewhere in *Troilus and Criseyde* [1.394, 5.1653], but Chaucer's near-contemporary, the Florentine Giovanni Boccaccio—with a great deal of freedom, translating the Italian's *Il Filostrato* closely in some parts of the poem but inserting massive amounts of new material and altering the tone and spirit of his predecessor time and time again.)[7] The narrator of *Anelida*, notwithstanding his claim to resurrect a neglected "olde storie" in Latin, admits almost at once that he is following not one but two sources: the Latin epic poet Statius and a more elusive "Corinne" (perhaps a deliberately misleading reference of Ovid's *Amores*). Despite the fact that a few lines of Statius's post-Vergilian *Thebaid*—the epic tale of the destruction of Thebes through fraternal strife betweeen the two male offspring of Oedipus's incestuous union with his mother—are quoted and closely translated shortly after the narrator's avowal, there is nothing else of that auctor in the poem, which settles instead into a brief tale of the betrayal of a naively virtuous woman by a two-timing cad. As for the "Legend of Dido," it borrows its image of following the auctor's lantern from Dante's *Purgatorio* 22, where that same Statius, appearing to Dante and Vergil, praises the latter, though himself a pagan, for leading his poetic successor to Christianity, even as a man walking in the darkness may shine a lantern behind him so that its light, which cannot benefit him, aids those who follow him. (This medieval appreciation of Vergil as a proto-Christian derives from the fact that many commentators of that era believed that Vergil's fourth *Eclogue* contained a thinly veiled prophecy of the birth of Christ.)[8] The Chaucerian narrator appears to place himself into an analogous, albeit non-creedal, status of dependency on "Virgil Mantoan," at least with respect to the story of Aeneas's love for and abandonment of Dido in *Aeneid* 4. But the real significance of "as I can" is immediately revealed by the succeeding lines, in which the narrator admits he will fabricate a general outline from not one but two classical poets (who offer opposing perspectives on Dido, by the way) while adding the "grete effectes" (the high points? the special details? the real meaning?) himself.

What these examples teach us is not so much that Chaucer makes fraudulent claims about his fidelity to his poetic antecedents—although he does that, certainly—as that "folwen if (or as) I konne" seems to mean something like, "faced with the stature of both classical and modern auctores, I will appropriate them in the way that best serves my poetic needs." Behind the mask of humble servitude to the auctor lurks the eye of the opportunist, ready to appropriate auctorial achievement to his own devices.[9]

T he supple, irreverent ways in which Chaucer dealt with his culture's auctores, and with issues of literary and cultural authority alluded to in *Troilus and Criseyde*, are on view in two earlier poems cast in the then-popular literary form of the dream vision. The *Troilus* narrator's insistence on the fragility of authority across time and space, owing to changes in language—"wordes tho / That hadden pris now wonder nyce and straunge / Us thynketh hem" (*TC* 2.23–25)—and customs—"forto wynnen love in sondry ages, / In sondry londes, sondry ben usages" (*TC* 2.27–28)—is anticipated in *The House of Fame* (*HF*), a highly skeptical meditation on the reliability of all authority, indeed all information and knowledge, transmitted by language from age to age or place to place.[10]

The inspiration for *HF* is impeccably auctorial: it is the depiction of Fame's dwelling in book 12 of Ovid's *Metamorphoses*, which in turn adapts Vergil's description of Fame, in book 4 of the *Aeneid*, as a malevolent creature of many eyes and ears who rushes around the world, spreading the harmful news of Dido's love affair with Aeneas:

Extemplo Libyae magnas it Fama per urbes,
Fama, malum qua non aliud velocius ullum.
mobilitate viget virisque adquirit eundo;
parva metu primo, mox sese attollit in auras
ingrediturque solo et caput inter nubila condit.
. . . pedibus celerem et pernicibus alis,
monstrum horrendum, ingens, cui, quot sunt corpore plumae,
tot vigiles oculi subter (mirabile dictu),
tot linguae, totidem ora sonant, tot subrigit auris.
Nocte volat caeli medio terraeque per umbram,
stridens, nec dulci declinat lumina somno;
luce sedet custos aut summi culmine tecti,
turribus aut altis, et magnas territat urbes,
tam ficti pravique tenax quam nuntia veri.

(*Aeneid* 4.173–77, 180–88)

(Then, swiftest of all evils, Rumor runs / straightway through Libya's mighty cities—Rumor, / whose life is speed, whose going gives her force. / Timid

and small at first, she soon lifts up / her body in the air. She stalks the
ground; / her head is hidden in the clouds. / . . . fast footed / and lithe of
wing, she is a terrifying / enormous monster with as many feathers / as
she has sleepless eyes beneath each feather / (amazingly), as many sounding tongues / and mouths, and raises up as many ears. / Between the
earth and skies she flies by night, / screeching across the darkness, and
she never / closes her eyes in gentle sleep. By day / she sits as sentinel on
some steep roof / or on high towers, frightening vast cities; / for she
holds fast to falsehood and distortion / as often as to messages of truth.)

(Mandelbaum trans., 87)

Ovid's adaptation—less overtly hostile, more focused on social interchange—
stresses the instability of *fama*, or what we would call news and rumor, as it
passes from mouth to mouth, growing and changing as it goes:

> Orbe locus medio est inter terrasque fretumque
> caelestesque plagas, triplicis confinia mundi;
> unde quod est usquam, quamvis regionibus absit,
> inspicitur, penetratque cavas vox omnis ad aures:
> Fama tenet summaque domum sibi legit in arce,
> innumerosque aditus ac mille foramina tectis
> addidit et nullis inclusit limina portis;
> nocte dieque patet: tota est ex aere sonanti,
> tota fremit vocesque refert iteratque quod audit;
> nulla quies intus nullaque silentia parte,
> nec tamen est clamor, sed parvae murmura vocis. . . .
> Atria turba tenet: veniunt, leve vulgus, euntque
> Mixtaque cum veris passim commenta vagantur
> Milia rumorum confusaque verba volutant;
> e quibus hi vacuas inplent sermonibus aures,
> hi narrata ferunt alio, mensuraque ficti
> crescit, et auditis aliquid novus adicit auctor. . . .
> Ipsa [i.e. Fama], quid in caelo rerum pelagoque geratur
> et tellure, videt totumque inquirit in orbem.

(*Metamorphoses* 12.39–49, 53–58, 62–63)

(There is a place / At the world's center, triple boundary / Of land and
sky and sea. From here all things, / No matter what, are visible; every
word / Comes to these hollow ears. Here Rumor dwells, / Her palace

high upon the mountain-summit, / With countless entrances, thousands on thousands, / And never a door to close them. Day and night /
The halls stand open, and the bronze re-echoes, / Repeats all words, re-
doubles every murmur. / There is no quiet, no silence anywhere, / No
uproar either, only the subdued / Murmur of little voices. . . . / The halls /
Are filled with presences that shift and wander, / Rumors in thousands,
lies and truth together, / Confused and confusing. Some fill idle ears /
With stories, others go far-off to tell / What they have heard, and every
story grows, / And each new teller adds to what he hears. / . . . [A]nd
she, their goddess, / Sees all that happens in heaven, on land, on ocean,
searching the world for news.)   (Humphries trans., 286–87)

Chaucer's poem proceeds to enlist these representations of Fame for use in a
variety of ways as ammunition against the elevated cultural status of their cre-
ators (remember what I said about comic poets biting the feeding hand). In
book 1 of *HF*, for example, the narrator dreams of wandering alone in a temple
of Venus, on the walls of which he finds graven (*HF* 157, 193; the word can mean
"written" or "engraved") the story of the Aeneid:[11]

But as I slepte, me mette I was	*I dreamed*
Withyn a temple ymad of glas,	
In which ther were moo images	*more*
Of gold, stondynge in sondry stages,	*variously mounted*
And moo ryche tabernacles,	
And with perre moo pynacles,	*precious gems*
And moo curiouse portreytures,	*skillful paintings*
And queynte maner of figures	*clever types*
Of olde werk, then I saugh ever.	
For certeynly, I nyste never	*had no idea*
Wher that I was, but wel wyste I	
Hyt was of Venus redely,	*truly*
The temple; . . .	
But as I romed up and doun,	
I fond that on a wall ther was	
Thus writen on a table of bras:	*plaque*
'I wol now synge, *yif I kan*	
The armes and also the man	
That first cam, thurgh his destinee,	
Fugityf of Troy contree,	

In Italye, with ful moche pyne   *suffering*
Upon the strondes of Lavyne.'   *shores*
                              (HF 119–31, 140–48; emphasis added)

The poem's rendering of Vergil's famous opening line, "Arma virumque
cano," as "I wol now singe, yif I kan, / The armes and also the man," suggests
that Chaucer cannot resist transfering to Vergil his own sense of the contin-
gencies of translation. Indeed, HF's version of the *Aeneid* is an exercise in following an auctor "as I konne," for it inserts into the account of Aeneas's affair
with Dido a segment of the pathetic lament Ovid wrote for her in his *Heroides*,
casting the Trojan hero in a much less favorable light. The Chaucerian narrator
also interrupts the Vergilian narrative to add a warning to women—beware
the verbal trickery of false lovers!—that owes a general debt to similar admonitions directed at the elegant young women of Rome by Ovid's *magister amoris*
in book 3 of the *Ars amatoria*:

Therfore be no wyght so nyce   *no one should be so foolish*
To take a love oonly for chere,   *looks*
Or speche, or for frendly manere,
For this shal every woman fynde,
That som man, of his pure kynde,   *from his very nature*
Wol sheweth outward the fayreste,   *will make the best posible*
                                        impression

Tyl he have caught that what him leste; *what he wants*
And thanne wol he causes fynde   *excuses*
And swere how that she ys unkynde,
Or fals, or privy, or double was.   *has guilty secrets*
                                        duplicitous
                                                        (HF 276–85)

The result is a Vergil-Ovid amalgam that testifies, among other things, to the
instability, dubious integrity, and unverifiability of transmitted stories. The narrator speaks later of "Aventure / That is the moder of tydynges [spreader of ru-
mors]" (1982–83), reminding us of the role chance inevitably plays in the transmission, suppression, or distortion of narratives, that is, in the process that
constitutes *fama*.

   In a wry, albeit implied, comment on the inscrutability of fame, the narrator's dream version of the *Aeneid* shows Dido lamenting the damage done her
reputation by her affair with a man who has abandoned her, convinced that

"wikke Fame" will insure her condemnation by future ages. Meanwhile, the very text that reports this despairing comment passes a negative judgment not on her but on Aeneas. Finally, as if to illustrate the process of transmission plus addition that Ovid attributes to all the information that comes to and is circulated in Fame's palace (*Metamorphoses* 12.57–58), the narrator puts some words in Dido's mouth for which only he is responsible, not Vergil or Ovid:

> In suche wordes gan to pleyne   *lament*
> Dido of hire greete peyne;
> As me mette redely;   *I truly dreamed*
> Noon other auctor allege I.
>
> (*HF* 311–14)

This hybrid version of the *Aeneid* is a multimedia presentation, in pictures as well as words—see, for example, *HF* 209–11: "Ther saugh [saw] I such tempeste aryse / That every herte myght agryse [shudder] / To see hyt peynted on the wal"—that, together with its architectural setting, presents the classical tradition as a living, multiply communicating structure of great beauty and complexity, into which the modern poet ventures by acts of individual and cultural memory (here conventionally figured as dreaming). In addition, the dream temple's dedication to Venus suggests the continuing impact of classical story on late-medieval representations of desire (such as *Troilus and Criseyde*), but the poem suggests that this pervasive influence is not without its downside. The fact that the temple is empty except for the narrator, and is located in a huge sandy desert, inscribes the dreamer's fear that paraphrasing classical poetry in the vernacular (as he has just done with the *Aeneid*) is a sterile exercise in venerating literary traditions that, for all their "noblesse" and "richesse," remain the fantasies of an abandoned "chirche"—cultural illusions that shut the poet off from a lived experience fertile with potential for the narrative imagination:

> When I had seen al this syghte
> In this noble temple thus,
> 'A, Lord,' thoughte I, 'that madest us,
> Yet sawgh I never such noblesse
> Of ymages, ne such richesse,
> As I saugh graven in this chirche: *drawn/written*
> But not wot I whoo did hem wirche,   *who made them*
> Ne where I am, ne in what contree. . . .'
> When I out at the dores cam,

I faste aboute me beheld.
Then sawgh I but a large feld,   *nothing but*
As fer as that I myghte see,
Withouten toun, or hous, or tree,
Or bush, or grass, or eryd lond;   *cultivated*
For al the feld nas but of sond. . . .   *consisted of nothing but sand*
Ne no maner creature
That is yformed be Nature
Ne sawgh I, me to rede or wisse.   *to advise or guide me*
'O Crist,' thoughte I, 'that art in blysse,
Fro fantome and illusion
Me save!'

                                    (*HF* 468–75, 480–86, 490–94)

Having skewered the auctoritee of classical antiquity's greatest Latin epic in its first book, *HF* delivers a deathblow to historical and poetic authority in book 3 via its depiction of the hit and miss way in which information is actually disseminated from the dwelling place of Fame, a site high in the sky to which all sounds uttered in the world must inevitably rise. Fame sits enthroned in her temple built on a hill of ice (with the result that the names of noteworthy people engraved on its sunny side quickly melt away, while those on the side shaded by the temple long remain sharp and clear); the temple's façade teems with niches containing all manner of popular performers "that tellen tales / Both of wepinge and of game, / Of al that longeth unto Fame" (*HF* 1198–1200)—quintessentially unauthoritative entertainers who provide a ubiquitous conduit for the spread of gossip, rumors, and outright fabrications—and, in its great hall, on either side of Fame's throne, pillars of nonprecious metal depict the epic poets and historians of antiquity supporting, by their writings, the fame of various peoples and civilizations (*HF* 1419–1512). As the dreamer summarizes, with a touch a distaste:

What shulde y more telle of this?
The halle was al ful, ywis,   *as full   certainly*
Of hem that writen olde gestes   *those who   stories*
As ben on trees rokes nestes;   *rooks' nests*
But hit a ful confus matere   *it would be very confusing*
Were alle the gestes for to here   *to hear all the stories*
That they of write, or how they highte.   *were named*

                                    (*HF* 1513–19)

The record of the past—its "fame" through the ages— is here reduced to a disorienting babel, the accuracy of which is far from assured (hence the baser metals of the columns?): in the most notorious instance, the fame of Troy is borne (or, as we would say, propagated) by a phalanx of poets who are at odds about the truth of the matter:

Betwex hem was a litil envye.   *between*   *ill-will*
Oon seyde that Omer made lyes,
Feynynge in hys poetries,
And was to Grekes favorable:
Therfor held he hyt but fable.   *a fiction*

                           (HF 1476–80)

Meanwhile, suppliants who arrive at Fame's temple seeking a good reputation for deeds performed are variously rewarded by the fickle goddess with good fame, no fame, and evil fame, based on no evident criteria except her momentary pleasure: responding to the plea of those suitors who request good reputations

In ful recompensacioun
Of good werkes, . . .
'I werne yow hit,' quod she anon;   *deny*
'Ye gete of me good fame non,
Be God, and therfore goo your wey.'   *by*
'Allas,' quod they, 'and welaway!
Telle us what may your cause be.'
'For me lyst hit noght,' quod she.   *because I don't want to*

                           (HF 1557–64)

The same inscrutable fate awaits those seeking ill-fame, or mere oblivion. The result is to establish the complete amorality and unreliability of fame's judgments. (That such judgments are in direct opposition to those of the deity is suggested by the implicit comparison between Fame and the enthroned Christ in the Book of Revelation [see HF 1381–85: "For as feele eyen [many eyes] hadde she / As fetheres upon foules [birds] be, / Or weren on the bestes foure / That Goddis trone gunne honoure [honored, worshipped], / As John writ in th'Apocalips"].) And this arbitrariness of authority on Fame's part clearly underscores the crisis of authority for those empillared poets and chroniclers, already mentioned, whose back-breaking labors the text of HF places in fatal proximity to the fickle goddess. (It should be noted that some years after Chaucer composed HF, a similar arbitrariness of judgment was attributed to Richard II in the "Articles of Deposition" drawn up by supporters of his supplanter, Henry Bolingbroke, to justify the latter's usurpation of the throne.)[12]

After leaving Fame's palace, the narrator visits a huge ("sixty myle of lengthe" [HF 1979]), whirling house of wicker construction, crammed full of people and their stories. This is the place to which all news from earth first ascends—"and eke [also] this hous hath of entrees / As fele [many] as leves ben in trees / In somer" (HF 1945–47; cf. *Metamorphoses* 12.44–45)—before proceeding to Fame's throne room to be judged. I take the liberty of quoting myself:

> The bizarre, revolving house stands in relation to Fame's temple as an out-building to a manor house: it is a depot or workshop where the raw materials are received and prepared. Chaucer has taken certain Ovidian details— the chain of retellings by which Fama pursues her ever-expanding existence; the multiple openings into Fama's dwelling; its crowdedness— and augmented them (to out-Ovid Ovid), creating the enormous, grotesque space in which Fame actually begins to breed.[13]

Here in this "workshop of Fame," the process of spreading and distorting the word seems to be in the hands of the lowest rank of tale tellers—shipmen, pilgrims, pardoners—who move about the earth collecting and transmitting news, gossip, rumor, what have you. (They will, eventually, become the dramatis personae of Chaucer's *Canterbury Tales*.) The narrator watches as a true and a false "tydyng [story, report]" engage in a shoving match, while each attempts to squeeze first out of a narrow window in order to proceed to the fickle goddess's summary judgment. Their strife ends with an agreement to combine; after this Ovidian moment of metamorphosis, the new entity, "soth [true] and fals compouned,"[14] exits, leaving behind no doubt whatsoever as to the value of information gained from any link in the chain of narration that extends from bit of juicy gossip, through heraldic genealogy, to classical epic.

The sudden appearance of someone who seems "a man of greet auctoritee" in a corner of the whirling house causes a stir among its sardined occupants, but at that point the poem breaks off, having by now rendered effectively null and void any viable idea of historical or cultural authority.

*T*he *Parlement of Foules* offers another good example of Chaucer's aptitude for (to paraphrase a medieval bon mot on the subject) twisting the wax

nose of (poetic) authority.[15] This poem also supports, proleptically, the narrator's contention to his audience in *Troilus and Criseyde* that "forto wynnen love
in sondry ages, / In sondry londes, sondry ben usages," and, furthermore, that
"scarsly ben ther in this place thre / that have in love seid like and don in al." The
Parlement uses materials as diverse as a philosophic dream vision, Italian erotic
allegory, bird lore drawn from the bestiary tradition, and sociopolitical antago-
nisms aired through a comic simulacrum of parliamentary debate to dramatize
divergent perspectives on the satisfaction of desire.

I've already quoted the opening stanza of *PF* in which its narrator expresses
wonder and fear at the "wonderul werkynge" of love, which, like the *Troilus* narrator, he knows about only from reading, as the poem's second stanza makes clear:

> For al be that I knowe nat Love in dede,
> Ne wot how that he quiteth folk here hyre,   *repays people for their*
>   *service (to him)*
> Yit happeth me ful ofte in bokes reede
> Of his myrakles and his crewel yre.
>
> (PF 8–11)

After perusing the "Somnium scipionis" ("Dream of Scipio"), a Stoic-Platonic
parable that concludes Cicero's *De republica* by inculcating detachment from
worldly concerns and service to "the commun profyt" (*PF* 75) or *res publica*, the
narrator dreams that Affrican (*Scipio africanus*), the wisdom figure from Scipio's
dream, brings him to a garden, on the gate of which are inscribed starkly contrary messages. One promises joy and pleasure within while the other (modeled
on the inscription over the entrance to hell in Dante's *Inferno*) warns of disaster
and counsels avoidance. Together they suggest proleptically (though from a different perspective) the debates to follow within:

> 'Thorgh me men gon into that blysful place
> Of hertes hele and dedly woundes cure;   *well-being*
> Thorgh me men gon unto the welle of grace,
> There grene and lusty May shal evere endure.
> This is the wey to al good aventure.   *fortune*
> Be glad, thow redere, and thy sorwe of-caste;
> Al open am I—passe in, and sped thee faste!'
>
> 'Thorgh me men gon,' than spak that other side,
> 'Unto the mortal strokes of the spere

Of which Disdayn and Daunger is the gyde,   *(the lady's)*
                                                   resistance
                                                   guide

Ther never tree shal fruyt ne leves bere.
This strem yow ledeth to the sorweful were   *stream   weir*
                                                   (fish trap)

There as the fish in prysoun is al drye;
Th'eschewing is only the remedye!'

                                                           (PF 127–40)

Reassured by his guide that the messages are not intended for nonlovers, the narrator enters and passes in quick succession through a beautiful landscape of perpetual spring, vibrant with animal life and harmonious bird song (*PF* 172–210), and then a temple of love and desire, staffed by allegorical abstractions who represent facets (mostly discouraging) of a lover's experience, presided over by Venus and the lustful phallic god Priapus (his scepter in his hand, we are euphemistically informed) and populated by troops of famous, mostly tragic lovers (*PF* 211–94). Each of these phases of the dream represents a literary response to the fact of desire: the beautiful landscape is borrowed from *The Romance of the Rose* (*RR*), an influential French allegory of love; the allegorical temple of Venus and Priapus from Boccaccio's epic-romance, the *Teseide*; the figure of Priapus, portrayed at the moment he is prevented by the wake-up bray of a jackass from raping a sleeping nymph, from Ovid's *Fasti*; and the catalogue of lovers from Dante's *Commedia, Inferno* 5. In effect, the narrator, awake and asleep, is reading his way through his library of auctores, old and new, in search of what he calls early in the poem "a certeyn thing," a delightfully ambiguous phrase that can mean either, "something or other," or "certainty," presumably as a relief from his confusion about love ("Nat yoore [long] / Agon it happede me for to beholde / Upon a bok, was write with lettres olde / And therupon, a certeyn thing to lerne, / The longe day ful faste [eagerly] I redde and yerne [*PF* 17–20]).

One last book remains to be opened: the dreaming narrator now comes upon a kind of natural temple of shade trees (as opposed to Venus's shrine of brass) amid which, surrounded by birds of every species arranged in large categories according to their eating habits, sits the goddess Nature, looking "ryght as Aleyn, in the Pleynte of Kynde, / Devyseth [shows] Nature of aray [dress] and face" (*PF* 316–17; *The De planctu naturae*, [*The Plaint of Nature*] by Alan of Lille, a late-twelfth-century grammarian and theologian, was a widely disseminated dream-vision allegory about fallen human sexuality, supposedly as exemplified by clerics and courtiers.)[16] The birds have assembled to choose their mates on St Valentine's Day, under Nature's supervision. Does their orderly disposition around "Nature, the vicaire [deputy] of the almighty Lord, / That hot, cold, hevy, light, moyst, and dreye / Hath knit by evene noumbres of accord [combined in coordinated proportions]" (PF 379–81), mean that the narrator's quest for certainty about love has ended at last in a bookish epiphany of marital harmony as the "commun profyt" at which desire must aim?[17] Nature now announces her "ryghtful ordenaunce . . . that he that most is worthy shal begynne" the mating process, and calls on the noblest bird present, "the tersel [male] egle . . . the foul royal above yow in degre [rank, status]" to choose a mate first, "and after hym by ordre shul ye chese [you will choose in order], / After youre kynde, everich as yow lyketh [each of you as it pleases you]" (PF 390, 392–94, 400–401). By this exercise of her authority, the goddess imposes a social hierarchy—proposed as an expression of the natural order, not just a human construct—on the universal pursuit of desire's satisfaction, along with the "condicioun . . . / that she [i.e., the female chosen] agre to his eleccioun [choice of her], / Whoso he be that shulde be hire feere [wants to be her mate]" (PF 409–10). Accordingly, the royal tercel chooses the beautiful female eagle, perched in a privileged position on Nature's wrist; in an extended speech conforming to the discourse of courtly wooing, he bases his plea for his lady's mercy on his exemplary devotion and service (PF 416–41). So far, so good; but not to be outdone, two other tercels, lower in rank, counterpropose their merits in equally hyperbolic speeches (PF 449–83), introducing division and uncertainty where harmony was to reign: which suitor will the female eagle choose?

The narrator, catching the tone of the proceedings, praises what he has heard, in some extravagant rhetoric of his own: "So gentyl ple [such refined pleading] in love or other thing / Ne herde never no man me beforn [i.e., until now]," while admitting that the high-toned speeches lasted "from the morwe [morning] . . . / Tyl downward went the sonne wonder fast," that is, all day (PF 485–86, 489–90). At which point, all avian hell breaks loose: the fowl of lower ranks make their impatience felt, both at the delay in their satisfying their desires and at the elaborate quadrille of avowals and counter-avowals by which each of the formel's three suitors has been seeking to outdo his rivals:

The noyse of foules for to ben delyvered
So loude rong, 'Have don!, and lat us wende!'   *go (now)*
That wel wende I the wode hadde al toshyvered.   *woods   shattered*

'Come of!' they cride, 'allas, ye wol us shende!	*hurry up*
	you're ruining us
Whan shal youre cursede pletynge have an ende?'	*arguing*
	(PF 491–95)

This intervention transforms a natural occasion (birds mating) into a socio-political one, with status difference expressed in different idioms—no self-respecting tercel, we are sure, would allow himself to say "Have don!" or "Come of!" no matter how upset—but also in different perspectives on wooing strategies. The humbler birds regard courtly rhetoric as "cursede pletynge," and lengthy expressions of devotion as detrimental to their own quite urgent interests, as well as being susceptible to a pointedly rational skepticism: "Howe sholde a juge [judge] eyther parti leve [believe] / For ye or nay without-outen any preve [proof]?" (PF 496–97). That is, on what grounds can the formel choose among these three windbags who offer no supporting evidence for their extravagant claims? (The question has a sting in its tail for the repute of auctores, between whose contradictory claims—e.g., Vergil and Ovid on Dido's innocence or guilt—Chaucer and his contemporaries would have no way of adjudicating.)

This is not to suggest that the poem necessarily takes the side of the lesser ranks in their dissent, or endorses their idiom, which it repeatedly refers to as "noise," the preferred term of hostile chroniclers to describe the outcry of the rebels in the Great Rising (aka the Peasants' Revolt) of 1381, soon after which the *Parlement of Foules* may have been written.[18] In addition, *PF* depicts the spokesbirds for the anti-courtly view as prone to salting their arguments with mere birdspeak:

The goos, the cokkow, and the doke also	*duck*
So cryed, 'Kek! Kek! kokkow! quek quek!' hye	
That thourgh myne eres the noyse wente tho. . . .	
And for the water foules tho bigan	*then*
The goos to speke, and in hire kakelynge	
She seyde, 'Pes' . . .	*peace*
'Ye queke!' seyde the goos, 'ful wel and feyre.'	
	(PF 498–500, 562–63, 594)

Nonetheless, despite these signs of entrenched class snobbery, the poem allows the avian "lewednesse [uncultured ignorance]," as it is called at one point

(PF 520), to make several telling critiques of the eagles' modus operandi in wooing: to one tercel who claims he will love the formel until he dies, even if she refuses his pleas to take him as her mate, the goose replies, self-interestedly but
with unexceptionable logic: "my wit is sharp; I love no taryinge; / I seye I rede
[advise] him, though he were my brother, / But [unless] she wol love hym, lat
hym love another!" (PF 565–67). To such admittedly unromantic suggestions
the tercels can only reply with the scorn of lords for revolting (in both senses of
that word) peasants and by recourse to what might be called playing the class
card, but with no good counterargument:

> Lo here a parfit resoun of a goos!
> ... Nevere mot she thee!   *thrive*
> Lo, swich it is to have a tonge loos!   *loose tongue*
> Now parde, fol, yet were it bet for the   *by God*
> Han holde thy pes than shewed thy nycete.   *folly*
> It lyth nat in his wit, ne in his wille,
> But soth is seyd, 'a fol can not be stille.' ... *it's true what they say*
> Thy kynde is of so low a wrechednesse
> That what love is, thow canst nouther seen
>   ne gesse.'   *neither see*
>   (PF 568–74, 601–2)

So the poem, and the mating session, reach a standoff: no agreement on
moving forward can be reached because the two sides in the dispute have irrec-
oncilable perspectives on what should happen, and completely different discur-
sive registers in which to express them. Nature attempts to break the logjam by
proposing that the formel choose which of her three suitors she prefers, thereby
enacting a major new erotic paradigm, replacing the one in which men choose
and women can only agree or refuse to be chosen. But the formel rejects Nature's advice—another auctor dismissed—and all her three suitors, at least for
the next year:

> 'Almyghty quene, until this yer be don,
> I axe respit for to avise me,
> And after that to have my choys al fre. . . .
> I wol nat serve Venus ne Cupide,
> Forsothe as yit, by no manere weye.'   *yet, in truth*
>   (PF 647–49, 652–53)

Nothing in this plea for deferral guarantees that her "choys al fre" will be one of the tercels. But it does clear the way for the rest of the birds quickly to choose their mates in a joyful and sensual process that contrasts sharply with (as it turns out) the eagles' sterile exercise of courtly wooing—

> To every foul Nature yaf his make   *mate*
> By evene acord, and on here way they wende.   *mutual   their*
> And Lord!, the blisse and joye that they make!
> For ech of hem gan other in wynges take,
> And with here nekkes ech gan other wynde
>
> (PF 667–71)

—an irrepressibly comical but nonetheless touching accommodation of human love embraces to avian bodily configurations.

As they fly away, their desires (except, of course, for the eagles') happily satisfied, the birds sing a "roundel"—a lyric of French origin—in praise of springtime and love, recalling the harmonious birdsong that greeted the dreamer on his entrance into the garden that has offered him so many perspectives on desire, filtered through so many culturally authoritative texts. Within these melodious parentheses, however, there remains an unanswered question. Specifically, PF ends with no resolution of the difference between two contrasting approaches to mating—two "sundry usages," as the *Troilus* narrator would say—and no auctor who can leave the narrator with any "certain thyng" to hold on to (except, perhaps, that love is humanity's—and Nature's—most complex experience), though this outcome will not deter him from what seems likely to be a long, ultimately vain search for further enlightenment:

> I wok, and othere bokes tok me to,   *awoke*
> To reede upon, and yit I rede alwey.
> I hope, ywis, to rede so som day
> That I shal mete som thyng for to fare   *meet (or dream)*
> The bet, and thus to rede I nyl nat spare.   *better*
>
> (PF 695–99)

After composing *Troilus and Criseyde*, Chaucer turned his attention to two projects, each as different from the other as both are from *TC*: *The Canterbury Tales* and *The Legend of Good Women*, collections of short tales embodying divergent organizing principles and source materials. (He may have had the collections in mind even while or before writing *TC*; our information about the dating and sequence of the Chaucerian canon is exiguous nearly to the point of nonexistence.) Crises of desire and authority figure centrally in each collection, providing ample opportunities for comic treatment of cultural and political issues of obvious importance to the poet. Although understandably overshadowed by the brilliance and variety of *The Canterbury Tales*, *The Legend of Good Women* (*LGW*)—a compendium of stories adapted from Ovid, Vergil, Livy, and other classical (or supposedly classical) *auctores*, all depicting women whose faithfulness to their men is often not reciprocated and in any case leads to their suffering—has a special claim on my attention in this chapter, because its Prologue (unusual for its two extant versions, offering unique evidence of extensive Chaucerian rewriting) features a complex, amusingly oblique juggling of relevant concerns, including a "modern" poet's responses and responsibilties to cultural antecedents, both ancient and more recent; a court poet's obligations to (and anxiety about) the power of princes and patrons; and any poet's need to balance inspiration and audience expectation in the course of an evolving career. My comments are based primarily on the so-called G version of the Prologue, usually considered the later of the two, because I believe it contains Chaucer's latest extant comments on these important issues.[19]

A brief summary of the Prologue will give an initial idea of the number of balls Chaucer is keeping in the air. The first 103 lines constitute a waking "Prologue within the Prologue": the narrator begins (G 1–28) by praising books (especially "olde bokes") and the learning they contain, as "keys of remembrance" and necessary complements to lived experience. Despite his "reverence" for books, however, he abandons them in "the joly tyme of May" (G 36) to walk in the fields and take special pleasure in observing his favorite flower, the daisy, "of alle floures flour, / Fulfyld of vertu and of alle honour" (G 55–56), as it opens with the coming of day and closes again when the sun sinks to rest. After a day of daisy watching, late in May, he returns home, has a bed made up for him in his garden, and falls asleep outdoors.

In his dream, the narrator, while seeking daisies in the meadow, encounters the God of Love, accompanied by his queen, whose green cloak, golden hairnet, and white crown—a single pearl—"made hire lyk a dayeseye [daisy] for to sene" (G 156), and a substantial courtly entourage of women "trewe of love" (G 193). The god's stern look and subsequent angry words—"it were better worthi [it would be more worthwhile], trewely, / A worm to comen in my syght than thow" (G 243–44)—make clear his displeasure with the dreamer, whom he accuses of slandering and hindering the god's servants by translating the *Romance of the Rose* and "the bok / How that Criseyde Troilus forsok," (G 264–65). For such acts of betrayal, the God of Love now demands repentance.[20]

At this awkward moment, the Queen intervenes on the Dreamer's behalf, counseling her lord against hasty, unjust judgment of his subject and proffering a number of possible reasons to explain and excuse the latter. Her lawyerly defense shades off into a lecture on the difference between good and bad rulership, and, after rehearsing a catalogue of the poet's previous works as evidence of his meaning well, the Queen proposes that the God of Love not punish the poet, who will promise never to trespass again and to make appropriate amends, in the form of stories "Of women trewe in lovynge al here lyve" (G 428).

The god acquiesces, granting his consort authority over the Dreamer, whose belated protestation of innocence she quickly squelches, assigning him, as a "lyte" [little] penance (G 485), the task of writing "a gloryous legende / Of goode women," and of "false men that hem [them] betrayen" (472–76).[21] When the Dreamer confesses his ignorance of his intercessor's identity, the God of Love refers him to "a bok, lyth [lying] in thy cheste" (498), by one Agaton, which tells the story of classical antiquity's Queen Alceste, savior of her husband from the underworld, who for her loyal wifehood was transformed into a daisy. The Dreamer expresses surprise that "this goode Alceste" is also "the dayeseye and myn owene hertes reste [heart's comfort]" (506–7), who was later "stellified" [turned into a star]—a second metamorphosis—by Jove (513). The God of Love instructs the dreamer to make the tale of Alceste the climax of his legend of good women, which is to begin with Cleopatra. At this word, the dreamer awakes and, as we might say, hits the ground writing.

The Prologue to *LGW* is a complex and provocative document. Some questions immediately present themselves: Was Chaucer really criticized by important members of his audience for having translated *RR* and *TC*? Is the God of Love a stand-in for Richard II, and could the real monarch actually have become annoyed at the real Chaucer, whether for how he wrote about love or for other statements, spoken or written, that the king considered divisive and threatening to the peace of the realm? Is Alceste a coded version of Richard's queen, Anne of Bohemia (to whom, at the royal palaces of Eltham or Shene, Alceste, in the F Prologue, instructs the dreamer to deliver his completed "glorious legende of goode wommen" [F 483–84, 496–97]), and did Anne really intercede for Chaucer with her husband?[22]

In seeking to answer such questions, and arrive at a coherent interpretation of the Prologue, we must, I think, begin by recognizing what it owes to and how it differs from the most important antecedent to both it and the tales that follow it in *LGW*, namely *The Judgment of the King of Navarre* (*Jugement du roi de Navarre* [*JKN*; after 1350]), a poem by Guillaume de Machaut, a major, widely influential fourteenth-century French poet and composer.

The English poet was familiar with a broad range of Machaut's secular lyric and narrative poems (or *dits*)—Machaut also composed church music, including a Mass that has been widely performed and recorded within the early music revival of the last forty years—and had adapted significant aspects of the latter's popular *dit The Judgment of the King of Bohemia* (*Jugement du roi de Behaigne* [*JKB*; 1340s]) for *The Book of the Duchess*, with an excerpt from which the present chapter began. Since the central conceit of *JKN* makes it a (forced) response to and revision of *JKB*, I must first devote a few words to the latter poem.

In *JKB*, the poet-persona (a lineal descendent of the dreamer in the *Roman de la Rose*) overhears a debate between a knight and a noblewoman over whose grief is greater: his, for a beloved who has deserted him for another, or hers, for a faithful lover who has died. The narrator offers to resolve the dispute by bringing the contestants to the court of the noble and virtuous king of Bohemia (obviously Machaut's patron at the time), who, assisted by a courtly council of allegorical virtues, hears both sides and decides that the knight's is the greater grief, since he has been unjustly betrayed; the monarch also assures the noblewoman that her grief will pass and another lover may come into her life.

JKB constitutes a contribution by Machaut to the medieval genre, both courtly and learned, of debate poetry descended from the *controversiae* of Roman rhetorical schools, by which patrician young men were taught, among other things, to argue both sides of any legal case—however fictional, however outrageous—posited by their teachers, using every trick available to the well-trained lawyer or orator. (In the preceding chapter, I placed the *Ars amatoria* and *Remedia amoris* within the context of these *disputationes ad utramque partem* [arguments on either side].) Returning to the genre some years later in *JKN*, Machaut offers a seriocomic, deliberately unconvincing correction to the earlier poem's judgment, and thus a further proof of his virtuosity in scripting a *disputatio ad utramque partem*. But he complicates his model by making himself a participant in a debate that turns out to be more like a legal action with himself as the defendant, although what is ultimately on trial is the denouement of *JKB*.

Early in *JKN*, the narrator, while out hunting rabbits,[23] is summoned by a noble lady who, after some preliminary persiflage, angrily accuses him of having "sinned against women" (811), explaining that "the case against you is something / You've written in one of your books" (866–67). When the narrator (addressed as "Guillaume" by his accuser) denies recalling any such affront, the

lady summarizies *JKB* and assures the narrator that he judged incorrectly, and
to the detriment of women, in awarding the palm for greater grief to the man
in that poem. Note that it is the poet, not his surrogate, the king of Bohemia,
whose judgment is faulted; within the fiction of *JKN*, that is, the poet is held
accountable for the opinions expressed by his characters. (Guillaume accepts
this responsibility [1068–70].)

The lady now asks "Guillaume" to reverse his judgment (1034–36), which he
refuses to do (1044–46; 1065–70), although this is precisely what Machaut the
poet will undertake, through "Guillaume's" opponents, in the remainder of *JKN*,
with a view to entertaining an audience (presumably courtly) that appreciates
debates pursued with more virtuosity than scrupulosity, as, in a nicely ironic
touch, the noble lady's subsequent indictment of "Guillaume" to the king of
Navarre makes clear: "You see there Guillaume de Machaut. / He's a man who
doesn't concern himself / With upholding either wrong or right; / In fact he'd
just as soon sustain / The wrong as the right" (1499–1503).

Once the noble lady nominates and Guillaume accepts the king of Navarre
(obviously Machaut's current patron) as the ideal judge to hear and decide between their arguments, the remainder of the poem becomes a distinctly (and
amusingly) one-sided forensic exercise, with Guillaume on trial and under attack by the twelve allegorical virtues (Reason, Understanding, Generosity, and
so on), who, having been introduced as the noble lady's entourage, are subsequently borrowed by the king of Navarre as his councillors, thereby making
their support of their mistress's claim, and their consistent denigration of
Guillaume's, a foregone conclusion. The pleasure of the situation arises from
the kinds of exemplary material drawn on by both sides to support their positions and the rhetorical tricks—twisted reinterpretations of the opponent's
arguments (known as colors—cf. chapter 1, page 55), incomplete citations of
supposedly corroborative sources, and others—they deploy to bolster their
own position and discredit the opposing one. Thus the debate becomes a comic
exercise in sleazy declamation.

After a good deal of such eloquent byplay, Reason pronounces threefold
judgment on Guillaume, confirmed to the kneeling poet by the king himself:
he has not only judged incorrectly the relative priority of love-inspired sorrows
but also acted foolishly in not repenting of his errors when the noble lady cen-
sured him (3800–3804); finally, Reason asserts,

'I know of no high personage,
So far as the world extends,
No prince or duke, no count or king,

Who would dare perpetrate such an outrage,
Guillaume, as did you,
When you entered into debate against her. . . .
And thus you have stripped your mind
Of courtesy and due respect.'

(3819–24, 3828–29)

The real significance of Guillaume's trial becomes clear when the noble lady is named, at last, as the personification of Bonneürté—Good Fortune, or Success—clearly not a personage, that is, a condition, with which a poet can afford to be at odds in the conduct of his career. In sum, *JKN* ruefully but lightheartedly proposes that a poet working in courtly genres and a courtly ambience—where, according to Reason, Bonneürté resides, summoned by honor—has to be ready to make adjustments, to find new subjects or revisit old ones from new, even opposing, perspectives if he is to remain on good terms with Fortune, that is, to enjoy success over time (which the historical Machaut did). Within the fiction of *JKN*, Guillaume, by arguing in *JKB* against (his own) Good Fortune—that is, his popularity with women—has erred badly; you can't quarrel with success, as that argument will always, even if unfairly, be stacked against you.

The king, his deliberations complete, informs Guillaume of his threefold penitence (4047): he is to compose, without grumbling, a compensatory *lai*, *chanson*, and *balade*: "Now don't act like you're sick about this, / But respond happily" (4190–91). Machaut concludes the poem with Guillaume's statement that he will now offer it to madame, "Li priant que tout me pardoint [begging her to pardon me]" (4205)—in other words, in full recognition that nothing succeeds like success—and set to work at once on "a lay about love" (4212).

JKN is a lighthearted meditation on the twists and turns of a poet's road to repute, replete with risks and obstacles—a road, moreover, on which looking backward is often a necessary part of moving forward. Judging from its impact on the Prologue to *LGW*, Machaut's *dit* attracted Chaucer by raising the issue of a poet's reception, specifically his being challenged about his earlier writings on women and love by powerful figures whose favor he needs—an extension up the sociopolitical ladder, we might say, of the concerns about reception comically articulated in the Proem to book 2 of *Troilus and Criseyde*. Such a representation of the poet's potential responsibility, at any given moment in his career, for all his works—Alceste, in defending the Dreamer to the God of Love includes a catalogue of Chaucer's works (perhaps including some he had not yet written or circulated) ostensibly as proof that "he hath maked lewed [humble,

ignorant] folk to delyte / To serven yow, in preysynge [praising] of youre name"
(403–4)—has as its corollary that this poetic career constitutes an important
part of his identity,[24] albeit one that leaves him open to judgment from the perspective of both cultural and political authority. (Were the god to acquaint
himself with this Chaucerian bibliography, he would find little to support Alceste's claim, though he might have taken the translation of "Orygenes upon the
Maudeleyne" [418], if Chaucer in fact ever undertook it—it is in any case not
extant—as a hopeful portent, as its theme is repentance for sinful deeds.)

Beyond this catalogue, and building on *JKN*'s revisionary recourse to an
earlier Machaudian text, the Prologue to *LGW* contains verbal or thematic recalls, revisions, and theoretical justifications of several earlier Chaucerian texts—
a technique perhaps best compared with Beethoven's brief quotations of
themes from the first three movements of his Ninth Symphony in the early
measures of its last movement. In both cases, the recalls prepare us for more
complex or profound statement of artistic endeavor; for Chaucer, I'd argue, the
Prologue offers—with characteristic comic nuancing—mature considerations
of the challenges presented to a poetic career by established traditions of representing desire and by the often competing claims of cultural and political authority, as well.

The narrator's dream begins with his perambulation through the meadow
where, waking, he sought out the daisy. It is springtime and the birds

[songen clere / Layes] of love ...
In worshipe and in preysyng of hire make;   *mates*
And for the newe blysful somers sake,   *springtime's*
[They] sungen, 'Blyssed be Seynt Valentyne!
For on his day I ches yow to be myn,
Withoute repentynge, myn herte swete!'
And therwithal here bekes gonne mete,   *their beaks met*
Yelding honour and humble obeysaunces;   *deference*
And after diden othere observaunces
Ryht longing unto love and to nature.   *appropriate to*
                              (*LGW* G 127–37; emphasis added)

These lines recapitulate the end of the dream in *PF*, where the lower avian
ranks, in keeping with the purpose for which Nature has assembled them on
Valentine's Day, engage in joyful mating, once the courtly wooing of the nobler
eagles has come to naught. Here, however, the scene initiates, rather than con-

cluding, a dream, and instead of sending the waking dreamer back to his books
in search of the elusive "unified theory" of love, as in the *Parlement*, the birds'
expressions of mutual affection spark his attention and comprehension: "This
song to herknen I dide al myn entente [tried my hardest], / For-why I mette I
wiste [because I dreamt I knew] what they mente" (139–40). This act of recol-
lective metamorphosis on the dreamer's part is also an act of acquiescent reception, both of the poet's own earlier work, and of the *Romance of the Rose*, ultimate literary ancestor of this preparatory, springtime-and-birdsong dreamscape.
As such, it provides a contrast to what will immediately follow: the resistant,
indeed, outraged reception of the God of Love—thus a foil to the benevolent
goddess Nature—of the dreamer's translation of this same *Romance of the
Rose*. On the other hand, the marital harmony of the birds anticipates the
central presence in the dream of Alceste, the famous exemplar of marital devotion, whose trip to the underworld to rescue her husband is in turn recapitulated by her rescue of the dreamer from the "hell" of the God of Love's
condemnation.[25]

By contrast with its textual citation of *PF*, the Prologue's recall of the translations of *RR* and *TC* is inserted not so much as a reference to those texts but
rather to trigger seriocomic consideration of matters of importance, and indeed
potential risk, to a poet working in a court milieu or, in any case, within the
purview of superior political authority: issues of choice of subject, reception,
reputation, and patronage. The God of Love, presented throughout the Prologue as a king, takes umbrage at those translations, which he understands as
exercises in slander, disloyalty, and the denigration of women:

'Thow art my mortal fo and me werreyest,	*(you) wage war against me*
And of myne olde servauntes thow mysseyest,	*slander*
And hynderest hem with thy translacyoun,	
And lettest folk to han devocyoun	*prevent from having*
To serven me, and holdest it folye	
To truste on me. Thow mayst it nat denye,	
For in pleyn text, it nedeth nat to glose,	*no need to gloss it*
Thow hast translated the Romaunt of the Rose,	
That is an heresye ageyns my lawe,	
And makest wise folk fro me withdrawe;	

And thynkest in thy wit, that is ful col,	*completely dull*
That he nys but a verray propre fol	*true and complete fool*
That loveth paramours to harde and hote. . . .	*with too intense a*
	romantic passion
Hast thow nat mad in Englysh ek the bok	
How that Criseyde Troylus forsok,	
In shewynge how that wemen han don mis?'	*wrong*
	(G 248–60, 264–66)

The Dreamer's crime, according to this resistant monarchic reader, is treason, or even heresy, and it demands his public repentance—or else:

'By Seynt Venus, of whom that I was born,	
Althogh thow reneyed hast my lay,	*have denied my*
	creed
As othere olde foles many a day,	
Thow shalt repente it, so that it shal be sene!'[26]	
	(G 313–16)

The God of Love's diction suggests that he has brought a distinctly religious perspective to his reading (and condemnation) of the Dreamer's efforts: "the Romaunt of the Rose / . . . is an heresye ageyns my lawe; . . . / But yit, I seye, what eyleth the [is wrong with you] to wryte / The draf [chaff] of storyes and forgete the corn? . . . / thow hast reneyed my lay / . . . Thow shalt repente it" (255–56, 311–12, 314, 316; the reference to "draf" and "corn" borrows a well-established metaphor from biblical exegesis to distinguish between the surface meaning and true, inner significance of a scriptural passage.) Nor is his animus placated by the repentance that Alceste claims for the Dreamer and the penance, on the god's behalf, that she assigns him; even after agreeing to this settlement, the testy monarch cannot resist getting in one last dig at a subject who has managed to avoid the royal punishment he deserved, asking him if he knows who the woman is "that hath so lytel penaunce yiven the [imposed on you], / That hath deserved sorer for to smerte [to suffer greater pain]?" (489–90). The wording suggests that the God of Love, thinking as much like a bishop as a king, would relish the idea of a long stay in Purgatory for the Dreamer.[27]

Since the offending texts are English translations, it may well be that Chaucer is using *RR*, *TC*, and the God of Love as covers for a pointed critique of the condemnation, by the contemporaneous institutional religious establishment, of those religious dissenters—collectively and derogatorily called "Lollards" by their detractors—whose reforms included translating the Bible into English, to make it available for direct study by layfolk. (Another, probably later Chaucerian Prologue, to his *Treatise on the Astrolabe*, defends English translations in language that closely approximates similar arguments by his contemporary, John Trevisa, chaplain to the powerful Lord Thomas Berkeley, translator of several Latin texts and widely presumed suppporter of the religious reformers.)[28]

Or could Chaucer even be casting his poet-persona as a latter-day Ovid, threatened by the God of Love as a latter-day Augustus? The Ovidian presence throughout the Prologue and Tales of *LGW* makes this latter possibility a tempting one. Beyond these hypotheses, another should be acknowledged, namely, that the decision to translate into English poetry about love that, even if not specifically written with the court in mind, might be read (or even presented orally) in a court milieu where French was the preferred language of social intercourse, was a decision that entailed the risk of raised eyebrows and a less than enthusiastic reception (if not one as hyperbolically hostile as the God of Love's).

Besides serving as a comically inflected figure of political authority who interprets the poet's poems about the vagaries of desire in a narrowly self-interested and threatening manner (Kiser calls him an "incompetent literary critic" who exhibits "demanding stupidity"),[29] the God of Love also has his own, politically correct (or at least personally palatable), agenda for what the Dreamer should have written:

'But natheles, answere me now to this:
Why noldest thow as wel han seyd goodnesse   *good things*
Of wemen, as thow hast seyd wikednesse?
Was there no good matere in thy mynde,
Ne in alle thy bokes ne couldest thow nat fynde
Som story of wemen that were goode and trewe?'

                                        (G 267–72)

I'll return to the kinds of stories the god is promoting; first I want to examine what the Prologue has to say about the Dreamer's possible reasons, and responsibility, for what he wrote instead, thereby earning his sovereign's displeasure. The spectrum of opinions offered by the God of Love, Alceste, and the Dreamer himself is comic in tone and diction but also, I believe, indicative of heightened ambiguity within Chaucer's England about who actually exerts ultimate authority over the reception of new (perhaps audaciously new) English versions of love stories already well established in other languages: the translating poet or his multifaceted, multilingual audience?

The God of Love has emphatic answers for his own question: the Dreamer's putative condemnation of "paramours" as folly (257–60) is the result (or manifestation) of a senescent denial of lost libido:

> 'Wel wot I therby thow begynnyst dote,   *to be senile*
> As olde foles whan here spirit fayleth;   *vitality*
> Thanne blame they folk, and wite nat what
>   hem ayleth.'
>   *don't know what ails*
>   *them*
>   (G 261–63)[30]

The same notion of failing powers of judgment underlies his preference for the story of faithless Criseyde over more wholesome tales of "trewe wyves and of here labour" (G 306): "But yit, I seye, what eyleth the to wryte / the draf of storyes, and forgete the corn?" (G 311–12). And then there is his final dig at the dreamer's expense, for writing about Criseyde instead of Alceste, the "calandier . . . of goodnesse": "Thy litel wit was thilke [at that] tyme aslepe" (G 533–34, 537; an ironic comment, addressed as it is to a dreaming poet by a character in his dream).

Taking up the cudgels for the Dreamer, Alceste urges the God of Love to listen before condemning:

> 'God, ryght of youre courteysye   *because of*
> Ye moten herkenen if he can replye   *must*
> Ageyns these poynts that ye han to   *things you've accused*
>   hym meved.'   *him of*
>   (G 318–20)

In other words, the audience, however powerful its authority and set in its opinions, should take into account the poet's aims in writing. She then traverses a broad spectrum of exculpatory hypotheses: first, the Dreamer's intentions have been misrepresented through envy:

> 'Al ne is nat gospel that is to yow pleyned;   *every complaint you*
>   *receive isn't true*
>
> The god of Love hereth many a tale yfeyned.
> For in youre court is many a losengeour,   *flatterer*

And many a queynte totelere accusour,   *clever peddler of
                                                 slander*

That tabouren in youre eres many a thyng   *who drum*
For hate, or for jelous ymagynyng,
And for to han with you som dalyaunce.'   *in order to get on your
                                                 good side*
                                                            (G 326–32)

Envy is a constant resident of "the grete court," she adds; hence "this man to yow may wrongly ben acused, / Wheras by ryght him oughte ben excused" (G 338–39). The omnipresence of envy within the climate of competiton at any "grete court" and its role as a stimulus to backbiting and false accusations, with a view to advancement at another's expense, is a commonplace of medieval and Renaissance considerations of court life. Its possible effect on the attempt of a poet writing in English to gain favor at Richard II's court could be of concern to Chaucer, whether or not he felt himself to be victimized there by "jelous ymagynyng."[31]

Second (and hardly flattering to her client), he pays no attention to the meaning of what he translates:

'Or elles sire, for that this man is nyce,   *foolish*
He may translate a thyng in no malice,
But for he useth bokes for to make,   *because he's used to
                                                   writing*

And taketh non hed of what matere he take,
Therfore he wrot the Rose and ek Criseyde
Of innocence, and nyste what he seyde.'   *didn't know*
                                                            (G 340–45)

Behind this outrageous claim of heedlessness lies a question of potentially vital interest to any translator: To what extent can he (or she) be held responsible for the content and perspectives of the work translated? Can allowance not be made for motives other than coincidence of viewpoint that might induce a poet to render in English "classic" representations of desire's peaks and perils? Indeed, one such motive (of obvious relevance to Chaucer's society) could be patronage: "Or hym was boden make thilke tweye [he was ordered to compose those two] / Of [by] som persone, and durste it nat withseye [dared not refuse]" (G 346–47).

Or perhaps these translations are just pardonable aberrations:

'For he hath write many a bok er this.
He ne hath nat don so grevously amys
To translate that olde clerkes wryte,   *what*
As thogh that he of maleys wolde endyte   *out of malice   compose*
Despit of love, and hadde hymself ywroght.'   *scorn of his own*
                                         making

                                      (G 348–52)

And even if the Dreamer did translate out of "maleys" this time—"I not wher he be now a renegat [apostate]," his lawyer admits (G 401)—

'The man hath served yow of hys konnynge,
And forthered wel youre lawe with his makynge.   *poetry*
Whil he was yong, he kepte youre estat. . . .   *was loyal to*
                                    your dignity

He hath maked lewed folk to delyte   *simple*
To serven yow, in preysynge of youre name.'

                      (G 398–400, 403–04)

There follows the already mentioned catalogue of Chaucer's own works.

Having mounted this not entirely consistent defense of the (more or less) innocent Dreamer, Alceste ends her argument to the God of Love with a plea bargain, proposed without even consulting her suddenly guilty client:

'I axe yow thys man, ryght of youre grace,   *(concerning)*
                                    this man

That ye hym nevere hurte in al hys lyfe;
And he shal swere to yow, and that as blyve,   *right away*
He shal no moore agilten in this wyse.'   *be guilty*

                                (G 423–26)

Instead, he will make amends by writing about

'women trewe in lovynge al here lyve, . . .   *their lives*
And fortheren yow as much as he mysseyde   *support*
                                  slandered (you)

Or in the Rose or elles in Criseyde.'

                       (G 428, 430–31)

That is, a poet writing under the eye of those in political authority may find such attention playing a role, welcome (as patronage) or not (as disapproval), in how he shapes his career.

The last word on motive and responsibility in undertaking translations belongs to the narrator, who, after thanking Alceste for rescuing him from royal displeasure—"Foryelde yow [may you be rewarded] that ye the God of Love / Han maked me his wrathe to foryive [have made the God of Love abjure his anger toward me]" (G 447–48)—nonetheless demurs from her admission of his guilt:[32]

'But trewely I wende, as in this cas,	
Naught have agilt, ne don to love trespas.	*that I'm not guilty*
For-why a trewe man, withoute drede,	*because an honest man*
Hath nat to parte wyth a theves dede;	*shouldn't share blame*
Ne a trewe lovere oghte me nat to blame	
Thogh that I speke a fals lovere som shame.	*say shameful things about*
They oughte rathere with me for to holde	*be on my side*
For that I of Criseyde wrote or tolde,	
Or of the Rose; what so myn auctor mente,	*whatever my source intended*
Algate, God wot, it was myn entente	
To forthere trouthe in love and it cheryce,	*fidelity*
And to be war fro falsenesse and fro vice	*[to tell others] to avoid*
By swich ensaumple; this was my menynge.'	

$$(G\ 452–63)$$

To depict evil is not to sympathize with it; the translator-poet's aim may in fact be to offer it as an exemplary warning, even if in doing so he he may ignore (or even distort) the intention of the original "auctor." Stepping back from this somewhat overdetermined exercise in self-exculpation, we can, I think, take a larger view of it as an indirect suggestion that the relationship between a translator and his original may be complicated and difficult to fathom, in which case sweeping and moralistic judgments of intention (such as the God of Love's) are of dubious merit.[33]

In any case, the ambiguous impact of political authority on poetic practice shines through two adjacent comments by Alceste to the Dreamer. First, after

announcing "what penaunce thow shalt do / For thy trespas," namely, spending most of his time each year composing the "gloryous legende / Of goode
women," she summarizes her (and the God of Love's) unrefusable commission: "Spek wel of love; this penaunce yeve I thee" (G 469–70, 473–74, 481).
This is the great and defining comic line of the Prologue, and of *LGW* as a
whole: to write about women and love in a consistently and seriously encomi-
astic mode—to sacrifice exploring the human complexities of desire in favor
of a monochromatic, ideologically inspired and sponsored catalogue of exempla uniformly praising one sex and condemning the other—would indeed be a
penitential exercise for a poet of Chaucer's humane interests and comic abili-
ties, but one he circumvents, throughout the tales constituting *LGW*, by nar-
rational and narratorial methods that effectively undermine the fictive obligation under which the Prologue, through its figures of political authority,
places him.

Alceste then follows her assignment of penace with compensatory promise:

> 'And to the God of Love I shal so preye
> That he shal charge his servaunts by any weye   *any way they can*
> To fortheren the, and wel thy labour quyte.'   *advance   reward*
>   *well*
>
>   (G 482–84)

In other words, the political powers that be also have potentially vast powers of direct or indirect patronage that can bring rewards and career enhance-
ments to the compliant poet. There may be a joke hidden in these lines about
Chaucer's own experience, or lack of it, with patrons; aside from the somewhat
cryptic remark in the so-called F Prologue of *LGW* that the Dreamer should
present his completed "legend" to "the Queen," that is, to Anne of Bohemia,
Richard's queen—he did receive various rewards from Richard II for his political and civil service—*The Book of the Duchess*, with its obvious link to John of
Gaunt, is the only putative case of poetic patronage we can find in Chaucer's
career, and we do not even know whether Gaunt actually solicited that poem
or Chaucer wrote it on spec.[34]

Different again from Chaucer's citational recall of *The Parlement of Foules*
and his use of his translations, *RR* and *TC*, as the trigger for a consideration of
crises of political authority—potentially initiated by translating into English
texts with (contested) cultural authority in other vernaculars—is the poet's
more submerged but important recourse to *The House of Fame* in his construction of the Prologue to *LGW*, specifically with respect to the question of the

cultural authority of "olde bokes," that is, the classical auctores from whom most of the *Legend*'s stories are appropriated. (*LGW*'s idiosyncratic concern with and use of stories derived from classical antiquity pobably reflect Chaucer's recognition of the comic potential in Machaut's manipulative use of old, exemplary stories, including those of Ariadne, Medea, Thisbe, and others who reappear in the English collection.)[35]

From the Prologue's opening lines onward, the importance and authority of such books is almost constantly under discussion. The narrator begins by noting that the limitations imposed on knowledge by experience—we have no direct evidence of "joye in heven and peyne in helle" (G 2)—can only be transcended by recourse to books:

Thanne mote we to bokes that we fynde,	*we must [turn]*
Thourgh whiche that olde thynges ben in mynde,	
And to the doctryne of these olde wyse	*teachings savants*
Yeven credence, in every skylful wyse,	*reasonable way*
And trowen on these olde aproved storyes. . . .	*believe in*
And if that olde bokes weren aweye,	
Yloren were of remembraunce the keye.	*the key to remembering would be lost*
	(G 17–21, 25–26)

The last lines of this prologial exhortation sum up the narrator's position, but in doing so, slightly diminish, it seems to me, the actual authority of books by reversing the order of priority established a few lines before: First we are warned, "But Goddes forbode but men sholde leve [that we not believe] / Wel more thyng than men han [have] seyn with ye! [(their own) eyes]" (10–11); but less than twenty lines later, the narrator's message has moderated to, "Wel oughte us thanne on olde bokes leve [believe], / There as there is non other assay by preve [evidence from experience]" (27–28). This more cautious assessment appears to elevate "preve" above "olde bokes," and in retrospect supports the general skepticism implied in the lines just after those stressing the importance of believing what one has not seen: "Men shal nat wenen [assume] *every thyng a lye* / For that he say [saw] it nat of yore ago [in the past]" (G 12–13; emphasis added). Just such a skepticism about the truthfulness and thus the authority of information transmitted from the past ("fame" in the form of written record) is the hallmark of *HF*.

The subject returns once the narrator, abandoning the "bokes" for which he has such "reverence" (G 30–31), ventures into the meadow to pursue his voyeuristic relationship with the daisy. Distancing himself from the courtly poetry, or "making," associated with the botanical denizens of beautiful landscapes—a career strategy requiring our proximate attention—he restates both his faith in and, paradoxically, underlying skepticism of the cultural authority residing in "olde bokes," noting that taking sides in the supposed rivalry between the flower and the leaf

nys nothyng the entent of my labour.	*not at all*
For this werk is al of another tonne,	*comes off a different shelf*
Of olde story. . . .	
But wherfore that I spak, to yeve credence	
to bokes olde and don hem reverence,	*offer them*
Is for men shulde autoritees beleve,	
There as there lyth non other assay by preve.	*[cf. line 28, almost identical]*
For myn entent is, or I fro yow fare,	*before I leave you*
The naked text in Englysh to declare	*literal*
Of many a story, or elles many a geste,	*(historical) deed*
As autors seyn, leveth hem if yow leste.	*believe if it pleases you*
	(G 78–88; emphasis added)

There is even a hint, in the last line quoted, that "autoritees" only have exalted cultural status because people may believe they do, not because of any inherent truth value.

Within the narrator's dream, his (apparently ambivalent) commitment to the stories told by classical auctores manifests itself in new, ultimately oppressive ways, even as their putative cultural authority becomes compromised by its intersection with, and appropriation by, political power intent on defending its reputation and authority As the Dreamer encounters the God of Love, his queen, Alceste, and their courtly entourage of women "trewe of love" (G 193), the latter group sing a *balade* in praise of the Queen while dancing around the daisy (Alceste's metamorphic avatar, as the Deamer will later discover), the point of which is that Alceste outshines in virtue the heroines (and one hero, the biblical Jonathan) whose excellence (and indeed whose identity) can only be known through "olde story." Many of the names on this list will become (or, reading backward from tales to explanatory, justificatory Prologue, have become) the subject of the tales that make up *LGW* proper. In terms of the poetic logic behind the fictive dream, this *balade* represents the seeds or initial inspiration of a project that will transform the narrator's general reverence for old books and their auctores into the "many a story" of which he will soon declare the "naked text in English."

The project is further defined and its function clarified (or distorted) by the God of Love, as part of his angry chastisement of the Dreamer for having translated *RR* and *TC* into English. In a passage that may or may not tell us something about Chaucer's library, the god asks peevishly,

> 'In al thy bokes ne coudest thow nat finde
> Som story of wemen that were goode and trewe?
> Yis, God wot, sixty bokes olde and newe
> Hast thow thyself, alle ful of storyes grete,
> That bothe Romayns and ek Grekes trete   *in which*
> Of sundry wemen, whych lyf that they ladde,
> And evere an hundred goode ageyn oon badde.'   *opposed to one*
>   (G 271–77)

He proceeds to offer yet another list, this one of (mostly) classical authors who created the record of "clene [pure] maydenes," "trewe wyves," and "stedefaste widewes" so faithful to their lovers

> 'that, rathere than they wolde take a newe,   *new (man)*
> They chose to be ded in sondry wyse,
> And deiden, as the storye wol devyse.'
>   (G 282–83, 289–91)

Although heathen, the monarch insists, these women were so dedicated to

> 'verray vertu and clennesse   *true   purity*
> . . . That in this world I trowe men shal nat
>   fynde
> A man that coude be so trewe and kynde
> As was the leste woman in that tyde.'   *at that time*
>   (G 297, 302–4)

Since "al the world of autours maystow here [you may hear], / Cristene and hethene, trete of swich matere [such themes]" (G 308–9), what could possibly have led the Dreamer to choose "draf" over "corn," thus meriting the (strangely ecumenical) God of Love's negative judgment and summons to swift repentance?

The point of this royal exercise in literary history and advocacy is to suggest that within a poetic career a work may be undertaken in expiation, correction, or (to put it less judgmentally) balancing of a previous one, but also that the auctoritas of "olde bokes" can be pressed into service supporting the ideological predispositions of those possessing political power, potentially compromising its supposed objectivity as a conduit of truth.

The potential damage to the status of "olde bokes" is actualized when the God of Love's queen, as already noted, ends her defense of the Dreamer by promising her lord that, in return for the remission of punishment for past misdeeds ("in the Rose or elles in Criseyde"), her client will tell tales "of women trewe in lovynge." This arrangement requires the effective recasting of a considerable portion of the classical literary inheritance—its tales of desire and passion—into a set of variations on a theme: women are good; men are evil. The Dreamer's resistance is futile: "For Love ne wol nat counterpletyd be [be argued against]" (466), warns Alceste, and neither will she. In a situation of power imbalance, political authority trumps, and controls to its purposes, cultural authority. Put differently, the result of the God of Love's intervention is to render cultural authority moot.

This point is made repeatedly in the tales that follow the Prologue. The very fact that the collection is called a "legend" (see note 21), and that in some manuscripts the women whose tales are told are called martyrs,[36] reminds us of the God of Love's theologically and exegetically inflected condemnation of the Dreamer's previous translations. By contrast, these translations will be tailored to reflect the orthodoxy the god and his consort have imposed, as penance, on the errant poet.[37] The narrator's references to his auctores—"But who wol al this letter have in mynde, / Rede [should read] Ovyde, and in hym he shal it fynde" (LGW 1366–67)—are invitations by Chaucer to discover how his narrator is editing his sources to make them conform to the God of Love's agenda.[38]

Two instances from "The Legend of Philomela" must suffice to support my estimate of how the tales of LGW serve as exempla not only of virtuous women and vicious men but of how fragile the cultural authority of "olde bokes" can be. In Ovid's version (Metamorphoses, book 4), Tereus, though married to Procne, rapes her sister, Philomela, and then cuts out her tongue so that she cannot reveal her assailant. The muted sister communicates the truth to Procne by weaving it into a fabric; as a result, the two sisters conspire to kill Tereus and Procne's young son, dismember and cook him, and serve him as dinner to his father, only revealing the truth after the act of unwitting cannibalism. Chaucer's version omits this barbaric revenge entirely; after Procne finds her "dombe sister" in Bacchus's temple, the two mistreated women embrace in sorrow, "And thus I late hem [leave them] in here [their] sorwe dwelle," the narrator announces, "The remenaunt is no charge [not my duty] for to telle" (*LGW* 2382–83)—and, indeed, must necessarily be omitted if the two women are to be presented, as prescribed from on high, as good women martyred by an evil man. The narrator's *moralitas* to his (supposedly) female audience comically exudes what might be called qualified indignation:

Ye may be war of men, if that yow liste,	*if you're smart*
For al be it that he wol nat, for shame,	*a man will not*
Don as Tereus, to lese his name,	*behave like Tereus lest*
	he ruin his reputation
Ne serve yow as a morderour or a knave,	
Ful litel while shal ye trewe hym have—	*faithful*
That wol I seyn, al were he now my	
brother—	*even if he were*
But if so be that he may have non other.	*unless he can find*
	no one else

$$\text{(LGW 2387–93)}$$

In other words, your lover/husband is sure to be a louse; don't feel good if he's faithful to you; it's not because he's virtuous or finds you attractive and lovable but only because no one else is available with whom he can betray you (hardly words designed to make a woman feel good about herself or her partner).

Despite his initial resistance, the narrator eagerly embraces his role as spokesperson for the God of Love. For example, in setting out to tell the legend of Jason and Hypsipyle, he adopts toward Jason a tone of strident animosity modeled on the god's toward him in the Prologue, even imitating his patron's penchant for religious terminology:

O, often swore thow that thow woldest dye	
For love, whan thow ne feltest maladye	
Save foul delyt, which that thow callest love!	*but lust*
Yif that I live, thy name shal be shove	*spread about*
In English that thy *sekte* shal be knowe!	*(heretical) sect*
Have at thee, Jason! Now thyn horn is blowe!	*your infamy is*
	published

$$\text{(LGW 1378–83; emphasis added)}$$

Indeed, at the end of the "Legend of Phyllis," the narrator assumes the role of an earthly alter ego of Eros—or perhaps of a latter-day Ovidian *praeceptor amoris*:

> Be war, ye wemen, of youre subtyl fo,
> Syn yit this day men may ensaumple se;
> And trusteth, as in love, no man but me.
>
> (*LGW* 2499–2501)[39]

The damage done to the authority of "olde bokes" by the imposition on them of such partisanship illustrates, and thus confirms, the point Chaucer is making in the Prologue to *LGW* about the misuse of auctores to shore up despotic political authority, resulting in the diminution of their cultural status.[40]

Beyond the recalls of his earlier poems that I've just catalogued, Chaucer includes in the Prologue a recollection of a key feature of Machaut's *JKN*: the lady Bonneürté, whose reconception by the English poet as Queen Alceste provides a seriocomic focus for his meditation on actual or hypothetical tensions between representations of desire, on the one hand, and exigencies of cultural and political authority, on the other, in the shaping of a poetic career. Machaut, you will recall, uses Bonneürté to figure the poet's sometimes fraught relationship with success, the inevitable goal of his efforts. By contrast, Alceste represents not success as a goal but appropriation and metamorphosis as a strategy, as well as a metaphor for the peculiar nature and function of poetic inspiration.[41]

The key to Alceste is precisely her many identities, or manifestations, in the Dreamer's waking and dreaming life. She first appears as an alternative to—one might say, a relief from—his profound attachment to the "olde bokes" to which he attributes such probative value in *LGW*'s opening lines but which, as I've suggested, the remainder of the poem genially undercuts, or at least puts in question:

> On bokes for to rede I me delyte,
> And in myn herte have hem in reverence,
> And to hem yeve swich lust and swich credence   *give such pleasure and belief*
>
> That there is wel unethe game non   *hardly any amusement*
>
> That fro my bokes make me to gon,
> But it be other upon the halyday,   *either*
> Or ellis in the joly tyme of May. . . .   *lovely*

Farwel my stodye, as lastynge that sesoun! . . . *as long as that*
                                                  season lasts

Thanne love I most these floures white and rede,
Swyche as men calle dayseyes in oure toun.

(G 30–36, 42–43)

What most attracts the narrator to the daisy is its heliotropism:[42]

To sen these floures agen the sonne sprede   *responding to*
                                              open
Whan it up ryseth by the morwe shene. . . .   *clear*
And whan the sonne gynneh for to weste,   *set*
Thanne closeth it, and draweth it to reste,
So sore it is afered of the nyght,   *afraid*
Til on the morwe that it is dayes lyght.

(G 48–49, 51–54)

This characteristic and description of the daisy both prefigures and oversimpli-
fies the role played by Alceste in the narrator's dream. There, as queen to the
God of Love—whose face, like the sun, shines so brightly that the dreamer
cannot directly behold it (G 162–65)—and daisy lookalike (G 146–57, summa-
rized earlier, page 125), she does indeed symbolically bend toward her lord, in
order to plead for the Dreamer's escaping punishment for his translations, but
also to counsel him against tyranny and other unjust forms of rulership. Moreover, as her name, "daisy (= day's eye), suggests, in mimicking the sun she in
effect becomes one her self: the eye of the day. As such, she sheds light (perhaps
rather too much light) on the poet's possible motives for composing the translations offensive to the God of Love, and also enlightens the poet/Dreamer as
to which his next poetic task will be. In effect, she is an externalization of the
poet's strategy of fabricating reasons for writing what he does—and thus escaping patronal displeasure or danger—and also of his processes of deciding
what his next composition will be.

These are not the only ways in which Alceste seems to represent the
Dreamer's—and, by extension, Chaucer's—Muse.[43] In her guise as the daisy,
she represents his debt to, distancing from, and transformation of the French
tradition of courtly poetry, or "making." At the beginning of the Prologue, the
narrator's admiration for the daisy introduces a gesture at popular fashions in
this poetry: he wishes to praise the daisy,

    if I coude aryght;
But wo is me, it lyth nat in my myght.
For wel I wot that folk han here beforn   *have before this*
Of makyng ropen, and led awey the corn;   *i.e., harvested all the*
                                                  good poetry
And I come after, glenynge here and there,   *[cf. the idea of "folwing"*
                                                  an "auctor" in TC]
And am ful glad if I may fynde an ere   *a stalk*
Of any goodly word that they han left.

                                              (G 59–65)

He adds that if he should happen to repeat what these forerunner poets have composed, he's to be forgiven, for such imitation is an homage to "hem that eyther serven lef or flour" (G 70); which is not to say, he adds hastily, that he has taken sides in the rivalry between partisans of flower or leaf:

For, as to me, is lefer non, ne lother.   *I prefer neither one*
                                                nor the other
I am witholde yit with never nother;   *I'm a paid retainer*
                                                of neither party
I not who serveth lef ne who the flour.
That nys nothyng the entent of my labour.

                                              (G 75–78)

Rather, his poetry will be "Of olde story, er swich strif [such rivalry] was begonne" (G 80).

The Prologue here alludes to daisy poems composed by Machaut (*Dit de la marguerite*) and other French court poets, and to poems celebrating a suppposed rivalry between court factions allied to the flower or the leaf.[44] The narrator's suggestion that he might "rehersen" some of the poetry involved (as Chaucer adapted French lyric and narrative poems in English throughout his career) but cannot undertake "the naked text in English to declare" (G 86) of any of it, supposedly out of belatedness or ignorance, is Chaucer's typically oblique and self-mocking way of ruling out any wholesale, uninflected imitation of this kind of writing in *LGW*. (Both "flour" and "lef" are literary quibbles as well as poetic subjects, the former alluding to the "flowers," or devices, of rhetoric, the latter to the leaf, or page, of a manuscript.)[45]

Instead, by means of the narrator's dream, the Prologue plots a journey toward a comic poetry richer in irony and complexity than any straightforward recapitulation of established French forms. Initially, the Dreamer's search for the daisy leads him through a *paysage idéale*, complete with harmoniously singing birds, clearly inspired by the *Romance of the Rose* and its many subsequent French imitators. This spatial encoding of French influences incorporating, as I've already noted, a glance backward at the *Parlement of Foules*, prepares for the arrival of Alceste, whose regalia, combining daisy colors with the great pearl that is her crown (G 153–54) materializes the double significance of the French word *"marguerite,"* meaning both daisy and pearl, while her "real habyt al of grene" (G 146) not only completes the daisy effect— "the white coroun above the grene / Made hire lyk a dayesye for to sene" (G155–56)—but contributes to her embodiment and harmonization of "flour" and "lef." But she is more than the sum of these parts: she is also Alceste, superior to all other virtuous and "trewe" women of classical antiquity, whom Hercules rescued from the underworld, preparing for her double metamorphosis into daisy and then star (a Chaucerian invention, as is Agaton [cf. G 514], supposed chronicler of at least the latter change). Alceste thus signifies both the poet's debt to Ovid and his uniquely humorous synthesis, in English, of French courtly and Latin learned materials—an ingenious metamorphosis of Machaut's *JKN*.

Alceste's significance does not end with this intertwining, in her person, of her poet's major cultural authorities, and her resultant status as an emblem of what he accomplishes in "translating" his Machaudian antecedent. It's through her, in her manifold and changing relationship to both the Deamer and the God of Love, that Chaucer places his poetic production in the context of a literarily distorted Ricardian court and monarchy (his self-protective version of the comic mirror?) and limns, always under this cover, the situation and potential perils of a poet working, willingly or unwillingly, within the orbit of political authority at once potentially hostile to and (through patronage) potentially rewarding of his efforts.

Alceste's defense of the Dreamer against the God of Love's angry accusations of slander, treason, and even heresy, committed or encouraged in his translations of *RR* and *TC*, is, as I've suggested, rife with comic elements of special pleading, condescension, overdetermination, and downright self-contradiction. Nonetheless, her attempt to placate the miffed monarch also conforms to the widespread late-medieval European assumption that a major responsibility of any queen was to intercede with her spouse, seeking his mercy on behalf of those upon whom, in copious measure, the royal wrath was about to fall.[46] Doubtless the most famous instance of such intercession, at least to modern readers, occurs in the *Chronicles of Jean Froissart* (here adapting an episode in Jean le Bel's *Chronicle*), when, after Edward III's successful siege of Calais in

1347, the king's pregnant wife, Philippa of Hainault, intervenes, throwing herself at Edward's feet to prevent him from executing its leading citizens—the
subjects of Rodin's famous sculpture—for their role in the city's long resistance
to the besieging English army.[47] Furthermore, there are obvious parallels between this secular intercession by queens and the role widely attributed to the
Virgin Mary in high- and late-medieval Christian theology, as intercessor with
her son to prevent him from judging humanity with the severity its sinfulness
otherwise merits. Given the God of Love's penchant for theologically tinged
judgments, and the original Alceste's role in saving her husband from the underworld, a further, implied reference to Mary in the Prologue's portrait of the
daisy queen seems to me highly likely.[48]

As imagined by Chaucer, Alceste is not a woman inclined to throw herself at
anyone's feet. Instead, in a move that is logically consistent if historically unlikely,
she frames her queenly intercession for the Dreamer in some political advice to
the God of Love, concerning proper attitudes and behavior toward his subjects:

'A god ne sholde nat thus ben agreved,
But of his deite he shal be stable,   *because of his*
                                                              godhead
                                                              even-tempered
And therto ryghtful, and ek mercyable.   *just*
He shal nat ryghtfully his yre wreke
Or he have herd the tother partye speke. . . .   *before   has heard*
This shulde a ryghtwys lord han in his
    thought,   *just*
And nat ben lyk tyraunts of Lumbardye,   *not be*
That usen wilfulhed and tyrannye.   *rely on arrogance*
For he that kyng or lord is naturel,   *i.e., by birth*
Hym oughte nat be tyraunt and crewel. . . .
He moste thynke it is his lige man,   *he is dealing with his*
                                                              sworn retainer
And that hym oweth, of verray duetee,   *it behooves him, as is*
                                                              his duty
Shewen his peple pleyn benygnete,   *profound good will*
And wel to heren here excusacyouns. . . .   *their*
This is the sentence of the Philosophre,   *judgment*
A kyng to kepe his lyges in justice;   *should preside over*
                                                              his subjects

Withouten doute, that is his office. . . .	*obligation*
And for to kepe his lordes hir degree,	*to protect the status of*
As it is ryght and skylful that they be	*reasonable*
Enhaunsed and honoured, and most dere—	*advanced*
For they ben half-goddes in this world here—	
This shal he don bothe to poore and ryche,	
Al be that her estat be nat alyche,	*even though rank*
	equal
And han of pore folk compassioun.'	

(G 321–25, 353–57, 359–62, 365–67, 370–76)

Chaucer would have been familiar with these exhortations from the many late-medieval manuals on the instruction of princes—inspired in good part by the recent availability of Aristotle's *Ethics* and *Politics* (he is the "Philosophre" of line 365), translated first into Latin, then into various European vernaculars.[49] Although Alceste's reminder that the god-king should be respectful of the rank of his lords has no relevance for the Dreamer, it would surely have reminded Chaucer's audience of the real King Richard's fraught relationship with many of his barons during the mid-to-late 1380s, leading to his impeachment and near deposition by the so-called Appellant Lords (1388); similarly, the equally commonplace recommendation that the king shall "han of pore folk compassioun" may well have taken on topical resonance in the aftermath of the Rising of 1381, a period of great repression of all those peasants and artisans suspected of being rebels. In any case, the effect of these passages is to endow Alceste with yet another function, as the dream-vision-disguised voice of her creator, a comic poet making a rare (and potentially risky) foray into politics.[50]

The irony of Alceste's advice to her lord that, like a compassionate ruler, he listen patiently and react mercifully to his servant's excuses is that she does not in fact let the Dreamer plead his own case—she is less a traditional queenly intercessor than a none too scrupulous trial lawyer—and, when he finally attempts to argue his innocence, she silences him peremptorily by, in effect, denying that her counsel has had any impact on its intended recipient: "Lat be thyn arguynge," she snaps,

'For Love ne wol nat counterpleyted be
In ryght ne wrong; and lerne this at me!
Thow hast thy grace, and hold the ryght therto.'

(G 464–67)

In other words, shut up and be satisfied with what I've gained for you.[51] The strict, commanding tone of these words, and the "penaunce" that she now imposes on the Dreamer "for thy trespas"—a lifetime of writing and rewriting the same story, of good women and false men—effect one last transformation of Alceste: into a stern Father (Mother?) Confessor, or (to switch institutional metaphors) a kind of artistic superego at work within a poet's mind and imagination, creating dissatisfaction with what has been accomplished and thus spurring on, as a personal imperative, the next (compensatory? better?) project.

In sum, Alceste is the Muse that helps the poet (some version of the historical Geoffrey Chaucer), as his career unfolds, negotiate the challenges of being a translational, metamorphic poet: one writing in English, hitherto not a courtly vernacular, a love poetry more complex than the French makers (crisis 1), and the challenges of cultural and political authority (crisis 2). She rescues him but also draws him into the courtly circle from his position as an outsider/onlooker (cf. G 234–40: the Prologue's initial situation of the Dreamer on the edge of, rather than of, the dancing, caroling, daisy-praising court of the God of Love may telegraph Chaucer's actual position as someone as much outside as within the court's ambience). Alceste muzzles him and even puts him in a subservient position, where instead of engaging in his translational poetic to tell truths about love and power through poetry, he must distort his auctores in order to meet political/patronal ends and avoid patronal anger. At the same time, each new work becomes "penance" for the one before—an attempt to make up for its shortcomings, hit new highs, avoid previous mistakes, and so on. New work is (always?) an act of "penance" undertaken in response to its predecessors and their reception; in other words, justification of one's past work—to oneself, to others—is a necessary, often fraught part of the gestation of new poems.

In so far as part of the import of *LGW* as a whole is that the poet's impulse to do more and more satisfactory composing can be complicated by the need to propitiate powerful critics or please powerful patrons, Chaucer's (at least imagined) response operates at two levels: at the first the poet does become the mouthpiece of his patron's or ruler's agenda and ideology,[52] creating and recreating what his political superior wants said and heard; at the second level, however, the tales that make up *LGW* are studies in the subversion of ideology by comic indirection, as well as demonstrations of the dubious authority of auctores who can so easily be manipulated to conform to an imposed *moralitas*, then twisted further into parody through the voice and choices of a fussy, self-important narrator.[53]

There is no evidence that Richard II knew *LGW* or, if he did know it, understood its encrypted messages.[54]

A nd now for something completely different, namely, Chaucer's other, far more illustrious tale collection, *The Canterbury Tales* (*CT*), which differs radically from *LGW* in its choice of stories that lack a common theme and are drawn from a wide variety of sources: classical *auctores*; learned medieval writers, both secular and religious; and popular tales, of no fixed authorship or abode, that circulated widely within medieval European culture, both orally and in writing. Across this wide spectrum of material, *CT* continues to ring inventive, comic changes on crises of desire and of authority, both cultural and political.

Chaucer gathers his tales within the larger, framing fiction of a pilgrimage from the disreputable London suburb of Southwark to the shrine of St. Thomas Becket at Canterbury.[55] Harry Bailly, the large, boisterous, and self-important Host of Southwark's Tabard Inn, establishes the raison d'etre of the storytelling to follow when he tells the pilgrims, during the evening before they set out from his hostelry,

> 'Ye goon to Caunterbury, God yow speede.
> The blisful martir quite yow youre meede!   *reward you for it*
> And wel I woot, as ye goon by the weye,
> Ye shapen yow to talen and to pleye;   *you're planning to tell*
>   *tales*
>
> For trewely, confort ne mirthe is noon
> To ride by the weye doumb as a stoon.'
>
> (*CT* 1.769–74)[56]

To further enliven the trip, Harry proposes that the inevitable tale telling be arranged as a contest with himself as judge (he will come along at his own expense) and the prize for the winner "a soper at oure aller cost / Heere in this place [i.e., the Tabard] . . . / Whan that we come again fro Caunterbury" (*CT* 1.799–801). Harry's overt argument is that competitive storytelling is more fun than mere storytelling; his hidden agenda is to get this group of twenty-nine pilgrims to return to his own hostelry to spend more money at the dinner that will reward "which of yow that bereth him [performs] best of alle— / That is to seyn, that telleth in this caas [on this occasion] / Tales of best sentence [instruction] and moost solaas [pleasure]" (*CT* 1.796–98).[57] The tales themselves, he makes clear, are to concern "aventures that whilom [once] han bifalle" (*CT* 1.795), a recipe for popular rather than learned storytelling.

The result of Harry's proposal is an ambulatory community that creates and sustains itself entirely by telling stories (Harry's phrase, "ye shapen yow to talen and to pleye," features a verb, "shapen," that can mean "to create"). And this allows the conjecture, at least, that in his last, unfinished work—incomplete as to number of stories, imperfect as to their organization into subgroups (cf. note 56)—Chaucer undertakes to define and exemplify human society not as a putatively stable hierarchy (as it was frequently defined in medieval political and social theorizing, and, by implication, by Nature in *The Parlement of Foules*) but as an ongoing process—incorporating yet transcending established social and occupational orders—driven by the exchange of fictions—about oneself, others, and the world—and having as its goals successful competition; the outwitting of opponents; the earning of praise, respect, or influence; and the effective expression of or resistance to prejudices and stereotypes. Persuasive narration and critical reception—in ancient Rome the hallmarks of the rhetorical education designed exclusively for a small social eltite—thus become important tasks of all constituent members of society. Such narrative and critical skills are, however, always deployed within—and must therefore be cognizant of—contexts defined by culturally and politically authoritative discourses and traditions.

Perhaps *The Canterbury Tales'* most interesting and idiosyncratic representation of how a poet can respond to the issue of cultural authority comes within the introductory material assigned to the Sergeant of Law—an influential if (according to popular satire) highly self-aggrandizing figure in England's secular legal system—where Chaucer stages what we might call a comically displaced version of literary crisis, casting himself as an (absent) auctor whose writings on love and desire force a would-be teller of similar stories into a position of frustrated belatedness, from which he must take refuge in new sources of inspiration. (The situation parallels, albeit with greatly changed particulars, the frustration of the *LGW* narrator vis-à-vis the spate of daisy-praising poems produced by courtly "makers.") In this oblique, irony-laden manner does the poet theorize a new literary form in which crises of desire and authority, articulated via stories of multiple (not just learned, auctorial) origin, function within a social system conceptualized by him as dynamic and contested, rather than as static and simply hierarchical.

The episode in question begins when Harry Bailly, having exhorted the pilgrim compaignye, "Leseth [lose] no tyme, as ferforth as ye may," because "the tyme wasteth nyght and day" (*CT* 2.19–20), turns to the Sergeant: "'Sire Man of

Lawe,' quod [said] he, 'so have ye blis [salvation], / Telle us a tale anon, as forward is [as you agreed]'" (*CT* 2.33–34). Despite the Host's ostensible urgency,
his twenty-three-line speech of exhortation is in fact a show-off's exercise in
rhetorical amplification, or *dilatatio*—the arch-enemy of expeditiousness; indeed, his appeal to "Senec and many a philosophre" [*CT* 2.25] to support his
contention about the passage of time, like his paraphrase of a statement on the
subject in one of Seneca the Younger's letters [*CT* 2. 27–28], marks the speech as
an innkeeper's half-parodic attempt at learned discourse, which he apparently
understands as saying little in many words. Similarly, the legal terminology he
uses in pressing the lawyer to tell the next tale constitutes both a parody of and
challenge to the latter's professional loquacity:

> 'Tell us a tale anon, as forward is.
> Ye been submytted, thurgh youre free assent,
> To stonden in this cas at my juggement.
> Acquiteth yow now of youre biheeste,   *fulfill your promise*
>   *now*
> Thanne have ye do youre devoir atte leste.'   *done   duty*
>   (*CT* 2.34–38)

Like most acts of mimickry, Harry's words to the Sergeant are playful but
also antagonistic; they establish a little one-on-one contest within the larger
tale-telling competition, with the Host asserting not only his temporary,
occasion-specific authority over the otherwise more culturally authoritative
legal bigshot—by ordering him, as would a judge, to pay his debt to the pilgrimage society—but also his control over (and skepticism about) his "opponent's" occupational jargon.[58]

The lawyer mounts a double riposte to the Host's challenge. Acceding to
Harry's pro tem authority, he agrees to tell a tale but accepts his obligation
with a counterappeal to legal process and precedent, as if to reclaim his professional status:

> 'Hooste,' quod he, 'depardieux, ich assente;   *in God's name   I*
> To breke forward is nat myn entente.
> Biheste is dette, and I wol holde fayn   *a promise is a debt*
>   *(obligation)*
>   *certainly*
> Al mi biheste, I kan no bettre sayn.
> For swych lawe as a man yeveth another wight,

He sholde hymselven usen it, by right;   *abide by it*
Thus wole oure text.   *says   law code*
                                                          (CT 2.39–45)

He then easily outdoes Harry's exercise in dilation: where the Host of the Tabard took twenty-three lines to say, in effect, "It's your turn to tell the next
story," the Man of Law takes nearly ninety to say, "All right, and here's the only
story I can think of" (CT 2.45–133). Adding a further ironic dimension to the
moment, this colossal, pompous exercise in deferral by a man whose professional competence consists largely in his ability to cite authoritative precedents
(cf. CT 1.323–24) becomes the occasion for an important, if comically couched,
two-pronged statement by Chaucer about both his proficiency in appropriating to his needs the authoritative discourse of desire inherited from classical
antiquity, and his experimentation in *The Canterbury Tales* with new kinds of
storytelling, based on tales of love and other central human concerns that cir-
culate outside the orbit of the classical auctores.

The Man of Law proceeds to obsess about Chaucer (!) as an impoverishing
poetic predecessor:[59]

'I kan right now no thrifty tale seyn   *appropriate*
That Chaucer, thogh he kan but lewedly   *has only basic*
                                                          knowledge

On metres and on rymyng craftily,
Hath seyd hem in swich Englissh as
    he kan. . . .   *hasn't already told*
                                                          them

And if he have noght seyd hem, leve brother,
In o book, he hath seyd hem in another.
For he hath toold of loveris up and doun
Mo than Ovide made of mencioun
In his Episteles that been ful olde.   *i.e., the Heroides*

He adds, querulously, "What [why] sholde I tellen hem, syn they been [have
already been] tolde?" (CT 2.46–49, 51–56), and there follows a recapitulation
(CT 2. 57–76) of Chaucer's adaptations of stories of desire (often star-crossed)
from Ovid's *Heroides* and *Metamorphoses*, mostly in *LGW*, here refered to as
"the Seintes Legende of Cupide" (CT 2.61; the list includes tales of "seintes" he
never wrote, or at least that have not survived).

Through the screen of genial Chaucerian self-mockery at the hands of his surrogate, and beyond the self-advertisement implied in this canon of classically derived love poetry, these lines raise serious issues. Line 56, for example, asks us to consider the discomfort of belatedness, vis-à-vis the classical auctores, that any modern poet must eventually, even constantly, confront; it may even suggest Chaucer's growing uncertainty about the personal and cultural benefit of recycling stories long since canonized in medieval Europe's inheritance from classical auctores.[60]

After granting that Chaucer has at least avoided the "unkynde [unnatural] abhomynacions" of tales centering on incest—"Of swyche cursed stories I sey fy!" the Sergeant harrumphs, allowing Chaucer to offer a friendly (?) poke in the eye to his contemporary, John Gower (and perhaps even to himself)[61]—the Man of Law concludes his meditation (and arguably Chaucer's) with these lines, expressing the burdens and options of poetic belatedness in what we might call an externalized inner dialogue:

'But of my tale how shal I doon this day?
Me were looth to be likned, doutelees,   *I certainly don't want
                                             to be compared*

To Muses that men clepe Pierides—   *call*
Metamorphosios woot what I mene;   *knows*
But nathelees, I recche noght a bene   *I don't give a damn*
Though I come after hym with hawebake.
I speke in prose, and lat him rymes make.'

(CT 2.90–96)

The first four lines appear to articulate a refusal to engage in a storytelling contest with Chaucer (yet another one-on-one rivalry, echoing the Host's and Sergeant's), presumably by retelling a tale he has already told (even as Chaucer has retold many of Ovid's stories); such an act of mimicry, the Man of Law suggests, would be akin to the challenge posed to the nine Muses (in Ovid's *Metamorphoses*, book 5) by the nine daughters of King Pierus, who were punished by being turned into magpies, birds that jabber meaninglessly in other people's voices. But, as Helen Cooper has pointed out, there is a crucial ambiguity in the Lawyer's expression of unwillingness, since the Muses themselves were often called Pierides in classical writings, based on their supposed home (and center of worship), Pieria.[62] Hence, if the Man of Law's statement, when read from one perspective, implies Chaucer's own reluctance to continue composing poetry that imitates, however freely and ingeniously, the legacy of classical *auctores*, from another it suggests that all storyteller-poets are at once imitators and innovators: there can be no discoverable point of origin for the human penchant for narration, and therefore no stigma in retelling tales.

But even as the Sergeant resigns himself to belatedness—"coming after" Chaucer; cf. "myn auctor shal I folwen"—he commits himself to a different kind of storytelling, which he characterizes as "hawebake" (an inferior bread made from hawthorn berries) and "prose." What he means by this only becomes evident after another thirty-four lines of digression and dilation, this time on the horrors of poverty and, by contrast, the many blessings enjoyed by rich merchants, whom he then addresses in lines that form a transition (finally!) to his tale:

> Ye seken lond and see for yowre wynnynges;
> As wise folk ye knowen al th'estaat   *condition*
> Of regnes; ye been fadres of *tidynges*   *kingdoms*
> And *tales*, both of pees and of debaat.   *[important descriptors*
>   *in the "workshop of*
>   *Fame" in HF]*
>   *peace   conflict*
> I were right now of tales desolaat,   *completely lacking*
> Nere that a marchant, goon is many a yeere,   *were it not*
> Me taught a tale, which that ye shal heere.
>
> (CT 2.127–33; emphasis added)

That is, the merchant-purveyed "hawebake" that the Man of Law has no choice but to offer to the Canterbury pilgrims is, he claims, one of those myriad stories—some little more than jokes—that, lacking any cultural cachet, circulated all over Europe and Asia, transmitted by merchants and other travelers (including pilgrims, of course), and that Giovanni Boccaccio made the basis of his immensely successful tale collection, the *Decameron*, which Chaucer probably knew through his professional involvement, as a customs officer and the son of a wine merchant, with London's large colony of Italian merchants, arguably Boccaccio's most enthusiastic audience. Many of the *Canterbury Tales*, including several that deal with desire, are of this unauthorized type, though elevated by Chaucer's art. (The Man of Law's Tale, in a further joke, has folktale antecedents but more immediately came to Chaucer through literate antecedents, both Latin and venacular.) They represent for him an opportunity to demonstrate that as a comic poet of love, he can be more than an Ovidian magpie, and his declaration of independence, as so often by indirection, is couched in the orotund tones of a self-important lawyer.

Chaucer explores the dangers posed to the poet by political authority—an issue, as we've seen, centrally embedded in the Prologue to *The Legend of Good Women*—with characteristic obliquity in several ways throughout *CT*. He builds it into the poem's framing fiction through his creation of Harry Bailly, who puts himself in charge of this "companye / of sondry folk by aventure yfalle / in felaweship, and pilgrims were they alle / That toward Caunterbury wolden ryde" (*CT* 1.24–27). After outlining the storytelling contest and the prize, as recapitulated above, Harry continues, "I wol myself goodly [happily] with yow ryde, / . . . And whoso wole my juggement withseye [contradict] / Shal paye al that we spenden by the weye" (*CT* 1.803, 805–6). That is, in addition to serving as "juge and reportour" (*CT* 1.814) of the stories, Harry demands, and receives, the pilgrims' acquiescence in his being "oure governor" (*CT* 1.813). Harry's imposition of himself as de facto and de jure ruler of this ad hoc storytelling community represents a major development in its formation as a polity. Early in the so-called General Prologue which establishes the framing fiction, the narrator encounters the other pilgrims "in Southwerk, at the Tabard as I lay, / redy to wenden on my Pilgrimage / To Caunterbury, with ful devout corage [spirit]" (*CT* 1.20–22); he attaches himself to the nascent "compagnye" in a series of conversations that result in some amicable and quite unhierarchical decision making: the pilgrims "made forward [agreement] erly for to rise / To take oure wey ther as I yow devyse" (*CT* 1.33–34). Until Harry demands everyone's subordination to his "juggement," there is no evidence of the need for a ruler. The Host reiterates the absolute nature of his authority the next morning, as the pilgrims set out on the Canterbury road: "As evere mote I drynke wyn or ale, / Whoso be rebel to my juggement / Shal paye for al that by the weye is spent" (*CT* 1.832–34).

Tension appears early in the Canterbury pilgrimage as Harry's authority is challenged by the drunken Miller, described in the General Prologue by the narrator as a strong, bold, and dishonest fellow with animal-like features. (Such features and deportment were often attributed to the rebels of 1381 by their ecclesiastical and noble detractors.) When the Knight, the highest ranking secular pilgrim, finishes his tale of love, chivalry, and rulership, and Harry calls on the Monk, the ecclesiastic of equivalent status, to tell "somwhat to quite [i.e., accord or match] with the Knyghtes tale" (*CT* 1.3119), it becomes clear that the Host intends to align the order of the storytelling with the social hierarchy of the pilgrims. But rebellion quickly rears its head:

The Miller, that for dronken was al pale,	*who, being drunk*
so that unnethe upon his hors he sat,	*barely*
He nolde avalen neither hood ne hat,	*would not doff*
Ne abyde no man for his curtesie,	*give way to out of*
But in Pilates voys he gan to crye,	*Pilate's voice (see note)*
And swoor, "by armes and by blood and bones,	*[Christ's] arms, etc.*
I kan a noble tale for the nones,	*for this occasion*
With which I wol now quyte the Knightes Tale.	(CT 1.3120–27)[63]

This outburst not only challenges the ruler and the social order but also the univocity of language: in Robin Miller's mouth, and rage, the locution, "a noble storie" (such as the Knight had just told), becomes an exercise in sarcasm, and to "quite" morphs in meaning from "accord with" to "pay back," "get even with."

Harry seeks to put the Miller in his place by a patronizing appeal to his sense of rank—"som bettre man shal telle us first another" (CT 1.3130)—but Robin's response is to issue an ultimatum: "For I wol speke or elles go my wey." This threat hits Harry where it most hurts, in the pocketbook; not wishing to lose a customer, he gives in with bad grace: "Tel on, a devel way; / Thou art a fol; thy wit is overcome" (CT 1.3134–35). The phrase, "a devel way," is telling because it alludes to Lucifer, the ur-rebel against an established order, whose attempted usurpation of divine power and authority in heaven resulted in his banishment to hell as Satan, the devil. From one perspective— Harry's certainly, and perhaps every early listener or reader of this passage who remembered the horrors of the Great Rising of 1381—the Miller's disruption of Harry's plan for the pilgrimage embodies the threat posed to English society by lower-class rebels. But there's another, less obvious allusion in this passage, to Ovid in fact, that hints at a different interpretation. Recall the words that introduce Robin: "The Miller, that for dronken was al pale, / So that unnethe upon his hors he sat." This description of a tipsy, barely stable rider is in fact a close paraphrase of a line in book 1 of Ovid's *Ars amatoria* describing Silenus, the companion of Bacchus, who follows the wine god riding on a mule from which he keeps threatening to fall thanks to his state of chronic inebriation ("Ebrius, ecce, senex pando Silenus asello / Vix sedet [Here comes plastered old Silenus, barely keeping his own ass on the ass swaying beneath him]" *Ars* 1.543–44). Taking a hint from this hint, as it were, a different interpretation of the Miller's interruption will see in it a version of Bacchic inspiration—a freeing of the tale telling from a preconceived, socially determined order, substituting instead a principle of reaction and rivalry that links tale telling to a competitive spirit grounded not in Harry's (commerically advantageous) holiday scheme but in the social reality of clashing personal and professional agendas.

Chaucer also uses Harry to dramatize a worst-case scenario of artistic differences (to put it mildly) with political authority when the Host calls on the narrator of the pilgrimage, Chaucer's stand-in, to tell a tale. The result is the rambling, anticlimactic account of the adventures of Sir Thopas, a parody of popular English "tail-rhyme" romances, albeit with satirical overtones aimed at the Flemish, England's political and commecial rivals.[64] After several dozen jogging stanzas, Harry harshly interrupts the performance:

> 'Namoore of this, for Goddes dignitee!
> . . . for thou makest me
> So wery of thy verray lewednesse   *weary   complete*
>   *stupidity*
> That, also wisly God my soule blesse,
> Myne eres aken of thy drasty speche.'   *ache   crappy*
>   (CT 7.919–23)

When the narrator asks why he alone of all the pilgrims has been prevented from completing "the beste rym I kan," Harry replies curtly, "By God . . . for pleynely, at [in]a word, / Thy drasty ryming is nat woorth a toord!" (CT 7.928–30).

Every reciting poet's nightmare: the most powerful member of his audience exercises his unchallenged authority to interrupt and condemn the performance on the grounds that it is "nat worth a toord." Such poetic truncation must hurt almost as much as the more physical truncation with which the same Harry Bailey elsewhere, and with analogous excremental emphasis, threatens the (already ambiguous) masculinity of another pilgrim, the Pardoner:

> 'I wolde I hadde thy coillons in myn hand   *wish   balls*
> In stide of relikes or of seintuarie   *stead   reliquary*
> Lat kutte hem of, I wol thee helpe hem carie;
> They shul be shryned in an hogges toord.'
>   (CT 6.952–55)

To return to "The Miller's Tale": it is the first of several comic contributions to the storytelling contest in which male figures of domestic authority show themselves lacking in prudence and pay the price. Specifically, men who marry unwisely and then, out of sexual jealousy, impose unreasonable restraints on their wives to protect themselves from being cuckolded are condemned to comic complicity in bringing about the very situation they most wish to avoid. As the Miller puts it about old John the carpenter, the butt of his tale (predictably a fabliau, or bawdy story),

> 'This carpenter hadde wedded newe a wyf,
> Which that he lovede moore than his lyf;
> Of eighteteene yeer she was of age.
> Jalous he was, and heeld hire narwe in cage,   *kept her under tight control*
>
> For she was wylde and yong, and he was old,
> And demed hymself been lik a cokewold.
> . . . Men sholde wedden after hire estaat,   *in accord with their situation*
>
> For youthe and elde is often at debaat.
> But sith that he was fallen in the snare,   *since he had*
> He moost endure, as oother folk, his care.'
>
> (CT 1.3221–26, 3229–32)

The key image here is "narwe in cage," as if the wife were a captive bird. This image, which Chaucer uses more than once in CT to interesting effect, brings together crises of desire—the husband's to have exclusive sexual control of his wife, the wife's to escape from such imprisonment—and of authority, as the husband, as head of the household, attempts, usually without success, to impose his on his spouse.

The caged bird appears literally in "The Manciple's Tale," as one of Chaucer's innovations in a story that has antecedents as far back as Ovid but exists in a variety of versions in medieval tale collections. The plot is simple enough: a bird distinguished by its bright plumage and ability to communicate directly with human beings tells a powerful man or a deity (usually Phoebus Apollo, god of light and song) that the woman he loves, wife or mistress, is playing him false with another. In jealous rage the distraught man kills her, too late experiences remorse for his hasty reaction, and turns on the bird, blaming him entirely for what has happened and stripping him of his voice, his bright plumage, or both. The lesson usually drawn from this exemplary tale is not to be the bearer of bad news, even if it is true. Other obvious morals—don't take pleasure in revealing other peoples' faults; don't allow your emotions to get the better of you in ways you'll later regret; don't blame others for your own lack of self-control—seem rarely, if ever, to be drawn.[65]

Chaucer takes the cynical and incomplete nature of this tale's traditional moralization as the starting point for his placement of it within his Canterbury collection. In his hands, a seemingly straightforward parable of the dangers of truthtelling is bent and subverted in a variety of ways that make plain dealing, irrational power, and counsels of prudence all look bad. He puts the story in the mouth of the Manciple, a dubiously honest purchasing agent, who, responding to the helpless inebriation of another pilgrim, the Cook—who is slated, but unable, to tell the next tale—takes obvious and malicious pride in delivering this brutal, hyperbolical reprimand:

> 'Of me, certeyn, thou shalt nat been
>   yglosed. . . .   *flattered*
> Hoold cloos thy mouth, man, by thy fader kyn!   *for God's sake*
> The devel of helle sette his foot therin!
> Thy cursed breeth infecte wole us alle.
> Fy, stynkyng swyn! Fy, foule moote thee falle!'   *you should suffer*
>   *for this*
>   (CT 9.34, 37–40)

The Host exercises his authority to excuse the Cook from his narratorial obligation and substitute the Manciple; but he warns the latter of the Cook's potential retaliation for his attack:

> 'I meene, he speke wole of smale thynges,
> As for to pynchen at thy rekenynges,   *make trouble about*
>   *account keeping*
> That were nat honest, if it cam to preef.'   *might not be legitimate*
>   *when examined*
>   (CT 9.73–75)

To which the Manciple replies with heavy sarcasm,

> 'No . . . that were a greet mescheef!   *would be disaster*
> So myghte he lyghtly brynge me in the snare.   *easily get me into*
>   *trouble*
> Yet hadde I levere payen for the mare
> Which he rit on, than he sholde with me stryve.

> I wol nat wratthen hym, also moot I thryve!
> That that I spak, I seyde it in my bourde.'   *in jest*
>
>   (CT 9.76–81)

Lest anyone mistake these words for an expression of real worry, he adds that, as
"'a good jape,'" he will now buy the Cook's good will by offering him "'a draughte
of wyn, ye, of a ripe grape,'" which he will not refuse; sure enough, "the Cook
drank faste" and even "thanked [the Manciple] in swych wise [however] as he
koude" (CT 9.83–84, 88, 93). It is against this backdrop of cynical, insincere regret for indulgence in verbal abuse under the guise of telling unpleasant truths
that the Manciple will tell his tale, as a supposed caution against plain speaking
but in a manner so parodically excessive as to make clear his scorn for the story's
traditional exemplary message.

The tale is set in the period "Whan Phebus dwelled heer in this erthe adoun,"
as a compendium of all desirable human qualities:

> He was the mooste lusty bachiler   *vigorous young man*
> In al this world, and eek the beste archer. . . .
> Pleyen he koude on every mynstralcie,   *instrument to*
>   *accompany singing*
>
> And syngen that it was a melodie
> To heeren of his clere voys the soun.
> . . . Therto he was the semelieste man
> That is or was sith that the world bigan. . . .   *since*
> He was therwith fulfild of gentilesse,   *a model of refinement*
> Of honour, and of parfit worthinesse.   *excellence*
> . . . [the] flour of bachilrie,   *noble youth*
> As wel in fredom as in chivalrie.   *generosity   knightly*
>   *prowess*
>   (CT 9.105–8, 113–15, 119–20, 123–26)

The household of this paragon contains two other members, a wife and a bird,
whom he treats with analogous devotion—and possessiveness:

> Now hadde this Phebus in his hous a crowe
> Which in a cage he fostred many a day,
> And taughte it speken, as men teche a jay.   *to speak*
> Whit was this crowe as is a snow-whit swan,
> And countrefete the speche of every man

He koude, whan he sholde telle a tale.
Therwith in al this world no nyghtyngale
Ne koude, by an hondred thousand deel,   *fold*
Syngen so wonder myrily and weel.
Now hadde this Phebus in his hous a wyf
Which that he lovede moore than his lyf,
And nyght and day dide evere his diligence
Hir for to plese and doon hire reverence,
Save oonly, if the sothe that I shal sayn,   *if I'm to tell the truth*
Jalous he was, and wolde have kept hire fayne,   *gladly have kept her*
                                                        under guard
For hym were looth byjaped for to be,   *he didn't want to be*
                                                        cheated
And so is every wight in swich degree.   *as is every man in*
                                                        such a place
                                                        (CT 9.130–46)

The exact parallel between the line that begins each of these descriptions, "now had this Phebus in his hous a crow/a wyf,"[66] suggests that the first in some way stands for the second—indeed, in Chaucer's Middle English the word, "bryd," has both meanings—an interpretation reinforced by the extended simile, available to Chaucer in sources as diverse as Boethius's *Consolation of Philosophy* and *The Romance of the Rose*, with which the Manciple describes the futility of Phebus's attempt to keep his wife faithful by combining service and constraint:[67]

But God it woot, ther may no man embrace   *knows   no man can*
                                                      succeed
As to destreyne a thyng which that nature   *in constraining*
Hath natureelly set in a creature.
Taak any bryd, and put it in a cage,
And do al thyn entente and thy corage   *ingenuity*
To fostre it tendrely with mete and drynke
Of alle deyntees that thou kanst bithynke,
And keep it al so clenly as thou may,
Although his cage of gold be never so gay,
Yet hath this brid, by twenty thousand foold,   *would twenty*
                                                      thousand times
Levere in a forest that is rude and coold   *prefer*

Goon ete wormes and swich wrecchednesse.   *to go   such garbage*
For evere this bird wol doon his bisynesse
To escape out of his cage, yif he may.
His libertee this brid desireth ay.

(CT 9.160–174)

As the tale plays out, the Manciple's intrinsic nastiness and sour view of
humanity shines through his (and Chaucer's) further additions. The wife's inevitable adultery, the bestiality of which the teller has underscored using com-
parisons with the base appetites of cats and wolves, is in this version particularly depraved and thus demeaning to Phoebus:

This Phebus, which that thoghte upon
    no gile,   *who had no idea he was*
                                                  tricked

Deceyved was, for al his jolitee,   *attractiveness*
For under hym another hadde she,   *of lesser rank than he*
A man of litel reputacioun,
Nat woorth to Phebus in comparisoun.

(CT 9.196–200)

The crow's behavior is little better: he's presented first as a voyeuristic spectator
to the betrayal who does nothing to dissuade the wife and then as a tattletale
who takes obvious delight in rubbing his master's nose in the squalor of it all:

The white crow, that heeng ay in the cage,
Biheeld hire werk, and seyde never a word.
And whan that hoom was come Phebus,
    the lord,
his crowe sang 'Cokkow! Cokkow! Cokkow!'
'What, bryd?' quod Phebus, 'What song
    syngestow?   *are you singing*
Ne were thow wont so myrily to synge   *wasn't it your habit*
That to myn herte it was a rejoysynge
To heere thy voys? Allas, what song is this?'
'By God,' quod he, 'I synge nat amys: *I'm not singing badly*
Phebus,' quod he, 'for al thy worthynesse,
For al thy beautee and thy gentilesse,   *nobility*
For al thy song and al thy mynstralcye,   *music making*

For al thy waityng, blered is thyn ye   *surveillance   you've*
                                                         been tricked

With oon of litel reputacioun,   *by*
Noght worth to thee, as in comparisoun,
The montance of a gnat, so moot I thryve!
For on thy bed thy wyf I saugh hym swyve.'   *screw*

                                              (CT 9.240–56)

The literal caging of the bird—whose obvious status as an emblem of a poet who, like Chaucer, can tell tales in many voices,[68] makes his imprisonment a parable of patronal or royal constraint—like the metaphoric caging of the wife (which the Manciple, on the authority of "olde clerkes" [CT 9.154], deems "verray nycetee [complete stupidity]" [CT 9.152]), liberates in both wife and bird the capacity for despicable behavior that becomes the nemesis to Phebus's hubris in exercising coercive authority over both his paterfamilial possessions.[69]

The remainder of the story follows its preordained path: Phebus in a fury kills his wife, only to undergo an intense emotional reaction in which he not only regrets his hasty action but endows the victim with an entirely unwarranted innocence:

'O deere wyf! O gemme of lustiheed!   *jewel [my] delight*
That were to me so sad and eek so trewe,   *completely devoted*
Now listow deed, with face pale of hewe,   *you lie*
Ful giltelees, that dorste I swere, ywys.'

                                              (CT 9.274–77)

He then turns on the bird, not only taking away its beautiful voice and white feathers but "out of dore hym slong / Unto the devel, which I hym bytake [to whom I send him]" (CT 9.306–07). Behind the Manciple's ostensible repudiation of the bird who sounds suspiciously like him (see note 68) lies the indisputable fact, to my knowledge first pointed out by David Raybin, that Phebus's actions, for all their punitive harshness, result in the bird's gaining what the Manciple has said all birds wish: "For evere this bird wol doon his bisynesse / To escape out of his cage, yif he may" (CT 9.172–73).[70] The crisis of Phoebus's desire and authority created by his wife's adultery—her attempted escape from her too narrow "cage of gold"—ultimately, and ironically, fulfills his avian captive's desire for freedom from his literal cage—within which the poetic gift of "counterfeiting" voices has been, it would seem, a function of the bird's subordination to his master's power.

The tale ends with the Manciple's fulsome warning against speech of any kind, put in the mouth of his old mother, who concludes her overlong, overly sententious tirade, "Kepe [restrain] wel thy tong and thenk upon the crowe" (*CT* 9.362). With such a final flourish of insincerity—or perhaps of indirect praise for the crow's astute use of hurtful language—does the Manciple embellish his cynically reductive appropriation of an oft-told tale, already more celebratory of self-protection than of virtue, through which he repays the insult that Harry Bailley had earlier aimed at him, when, under the guise of counseling prudence in speech, the Host alluded to the Manciple's dishonest business practices. But lurking behind this further instance of pilgrim "quyting," directed at the Host's authority, is a still darker meditation on the potentially perilous, even fatal, impact of the unbridled exercise of authority on desire and poetic expression.

Let me close on a lighter note, with a crisis of desire in *The Canterbury Tales* more playful, if no less serious, and again involving birds—in this case talking, anthropomorphic chickens—who live in a cage, or more precisely a coop—that is literally, not metaphorically, too narrow. The "Nun's Priest's Tale" features Chauntecleer, a proud and colorful rooster who has a terrifying dream (that later comes true) in which he's carried off by a fox who sneaks into the barnyard. After he wakes from his dream, Chauntecleer and the favorite of his seven clucking paramours, Pertelote, engage in an argument over its credibility, with the hen insisting that she has no interest in a lover who responds in cowardly wise to a dream—"have ye no mannes herte, and han a berd [have a beard]?" (*CT* 7.2919), she asks the rooster (thereby, in one line, toppling the creaky superstructure of avian moral fabulation)—especially, she insists, since dreams have no predictive validity; Chauntecleer's has undoubtedly resulted from indigestion, so her advice is, "For Goddes love, as taak som laxatyf!" Her prescription is precious:

'A day or two ye shal have digestyves
Of wormes, er ye take youre laxatyves
Of lawriol, centaure, and fumetre,   *[these are all*
                                                          bad-tasting
                                                          herbs]

Or elles of ellebor, that groweth there,
Of katapuce, or of gaitrys beryis,   *berries*
Of herbe yve, growyng in oure yeerd, ther mery is.'   *ivy   where*
                                                          it's pleasant

And the coup de grace, a marvellously onomatopoeic line that catches the rhythm of the cock putatively following her instructions: "Pekke hem up ryght as they growe and ete hem yn [eat them up]" (CT 7.2943, 2961–67).

As a retort to Pertelote's pharmacopeia—he rejects laxatives "for they been venymes [venomous], I woot it weel; / I hem diffye [reject them], I love hem never a deel [not in the least]!" (CT 7.3155–56)—Chauntecleer marshalls an array of auctores who attribute veracity to dreams and offers two exemplary stories in support of that thesis. Having, as he feels, proven his point, the learned rooster then reverses himself completely, jettisoning cultural *auctoritas* and giving as his reason the inspiration to his courage that comes from his desire for Pertelote— but in the process being forced to confront that desire's ultimate frustration of being held "narwe in cage": "For whan I feele a-nyght your softe syde—Al be it that I may nat on yow ryde, / *For that oure perche is made so narwe, allas*—I am so ful of joye and of solas [pleasure], / That I diffye bothe sweven [dream] and dreem" (CT 7.3167–71; emphasis added). As with "The Manciple's Tale," so beneath the at times convulsive humor of this parodic animal fable run darker currents, and the image of chickens too tightly wedged into their perch—still a problem for twenty-first-century proponents of animal rights!—to be able to make love can stand as a pathetic emblem of the human condition, in which the quest for personal satisfaction is thwarted by the external structures—of political authority? economic imperatives? Augustan legislation against adultery?— imposed upon it. At the same time, a better example of a situation that is always hopeless but never serious than that of Chantecleer, seeking in vain to get a leg up on his libidinal situation, would, I believe, be very hard to find.

As I hope the few examples offered in this chapter demonstrate, Chaucer's poetry is serious play in its comic attention to crises of desire and authority in very human situations (even if the humans sometimes have feathers). The balancing of comedy and concern is an important part of Chaucer's legacy to us; we do well to ponder that legacy.

NOTES

1. All Chaucer citations follow *The Riverside Chaucer*. On the *Book of the Duchess*, see Minnis, *Oxford Guides*, 73–160; Hanning, "Chaucer's First Ovid."

2. The best recent biography (necessarily in part hypothetical, given gaps in records) is Pearsall, *The Life of Geoffrey Chaucer: A Critical Biography*. See Crow and Olson, eds., *Chaucer Life Records*, for the extant documents that refer to Chaucer's various appointments. On Chaucer's circle see Strohm, *Hochon's Arrow*,

chapter 2, "'A Revelle!': Chronicle Evidence and the Rebel Voice," and chapter 5, "Queens as Intercessors"; Kerby-Fulton and Justice, "Langlandian Reading Circles."

3. See Dane, *Who Is Buried in Chaucer's Tomb?*; Lerer, *Chaucer and His Readers*; and Fisher, *The Importance of Chaucer*, on the evolution of Chaucer's reputation and stature in the decades after his death.

4. "The term *auctor* denoted someone who was at once a writer and an authority, someone not merely to be read but also to be respected and believed" (Minnis, *Medieval Theory*, 10).

5. Cooper, "Chaucer and Ovid," 72.

6. See Donaldson, "Chaucer the Pilgrim."

7. See Chaucer, *Troilus and Criseyde*, ed. Windeatt, 3–24.

8. "Facesti come quei che va di notte, / che porta il lume dietro e sé non giova,/ ma dopo sé fa le persone dotte" (*Purgatorio* 22.67–69). "You were like the one who goes by night and carries the light behind him and profits not himself, but makes those wise who follow him." Immediately after these lines, Dante translates the key lines from Vergil's fourth *Eclogue*. See Comparetti, *Vergil in the Middle Ages*, chapter 6.

9. See Miller, *Poetic License*, 3–4, on the complicated attitudes toward authority implicit in the works of a poet such as Chaucer: "The poet's relation to authority usually seems complicated by a pull in two directions: does he rest upon his status as a reflector of an already authorized truth, a spokesman for something other than himself, or do his status and function reside in the exercise of his own creative power?"

10. See Hanning, "Chaucer's First Ovid," 141–58; Fyler, *Chaucer and Ovid*, chapter 2, "Chaucer's Faulty Vision: The House of Fame."

11. Whereas many dreams in French dream-vision poems take place in the springtime, the season appropriate to newly awakened desire, this dream is set on of December 10 (*HF* 111–12), suggesting an altogether less cheerful theme; it's also, according to the Julian calendar in use in Chaucer's day, almost the longest night of the year, allowing plenty of time for dreaming

12. See Simpson, "Ethics and Interpretation," 82–83, 82–83nn. 23–26; also Scanlon, "The King's Two Voices," 218–26.

13. Hanning, "Chaucer's First Ovid," 146–47.

14. Cf. Ovid, *Metamorphoses* 12.53–55: "Atria turba tenet: veniunt, leve vulgus, euntque / mixtaque cum veris passim commenta vagantur / milia rumorum confusaque verba volutant." "The halls / Are filled with presences that shift and wander, / Rumors in thousands, lies and truth together / Confused, confusing" (Humphries trans., 287).

15. The saying is Alan of Lille's (see this chapter, pages 120–21); cited in Minnis, *Medieval Theory*, 265n. 100.

16. For interpretation of *The Plaint of Nature*, see Economou, *The Goddess Natura*; Wetherbee, *Platonism and Poetry*, chapter 5.

17. On Chaucer's possible role in establishing St. Valentine's Day as a day for professing one's love or choosing a mate, see Oruch, "St. Valentine, Chaucer, and Spring."

18. See Ganim, *Chaucerian Theatricality*, chapter 7, "The Noise of the People"; Strohm, *Hochon's Arrow*, chapter 2; Crane, "The Writing Lesson"; Justice, *Writing and Rebellion*, chapter 5, "Insurgency Remembered." Cf. the use of animals, making animal noises, to stand for the rebels of 1381 in the harshly judgmental first book of the Latin poem *Vox clamantis* (The voice of one crying [in the desert]"), by Chaucer's contemporary, John Gower. esp. chaps. 1–11; Justice thinks that the noisy barnyard chase in Chaucer's animal fable "The Nun's Priest's Tale" of *The Canterbury Tales* (see this chapter, pages 166–67) is a parody of Gower. It does in any case mention Jack Straw, one of the leaders of the rebellion.

19. There's near unanimity that the sequence of versions of the Prologue is F before G; for a defense of the opposite sequence, see Delany, *The Naked Text*, chapter 1. Cowen and Kane defend the authenticity of the G text in their edition of *LGW* (124–39). After a long period of neglect, *LGW* has been much studied in recent years; for a review of scholarship and a general interpretation, see Minnis, *Oxford Guides*, 322–454. My reading of the tales constituting the body of *LGW* is close to Fyler's (*Chaucer and Ovid*, chapter 4, "The Legend of Good Women*: Palinode and Procrustean Bed"), while my reading of the G prologue focuses on its depiction of the trajectory of a poetic career during which the poet must confront, and negotiate, challenges posed by political authority, translation, and "courtly" composition in the English vernacular. By contrast, Wallace sees "the ultimate effect of the G revision" as "an attempt to save or withhold the text from history by denying it the force of occasion" (*Chaucerian Polity*, 370).

20. Wallace, *Chaucerian Polity*, 354: "Once the deity's gaze falls upon him, the deamer is subjected to intensive scrutiny as the court shifts from Hof to Gericht, from court of love to court of law."

21. "Legende" (from Latin *legenda*, that which should be read) has a somewhat different meaning from today's "legend"; it implies a narrative of moral or religious edification, such as the lives of saints read aloud in medieval monasteries while the monks or nuns ate their main meal of the day.

22. The most thorough-going, political reading of the F Prologue is in Wallace, *Chaucerian Polity*, 357–70, who offers a learned and provocative, though speculative, interpretation of the Dreamer's relationship to Alceste in that version as a fictional inflection (and deflection) of the coincidence of interests between Chaucer and Richard's queen, Anne of Bohemia (whom Richard married in 1382), in seeking to restrain the monarch's tendencies toward an Italian-style absolutism that Alceste identifies with "tyrants of Lombardy" (see this chapter,

page 148). But cf. Staley's convincing argument ("Gower," 70–77) that *LGW*, like contemporaneous works by Gower and Clanvowe, "need[s] to be seen as emerging from a more congenial courtly environment and as directed toward a king who was receptive to and conversant in the festively serious modes of princely advice" (70); in this account, the later recomposition of the G Prologue has less to do with Queen Anne's death in 1394 than with the poet's retreat from direct, courtly engagement with a monarch grown more tyrannical. For recent considerations of the nature, evolution, and policies of Richard II's monarchy, and its violent end in his removal and murder by Henry of Lancaster, crowned as Henry IV in 1400, see Saul, *Richard II*, and the essays in Goodman and Gillespie, *Richard II: The Art of Kingship*.

23. To quote Palmer, in his note to this passage, "Rabbit-hunting in the courtly texts of the period is often a slyly oblique way of referring to the pursuit of women (based on an obscene double entendre [*con/conil*]). Machaut does not reproduce the double entendre here, so it is not certain whether he meant the passage to be read in other than a literal sense" (*JKN* 215). The poet's extended and rather coy description of his hunt for "lievres [hares]" (505) does suggest an invitation to be read metaphorically (and erotically).

24. Cannon, "The Lives of Geoffrey Chaucer," 46, defines the list of Chaucer's works as "a surprisingly assertive self-defense."

25. Wallace, noting that "Chaucer, in representing his relationship with a figure of . . . authority, chooses to position an eloquent wife between himself and his lord" (*Chaucerian Polity*, 364), proposes that "Chaucer's dedication to exploring the domestic dynamics and political efficacy of female eloquence [in *LGW* and various *Canterbury Tales*] . . . seems peculiarly a phenomenon the years of Richard [II]'s first marriage, 1381–94" (376).

26. Chaucer has transferred to the God of Love the anger expressed in Machaut's poem by the lady Bonneürté, in effect politicizing the poet's transgression.

27. Cf. Wallace, *Chaucerian Polity*, 354: "The God of Love clearly arrogates both religious and secular authority to his own person."

28. Simpson, "Ethics and Interpretation," 81n. 22, suggests that by the time Chaucer wrote the G version of the Prologue (after 1394?), "its references to heretical textual practices, and their punishment, must have been more pressing in the context of Lollard activity." (He mentions unpublished papers by Wendy Scase and Helen Phillips supporting such a view.) Cf. *Treatise of the Astrolabe*, Prologue (*Riverside*, 662); interestingly, Chaucer refers in the Prologue to King Richard as "lord of this langage," i.e., English. On Lollardy, see Hudson, *The Premature Reformation*; on Lollards and English translation, see Watson, "Censorship and Cultural Change"; on Trevisa—his service as vicar of Berkeley and relationship with Thomas IV, Lord Berkeley; his translations; and his possible role in the English translation of the Bible under Wyclif's direction—see Fowler, *The Life and*

Times. Trevisa's two dialogues on translation have been edited by Waldron. See further Delany, *The Naked Text,* 83–85, 120–21, on echoes of Wycliffite Bible translation issues in *LGW.*

29. Kiser, *Telling Classical Tales,* 71, 94.

30. The Wife of Bath, in *The Canterbury Tales,* accuses clerics who hate women and marriage of the same senility-induced antagonism; see her Prologue, *CT* 3.707–10.

31. Cf. Wallace, 356: "It is certain that Chaucer was learning a great deal about the art of calumny and betrayal at court in this desperate period" (i.e., 1386–88).

32. See Simpson, "Ethics and Interpretation," 81.

33. Note the continuity between the Proem to Book 2 of *TC,* discussed earlier in this chapter, and the present passage, with respect to the poet's worry that his audience will misjudge, or judge harshly, his good faith efforts.

34. If *LGW* was really, commissioned or not, destined for Queen Anne, the poet must either have had a high estimate of her sense of humor or a very low estimate of her ability to comprehend English; she was Bohemian. But cf. Wallace, *Chaucerian Polity,* 355–70.

35. For example, Franchise, as part of her attack on Guillaume's hierarchy of griefs in *JKB,* extrapolates from the classical stories of Jason's betrayal of Medea and Theseus's of Ariadne this hyperbolical conclusion: "So Guillaume, that's the most important point: / No man ever is as loyal / As women are" (2809–11). To which Guillaume fairly snorts this deconstructive reply: "Damsel, the treason / Of either Theseus or Jason / Has nothing to do with the issue we're arguing, / And this is hardly the first, / Nor will it be the last betrayal / To be discovered among lovers, / Both women and men. / I wouldn't give two apples / For proving your point / By the introduction of examples such as these ["par si fais exemples trouver"]. / For if I intended to argue my case / With examples, I could find more than / Ten, truly more than twenty of them" (2823–36). Having thus dismissed the worth of "historical" examples, he proceeds to introduce several of his own—the lover of the Chatelaine de Vergy, Lancelot, Tristan—from more recent literature in support of a conclusion contrary to Franchise's.

36. See *Riverside,* 1178, for a list of MSS containing *LGW* (none is complete) and 1179 for those containing locutions such as, "Explicit Legenda Didonis martyris" ("Here ends the legend of Dido the martyr").

37. Fyler, *Chaucer and Ovid,* 97, suggests that Chaucer was inspired in part by the relationship between book 3 of Ovid's *Ars amatoria*—a supposed "arming" of women against men's erotic strategies—and the two preceding books.

38. These lines conclude the legend of Dido, which Chaucer adapted from both Vergil's *Aeneid,* book 4, and Dido's supposed letter to the fleeing Aeneas in Ovid's *Heroides.* That Chaucer's version follows the orders given the Dreamer by Alceste and the God of Love is clear from interventions such as this one: "O sely

wemen, ful of innocence [foolish], / Ful of pite, of trouthe [fidelity] and con-
science [tender feelings], / What maketh yow to men to truste so? / Have ye
swych routhe [such pity] upon hyre [their] feyned wo, / And han swich olde en-
saumples yow beforn [have before you]? / Se ye nat alle how they ben forsworn
[traitors]?" (LGW 1254–59).

39. Some of Chaucer's earlier poems deploy admonitions against male reprobacy
proleptic of LGW's narratorial rants. I've already mentioned the HF narrator's
cautionary comment on Aeneas's abandonment of Dido (see page 114), a passage that begins, "Loo, how a woman doth amys / To love hym that unknowen
ys! / For, be Cryste, lo, thus yt fareth [turns out] / 'Hyt is not al gold that glar-
eth.' / For also browke I wel [as I hope to keep] myn hed, / Ther may be under
godlyhed [(apparent) goodness] / Kevered many a shrewed [cursed] vice" (HF
269–75).

Even more apposite to LGW is the dry run for it at the end of TC. With a
nervousness that betrays his fear of adverse reaction, and possibly his bad con-
science, the narrator stumbles awkwardly from an apology for having retold a
famous story of female betrayal to an overly emphatic, and irrelevant, warning
against male betrayal: "But for that I to writen first bigan / Of [Troilus's] love, I
have seyd as I kan / . . . Bysechyng every lady bright of hewe, / And every gentil
womman, what she be [of whatever station], / That al be that Criseyde was un-
trewe, / That for that gilt she be nat wroth with me. / Ye may hire gilt in other
bokes se; / And gladlier I wol write, yif yow leste, / Penelopeës trouthe [loyalty]
and good Alceste." (Is the God of Love, *mutatis mutandis*, already waiting in the
wings? Or will be he subsequently created in the alchemy of Chaucer's imagination from a synthesis of the skeptical, putatively male audience defensively
evoked in the "Proem" to TC's book 2 and the equally hypothetical (and analogously threatening) "lad[ies] bright of hewe" here propitiated?) "N'y sey nat this
al oonly for thise men, / But moost for wommen that bitraised [betrayed] be /
Thorough [by] false folk—God yeve hem sorwe, amen!— / That with hire grete
wit and subtilte / Bytraise yow. And this commeveth [compels] me / To speke,
and in effect yow alle I preye, / Beth war of men, and herkneth what I seye!" (TC
5.1768–69, 1772–85).

The oracular, universal (and bathetic) condemnation-cum-self-puffery that
concludes this passage is particularly proleptic of the LGW narrator's bombast
at the end of the legend of Phyllis.

40. Cf. Fyler, *Chaucer and Ovid*, 98–115.

41. Wallace, *Chaucerian Polity*, 364, speaks of LGW's "intimate imagining of a relationship between an eloquent queen and a productive poet."

42. Travis, "Chaucer's Heliotropes," 411–16, sees the heliotropic daisy as an entry
point for a consideration of the notion of metaphor as explored in the French
daisy poems and in Chaucer's poetry.

43. Among recent critics of *LGW* known to me, Williams comes closest to my emphasis on Alceste's multiple significances, albeit pointing toward a different explanation: "A faithful wife, a daisy, a literary character, a queen, and an object of desire . . . , Alceste's many hats gesture towards the multivalent acts of interpretation required of readers of the dream vision" ("The Dream Visions," 175). An earlier essay, Carlson, "Alceste and Chaucer's View of Poetry," which came to my attention after I completed this discussion of *LGW*, also anticipates some aspects of my argument, noting that "as the poet's inspiration, his subject, his patron, and his audience, Alceste becomes a model of the poet's dynamic and unpredictable relationships to both his art and his audience. . . . [I]n her, Chaucer explores the sometimes confusing, often confounding realities of the sources and powers of poetry" (185). Carlson's analysis of the *LGW* Prologue deals primarily with the so-called F Prologue.

44. On daisy poetry see Fyler, *Chaucer and Ovid*, 116–18; Lowes, "The Prologue"; Wimsatt, *The Marguerite Poetry*; Travis, "Chaucer's Heliotropes," 403–5. For part of Machaut's daisy poem, see Travis, "Chaucer's Heliotropes," 404. For the courtly conventions of flower and leaf rivalries, see Minnis, *Oxford Guides*, 296–98, 327–29; Pearsall, *The Floure and the Leafe*, 20–29.

45. I owe this observation to Karen Bezella-Bond's Columbia University Ph.D. dissertation, "Florescence and Defloration: Maytime in Chaucer and Malory." For the quibble on flowers, see further Travis, "Chaucer's Heliotropes," 399–401.

46. See Strohm, *Hochon's Arrow*, chapter 5, "Queens as Intercessors."

47. See Strohm, *Hochon's Arrow*, 99–102, on this episode, including excerpts from Froissart's text, and for the context, his chapter 5, 95–119.

48. See Kiser, *Telling Classical Tales*, 28–49, on Alceste as an emblem of poetry's mediating role as "an earthly version . . . of some heavenly truth" (50).

49. Burnley, *Chaucer's Language*, chapters 1–3; Ferster, *Fictions of Advice*, chapters 1–3.

50. On Richard's relations with his barons, cf. Wallace, *Chaucerian Polity*, 367. Chaucer's *balade*, editorially entitled, "Lak of Stedfastnesse," is said in some manuscripts to have been addressed to Richard II, in accord with its concluding *envoy*, or message to the recipient; its admonitions to the "prince" (22–28) are extremely general, in the tradition of advice to rulers mentioned in this paragraph. Wallace, noting that in 1388 Simon Burley, Richard's tutor and Anne's ally at court, was executed by the Appellants despite Anne's attempted intercession for him, opines that "the helplessness of king and queen before the events of 1388 makes the delicate politics and rhetoric of the F Prologue seem anachronistic . . . almost as soon as they were written" (371), thus preparing the way for Chaucer's depoliticized G version, which, Wallace suggests, at a certain point "loses contact with (or washes its hands of) contemporary history" (374); in his reading, Anne's death "sapped the text of its political vitality and its occasional (that is, historical) force" (375).

51. Cf. Wallace, *Chaucerian Polity*, 369; Simpson, "Ethics and Interpretation," 80: "however much Chaucer is 'excused,' the real 'trial' is conducted wholly within the dynamics of Cupid's relationship with Alceste, the narrator's own defense being wholly irrelevant."

52. Wallace, *Chaucerian Polity*, 369: "Chaucer must accept the social and judicial reality of his 'trespas' and serve the life sentence of supervised 'makyng' that is handed down to him."

53. Simpson, "Ethics and Interpretation," 92, puts it elegantly: the narrator, in effect, "asks us to read . . . with an eye to authorial intention, an intention that is visible precisely in the traces of its effacement."

54. Cf. Staley, "Gower," who appears to believe that Richard and his queen would have known *LGW* with the F Prologue.

55. Thomas Becket, archbishop of Canterbury and formerly close associate of King Henry II, was murdered in Canterbury Cathedral in December 1170, by four knights possibly acting at Henry's behest. A shrine erected on the site of his martyrdom quickly became a major goal of Christian pilgrims from all over Europe, but by Chaucer's day it had long since been exceeded in popularity by other European sites and, in England, by the shrine to the Virgin Mary at Walsingham. See Kendall, *Medieval Pilgrims*, 109–117 (with medieval illustrations); Sumption, *Pilgrimage*; and Dyas, *Pilgrimage in Medieval English Literature*, part 3.

56. On the standard ordering of the sections, or fragments, that make up *CT* in all its manuscripts but vary widely in their ordering from manuscript to manuscript, see Cooper, *Oxford Guides*, 6–8. The order usually followed is that of the so-called Ellesmere MS of *CT*, a deluxe copy made within a few years of Chaucer's death, perhaps commissioned by his son, Thomas.

57. The commercial motive behind the Host's proposal is hinted at in line 719 of the "General Prologue," which tells that Harry Bailly's "gentil hostelrye" (718) is called "the Tabard, faste by the Belle"; that is, it is in close proximity to, and constant competition for pilgrim custom with, its neighboring taverns and (as we would say) B&Bs.

58. On the legal language and underlying legal concepts evoked in Harry's request and the Lawyer's reply, see, e.g., Hornsby, *Chaucer and the Law*, 33–35; also Braswell, "Chaucer's Court Baron."

59. On the argument that follows concerning the Man of Law's excursus, cf. Hanning, "'And countrefete the speche,'" 33–36.

60. See Shoaf, "'Unwemmed Custance,'" 298, on "the inexorable fact of belatedness." Cf. Miller, *Poetic License*, 20: "The relation between predecessors and successors is but one manifestation of the general tension between the assertion and denial of authorship, between the attribution of authority to self and to other sources."

61. John Gower's *Confessio amantis* (The lover's confession), a framed collection of tales broadly contemporaneous with Chaucer's work on *LGW* and *CT*—all

dating is hypothetical—contains stories of Apollonius of Tyre and Canacee that include incest. But many versions of the story that Chaucer adapts as "The Man of Law's Tale" also depict, or hint at, incest. See Shoaf, "'Unwemmed Custance'"; Archibald, "The Flight from Incest." Canacee is a character in the tale told by the Squire in *CT*, though the tale breaks off before indicating whether or not incest will figure in it.

62. Cooper, "Chaucer and Ovid," 81: "Chaucer is the ventriloquist behind the Man of Law: the poet can function as both Muse and magpie."

63. On Pilate's voice and all the references to medieval mystery plays in the Miller's Tale, see Prior, "Parodying Typology."

64. See Askins, "All That Glitters."

65. For other versions of the story, beginning with the one in Ovid's *Metamorphoses*, book 2, see Wheatley, "The Manciple's Tale." With respect to the last of these potential morals, the situation is a perfect illustration of the "cognitive dissonance" described by Tavris and Aronson, *Mistakes Were Made*. Cf. Hazleton ("The Manciple's Tale," 4): "Chaucer seems to have noted what escaped all the moralizers: namely, that this 'moral' fable creates more moral problems than it solves. Indeed, the 'moral' traditionally imposed on the fable is all wrong. The fact that the well-meaning truth-teller is often rewarded with punishment rather than praise lends itself to paradoxical or ironic statement, but it is not a secure ground on which to build a serious moral argument for the wisdom of holding one's tongue." I would only demur from Hazleton's description of Phoebus's crow as "well-meaning"; in my argument, "self-serving" seems a more accurate characterization (see page 165). On the perils of bringing bad news, see the comic treatment of the theme in Ovid, *Amores* ii.2, 47–54, 59–62; the poet is pleading with his *puella*'s eunuch/guardian to let him spend time with his beloved and to say nothing to the husband. Don't forget the trouble people get into by telling husbands they've been cuckolded, he counsels. The *New York Times* for January 18, 2006, reports a contemporary "version" of this oft-told tale—Sarah Lyall, "Kiss and Tell: She Kisses and the Parrot Tells"—in which a London woman's secret lover is revealed to her "official" boyfriend by the latter's parrot, who has observed (and perfectly imitates) the live-in girlfriend's amorous encounters while the boyfriend is not at home. The outraged "cuckold" divests himself of both woman and parrot, leading the offending ex-girlfriend to say (as quoted in a London newspaper), "I'm surprised to hear he's got rid of that bloody bird. He spent more time talking to it than he did to me." No comment from the parrot.

66. Cf. Raybin, "The Death of a Silent Woman," 21.

67. Economou, "Chaucer's Use of the Bird"; Raybin, "The Death of a Silent Woman," 23–25.

68. Of the crow, we're told, "And countrefete the speche of every man / He koude, whan he sholde tell a tale" (*CT* 9.134–35). As Axton notes ("Gower," 34), "The

syntax is ambiguous here. Who originates tales, a man or the crow? The crow is a mimic, but does he counterfeit the speech of a man-telling-a-tale or does he counterfeit the speech of the right sort of man when he (the crow) wants to tell a tale?" This insight is especially relevant to the climax of the tale, when the crow, apprising Phoebus of his cuckoldom, not only does so by imitating the voice of another bird, the cuckoo—famous in European folklore as an announcer to husbands of the bad news of their wives' adultery—or perhaps the voice of a man singing a song with a "cuckoo, cuckoo" refrain (cf. Askins, "The Historical Setting," 93–94), but also by lapsing into the Manciple's own nasty and cynical "tale-telling voice." (In none of the many versions of the story Chaucer could have known does the crow speak so harshly to his master.) Cf. Hazleton, "The Manciple's Tale," 27: the Manciple's "curious projection of himself into the role of the crow, to the point of identification, is worth noticing. . . . [T]here is more here than a vague resemblance between a plain-speaking narrator and a plain-speaking bird. The two use the same language."

69. Cf. Raybin, "The Death of a Silent Woman," 24–25: "Throughout his career, Chaucer uses women (and, curiously, birds too) as a principal vehicle for talking about such issues as free will, sinfulness, and determinism, often bringing patriarchal structures into question. . . . Phebus's wife . . . rebels against her jealous spouse, taking a lover apparently not for his superiority, for he has none . . . , but, as far as one can tell, for the sake of taking a lover—that is, for the freedom from enforced restraint obtainable only by this independent action."

70. Raybin, "The Death of a Silent Woman," 26–31.

REFERENCES

Chaucer

Legend of Good Women. Ed. Janet Cowen and George Kane. East Lansing, Mich.: Colleagues Press, 1995.
The Riverside Chaucer. 3rd ed. Gen. ed. Larry D. Benson. Boston: Houghton Mifflin, 1987.
Troilus and Criseyde. Ed. B. A. Windeatt. London: Longman's, 1984.

Other Primary Texts

Alan of Lille. *The Plaint of Nature*. Trans. James J. Sheridan. Toronto: Pontifical Institute of Mediaeval Studies, 1980.
Crow, Martin M., and Clair C. Olson, eds. *Chaucer Life Records*. Oxford: Clarendon, 1966.
Dante. *Purgatorio*. Trans. Charles Singleton. Princeton, N.J.: Princeton University Press, 1973.

Gower, John. *The Voice of One Crying* [*Vox clamantis*]. In *The Major Latin Works of John Gower*. Trans. Eric W. Stockton. Seattle: University of Washington Press, 1962.

Guillaume de Machaut. *The Judgment of the King of Bohemia*. Ed. and trans. R Barton Palmer. New York: Garland, 1984.

——. *The Judgment of the King of Navarre*. Ed. and trans. R. Barton Palmer. New York: Garland, 1988.

Ovid. *Metamorphoses*. 2 Vols. With a translation by Frank Justus Miller. Loeb Classical Library. Cambridge, Mass.: Harvard University Press, 1971; London: William Heinemann, 1971.

——. *Metamorphoses*. Trans. Rolfe Humphries. 1955. Repr., Bloomington: Indiana University Press, 1974.

Pearsall, Derek, ed. *The Floure and the Leafe and The Assembly of Ladies*. London: Thomas Nelson, 1962.

Vergil. *Aeneid*. Trans. Allen Mandelbaum. New York: Bantam, 1972.

——. *Works*. Rev. ed. 2 Vols. With a translation by H. Rushton Fairclough. Loeb Classical Library. Cambridge, Mass.: Harvard University Press, 1934; London: William Heinemann, 1934.

Secondary Sources

Archibald, Elizabeth. "The Flight from Incest: Two Classical Precursors of the Constance Theme." *Chaucer Review* 20, no. 4 (1986): 259–72.

Askins, William. "All That Glitters: The Historical Context of The Tale of Sir Thopas." In *Reading Medieval Culture: Essays in Honor of Robert W. Hanning*, ed. Robert M. Stein and Sandra Pierson Prior, 271–89. Notre Dame, Ind.: Notre Dame University Press, 2005.

——. "The Historical Setting of The Manciple's Tale." *Studies in the Age of Chaucer* 7 (1985): 87–105.

Axton, Richard. "Gower—Chaucer's Heir?" In *Chaucer Traditions: Studies in Honour of Derek Brewer*, ed. Ruth Morse and Barry Windeatt, 21–38. Cambridge: Cambridge University Press, 1990.

Bezella-Bond, Karen. "Florescence and Defloration: Maytime in Chaucer and Malory." Ph.D. diss., Columbia University. Ann Arbor, Mich.: University Microfilms, 2003.

Braswell, Mary Flowers. "Chaucer's Court Baron: Law and The Canterbury Tales." *Studies in the Age of Chaucer* 16 (1994): 29–44.

Burnley, J. D. *Chaucer's Language and the Philosophers' Tradition*. Cambridge: D. S. Brewer, 1979.

Cannon, Christopher. "The Lives of Geoffrey Chaucer." In *The Yale Companion to Chaucer*, ed. Seth Lerer, 31–54. New Haven, Conn.: Yale University Press, 2006.

Carlson, Paula. "Alceste and Chaucer's View of Poetry in the *Legend of Good Women*." *Mediaevalia* 11 (1985): 139–50.

Comparetti, Domenico. *Vergil in the Middle Ages*. 1885. Trans. E. F. M. Benecke, intro. Jan M. Ziolkowski. Princeton, N.J.: Princeton University Press, 1997.

Cooper, Helen. "Chaucer and Ovid: A Question of Authority." In *Ovid Renewed: Ovidian Influences on Literature from the Middle Ages to the Twentieth Century*, ed. Charles Martindale, 71–81. Cambridge: Cambridge University Press, 1988.

——. *Oxford Guides to Chaucer. The Canterbury Tales*. 2nd ed. Oxford: Oxford University Press, 1996.

Crane, Susan. "The Writing Lesson of 1381." In *Chaucer's England*, ed. Barbara Hanawalt, ed., 201–21. Minneapolis: University of Minnesota Press, 1992.

Dane, Joseph. *Who Is Buried in Chaucer's Tomb? Studies in the Reception of Chaucer's Book*. East Lansing: Michigan State University Press, 1998.

Delany, Sheila. *The Naked Text: Chaucer's 'Legend of Good Women.'* Berkeley: University of California Press, 1994.

Donaldson, E. Talbot. "Chaucer the Pilgrim." *PMLA* 69 (1954): 928–36.

Dyas, Dee. *Pilgrimage in Medieval English Literature, 700–1500*. Cambridge: D. S. Brewer, 2001.

Economou, George D. "Chaucer's Use of the Bird in the Cage Image in the *Canterbury Tales*." *Philological Quarterly* 54 (1975): 679–84.

——. *The Goddess Natura in Medieval Literature*. Cambridge, Mass: Harvard University Press, 1972. Repr., Notre Dame, Ind.: Notre Dame University Press, 2002.

Ferster, Judith. *Fictions of Advice: The Literature and Politics of Counsel in Late Medieval England*. Philadelphia: University of Pennsylvania Press, 1996.

Fisher, John Hurt. *The Importance of Chaucer*. Carbondale: Southern Illinois University Press, 1992.

Fowler, David C. *The Life and Times of John Trevisa, Medieval Scholar*. Seattle: University of Washington Press, 1995.

Fyler, John. *Chaucer and Ovid*. New Haven, Conn.: Yale University Press, 1979.

Ganim, John. *Chaucerian Theatricality*. Princeton, N.J.: Princeton University Press, 1990.

Goodman, Anthony, and James L. Gillespie. *Richard II: The Art of Kingship*. Oxford: Clarendon, 1999.

Hanning, Robert W. "'And countrefete the speche of every man / He koude, when he sholde telle a tale': Toward a Lapsarian Poetics for *CT*." Biennial Chaucer Lecture, presented at the New Chaucer Society Congress, Paris, 1998. *Studies in the Age of Chaucer* 21 (1999): 27–58.

——. "Chaucer's First Ovid: Metamorphosis and Poetic Tradition in *The Book of the Duchess* and *The House of Fame*." In *Chaucer and the Craft of Fiction*, ed. Leigh A. Arrathoon, 121–63. Rochester, Mich.: Solaris, 1986.

Hazleton, Richard. "The Manciple's Tale: Parody and Critique." *Journal of English and German Philology* 62 (1963): 1–31.

Hornsby, Joseph Allen. *Chaucer and the Law*. Norman, Okla.: Pilgrim Books, 1988.

Hudson, Anne. *The Premature Reformation: Wycliffite Texts and Lollard History*. Oxford: Clarendon, 1988.

Justice, Steven. *Writing and Rebellion: England in 1381*. Berkeley: University of California Press, 1994.

Kendall, Alan. *Medieval Pilgrims*. New York: G. P. Putnam, 1978.

Kerby-Fulton, Kathryn, and Steven Justice. "Langlandian Reading Circles and the Civil Service in London and Dublin, 1380–1427." *New Medieval Literatures* 1 (1997): 59–84.

Kiser, Lisa. *Telling Classical Tales: Chaucer and the Legend of Good Women*. Ithaca, N.Y.: Cornell University Press, 1983.

Lerer, Seth. *Chaucer and His Readers*. Princeton, N.J.: Princeton University Press, 1993.

——, ed. *The Yale Companion to Chaucer*. Hew Haven, Conn.: Yale University Press, 2006.

Lowes, John Livingstone. "The Prologue to the *Legend of Good Women* as Related to the French Marguerite Poems, and the Filostrato." *PMLA* 19 (1904): 593–683.

Miller, Jacqueline T. *Poetic License: Authority and Authorship in Medieval and Renaissance Contexts*. Oxford: Oxford University Press, 1986.

Minnis, A. J. *Medieval Theory of Authorship*. London: Scolar, 1984.

——. *Oxford Guides to Chaucer: The Shorter Poems*. Oxford: Clarendon, 1995.

Oruch, Jack B. "St. Valentine, Chaucer, and Spring in February." *Speculum* 56, no. 3 (1981): 534–65.

Pearsall, Derek. *The Life of Geoffrey Chaucer: A Critical Biography*. Oxford: Blackwell, 1992.

Prior, Sandra Pierson. "Parodying Typology and the Mystery Plays in the Miller's Tale." *Journal of Medieval and Renaissance Studies* 16, no. 1 (1986): 57–73.

Raybin, David. "The Death of a Silent Woman: Voice and Power in Chaucer's Manciple's Tale." *Journal of English and German Philology* 95, no. 1 (1996): 19–37.

Saul, Nigel. *Richard II*. New Haven, Conn.: Yale University Press, 1997.

Scanlon, Larry. "The King's Two Voices: Narrative and Power in Hoccleve's *Regement of Princes*." In *Literary Practice and Social Change in Britain, 1380–1530*, ed. Lee Patterson, 216–47. Berkeley: University of California Press, 1990.

Shoaf, R. A. "'Unwemmed Custance': Circulation, Property, and Incest in The Man of Law's Tale." *Exemplaria* 2, no. 1 (1990): 287–302.

Simpson, James. "Ethics and Interpretation: Reading Wills in Chaucer's *Legend of Good Women*." *Studies in the Age of Chaucer* 20 (1998): 73–100.

Staley, Lynn. "Gower, Richard II, Henry of Derby, and the Business of Making Culture." *Speculum* 75, no. 1 (2000): 68–96.

Stein, Robert M., and Sandra Pierson Prior, eds. *Reading Medieval Culture: Essays in Honor of Robert W. Hanning.* Notre Dame, Ind.: Notre Dame University Press, 2005.

Strohm, Paul. *Hochon's Arrow: The Social Imagination of Fourteenth-Century Texts.* Princeton, N.J.: Princeton University Press, 1992.

Sumption, Jonathan. *Pilgrimage: An Image of Mediaeval Religion.* London: Faber, 1975.

Tavris, Carol, and Elliot Aronson. *Mistakes Were Made (But Not by Me).* New York: Harcourt, 2007.

Travis, Peter. "Chaucer's Heliotropes and the Poetics of Metaphor." *Speculum* 72, no. 2 (1997): 399–427.

Waldron, R. A. "Trevisa's Original Prefaces on Translation: A Critical Edition." In *Medieval English Studies Presented to George Kane,* by E. D. Kennedy, R. A. Waldron, and J. S. Wittig, 285–99. Woodbridge, Suffolk: Boydell and Brewer, 1988.

Wallace, David. *Chaucerian Polity: Absolutist Lineages and Associational Forms in England and Italy.* Stanford, Calif.: Stanford University Press, 1997.

Watson, Nicholas. "Censorship and Cultural Change in Late Medieval England: Vernacular Theology, the Oxford Translation Debate, and Arundel's Constitution of 1409." *Speculum* 70, no. 4 (1995): 822–64.

Wetherbee, Winthrop. *Platonism and Poetry in the Twelfth Century: The Literary Influence of the School of Chartres.* Princeton, N.J.: Princeton University Press, 1972.

Wheatley, Edward. "The Manciple's Tale." In *Sources and Analogues of the Canterbury Tales,* ed. Robert M. Correale and Mary Hamel, 2:749–73. Cambridge: D. S. Brewer, 2005.

Williams, Deanne. "The Dream Visions." In *The Yale Companion to Chaucer,* ed. Seth Lerer, 147–78. New Haven, Conn.: Yale University Press, 2006.

Wimsatt, James L. *The Marguerite Poetry of Guillaume de Machaut.* Chapel Hill: University of North Carolina Press, 1970.

③

ARIOSTO'S *ORLANDO FURIOSO*:

CONFUSION MULTIPLY CONFOUNDED

OR, ASTRAY IN THE FOREST OF DESIRE

Come raccende il gusto il mutar esca,
così mi par che la mia istoria, quanto
or qua or là più varïata sia,
meno a chi l'udirà noiosa ha.
Di molte fila esser bisogno parme
A condur la gran tela ch'io lavoro.

(As varying the dishes quickens the appetite, so it is with my story; the more
varied it is, the less likely it is to bore my listeners. To complete the great
tapestry on which I am working I feel the need for a great variety of strands.)
—*Orlando Furioso*, 13.80.5–81.2 (W 136)

Quasi par un sogno a chi vi pensa.

(The whole thing seemed like a dream, if you thought about it.)
—*Orlando Furioso*, 15.78.5 (W 162)

—Signor mio,
ognun che vive al mondo pecca et erra . . .

(My lord, everyone who lives on earth sins and errs . . .)
—*Orlando Furioso*, 24.30.2–3 (W 286)

I n the second elegy of book 1 of Ovid's *Amores*, the narrator conjures up an imagined procession celebrating the god of love's triumph over his and many another heart. (Ovid's point of reference is the grand processional reentry into Rome of a victorious general, his army, and the captives [with their arms and standards] he has taken in battle.) Warming to his task, the newly vanquished lover-poet elaborates his allegory:

> Ducentur capti iuvenes captaeque puellae;
>   haec tibi magnificus pompa triumphus erit.
> Ipse ego, praeda recens, factum modo vulnus habebo
>   et nova captiva vincula mente feram.
> Mens Bona ducetur manibus post terga retortis,
>   et Pudor, et castris quidquid Amoris obest.
> Omnia te metuent: ad te sua bracchia tendens
>   vulgus "io" magna voce "triumphe!" canet.
> Blanditiae comites tibi erunt Errorque Furorque,
>   adsidue partes turba secuta tuas.

(The young men and women you've taken in battle will be herded along, and this show of force will be a great triumph for you. I'll be there myself, a recent victim with my wounds exposed, weighed down by the new chains around my captive heart. Peace of Mind will be led with hands tied behind her back, and Shame, and whoever else has tried to resist Love's siege. Everyone is terrified of you; the crowd, arms outstretched in fealty, chants, "Cupid Rules!" with one, great voice. Flatteries will be your companions, as will Error and Madness, permanent members of your mob of lackeys.)   (1.2.27–36)

The last two lines of this comic tableau, describing Cupid/Amor's entourage, and the contention that immediately follows: "his tu militibus superas hominesque deosque [with these troops you conquer men and gods]" (1.2.37) seem to me the conceptual if not actual point of origin for *Orlando Furioso* (OF), or *Roland Gone Mad*, by the confessed Ovidian Ludovico Ariosto—at 39,000 lines the longest, and arguably the greatest, monument of European comic poetry. To a great extent *error*—errancy, in its double but interanimating meanings of wandering and mistakenness—and *furor*—the abandonment of rationality that, in extreme cases, can lead to violent anger and even more destructive madness—generate the serious but uproarious comedy of the *Furioso*.

The comic force of the poem also derives from its polyphony (to borrow a term from the sister art of music), a rumbustious concert of narratorial and protagonistic voices, verging frequently on cacophony, that, at its outer limit, anticipates the brilliantly designated (and enacted) *quadro di stupefazione* brought to musical perfection in the comic operas of Ariosto's spiritual descendant, Gioacchino Rossini.

One of the major constituents of Ariostan polyphony is the expression of desire, and (as my putative Ovidian inspiration for the *Furioso* suggests) the driving force behind the poem's heavy investment in *error* and *furor* is desire in action, primarily erotic in nature, but also directed at a variety of other animate and inanimate objects: horses, swords, shields, suits of armor, even armorial bearings.[1] Indeed, in a poem whose broadest narrative scope is the furious (and, yes, error-prone) clash between Christian and Saracen civilizations, desire even becomes a function of ideology or belief and seeks nothing less than the annihilation of one's enemies, individual and collective.

Since desire is shown repeatedly, throughout the *Furioso*, to subvert rational deliberation and thus lead to behavior that is imprudent, self-defeating, and heedless of obligations other than its satisfaction, it also proves toxic to the exercise of authority. In general, authority, whether political or poetic, sustains hard knocks throughout the poem—this despite (or perhaps because of?) Ariosto's deep and constantly exhibited indebtedness to a wide range of classical and medieval authors, texts, and genres, on the one hand,[2] and, on the other, his nearly lifelong status as a courtier and retainer of one of late-Renaissance northern Italy's most celebrated (and most despotic) princely lineages.

In keeping with the major concern of these chapters, my attention to the *Orlando Furioso* will concentrate on those of the *molte fila* of its *gran tela* that represent the crises of desire and authority as they sow frustration, confusion, grief, and loss of control—even to the point of madness—among its myriad population of chivalric (and not so chivalric) knights, beautiful women (some of whom are themselves formidable warriors), magicians with powers of prophecy and illusion who compete to influence human events and fates, and monarchs whose high purposes are all too often brought low. This seriocomic pageant of the human condition plays out against two backdrops to which I will also (though only sketchily) allude. One is the horrendous condition of the Italian peninsula, which, beginning in 1494, had to suffer the destruction and brutality that accompanied successive invasions by the armies of European princes, as well as mutual animosity and score settling among the major indigenous powers such as the papacy, the Venetian republic, the dukes of Milan, and even the despotic dynasties of smaller city-states such as Ariosto's natal Ferrara. The other is the excitement and challenge of travel in an age of European exploration and discovery, which Ariosto, though no great traveler himself, followed keenly via a new generation of maps and travelers' accounts.[3]

I confess that my attempt, within the brief compass of a chapter, at a general appreciation of OF represents a triumph of delight and desire over intimidation and good sense. Since good sense—or prudence, the ability to make good choices in complicated situations—is precisely what most inhabitants of the *Furioso*'s comic universe lack, perhaps my attraction to this self-appointed task derives from seeing aspects of my life—and that of most people I know— reflected in the comic mirror that Ariosto holds up to his own troubled times. Indeed, the three major plots and a great many subordinate ones of the *Furioso* interrupt and intertwine with one another in such a way as to reduce the poem's readers (by authorial design, I'm convinced) to a state of confusion and lost direction quite similar to that in which its characters repeatedly find themselves within the ubiquitous forest of adventures. The resulting metaphoric equivalence between forest and book makes the experience of reading the *Furioso* a humbling reminder, and microcosm, of our all too frequent experience of life's frustrations, not the least of which stem from our own dealings with desire and authority.

L udovico Ariosto was born in 1474, one of ten children of a minor nobleman and functionary of the Este dynasty, which had ruled a princedom in northern Italy since the thirteenth century, in and around the valley of the river Po and centered on the city of Ferrara. Ludovico spent most of his adult life in service to his generation's leading male members of the Este family: first Ippolito, cardinal of the Roman Church, then Alfonso, duke of Ferrara. While discharging his duties as envoy, messenger, provincial governor, and military leader—and spending much of his adult life composing the *Furioso*, seeing it through three separate editions (1516, 1521, and 1532), the last appearing less than a year before his death in 1533—Ariosto also took part in the court culture for which the Este rulers had for generations been famous throughout central and northern Italy, a brilliant synthesis of two seemingly opposed cultural initiatives, both appropriated to the task of celebrating (that is, constructing) the magnificence and benevolence of the ruling family: "It was the Este who set the tone of Italian society in which the traditions of chivalry mingled with those of a free city, and public ceremonies were flavoured with classical culture."[4]

On the one hand, the Este rulers sponsored the educational and intellectual program of Renaissance humanism, dedicated to assimilating the Mediterranean legacy of classical antiquity and featuring flourishing schools presided over by celebrated humanist scholars;[5] they commissioned paintings on classical themes such as Titian's famous *Bacchus and Ariadne* (now in the National Gallery, London); and they patronized comedies inspired by Plautus and Terence that Ariosto (who also composed satires on a Horatian model) wrote and produced. On the other hand, the nostalgic (read: obsolete) ideals and colorful rituals of medieval chivalry, imported for the most part from France, undergirded their anachronistic spectacles such as jousts and tournaments, for espousal of a chivalric code by the despots of northern Italy, and especially the Este lords, spread a colorful gloss of dedication to noble ideals over their violent careers and extortionate rule.

It may seem strange to us that despotic princes who made a living as mercenary captains (and whose promotion of a sanitized culture of warrior virtues does not, alas, surprise) should have patronized renowned scholars and their schools; in fact, at that moment in peninsular history the enjoyment and encouragement of learning was considered a mark of princely virtue and magnificence. Baldesar Castiglione's *Book of the Courtier* (published 1528, but circulating in various drafts at least ten years earlier), the best guide to the complexities of high Renaissance court life and, along with *Orlando Furioso*, the summit of the age's literary endeavors, relates that Federigo di Montefeltro, lord of Urbino and, like Alfonso d'Este, a man who fought for a living as well as to preserve his rule, built a beautiful castle in Urbino and filled it with precious and wonderful paintings, sculptures, and furnishings. But his greatest treasures were the books, written in Greek, Latin, and Hebrew and bound in bejeweled covers, with which he filled his library.[6] The conspicuous consumption of rare and precious items, many imported at great cost from the East, was already a feature of noble self-definition in high-medieval Europe, but the inclusion of books in that self-definition was something new, and the humanists had a great deal to do with it.

In its version of the comic mirror, *OF* reflects the *discordia concors* of the Este synthesis of humanism and chivalry by its own synthesis of episodes and motifs borrowed (and suitably revised) from the literature of classical antiquity, especially Ovid but also Vergil and others, including Seneca, whose *Hercules furens* provided Ariosto with crucial inspiration; from Dante's *Commedia*, Petrarch's lyrics, and the *novelle* of Boccaccio's *Decameron*; and from the medieval narrative traditions of Charlemagne, Arthur, and their knights, as mediated by the popular art (pulp fiction *avant la lettre*) of the *cantastoria* (storytellers who performed in the *piazze* of Italian towns and cities) and its adaptations in the learned poetry of Luigi Pulci's *Morgante*, written in Lorenzo de' Medici's Florence, and, above all, the *Orlando Innamorato* (*OI*; 1482–1494), by Matteo Maria Boiardo, lord of Scandiano, Ariosto's predecessor at the Este court. To this epic-romance of Orlando in love (left incomplete at the author's death), the *Furioso* is ostensibly a continuation (though actually a reimagining).[7] By adding to this hybrid inheritance the narratorial personae of frustrated lover and obsequious Este courtier and a host of new themes clothed in fantastic, often hilarious episodes, Ariosto attained a summit of creativity rarely matched in European literary history.

OF's tongue-in-cheek commentary on the Este cult of chivalry recognizes the persistent if delusory appeal of a code of courtesy and loyalty to those caught up in the morass of ruthlessness and betrayal that characterized the age's peninsular politics, even as it uses supposedly chivalric adventures to challenge comfortable assumptions about the boundaries between truth and fiction, reality and illusion, sanity and madness, and to raise troubling questions about the extent to which human beings can resist temptation, make rational decisions in the face of raging passions, and exercise authority over self or others in such a world.

A s we've seen, Ovid's strategy for developing a comic perspective on desire and authority involves what we might call *serial impersonation*: a poet-lover in the *Amores*, a lover turned expert on seduction techniques in the *Ars amatoria*. Ariosto opts instead for *narratorial polyphony*, featuring the successive entrance, in the opening octaves of *OF*, of three main narrative voices—the chronicler, the lover, and the courtier—that describe and respond to the poem's three major (and ultimately thoroughly intertwined) spheres of activity, respectively: martial, amorous, and dynastic.

First comes the chronicler, whose opening words assume responsibility for the elements of the *Furioso* derived from two divergent European traditions of warrior narrative, both originally Francophone: the chivalric romance and the feudal epic, also called the *chanson de geste*.

Le donne, i cavallier, l'arme, gli amori,
le cortesie, l'audaci imprese io canto,
che furo al tempo che passaro i Mori
d'Africa il mare, e in Francia nocquer tanto

seguendo l'ire e i giovenil furori
d'Agramante lor re, che si diè vanto
di vendicar la morte di Troiano
sopra re Carlo imperator romano.

(I sing of knights and ladies, of love and arms, of courtly chivalry, of courageous deeds—all from the time when the Moors crossed the sea from Africa and wrought havoc in France. I shall tell of the anger, the fiery rage of young Agramant their king, whose boast it was that he would avenge himself on Charles, Emperor of Rome, for King Trojan's death.)

(*OF* 1.1.1–8; W 1)

Balancing the initial roll call of archetypal romance protagonists and activities—"le donne, i cavalier, l'arme, gli amori, / le cortesie, l'audaci imprese"—is a prospectus analogously peculiar to epic: the fateful clash of two inimical civilizations originating in personal animosity (compare the rape of Helen, traditional cause of the Trojan War), as a Moorish army invades Europe from Africa, spurred on by the youthful rage of a young king seeking vengeance for the death of his father, Troiano (note the name), upon "re Carlo, imperator romano"—the Holy Roman Emperor Charlemagne, military and political head of Christendom. This Christian-Saracen confrontation constitutes the first, overarching plot of the *Furioso*, which eventually takes the quintessential epic form of a besieged city—in this case, Paris—in the process generating some of the most violent battle scenes in all European literature.

Octave 2 of the *Furioso* introduces the lover, who announces the narrative crisis that gives the poem its name: Orlando (Charlemagne's greatest warrior, the hero of the French national epic, *La Chanson de Roland*) driven mad by love, despite being reputed so rational, "si saggio":

Dirò d'Orlando in un medesmo tratto
cosa non detta in prosa mai né in rima:
che per amor venne in furore e matto,
d'uom che sì saggio era stimato prima.

(I shall tell of Orlando, too, setting down what has never before been recounted in prose or rhyme: of Orlando, driven raving mad by love—and he a man who had always been esteemed for his great prudence.)

(*OF* 1.2.1–4; W 1)

Besotted, like so many other male warriors in the *Furioso* (there are also two female ones), with the beautiful but unreceptive Angelica, princess of Cathay,[8] Orlando succumbs to violent madness—the product (as I'll suggest) of both frustrated desire and wounded honor—when he discovers that she has given herself (and her highly sought after virginity) to a young Moor, Medoro, vastly inferior to him in rank and accomplishment. This occurs at the exact midpoint of the poem, and only much later is he rescued from his existence as a naked and aggressive wild man by Astolfo, a travel-loving English lord who accidentally discovers Orlando's wits on the moon, lying in a vast junk heap of everything people have lost on earth through inadvertence or bad judgment, when he flies there on the back of a hippogryph—half horse, half gryphon—escorted by no less than St. John the Evangelist.[9]

In parallel with Orlando's crisis of desire comes the narrator's admission that he is in grave danger of suffering the same fate as his hero and will only be able to complete his chosen task if the hard-hearted woman who has, bit by bit ("ad or ad or"), robbed him of most of his sanity leaves him enough of it to do so:[10]

> Se da colei che tal quasi m'ha fatto,
> che 'l poco ingegno ad or ad or mi lima,
> me ne sarà però tanto concesso,
> che mi basti a finir quanto ho promesso.

(If she, who has reduced me almost to a like condition, and even now is eroding my last fragments of sanity, leaves me yet with sufficient to complete what I have undertaken.)   (*OF* 1.2.5–8; W 1)

The next two octaves accomplish yet another narratorial metamorphosis, this time into the voice and persona of the courtier, more precisely the deferential court poet, adept at the discourse of flattery and sly self-promotion appropriate for addressing a powerful patron, in this case Cardinal Ippolito d'Este:

> Piacciavi, generosa Erculea prole,
> ornamento e splendor del secol nostro,
> Ippolito, aggradir questo che vuole
> e darvi sol può l'umil servo vostro.

(Seed of Ercole, adornment and splendour of our age, Hippolytus, great of heart, may it please you to accept this which your lowly servant would, and alone is able to, give you.)   (*OF* 1.3.1–4; W 1)

This is the voice that, by means of Merlinic prophecies and elaborate ec-phrases of paintings and tapestries scattered through the next forty-six can-tos, glorifies the Este dynasty, from its legendary origin in the union of Rug-giero with Bradamante—sister of the great Christian warrior Rinaldo (another recruit from the French *chanson de geste*) and in her own right a su-perb knight-errant—to its contemporary exemplars, Cardinal Ippolito and Duke Alfonso. (Despite the narrator's parenthetical, self-serving assertion that he alone—"sol può l'umil servo vostro"—is capable of sounding this strain, such dynastic myths were an established subgenre of medieval histori-ography, here grafted by Ariosto onto the rhetoric of prince pleasing brought to a gleaming polish by humanists seeking places or rewards at the courts of popes, princes, and other high-Renaissance despots.)

It's worth noting two suggestive parallels drawn within these first four oc-taves, providing a note of cohesion to balance their narratorial variety. The first is between Agramante and Orlando, both possessed by *furore*, a word signifying extreme anger as well as downright madness. In stanza 1, Agramante's "ire e . . . giovenil furori" over the death of his father (killed by Orlando, in fact, in an ear-lier Italian epic-romance hybrid) is echoed in stanza 2 by Orlando, "che per amor venne in furore e matto," who goes mad for love. From the beginning, then, we are presented with powerful examples of rationality overcome by irresistible pas-sion, examples that suggest, via the word "*furore*," a common denominator of lost self-control even for human activities ostensibly as opposed in their nature as love and war.[11]

The second case of parallelism involves the narrator's subordinate status with relation first to his unnamed lady love (the "colei" of *OF* 1.2.5) and then to his pa-tron. Before each of these he stands as a suppliant with the fate of his poem at issue. The beloved, over whom he has already lost most of his wits, must allow him to hold onto what's left—presumably by offering him at least some show of pity, if not real sexual favors—if he is to accomplish what he has promised to do. And the cardinal, to whom he proposes to offer whatever writing he can to re-pay an unnamed (and presumably metaphorical) debt—"Quel ch'io vi debbo, posso di parole / pagare in parte, e d'opera d'inchiostro . . . quanto io posso dar, tutto vi dono [My debt to you I can repay in part with words, with an outlay of ink . . . for all I have to give, I give you]" (*OF* 1.3.5–8; W 1))—must be willing to put aside weightier thoughts—"vostri alti pensier cedino un puo" (*OF* 1.4.7)—to hear about Ruggiero, his putative progenitor, if all the narrator/poet's efforts are not to be rendered nugatory. By means of this parallelism, Ariosto suggests that real patronage is like poetry's unrequited love affair: both threaten autonomy and creativity.

Although the opening *ottava* of the *Furioso* states the major theme of the poem to be the struggle between Agramante and Charlemagne, the primacy given the poem's martial voice turns out to be something of a red herring. To be sure, that voice commandeers parts of *ottave* 5 and 6 to set the scene of epic confrontation with apposite bellicosity:

> sotto I gran monti Pirenei
> con la gente di Francia e de Lamagna
> re Carlo era attendato alla campagna,
>
> per far al re Marsilio e al re Agramante
> battersi ancor del folle ardir la guancia,
> d'aver condotto, l'un, d'Africa quante
> genti erano atte a portar spada e lancia;
> l'altro, d'aver spinta la Spagna inante
> a destruzion del bel regno di Francia.

(At the foot of the lofty Pyrenees, King Charlemagne and the hosts of France and Germany were assembled in their tented camp to force Kings Agramant and Marsilius once more to lament their rash stupidity—the one for leading from Africa as many men as could bear lance and sword; the other for inciting Spain to visit destruction upon the lovely realm of France.)   (OF 1.5.6–6.6; W 1)

But after this hyperbolic build-up, the two-line account of the battle is as anticlimactic as its outcome is disastrous: "Contrari ai voti poi furo I successi; / ch'in fuga andò la gente battezzata [The outcome, however, was not in keeping with their prayers: the ranks of the baptized were put to flight]" (OF 1.9.5–6; W 2). And then, except for a few brief mentions (see OF 2.24.6–2.26.2, 8.69–70), the warfare that will presumably decide the future of Christian Europe remains entirely out of view until the very end of canto 13. In its place, the *Furioso* offers its readers a tour of a different world, where Desire, attended, as in Ovid, by *error* and *furor*—and also by illusion—reigns supreme.[12]

The hegemony of desire over epic norms across great stretches of the Ariostan landscape receives emphatic confirmation at an emblematic moment in canto 2, when Bradamante, en route to rescue Ruggiero from his imprisonment in a sorcerer's mountaintop castle, is overtaken by a messenger from Marseilles—a city she had received (with surrounding lands) as a gift from Charlemagne—who pleads with her to return and protect it from disastrous Saracen invasion. There follows a brief but decisive inner debate, in which the imperatives of eros rout those of civic (and martial) obligation:

> Tra sì e no la giovane suspesa,
> di voler ritornar dubita un poco;
> quinci l'onore e il debito le pesa,
> quindi l'incalza l'amoroso foco.
> Fermasi al fin di seguitar l'impresa,
> e trar Ruggier de l'incantato loco;
> e quando sua virtù non possa tanto,
> almen restargli prigioneiera a canto.

> E fece iscusa tal, che quel messaggio
> parve contento rimanere e cheto.
> Indi girò la briglia al suo viaggio.

(Bradamant was in two minds whether to return or not; she was pulled one way by her sense of honour and duty, and the other by the promptings of love's passion. Finally she decided to pursue what she had undertaken and deliver Ruggiero from the enchanted castle; should this prove beyond her powers, at least she would remain a prisoner in his company. She made her excuse to such effect that the messenger seemed satisfied with it and remained silent. Then she turned her horse's head toward her journey.)   (OF 2.65, 66.1–3; W 19)

Nor is Bradamante alone in putting personal desire ahead of all other claims: Charles's two greatest paladins, Orlando and Rinaldo, betray their loyalty to the emperor by leaving him in order to pursue their quests for the same erotic prize. Orlando, stationed with Charles's army at Paris, dreams that Angelica is calling out to him for help. (She is, in fact, in dire straits at that point, tied naked to a rock on the island of Ebuda, about to be sacrificed to the Orca, a voracious sea monster.) Leaping out of bed and arming himself rapidly,

> Da mezza notte tacito si parte,
> e non saluta e non fa motto al zio [i.e., Charles];
> . . . .
> Con suo gran dispiacer s'avede Carlo
> che partito la notte è 'l suo nipote,

quando esser dovea seco e più aiutarlo;
e ritenir la còlera non puote.

(He stole off in the depth of night, greeting nobody and leaving no word
for his uncle. . . . Charles was profoundly displeased to discover that his
nephew had made off in the night, when he was most bound to stay with
him and lend his assistance. He could not restrain his anger.)

(OF 8.86.1–2, 8.87.1–4; W 80)

Similarly—and many, many adventures later—Rinaldo, when he learns
from his cousin, the sorcerer Malagigi, that Angelica has given herself to "un
vilissimo barbaro," is driven by jealousy to seek her out. He at least asks leave
from Charles but lies to the emperor that it is to seek his horse, stolen by a
Saracen.

Lasciollo andar con sua licenzia Carlo,
ben che ne fu con tutta Francia mesto;
ma finalmente non seppe negarlo,
tanto gli parve il desiderio onesto.

(Charles gave him leave to go; he and all of France was sorry to do so, but
he could not deny what appeared so honourable a request.)

(OF 42.43.1–4; W 502)

Much, though by no means all, of desire's realm is represented as a dark
and confusing forest ("selva oscura" [OF 1.22.5]; cf. *Inferno* 1)—the single most
memorable feature of the *Furioso*—along the winding and intersecting trails
of which ("calli obliqui") knights both Christian and Saracen wander inces-
santly, in unsuccessful quest of the object of their desire—usually a woman;
most usually, Angelica. When they unexpectedly meet, they duel fiercely,
though rarely conclusively, since one or both are called away, in medias res, by
yet another adventure that crosses their path or appears, mirage-like, in the
distance, thanks to the activities of the poem's large supporting cast of magicians and sorcerers.[13]

The spatial indecipherability of the forest asserts itself early in canto 1, when
Ferraù, one of Angelica's many Saracen pursuers, and Rinaldo, who, though
married, also lusts after the elusive beauty, come upon her and each other there.
During the resultant battle, their mutual prey, instead of waiting to be ravished
by the winner, escapes; breaking off, the two knights ride after her (sharing the

same horse, in comic contrast to their bellicose unwillingness to share a "ride" on Angelica).

> Da quattro sproni il destrier punto arriva
> ove una strada in due si dipartiva.
>
> E come quei che non sapean se l'una
> o l'altra via facesse la donzella . . .
> si messero ad arbitrio di fortuna,
> Rinaldo a questo, il Saracino a quella.
> Pel bosco Ferraù molto s'avvolse,
> e ritrovossi al fine onde si tolse.

(Goaded by four spurs, the charger came to a fork where the road divided. Here, not knowing which path the damsel had taken . . . they put themselves in Fortune's hands; Rinaldo took the one path, the Saracen the other. Ferraù thrust further and further through the wood, and in the end found himself at the place whence he had started.)

(OF 1.22.7–8, 23.1–2, 5–8; W 3)

In an even more egregious example at the end of canto 22, Bradamante leaves Ruggiero (with whom she has been reunited after searching for him since their brief meeting in canto 6) in order avenge herself on her arch-enemy, Pinabello, whose treachery in canto 2 almost led to her death. After killing the miscreant,

> Vòlse tornar dove lasciato avea
> Ruggier; né seppe mai trovar la strada.
> Or per valle or per monte s'avvolgea: . . . .
> Non vòlse mai la sua fortuna rea,
> che via trovasse onde a Ruggier si vada . . . .
>
> Ma non lo consentì sua dura sorte,
> che la fe' travïar per un sentiero
> che la portò dov'era spesso e forte,
> dove più strano e più solingo il bosco.

(She meant to return to where she had left Ruggiero, but she could not find her way. Over hill and dale she wandered . . . but her evil fortune never permitted her to find her way back to him. . . . she was destined to stray off down a path which took her into the thick of the forest, where it was at its most weird and lonely and intractable.)

(OF 22.98.1–3, 5–6, 23.5.4–7; W 266)

Meanwhile, another Christian knight, Zerbino, son of the king of Scotland, finds Pinabello's body and races off, following Bradamante's tracks, to confront his killer. But

poco dopo arrivò Zerbino, ch'avea
seguito invan di Bradamante i passi,
perché trovò il sentier che si torcea
In molti rami ch'ivano alti e bassi.

(he was back soon afterwards, having followed Bradamante's tracks in vain: the path, he found, twisted away into several offshoots, leading *upwards or down*.)   (OF 23.43.1–4; W 271, emphasis added)

As for Bradamante,

Di Vallombrosa pensò far la strada,
che trovar quivi il suo Ruggier ha speme;
ma qual più breve o qual miglior vi vada,
poco discerne, e d'ire *errando* teme.
Il villan non avea de la contrada
pratica molta; et *erreranno* insieme.
Pur andare a ventura ella si messe,
dove pensò che 'l loco esser dovesse.

Di qua di là si volse, né persona
incontrò mai da domandar la via.

(She decided to make for Vallombrosa, hoping to find her Ruggiero there; but she could not tell which was the best or the quickest way, and feared she might go astray—neither was the peasant [who is guiding her] all that familiar with the area, so they were sure to lose their way together. However, she set off at a venture, aiming at where she thought the monastery should be. She turned *this way and that* without meeting a soul to ask the way.)

(OF 23.19–20.2, emphasis added; W 268, emphasis added)

And after more travels, she finds her way out of the woods and sees a castle nearby—which turns out to be her home, Montalbano, so that in effect, like Ferraù in canto I, she has made a large circle and returned to where she started (OF 27.113–15).[14]

Grasped simply as a physical, spatial phenomenon, the movement of the *Furioso*'s chivalric exemplars through the dark and confusing forest anticipates the behavior and trajectories of children in bumper cars at an amusement park. At a deeper level, however, Ariosto has reimagined this central feature of medieval chivalric romance—the forest of adventures—by assimilating it, with parodic intent, to the symbolic landscape that begins Dante's *Commedia*, where the narrator finds himself "in una selva oscura, / che la diritta via era smarrita [in a dark wood where the straight path was obscured]" (*Inferno* 1.2–3). In OF there is no Beatrice, no Vergil, no guide back, even via a difficult journey through hell and purgatory, to the grace of Paradise. Instead, there is only a wilderness of randomness—this is Fortune's realm—and circularity, in which the bafflement of lost direction not only *brings about* the frustration of desire, as its objects elude discovery (Ruggiero) or capture (Angelica), but also *represents* it.[15]

This symbolic nature of the Ariostan forest, and its centrality to the poem's often wildly comic but also profoundly serious commentary on the crises born of humanity's subjection to desire,[16] is established through several complementary poetic strategies, of which the first, and most widely diffused throughout the *Furioso*, is a specific vocabulary of *wandering* that records the forest's negative impact on the attempts by Ferraù, Rinaldo, Bradamante, and Zerbino—already noted—and many others to make orderly progress through it toward the objects of their desires. The centerpiece of this vocabulary is the verb *errare*, to wander. Its centrality is supported, as Donald Carne-Ross famously noted years ago, by idiomatic phrases that ring the changes on random, undirected, and hence often frustrated motion: knights seeking one another or the women they desire or places where they might find them are said to move *di qua, di là; di su, di giù; in basso e in alto; l'una o l'altra; a questa o a quella*; and so on.[17] For example, when Orlando sneaks off from Charles's camp, and war, to seek Angelica, we're told, "Or questo, e quando quel luogo cercando / va, per trovar de la sua donna l'orma [Hither and thither he moved, intent on picking up traces of his lady]" (OF 9.4.3–4; W 81); again, seeking a boat to take him across a river, "con gli occhi cerca or questo lato o quello [with his eyes he searches now this shore, now that]" (OF 9.9.1; W 82, translation modified).

At one level of signification, the *Furioso*'s emphasis on wandering, or *errancy*, constitutes Ariosto's ironic reconception of the knight-errant of medieval French chivalric romance, who moved through the forest seeking adventures whereby to

burnish his reputation or right wrongs. By making the quest to find and possess
Angelica or another woman or an object in the possession of another (who often
has as much right to it as the seeker's) the main occasions for traversing the forest, and by rendering such occasions exercises in futility and frustration, the *Furioso* strips chivalry of those idealizing garments in which Ariosto's Este patrons
clothed their courtly pageants and military campaigns. In the third and last edition of the poem, irony at the expense of Este chivalry becomes even more
pointed in an episode in canto II that suggests the hypocrisy involved in being a
gun-toting, as opposed to sword-wielding, *cavaliere*. Orlando, as always seeking
Angelica *di qua, di là*, is distracted by the pleas of Olimpia, countess of Holland,
to rescue her fiancé from the clutches of a tyrant, Cimosco, who gains unfair advantage over his enemies by means of a new machine, called an *arcibuggio* (har-
quebus), that uses gunpowder to fire metal balls that kill and maim from a distance: as we would say, a gun. Orlando manages to kill him, using only the
weapons of chivalry, and has the diabolical engine taken out to sea and deep-
sixed, from which resting place, however, a sorcerer, guided by the devil, recovers
it. Now, the narrator laments, guns are everywhere in use:

> Come trovasti, o scelerata e brutta
> invenzion, mai loco in uman core?
> Per te la militar gloria è distrutta,
> per te il mestier de l'arme è senza onore;
> per te è il valore e la virtù ridutta,
> che spesso par del buono il rio migliore.

> (Wicked, ugly invention, how did you find a place in human hearts? You
> have destroyed military glory, and dishonoured the profession of arms;
> valour and martial skill are now discredited, so that often the miscreant
> will appear a better man than the valiant.)   (*OF* 11.26.1–6; W 109)

What gives bite to this parable decrying the *technological* progress that had
rendered chivalric notions of battle obsolete is the fact that Alfonso d'Este,
duke of Ferrara, was particularly famous for his expertise in the science of artil-
lery, honed in mercenary service to several larger powers during the prolonged
Italian warfare elsewhere bemoaned by Ariosto.[18] Titian painted a portrait of
Alfonso that shows the Duke more or less fondling one of his cannons, and at
OF 25.14 the narrator (in his courtier persona) praises him—and them—
referring (with an ironic distinction) to one piece of ordinance by its all too relevant name, "Gran diavol; non quel de lo 'nferno, / ma quel del mio signor [the

mighty Devil; not the one in hell—it's my Lord's Devil, I mean]" (*OF* 25.14.6–7; W 297).

Beyond serving as the vehicle for such deflation of chivalry, *errare* supplies Ariosto with a quibble crucial to his larger purposes thanks to its other, judgmental (as opposed to descriptive) meaning: to go astray, to wander from the right path, not only physically (as Bradamante fears she will do) but morally and ethically.[19] The verb's appositeness in describing *errant judgment* implicates forest wanderings as the objective correlative in the *Furioso's* representation of a world lacking ethical direction and the constant victim of its own bad judgment—its penchant for making bad choices.[20] Such imprudent behavior, errant because driven by desire or other strong emotions instead of rational deliberation, leads to frustration and loss and, at its most extreme, to madness. To give but one example, the passage in canto 8 where Orlando decides to quit Charles's camp and war in order to search for Angelica makes the connection between spatial and mental/moral errancy clear by its use of what I'm calling the phraseology of wandering to describe the paladin's inner state:

La notte Orlando alle noiose piume
del veloce pensier fa parte assai.
Or quinci or quindi il volta, or lo rassume
tutto in un loco, e non l'afferma mai:
qual d'acqua chiara il tremolante lume,
dal sol percossa o da' notturni rai,
per gli ampli tetti va con lungo salto
a destra et a sinistra, e basso e alto. . . .

che dal pastor sperando essere udita,
si va lagnando *in questa parte e in quella.* . . .

Intanto l'infelice (e non sa come)
perde la donna sua per l'aer fosco;
onde *di qua e di là* del suo bel nome
fa risonare ogni campagna e bosco.

(That night, Orlando imparted his fleeting thoughts to his restless bed. This way and that he drove them, and herded them all together, but could never pen them in. They were like the tremulous gleam which a limpid pool gives off under the rays of the sun or moon—high and low, to right and left it fans out. . . . [He dreams of Angelica like a little lamb.]

Hither and yon she wanders bleating, and hopes that the shepherd will
hear her. . . . Meanwhile [, as he dreams,] the hapless lover somehow or
other loses his lady in the failing light, and searches here and there
through the woods and moors calling her name.) [21]

(OF 8.71, 76.5–6, 82.1–4, emphasis added; W 78–80)

Supporting OF's imposition of symbolic significance on the chivalric forest
of adventures is the poem's embrace of the labyrinth, an artifact borrowed from
classical antiquity, as both simile and metaphor.[22] A passage at the end of canto
18 enacts the simile: two young Moorish warriors, Cloridano and Medoro, devoted to each other and to their captain, Dardinello, whose dead body now lies
on the field of battle, are driven by desire to honor their fallen leader to seek
and bury the latter's corpse, even if the effort costs them their lives.[23] After
finding Dardinello's body, they are spotted by a Christian patrol, led by Zerbino, and flee into the forest (Medoro weighed down by the body as Cloridano
races ahead), which is described thus in the canto's last octave:

> Era a quel tempo ivi una selva antica,
> d'ombrose piante e di virgulti,
> che come *labirinto*, entro s'intrica
> di stretti calli e sol da bestie culti.

(In those days there was an ancient wood there, thickly planted with
shady trees and shrubs; it formed a labyrinth of narrow paths and was
frequented only by wild beasts.)

(OF 18.192.1–4, emphasis added; W 216)

Sure enough, Medoro becomes its victim:

> Cercando già nel più intricato calle
> il giovane infelice di salvarsi;
> ma il grave peso ch'avea su le spalle,
> gli facea uscir tutti i partiti scarsi.
> Non concosce il paese, e la via falle,
> e torna fra le spine a invilupparsi.

(The unfortunate youth thrust his way through the most overgrown
paths in search of escape, but the heavy burden he carried on his shoulders [Dardinello] brought all his plans to nothing. The terrain was un-

familiar and he took a wrong turning which led him into impenetrable
thorns.) (OF 19.3.1–6; W 216–17)

Cloridano, seized by guilt at having abandoned his friend to a perilous situation, laments his perfidy, and "così dicendo, ne la torta via / de *l'intricata* selva
si ricaccia;/ et onde era venuto si ravvia [With these words he plunged back
along the tortuous trail, through the labyrinthine wood and retraced his steps]"
(OF 19. 5.1–3, emphasis added; W 217). Negotiating the labyrinth by following
his tracks backwards, he finds Medoro, only to receive his death at the hands of
the Christian soldiers.

The entrapment and consequent frustration that characterize the experience
of being caught in a physical labyrinth make it a powerful metaphor for those
trapped in desire and suffering from the delusions and dashed hopes that accompany that emotional state. A passage in canto 12 of the *Furioso* makes the
connection brilliantly. Atlante, Ruggiero's tutelary magician, who would keep
the young Saracen from his dynastic destiny as Este progenitor—a destiny that
carries with it the fate of an early death—uses his powers to fabricate a great
palace, on a beautiful plain at the edge of the forest (an obviously symbolic location), that attracts its prey by dangling before them as they pass by images of
objects of desire, to obtain which, be it a woman or a piece of armor, the victims
not only enter the palace but prowl through it night and day in search of a delusory satisfaction. The effect, as described in canto 12 in a passage that demands
extensive quotation, sounds much like a panoramic overview of collective insan-
ity but also like a repackaging in labyrinthine form of the forest wanderings described elsewhere in the poem.[24]

Orlando, seeking Angelica throughout Europe, "sente all'orecchia / una
voce venir, che par che piagna [a voice came to his ear, and what sounded like
weeping]" (OF 12.4.5–6; W 116); a knight on a "gran destriero [great charger]"
appears, carrying before him "per forza [by force]" a *donzella* who "fa sembiante
/ di gran dolore [gave evidence of utter sorrow]" (OF 12.4.7, 5.2–4; W 116) and
cries out to Orlando for assistance. Believing it to be Angelica—the narrator
notes with ironic ingenuousness, "Non dico ch'ella fosse, ma parea / Angelica
gentil ch'egli tant'ama [I do not say that she *was* sweet Angelica, his well-
beloved—but she looked like her]" (OF 12.6.1–2; W 117)—Orlando gives chase:

L'un fugge e l'altro caccia; e le profonde
selve s'odon sonar d'alto lamento.
Correndo, usciro in un gran prato; e quello
avea nel mezzo un grande e ricco ostello. . . .

Corse dentro alla porta messa d'oro
con la donzella in braccio il cavalliero.
Dopo non molto giunse Brigliadoro,
che porta Orlando disdegnoso e fiero.

(One fled, the other pursued [a situation that, as we'll see, mimics the actual relationship between Angelica, under her own steam, and her many
pursuers], and a high lament could be heard sounding through the deep
forest. They came galloping out into a broad meadow, in the middle of
which stood a magnificent great palace. . . . In through the gate, wrought
in gold, ran the knight [Atlante, magically transformed] with the lady in
his arms, followed shortly after by Brigliador carrying fierce Orlando.)
                                       (OF 12.7.5–8, 12.8.3–6; W 117)

Then his adventures within the labyrinth begin:

Orlando, come è dentro, gli occhi gira;
né più il guerrier, né la donzella mira.

Subito smonta, e fulminando passa
dove più dentro il bel tetto s'alloggia:
corre di qua, corre di là, né lassa
che non vegga ogni camera, ogni loggia.
Poi che i segreti d'ogni stanza bassa
ha cerco invan, su per le scale poggia;
e non men perde anco a cercar di sopra,
che perdessi di sotto, il tempo e l'opra.

    . . . *Di su di giù* va il conte Orlando e riede;
né per questo può far gli occhi mai lieti
che riveggiano Angelica, o quel ladro
che n'ha portato il bel viso leggiadro.

E mentre *or quinci or quindi* invano il passo
movea, pien di travaglio e di pensieri,
Ferraù, Brandimarte e il re Gradasso,
re Sacripante et altri cavallieri
vi ritrovò, ch'andavano *alto e basso*,
né men facean di lui *vani sentieri*;

e si ramaricavan del malvagio
invisibil signor di quel palagio.

Tutti cercando il van, tutti gli dànno
colpa di furto alcun che lor fatt'abbia:
del destrier che gli ha tolto, altri è in affanno;
ch'abbia perduta altri la donna, arrabbia;
altri d'altro l'accusa: e così stanno,
che non si san partir di quella gabbia;
e vi son molti, a questo inganno presi,
stati le settimane intiere e i mesi.

(Once inside, Orlando looked about him, but saw no sign of the knight nor
of the damsel. He jumped from his horse and stormed through into the
living quarters. He dashed hither and thither, never stopping until he had
looked into every room, every gallery; after vainly probing the secrets of all
the ground-floor rooms, he climbed the stairs and wasted no less time and
effort searching upstairs.... Upstairs and downstairs and all over again
Orlando hunted, but there was no joy for him: never did he set eyes upon
Angelica or the thief who had wafted her sweet delicate face away from his
sight. And while vainly pursuing his quest hither and thither, full of care
and anxiety, he came across Ferraù, Brandimart, King Gradasso, and King
Sacripant and other knights who were also searching high and low, pursuing a quest as fruitless as his own. They all complained about the malicious
invisible lord of that palace—the invisible lord for whom they were all
searching. All accused him of one theft or another; one was grieving over
the loss of his horse, another was raging over the loss of his lady; others had
other thefts to charge him with, and none of them could tear themselves
away from this cage—some there were, the victims of his deception, who
had been there for whole weeks and months.)

(*OF* 12.8.7–8, 12.9, 12.10.5–8, 12.11–12; W 117)

The *invisibil signor* and his *inganno* are, at one level, Atlante; at another, they
are but externalizations of the irrational, delusional desire to which all the unwilling guests in this labyrinthine "*palazzo altiero* [stately edifice]" (*OF* 12.8.2;
W 117) have succumbed.[25]

I'll mention one more verbal strategy (there are certainly others) by means
of which the *Furioso* both externalizes and characterizes the deleterious effects
of desire on its victims: nouns and verbs variously signifying entanglement,

confusion, and intrigue. A choice instance of externalization comes in the depiction of the labyrinthine forest in cantos 18 and 19, where the narrator describes the experience of Medoro and Cloridano—an experience both caused by and symbolic of their unrestrained love for each other and for the dead Dardinello—as one of being not only *lost* but *entangled*. The forest, "come *labirinto*, entro *s'intrica*/ di stretti calli e sol da bestie culti" (*OF* 18.192.3–4, emphasis added); Medoro struggles within it: "cercando già nel più *intricato* calle il giovane infelice di salvarsi" (*OF* 19.3.1–2, emphasis added). Meanwhile, Cloridano is seized by guilt at having left his beloved comrade behind, and "così dicendo, ne la torta via/ de *l'intricata* selva si ricaccia" (*OF* 19.5.1–2, emphasis added; see above for translations). As used here, the Italian verb *intricare* means to entangle or tangle; its reflexive form, *s'intricare*, likewise means to become entangled. *Intricato* means entangled and also confused.

The nominal form of the verb, *intrico* (not present in this passage) means a knot, and this connotation leads us directly to a notorious passage earlier in the *Furioso* that comes right after Ruggiero—who is betrothed to Bradamante—spies the beautiful Angelica, naked and tied to a rock as a sacrifice to the sea monster Orca, as he flies high above the earth on his extraordinary mount, the hippogryph. Even as he rescues her, she entangles him in desire, thanks to "gli occhi che già l'avean preso alla rete [her eyes which had already ensnared him]" (*OF* 10.109.4; W 105); after blinding the Orca by means of his magic shield (an updated version of how Perseus used Medusa's head to rescue Andromeda in the episode from book 4 of Ovid's *Metamorphoses* here appropriated by Ariosto), Ruggiero escapes with, but not from, Angelica, who now sits behind him on his winged steed:

> Così privò la fera de la cena
> per lei soave e delicata troppa.
> Ruggier si va volgendo, e mille baci
> figge nel petto e negli occhi vivaci.

> (Thus did he deprive the monster of a feast which was far too dainty and delicious for it. He kept turning around, and in his breast, and in his lively eyes a thousand kisses were a-smouldering.)
>
> (*OF* 10.112.5–8; W 105)

Suspending his planned itinerary, he lands in a nearby, obviously symbolic forest, whose equally symbolic avian resident (again borrowed from Ovid's *Metamorphoses*, this time an infamous rape scene) announces to the poem's humanistically educated readers the betrothed knight's planned infidelity, as does a characteristic turn of phrase:

> Nel propinquo lito il destrier pose. . . .
> Sul lito un bosco era di querce ombrose,
> dove ognor par che Filomena piagna;
> ch'in mezzo avea un pratel con una fonte,
> e *quinci e quindi* un solitario monte.

> (He put down at a neighboring shore. . . . By the shore there was a shady oak wood, which forever resounded with Philomena's lament; in the middle was a grassy clearing with a spring, and to either side, a solitary hill.)   (*OF* 10. 113.3, 5–8, emphasis added; W 105)

His desire growing (internally and externally), Ruggiero becomes the very model of a knight (judgmentally) errant, thanks to some changes rung on a well-established Boccaccian sexual metaphor:

> Quivi il bramoso cavallier ritenne
> l'audace corso, e nel pratel discese;
> e fe' raccorre al suo destrier le penne,
> ma non a tal che più le avea distese.
> Del destrier sceso, a pena si ritenne
> Di salir altri, ma tennel l'arnese.

> (Here the eager knight drew rein and set foot in the clearing; he had his charger fold his wings [leaving at liberty, however, another steed, who had now spread his even wider]. He dismounted, but could scarcely restrain himself from climbing onto a different mount; but his gear delayed him.)   (*OF* 10.114.1–6; W 105)

The stumbling rhythm of the following farcical lines mimics Ruggiero's literal, Chaplinesque entanglement in his armor, exacerbated by his lust-driven haste, which in turn mimics the emotional (and, we might say, judgmental) knots into which desire has tied him, the would-be violator of the woman he has just saved from (a different, but equally cruel) violation:

> L'arnese il tenne, che bisognò trarre,
> e contra il suo disir messe le sbarre.

Frettoloso, or *da questo or da quel canto,*
confusamente l'arme si levava.
Non gli parve altra volta star tanto;
Che s'un laccio sciogliea, dui n'annodava [a synonym for *intricare*].

(His gear delayed him, for he had to pull it off; it obstructed the impetus of
his desire. With hasty fingers he fumbled confusedly at his armour, now
this side, now the other. Never before had it seemed such a long business—
for every thong unlaced, two seemed to become entangled.)

(OF 10.114.7–8, 115.1–4, emphasis added; W 105–6)

With comic obliquity, Ariosto now skewers at least the male reader's complicity in Ruggiero's desire, making that reader share the errant knight's frustration by having the court-poet version of the narrator interrupt the pageant of
knotting and unknotting with an obsequious apology to his patron: "Ma troppo
è lungo ormai, Signor, il canto, / e forse ch'anco l'ascoltar vi grava [But this canto
has gone on too long, my Lord, and perhaps you are growing a-weary with listening to it]" (OF 10.115.5–6; W 106). The following canto opens with a sententious contrast between reining in a horse by means of a bridle (easy) and a "li-
bidinosa furia [rabid lust]" (OF 11.1.4; [W 106]) by means of "ragione" (almost
impossible—and a proleptic reference to the horrendous outcome of Orlando's
desire, many cantos on, for this same Angelica), and continues,

Qual raggion fia che 'l buon Ruggier raffrene,
sì che non voglia ora pigliar diletto
d'Angelica gentil che nuda tiene
nel solitario e commodo boschetto?
Di Bradamante più non gli soviene,
che tanto aver solea fissa nel petto.

(What argument can there be to stop Ruggiero and change his mind
about taking his pleasure with lovely Angelica, whom he holds naked
there in the convenient solitude of the glade? Bradamant he has quite
forgotten, though she had always reigned in his heart.)

(OF 11.2.1–6; W 106)

And even if he did remember his distant beloved, the narrator continues mis-
chievously, how could he resist the proximate charms of naked Angelica,
whose beauty would seduce even "quel crudo / Zenocrate [Xenocrates him-

self, that austere paragon]" (*OF* 11.3.1–2; W 106), the famous exemplar of stoic restraint?

In fact, however, Ruggiero's frustration, emblematized, like his desire itself, in those unyielding knots, cannot be denied, as Angelica escapes him thanks— cruel irony!—to the very magic ring that he had placed on her finger to shield her from the stunning effect of his equally magic shield, and which she uses to become invisible, thus eluding this would-be rapist as she has, and will, many others.

Two further variants of *intricare*—*intricato* in its meaning, "confused," and *intrigo*, cognate to English "intrigue" or plot (which entangles its victims)—have roles to play in the *Furioso's* panorama of what Shakespeare would subsequently call "lust in action," but I shall postpone weaving those strands into my own *tela* of appreciation in order to return to the poem's crucial quibble on *errare*, imply- ing both spatial and mental (or judgmental) errancy.

The poem has just begun when Orlando, having fought on Angelica's behalf in India and other Asian kingdoms, rescuing her from more perils than even Pauline could shake a stick at (all recorded in Boiardo's *Orlando Innamorato*), returns to Europe and, as a loyal vassal should, reports to Charles, whose army, as already noted (cf. *OF* 1.5–6), waits at the foot of the Pyrenees to counter the coming Saracen attack. He immediately has cause to regret his arrival, for Charles commandeers Angelica, seeking to avoid further conflict (which the emperor regards as "un grave incendio [a terrible fire]" [*OF* 1.7.8;]) between Or- lando and Rinaldo over Angelica. Presuming that this rivalry will cost him the undivided attention and support of both men, Charles gives Angelica to Namo, another of his lieutenants, for safe keeping, promising her to whichever of her two lovers contributes most to Frankish victory.

Responding to this imperial intervention, the narrator declares, "Ecco il gi- udicio uman come spesso erra"—behold, how often human judgment errs (my translation)—and then explains:

Quella che dagli esperii ai liti eoi
Avea difesa con sì lunga guerra,
Or tolta gli è fra tanti amici suoi,
Senza spada adoprar, ne la sua terra.

(The damsel, whom [Orlando] had defended so constantly all the way from the Hesperides to the shores of Sunrise, was taken from him now, now that he was surrounded by friends, in his own land, with not a blow struck.)   (*OF* 1.7.3–6; W 1–2)

But, we are entitled to ask, whose judgment in fact erred? Orlando's in returning to support his feudal lord? Charlemagne, in taking Angelica away from Orlando in order to make him fight the Saracens all the more fiercely to win her back? (The outcome of the battle opens that strategy to serious doubt.) Or Orlando's friends, in not sticking up for him? The operative line is not clearly linked to any of these possible culprits, leaving the reader with a vague and troubling sense that in any given situation, errant judgment may be the one characteristic shared by all its participants.[26]

As we've seen, however, "la gente batezzata" are trounced; their flight and the capture of Namo leave Angelica free to flee, which she proceeds to do— into the forest, of course, where (OF 1.10–11) she encounters first Rinaldo (whom, for reasons later explained, she hates as much as he loves her)[27] and then, as she flees from him, the Saracen Ferraù, who begins to fight over her with Rinaldo while Angelica flees from both of them. They pursue her and separate when the path they are following divides; as I've noted, Ferraù's branch circles back to the very place where we first saw him, attempting to fish out of a stream his battle helmet, which he carelessly dropped while slaking his battle-prompted thirst (in OI II.xxxi.4–5, 14). He is now confronted by the ghost of the helmet's former owner, who rises from the river to castigate Ferraù for not having sunk the helmet long ago, as he promised after killing Angelica's brother, who now speaks from the grave. Shamed, Ferraù sets out on a new quest, to find Orlando and take from him the helmet that that worthy had in turn taken from a pagan warrior in an earlier battle. (This is only the first of myriad descriptions of artifacts—and occasionally women—that pass through many hands, by accident, force, or fraud, during the course of OF. This mammoth circulation of desired objects assimilates the world of chivalry to that of commerce, doubtless by Ariostan design.) Meanwhile, Rinaldo, still in search of Angelica, instead crosses paths with his strangely missing charger, Baiardo; the horse ignores his master's plea that he stop, racing away with Rinaldo in hot pursuit.

All the characters and many of the events and situations in this opening segment of the first canto of OF—including Charles's sequestration of Angelica, Ferraù's loss of his helmet, and the love-hate relationship between Angelica and Rinaldo (all love on his side, all hate on hers)—are borrowed by Ariosto from the *Orlando Innamorato* but are infused with a new sensibility and new meanings. Of these activities, though they vary greatly in tempo from frantic haste on horseback, one or two on a horse, through much slower progress unhorsed and in armor, to riverbank stasis, what almost all have in common is a frustrated quest: Rinaldo and Ferrau for Angelica, Ferraù for his helmet,

Rinaldo for his charger. Frustration, at least for men, is thus quickly established as a fact of life in the *Furioso*'s world.

The exception is, of course, Angelica, who flees *from* rather than questing
toward.[28] But whereas the Christian army flees in defeat from a superior Saracen foe, the ravishingly beautiful princess of Cathay is spurred to flight by her
deeply felt need to escape the individual attentions of her many suitors, Christian and Saracen, or, put differently, by her fear of the consequences (read:
rape) should she fall into the hands of any of them. *OF* 1.13 offers, in its description of Angelica's flight from Rinaldo, a first, unforgettable portrait of a
crisis of desire, or more precisely a crisis of fear generated by the desires of
others, one that, thanks to a poetic exercise of pathetic fallacy, results in an
experience of the forest quite different from that of the desirous knights who
quest through it, even as it espouses the same verbal vocabulary of undirected
motion:

> La donna il palafreno a dietro volta,
> e per la selva a tutta briglia il caccia;
> né *per la rara più che per la folta*,
> la più sicura e miglior via procaccia:
> ma pallida e tremando, e di sé tolta,
> lascia cura al destrier che la via faccia.
> *Di su di giù*, ne l'alta selva fiera
> Tanto girò, che venne a una riviera.

(The damsel turned her palfrey's head and galloped off through the forest at full tilt. She made no attempt to choose the best and surest path, or
to avoid the thickets and the undergrowth; pale and trembling and quite
unstrung, she left it to her horse to find his own way through. High and
low, on and on through the deep, grim forest she coursed, until she came
to a river.)   (Emphasis added; W 2)

And again, in *OF* 1.33:

> Fugge tra selve spaventose e scure,
> per lochi inabitati, ermi e selvaggi.
> Il mover de le frondi e di verzure,
> che di cerri sentia, d'olmi e di faggi,
> fatto le avea con subite paure
> trovar *di qua di là* strani viaggi;

ch'ad ogni ombra veduta *o in monte o in valle,*
temea Rinaldo aver sempre alle spalle.

(Through fearful dark woods she fled, through wild, desolate and deserted places. The stirring of a branch, of a green leaf of oak, elm, or beech would make her swerve in fright; at each shadow she espied, whether by hill or dale, she imagined that Rinaldo was still close behind her.)

(Emphasis added; W 4–5)

As I've mentioned, Ariosto's Ferrarese milieu included paintings by Titian and other major artists, commissioned by Alfonso d'Este, and here the poet portrays in words, but with a painter's eye, the woman's headlong, indiscriminate rush through an encroaching forest that represents, even as it offers escape from, the lustful grasp of her admirers. The dominance of passion (in the form of terror) over rationality is symbolized by Angelica's ceding choice of direction to her horse, while her temporary loss of control over herself ("e di sé tolta" [*OF* 1.13.5]) finds expression in her terrified screams as she gallops ("gridando la donzella ispaventata [the damsel, screaming with terror]" [*OF* 1.15.2; W 2]).

In a world full of men committed to heroic acts and protected from harm by enchanted armor or by magic spells that render them (in mockery of Homer's Achilles) nearly invulnerable—Orlando, for instance, can be wounded only on the soles of his feet, Ferraù only in his navel—in such a world only Angelica is motivated entirely by fear, unprotected by anything but the speed of her horse, the control her beauty sometimes allows her to exert over men—and, from time to time, by a magic ring (Boiardo's invention) that passes in and out of her possession and that, when she puts it in her mouth, renders her invisible.(According to *OF* 10.108 and 11.4, it was stolen from her by the rascally Brunello—more on him soon—and from him by Bradamante, who gave it to the sorceress Melissa, to aid in her rescue of Ruggiero from his courtly, erotic enslavement to Alcina—more on her, too—after which, as we've seen, Ruggiero made the error—understandable, but an error nonetheless, given his lustful designs—of giving it [back] to its original owner, allowing her, just in time, to frustrate those designs.) And it is she, *Angelica che fugge*, who determines the priorities of so many of the other characters in the *Furioso*—they neglect wives, sweethearts, and feudal obligations to search for her—and who sets the tempo and scope of their movements as they rush, or wander, through the endless forest in this hopeless, frustrating quest.[29]

Hence the major crisis of human desire, as dramatized through the behavior of Angelica, is to have as its object that which fears rather than reciprocates, flees rather than welcomes it. And desire thus based on mistaken choice can only breed frustration, lost direction, and, finally, lost sanity. The image of Ruggiero, inflamed by desire, staggering about like a blind man seeking to embrace (and have his way with) the newly invisible Angelica, is yet another incarnation of the wanderer in love's forest:

> Intorno alla fontana
> brancolando n'andava come cieco.
> Oh, quante volte abbracciò l'aria vana,
> sperando la donzella abbracciar seco!

(He went groping around the spring like a blind man; many a time he hugged the empty air, hoping to clasp the damsel in the same embrace.
(OF 11.9.1–4; W 107)

Even Angelica finally surrenders to desire, and, becoming the poster girl for its irrationality, bestows her love on an insignificant young Saracen, Medoro, giving him, of her own free will, the "flower" that she had so jealously guarded from all those paladins who wanted nothing more in the world than to take it from her (with or without her acquiescence).[30] This quasi-universal male obsession with Angelica's virginity exemplifies an important and not yet mentioned dimension— one might almost call it the dirty little secret—of the crisis of desire that roars like a great emotional tornado through the fanciful landscape presented for our delectation and dismay in the comic mirror that is the *Orlando Furioso*.

For desire in the *Furioso* has this darker side: satisfying it brings not only joy (sexual joy if the object is a woman) but also the honor that comes from proving one's superiority to all other rivals in getting what one wants. In other words, throughout *OF*, desire is for possession and for honor, for the pleasure that comes less from obtaining the thing itself than from getting there first—from winning out over others who want the same thing, over whom, in their frustration, you can now lord your success. The inverse, of course, is that seeing someone else obtain the object of desire before you doubles your misery: with loss comes shame.

This troubling theme (at least to modern American sensibilities) is first sounded early in the *Furioso*, in connection (of course) with Angelica. After her mad dash through the fearsome forest with the specter of Rinaldo at her heels, she finds a place to rest undetected in a very different woodland environment, "un boschetto adorno [a pleasant grove]" (OF 1.35.3; W 5), described in pastoral terms.[31] Soon, however, a knight arrives—Sacripante, Saracen king of Circassia and yet another lover of Angelica—who, striking a melancholy pose— another instance of Ariosto's word-painting skills—utters a mournful lament,

expressing both misery and confusion consequent on his conviction that someone else has taken his beloved's virginity before he could:

> "Pensier (dicea) che 'l cor m'aggiacci et ardi,
> e causi il duol che sempre il rode e lima,
> che debbo far, poi ch'io son giunto tardi,
> e ch'altri a côrre il frutto è andato prima?
> a pena avuto io n'ho parole e sguardi,
> et altri n'ha tutta la spoglia opima.
> Se non ne tocca a me frutto né fiore,
> perché affliger per lei mi vuo' più il core?"

(He spoke: "you, thought, who set my heart afire and turn it to ice, and
cause the pain which ever gnaws within me, what am I to do? For I have
been late in coming, and another has been first to cull the fruit. Little has
fallen to me but words and looks while another has gathered the best of
the crop. If I am to be denied both fruit and blossom, why does my heart
keep aching for her?)   (*OF* 1.41; W 5–6)

The two remarkable features of this outburst are, first, that the source of Sacripante's woe is not that Angelica may love someone else instead of him, but that
some one has beat him to his goal of deflowering her, and then, that he can't
understand why, if he can no longer be the first to take her virginity, he should
still have feelings of desire for her. Taken together, these two constituents of
Sacripante's whine adumbrate a cultural system in which the real competition
among men involves the race to deflower a woman, as a result of which the successful seducer or rapist achieves superiority and shames his competitors, while
the woman in question loses (or should lose) much, if not all, her value as an
object of desire. (Pietro Germi gave trenchant, comedic immortality to this
Mediterranean triptych of virginity, its violation, and the victimization of
women in his 1963 film, *Seduta e abbandonata* [Seduced and abandoned].)

Sacripante's speech continues in lyric vein, sounding at first like a traditional
persuasion to love, but soon turning into something altogether more sour and
dismissive (not to say misogynistic), only to end, via yet another twist, in confusion and self-pity, caused by the contradiction between what he should feel toward a deflowered woman and what he does feel toward this one:

> "La verginella è simile alla rosa,
> ch'in bel giardin su la nativa spina

mentre sola e sicura si riposa,
né gregge né pastor se le avicina;
l'aura soave e l'alba rugiadosa,
l'acqua, la terra al suo favor s'inchina:
gioveni vaghi e donne inamorate
amano averne e seni e tempie ornate.

Ma non sì tosto dal materno stelo
rimossa viene e dal suo ceppo verde,
che quanto avea dagli uomini e dal cielo
favor, grazia e bellezza, tutto perde.
La vergine che 'l fior, di che più zelo
che de' begli occhi e de la vita aver de',
lascia altrui côrre, il pregio ch'avea inanti
perde nel cor di tutti gli altri amanti.

Sia vile agli altri, e da quel solo amata
a cui di sé fece sì larga copia.
Ah, Fortuna crudel, Fortuna ingrata!
trionfan gli altri, e ne moro io d'inopia.
Dunque esser può che non mi sia più grata?
dunque io posso lasciar mia vita propria?
Ah, più tosto oggi manchino i dì miei,
Ch'io viva più, s'amar non debbo lei!"

(A virgin is like a rose; while she remains on the thorn whence she sprang, alone and safe in a lovely garden, no flock, no shepherd approaches. The gentle breeze and the dewy dawn, water, and earth pay her homage; amorous youths and loving maidens like to deck their brows with her, and their breasts. But no sooner is she plucked from her mother-stalk, severed from her green stem, than she loses all, all the favour, grace, and beauty wherewith heaven and men endowed her. The virgin who suffers one to cull her flower—of which she should be more jealous than of her life—loses the esteem she once enjoyed in the hearts of all her other wooers. Let her be abhorred by those others, and loved only by him to whom she gave herself so abundantly. O cruel enemy, Fortune! The others triumph and I die of need. What then: am I to find her no longer pleasing? Am I to relinquish my own heart's life? Ah, let this day be my last, let me live no longer if I am no longer to love her.)[32]   (OF 1.42–44; W 6)

Listening to this tearful performance, Angelica, though unmoved by it (the narrator, buying into the system of male entitlement that demonizes women who won't give into male desire, calls her "dura e fredda più d'una colonna [hard . . . and cold as a stone pillar]" [*OF* 1.49.5; W6]), decides that she can turn Sacripante's self-torturing infatuation with her to her advantage, persuading him to be her protector on her long journey back to Cathay. Accordingly, she appears before him and assures him she is still a virgin, thanks to Orlando, who

> la guardò sovente
> da morte, da disnor, da casi rei;
> e che 'l fior virginal così avea salvo,
> come se lo portò del materno alvo.

(had frequently saved her from death and outrage and all manner of evils; and how her virginal flower was still as intact as the day she had borne it from her mother's womb.)   (*OF* 1.55.5–8; W 6)

The narrator scoffs, "forse era ver, ma non però credibile [maybe it was true, but nonetheless not credible]," (my translation) and condemns Sacripante's desire-driven gullibility: "che 'l miser suole / dar facile credenza a quel che vuole [for a poor wretch will readily believe whatever suits him]" (*OF* 1.56.1, 7–8; W 7).[33] But this information, accurate or not, wrenches the Circassian's train of thought in a new, more "orthodox" direction: he decides at once that he will not make Orlando's foolish error but rather will waste no time obtaining the real object of his affection—not Angelica, but her virginity—justifying what will be a rape by sophistry and stereotyping familiar to us (and to the poem's first readers) from Ovid's *Ars amatoria*, book 1:

> "Se mal si seppe il cavallier d'Anglante
> pigliar per sua sciochezza il tempo buono,
> il danno se ne avrà; . . .
> ma io per imitarlo già non sono. . . .
>
> Corrò la fresca e matutina rosa,
> che, tardando, stagion perder potria.
> So ben ch'a donna non si può far cosa
> che più soave e più piacevol sia,
> ancor che se ne mostri disdegnosa,

e talor mesta e flebil se ne stia:
non starò per repulsa o finto sdegno,
ch'io non adombri e incarni il mio disegno.

(If the knight of Anglant [i.e., Orlando] was so stupid as to neglect his opportunity, so much the worse for him. . . . Far be it from me to imitate him. . . . I shall pluck the morning-fresh rose which I might lose were I to delay. Full well I know that there is nothing that a woman finds so delectable and pleasing, even when she pretends to resent it and will sometimes burst into tears. I shall not be put off by any repulse or show of anger, but shall carry into effect what I propose.)

(OF 1.57.1–3, 6, 58; W 7)

Only the sudden appearance of Bradamante, who quickly defeats Sacripante in a duel, saves Angelica from ravishment.

Nearly at other end of the *Furioso*, Rinaldo learns that Angelica (whom, we recall, he also has pursued as the object of his desire) has given herself (and her virginity) to "un vilissimo [i.e., of very low status] barbaro" (OF 42.39.4); before he leaves Charles's camp to pursue her and Medoro (using the excuse, as we've seen, of searching for his warhorse, Baiardo), we are given this insight by the narrator into the great warrior's frame of mind:

La partita d'Angelica non molto
sarebbe grave all'animoso amante;
né pur gli avria turbato il sonno, o tolto
il pensier di tornarsene in Levante:
ma *sentendo ch'avea del suo amor colto*
un Saracino le primizie inante,
tal passione e tal cordoglio sente,
che non fu in vita sua, mai, più dolente.

. . . e come il caccia *la gelosa rabbia,*
dopo gran pianto e gran ramaricarsi,
verso Levante fa pensier tornarsi.
. . . .
Ha sempre in mente, e mai non se ne ne parte,
come esser puote ch'un povero fante
abbia del cor di lei spinto da parte
merito e amor d'ogni altro primo amante.

Con tal pensier che 'l cor gli straccia e parte,
Rinaldo se ne va verso Levante.

(Angelica's departure would not have greatly depressed the impassioned
lover, nor would the thought of returning to the East have dismayed him
or robbed him of his sleep. But the news that a Saracen had forestalled
him in gathering the first-fruits of his love left him feeling such anger and
misery that never in his life had he been in such agony. . . . And after a
spell of weeping and self-pity, [he] decided upon a return to the Orient,
driven by his passionate jealousy. . . . What he could never escape was
the thought of how a poor simple soldier could have displaced in her
breast the entire merits, the full ardour of all her previous suitors. His
heart torn by thoughts such as these, Rinaldo journeyed Eastwards.
            (*OF* 42.40, 42.41.6–8, 42.45.1–6, emphasis added; W 502)

What hurts Rinaldo most is not that Angelica doesn't love him but that she
should choose to love—and to give her *primizie* to—someone so far below her
other suitors in status and quality.

The key term here is "*la gelosa rabbia*." By its depiction of the strong feelings
of both Sacripante and Rinaldo, *OF* shows desire integrated into an honor/
shame culture, the worst consequence of which is the jealousy that results from
someone else obtaining the object of desire before you could—especially someone you consider your inferior. Women are only worth pursuing if they are
virgins, and the peril that attends the pursuit is the shame of seeing someone
else win the race and pluck the rose. To the burden of sexual frustration must
be added the crushing weight of shame, of honor lost. The same dynamic—
desire courting not just frustration but shame—applies even if the object of
desire is inanimate: a sword, a horse, a suit of armor.

The supreme instance of the potential for disaster in this imbrication of
desire in a personal value system driven by honor and shame comes at the midpoint of *OF*, when Orlando is driven mad (thus fulfilling the promise of the
poem's title) by his discovery that a lowlife like Medoro has culled the flower of
his beloved Angelica, in quest of whom he has been in almost constant movement, *di qua di là*, across the length and breadth of Europe throughout the
length and breadth of the poem (the parallelism is deliberate and interpretive).

Orlando has just parted company with his faithful companion, Zerbino—
the Italian lines, "feron camin diverso i cavallieri, / di qua Zerbino, e di là il
conte Orlando [then the knights took their separate ways, Zerbin hither,
Count Orlando yonder]" (*OF* 23.99.3–4; W 278) could serve as an epigraph

for the entire poem—and goes in search of his enemy, Mandricardo. But (also archetypically)

> Lo strano corso che tenne il cavallo
> del Saracin pel bosco senza via,
> fece ch'Orlando andò duo giorni in fallo,
> né lo trovò, né poté averne spia.

(The Saracen's steed had pursued so wild a course through the trackless wood that Orlando journeyed for two days to no avail; he found neither his quarry nor even a clue to where he was.)   (*OF* 23.100.1–4; W 278)

Having lost his opponent, the mighty paladin proceeds to lose himself: he wanders into the *paysage idéal* that has until recently sheltered Angelica and her lover, and there he receives the shock that will soon deprive him of his wits: unimpeachable testimony that the object of his desire his given herself to another:

> [V]ide scritti
> molti arbuscelli in su l'ombrosa riva.
> Tosto che fermi v'ebbe gli occhi e fitti,
> fu certo esser di man de la sua diva. . . .
>
> Angelica e Medor con cento nodi
> legati insieme, e in cento lochi vede.
> Quante lettere son, tanti son chiodi
> coi quali Amore il cor gli punge e fiede.

([He saw] inscriptions on many of the trees by the shady bank; he had only to look closely at the letters to be sure that they were formed by the hand of his goddess. . . . He saw 'Angelica' and 'Medoro' in a hundred places, united by a hundred love knots. The letters were so many nails with which Love pierced and wounded his heart.)

> (*OF* 23.102.1–4, 103.1–4; W 278)

Ariosto borrowed from Ovid's *Heroides*, that collection of highly emotional letters supposedly written by women (and a few men) famous in classical myth and legend, a detail from the fifth letter, sent to Paris by his former lover, the forest nymph Oenone, in which Oenone reminds him of his carving both their names into trees along with a promise, since broken, always to love her. As deployed in *OF*, names carved on trees take on a crucial double significance: they are the immediate occasion for Orlando's (and the poem's) climactic crisis of desire, but they also serve to commemorate in broader terms both Orlando's mistake in letting his love for Angelica, now revealed as hopeless, get in the way of his duty to Charlemagne and to his own welfare and Angelica's unaccountable judgment in allowing a nobody, rather than a famous and super-valiant Christian or Saracen warrior, to pluck the rose that, more than even her beauty, has been driving a raft of those warriors into the woods and into folly, frustration, and disgrace. In this latter function, the textually inscribed forest communicates a more global message about desire's profound implication in human error, and as such must be recognized as a metaphor for *OF* itself—a textual forest in which its readers, like its characters, wander about, frequently lost and forever surprised about what adventure they next meet or meet again. Finally, the knots (*cento nodi*) linking the lovers' names connect with the knots that impede Ruggiero's attempt to rid himself of his armor in order to ravish this same Angelica and with the insoluble intricacies of the labyrinthine forest to those seeking a way through it: images of frustration anticipating Orlando's plight even as they signal the union that will drive him mad.

Having discovered the names of Angelica and Medoro repeatedly carved into tree trunks and written upon every available wall—madness by graffiti, a strangely modern-seeming malady—Orlando experiences a downward spiral from jealousy and frustration to self-pity and profound misery. As his mind snaps, passion becomes anger, and the *furioso* (mad, but also furious in the English sense of the term) proceeds to leave his own, demented signature on the world around him, uprooting trees and slaughtering both man and beast (*OF* 23.130–136; 124.4–10).[34]

While Orlando's situation is extreme, the great chivalric heroes of *OF*, Christian and Saracen, are almost without exception victims, like him, of the toxic mixture of unregulated passions and commitment to the primacy of honor. Ariosto comments on this, the greatest crisis of male desire, by having his narrator gleefully (and heartlessly) rub the noses of the paladins in their collective agony of rejection, envy, and pain on learning that Angelica has given her virginity to Medoro:

O conte Orlando, o re di Circassia,
vostra inclita virtù, dite, che giova?
Vostro alto *onor* dite in che prezzo sia,
o che mercé vostro servir ritruova.
Mostratemi una sola cortesia

che mai costei v'usasse, o vecchia o nuova,
per ricompensa e guidardone e merto
di quanto avete già per lei sofferto.

Oh se potessi ritornar mai vivo,
quanto ti parria duro, o re Agricane!
che già mostrò costei si averti a schivo
con repulse crudeli et inumane.
O Ferraù, o mille altri ch'io non scrivo,
ch'avete fatto mille pruove vane
per questa ingrata, quanto aspro vi fôra,
s'a costu' in braccio voi la vedesse ora!

(O count Orlando! O King of Circassi! Tell me just what good your emi-
nent valour has gained you, what account has been taken of your *honour*
and nobility, what reward your attentions have merited! Show me one
single kindness the damsel ever did to you, at any time, to requite and reward you for all you have suffered for her sake! O King Agrican, if you
could return to life, how you would be pained, after the cruel merciless
way she rejected your advances! And Ferrau, and all you others I'll not
mention, who have done great deeds without number for this thankless
one, and all in vain—what a bitter blow it would be if you saw her now in
this boy's arms.)   (OF 19.31–32; W 220, emphasis added)

These lines not only skewer the vanity and insecurity underlying male chivalric
posturing about desire; they also, by their assumed indignation, reveal the fact
that within the "system" of male desire there is no sense that a woman has the
right to say no, to refuse you and choose another, to give herself or not to whom
she pleases.

But this narratorial nose-thumbing at a major component of his cast of
characters derives further seriocomic force from its location within the system
of Mediterranean gender and sexual relations, a system constructed on the
bedrock of a double standard. For women, in this system, chastity is the only
important virtue. As the Magnifico Giuliano de' Medici declares early in book
3 of Castiglione's *Book of the Courtier*, a *donna di palazzo* (the female equivalent
of the *cortegiano* [courtier]), whatever her other gifts of deportment and conversation, must above all protect her reputation for being chaste (206–8); the
reason for this is stated with brutal frankness, also in book 3, by Gasparo
Pallavicino:

From women's incontinence countless evils arise, as they do not from
men's. Therefore . . . it is wisely established that women are permitted to
fail in all other things without incurring blame, to the end that they may
devote all their strength to holding to this one virtue of chastity, without
which there would be uncertainty about offspring, and the bond would
be dissolved that binds the whole world through the blood, and through
each man's natural love for what he engenders. Hence, a dissolute life is
more forbidden to women than to men, who do not carry their children
within them for nine months.   (240)

This concern (one may call it an obsession) with the legitimacy of one's children becomes, under male hegemony, the cornerstone of a moral edifice, but
one actually intended to enclose only women. By contrast, and in subversion of
this chastity-based moral system, the highest aspiration of a man is to be the
first lover of any woman who takes his fancy—to take the virgin's flower. This
is not love, nor even primarily erotic desire, but rather behavior driven by the
desire for conquest, and for a sign that signals preeminence in the semiotics of
male rivalry, vis-à-vis other men who didn't get there first. So where the *Courtier* speakers insist that chastity is most important for practical familial/dynas-
tic reasons (based finally on the magical idea that "blood" is crucial, requiring
the transmission of noble "blood" through male sperm from generation to generation), in the *Furioso*'s distorted, comic mirror—and in the warped world of
Mediterranean male sexual/shame culture—the destruction of chastity becomes the great prize, the goal of the macho man; by getting there first he wins
honor among his fellows, shows them up by being superior in deflowering
virgins.[35]

Conversely, to let another get there first is to be shamed, shown up; the
sexual pleasure of deflowering is finally a power/prestige thing, not a physical/
sexual thing at all. The two halves of this paradigm imposed on desire, competing against each other, form a kind of crazy whole. Both express purely male
priorities: the first is that of the father and brothers who lose a valuable com-
modity for profit through advantageous marriage if the woman isn't chaste, or
of husbands who suffer loss of face if a wife isn't chaste, vis-à-vis all men who
expect husbands to keep their wives guarded, fathers to keep their daughters
under lock and key; the second is that of the would-be lover, violator/seducer/
rapist, concerned with achieving honor by outdoing other potential violators.

An extended episode (*OF* 4.51–6.16) evokes this double standard even as it
transfers from the forest to the court the theme of desire's entanglements, this
time centered on plots and intrigues which ensnare a wide range of characters

in dangerous illusions and misprisions. Initiating these intrigues is an evil courtier, Polinesso, whose emblematic name (suggestive of multiple intersections or knots) points to both his labyrinthine machinations and the episode's intricate intertwining of laudable and iniquitous desires.[36]

Set at the court of the king of Scotland, the story of the almost tragic love of Ginevra, the king's daughter, and Ariodante, an Italian knight whose valor has won the king's favor, offers Ariosto the chance to "colonize" the highly popular and influential French Arthurian prose romances while poking fun at the moral paradoxes at their center. Indeed, the combinative name (Ario[sto] + Dante) suggests the Italian literary tradition in temporary "residence" in a northern European genre, while Ginevra is the Italian equivalent of Guinevere; the peril, driven by misconceptions both malevolent and comic, that threatens their chaste love inverts, mirrorlike, the dire consequences, in the French narratives, of the adulterous love between Guinevere, Arthur's queen, and Lancelot, the king's best and favorite knight.

Paradoxically, what enables the multiple confusions and illusions of the Ginevra episode and Polinesso's role as their instigator is a Scottish law, described thus to Rinaldo, the accidental hero of the episode, by the monks of a Scottish abbey:

L'aspra legge di Scozia, empia e severa,
vuol ch'ogni donna, e di ciascuna sorte,
ch'ad uom si giunga, e non gli sia mogliera,
s'accusata ne viene, abbia la morte.
Né riparar si può ch'ella non pèra,
quando per lei non venga un guerrier forte
che tolga la difesa, e che sostegna
che sia innocente e di morire indegna.

(By the cruel and pitiless law of Scotland any woman, whatever her condition, who engages in union with a man, and is not his wife, must be put to death if an accusation is laid against her. And she has no recourse against death unless a mighty warrior come and undertake her defence, maintaining that she be innocent and not deserving of death.)

(OF 4.59; W 37)

As I've noted, Ginevra is loved by, and has promised to marry, Ariodante; Polinesso, the wicked duke of Albany, also loves Ginevra, but when she rejects him his love turns to hate. To take vengeance, he enlists the aid of his long-time

mistress, Dalinda, who, because of her position as Ginevra's primary attendant, has access to her mistress's quarters and wardrobe. Pretending that he
needs to exorcise his frustrated passion by a bout of play-acting, the evil duke
convinces the unsuspecting Dalinda to dress up as Ginevra (while the latter is
not in residence at the royal palace), stand on a balcony outside Ginevra's
rooms, and welcome Polinesso to her arms when he climbs up a ladder to join
her. These arrangements made, Polinesso urges Ariodante to abandon his honor-
able relationship with Ginevra, on the grounds that she has long since made
Polinesso her lover and admits him regularly to her chambers for a night of
lovemaking. The shocked Ariodante insists on proof, which Polinesso, spring-
ing the trap, promises to supply.

The next night, while Ariodante watches in horror and despair, Polinesso
and Dalinda perform their balcony scene. The Italian prepares to kill himself
with his sword but is prevented by his brother Lurcanio, whom Ariodante,
fearing an ambush, had brought with him. Here is where the "aspra legge di
Scozia" comes in: Lurcanio urges Ariodante to seek the false Ginevra's death
instead of his own, to which the traumatized lover pretends to agree; the next
morning, however, he disappears, and a week later, a traveler comes to the court
with the news that he witnessed Ariodante's suicide: the distraught lover threw
himself off a cliff into the sea, giving instructions to the passerby to tell Ginevra
that he is ending his life "sol perc'ho troppo veduto: / felice, se senza occhi io
fossi suto [simply because I saw too much; happy would I be, had I lived sight-
less]" (OF 5.58.7–8; W 45).

Ginevra, completely unaware of Polinesso's scheme, is horrified at the death
of Ariodante, and so is Lurcanio, who in his fury formally accuses Ginevra of
causing his brother's demise by her sexual depravity. So good a swordsman is
Lurcanio, and so credible does Ariodante's last message about seeing too much
make his brother's accusation, that no one steps forward in Ginevra's defense,
seeming to seal her doom.

The fact that Ariosto was a playwright for the Este court might lead the
reader to interpret this episode as a gloomy parable about the power of theatrical illusion. But it's much more centrally about yet another kind of errancy,
misperception, functioning here as a kind of communicable disease or plague
in which desire plays an important role as carrier. As Dalinda later admits, she
was too in love with Polinesso to notice the potential for malevolence in his
masquerade. And her willing participation in it leads both Ariodante and Lurcanio to completely errant judgments of Ginevra that motivate the former's
grief-stricken suicide leap and the latter's rage-induced invocation of the *aspra
legge* in order to take vengeance on an innocent woman.

Nor do these instances exhaust the episode's catalogue of errors, which begins with the unintentional arrival in Scotland of Rinaldo, blown off course— "quando a ponente e quando contra l'Orse" [one moment to the West, the next toward the Pole] (*OF* 4.51.3; W 36), the nautical equivalent of "di qua, di là"—by a storm at sea while on his way to England, where he has been sent by Charlemagne to raise new troops after that initial defeat by Agramante's hordes. Heedless as ever of the call of duty, Rinaldo leaves his ship to seek adventure in the Caledonian forest,

> che spesso fra gli antiqui ombrosi cerri
> s'ode sonar di bellicosi ferri.

> Vanno per quella [selva] i cavallieri erranti. . . .
> Chi non ha gran valor, non vada inanti; . . .
> Gran cose in essa già fece Tristano,
> Lancillotto, Galasso, Artù e Galvano,

> et altri cavallieri e de la nuova
> e de la vecchia Tavola famosi.

(where so often the clash of arms resounded amid the ancient shady oaks. Through it travel knights errant. . . . The man of little valour should not adventure there. . . . Great deeds were accomplished here by Tristan, and Lancelot, Galahad, Arthur, and Gawain, and other famous knights of the new Round Table, and of the old.)

(*OF* 4.51.7–8, 52.1, 5, 7–8, 53.1–2; W 36)

Wishing to follow in the footsteps of these famous knights errant, Rinaldo soon becomes an exemplar of the Ariostan ur-quibble: when he takes shelter for the night in an abbey within the forest, the monks tell him that he is committing an error in judgment; they warn him that while he can find adventures in this forest, they will not be noticed. He should go instead to where his deeds will win him fame, to the royal court where Ginevra is condemned to death under the *aspra legge* and the king, devastated by the prospect, is offering his daughter's hand in marriage to anyone brave enough to save her. This, the monks counsel, is an adventure worth pursuing. (This is not exactly the advice one would expect to hear from monks in retreat from the world—except perhaps in *OF*—but Ariosto's comic target is the kind of reasoning adopted by Federico Fregoso, one of the participants in book 1 of

Castiglione's *Libro del Cortegiano*, who advises the hypothetical perfect courtier to save his heroics in battle for moments when he will be widely observed doing them.)[37]

Instead of rejoicing in his good fortune, Rinaldo expresses great indignation at the law and its double standard; he insists on the right of women to reward with carnal favors the pleas and service of their lovers and vows to defend Ginevra not because he thinks her innocent of the charges (he admits ignorance on this score) but to defend her right to take a lover. (This is in fact a very self-serving argument for any man—except, of course, the woman's husband.) Having thus illustrated the narrator's claim, "ecco il giudizio uman come spesso erra," the paladin sets out for a showdown with Lurcanio. Here Fortune, which roams free in a world governed in good part by desire, intervenes, putting Rinaldo in the path of two of Polinesso's henchmen who are taking Dalinda away to kill her, lest she reveal what really happened on the balcony that night. Rinaldo rescues her and only then learns the true nature of the situation into which he is about to inject himself. What most affects his mission is Dalinda's news that a strange knight, unknown to all, has shown up, just in time, to fight Lurcanio. Armed with the truth, Rinaldo hurtles toward the city, where Dalinda's testimony stops the battle for Ginevra's life, and Rinaldo then challenges Polinesso, wounding him mortally after a brief struggle. All that's left is to discover the identity of the mysterious defender of Ginevra, who turns out to be . . . Ariodante, reports of whose death have been greatly exaggerated, thanks to (of course) the entanglement of even passersby in the episode's labyrinth of misperceptions:

> Adunque il peregrin mentir di quanto
> dianzi di lui narrò, quivi apparea;
> e fu pur ver che dal sasso marino
> gittarsi in mar lo vide a capo chino.
>
> Ma (come aviene a un disperato spesso,
> che da lontan brama e disia la morte,
> e l'odia poi che se la vede apresso,
> tanto gli pare il passo acerbo e forte)
> Ariodante, poi ch'in mar fu messo,
> si pentì di morire; e come forte
> e come destro e più d'ogn'altro ardito,
> si messe a nuoto e ritornossi al lito;

e dispregiando e nominando folle
il desir ch'ebbe di lasciar la vita,
si messe a caminar bagnato e molle,
e capitò all'ostel d'un eremita.

(It appeared, then, that the traveler had given a false account of him; and yet it was quite true that he had seen him plunge headfirst into the sea from the clifftop. But a man at his wits' end will often enough court death from a distance only to shun it on closer approach, so stark and grim do its jaws appear. Thus it was with Ariodant who, once he found himself in the sea, changed his mind about dying, and being strong, bold, and agile, he set to swimming and regained the shore. And, dismissing his death-wish as a piece of sheer folly, he walked off, soaking wet as he was, and came to the abode of a hermit.)   (OF 6.4.5–6.6.4; W 50)

From the hermit he learns of Ginevra's anguish at the (false) news of his death, and decides to defend her against his own brother—a tragic denouement avoided (indeed, rendered delusory) when Dalinda's confession lifts the scales from everyone's eyes, showing a way through the labyrinth of illusion to the morally satisfying victory of Rinaldo over Polinesso and the happy union of the two lovers.

Rinaldo is the hero of the Ginevra episode, saving Dalinda from assassination, Ariodante or Lurcanio from fratricide, and Ginevra herself from possible execution, but to do all this, he must himself be rescued from his own errant judgment, first by the Scottish monks, who point him toward a worthwhile exercise of prowess in arms, and then by Dalinda, who corrects his faulty assumptions about what is really at stake in Ginevra's case by revealing Polinesso's labyrinthine intrigues.[38] Much later in the *Furioso*, Rinaldo is again saved from errant judgment: this time he is liberated at last from his infatuation with Angelica by drinking from a fountain that turns desire into odium (and, yes, there's another nearby that has the reverse effect). While this may simply be another metaphor for Fortune's penchant for abruptly altering the circumstances of one's life, Rinaldo's liberation could also suggest that the effects of decision making driven by desire instead of rational deliberation can be reversed, or even simply outgrown. Be that as it may, Rinaldo soon demonstrates his return to rationality by a paradigmatic act of deliberation leading to prudent action: presented by a stranger with a chalice full of wine which he will only be able to drink without spilling if his wife has been faithful to him (talk about double standards!),

[q]uasi Rinaldo di cercar suaso
quel che poi ritrovar non vorria forse,
messa la mano inanzi, e preso il vaso,
fu presso di volere in prova pôrse:
poi, quanto fosse periglioso il caso
a porvi i labri, con pensier discorse. . . .

Pensò, e poi disse: "Ben sarebbe folle
chi quel che non vorria trovar, cercasse.
Mia donna è donna, et ogni donna è molle:
Lasciàn star mia credenza come stasse. . . .
[N]on vo' più saper, che mi convegna. . . .
[C]he tal certezza ha Dio più proibita,
ch'al primo padre l'arbor de la vita.

(almost persuaded to seek for what perhaps he would rather not have
found, Rinaldo reached out, grasped the chalice and made to undergo
the test. But then he considered the danger he might be incurring by setting it to his lips. . . . He thought, and then said, 'He would be an utter
fool who sought for what he had no wish to find. My wife is a woman,
and every woman is pliant. Let my faith remain undisturbed. . . . I desire
no further knowledge than is suitable. . . . God has proscribed this kind
of certainty, even more than he proscribed the Tree of Life to our first
father.')   (OF 42.104.1–6, 43.6.3–6, 43.7.4, 7–8; W 509, 510)

There is great irony in this passage, considering how *molle* Rinaldo has shown
himself to be during his all too recently eschewed adulterous passion for Angelica. Nonetheless, in its recognition that certainty in such matters is impossible, and therefore it's best not to put anyone's virtue to the test lest the result
be severe disappointment, Rinaldo's speech embodies prudence, based, as it
must be, on careful thought ("pensò, e poi disse").[39]
      Ariosto's account of the paladin's arrival at such a state of mind provides a
fascinating counterpoint to Orlando's crisis of desire. According to the *Orlando Innamorato*, Rinaldo had once hated Angelica while she pined for him;
more recently, their situations have been reversed, thanks, like the initial dis-
parity between their feelings toward each other, to what the *Furioso* calls the
"iniqua stella e fier destin [evil star and harsh fate]" (42.37.1; W 501) of the fountains from which he and Angelica have inadvertently drunk, one causing desire, the other hatred for the next person seen after imbibing. Like Boiardo,

Ariosto deploys these fountains as metaphors for the arbitrariness, fickleness, and, when misplaced, futility of erotic desire.

I've already recorded how Rinaldo's response to the information that Angelica has given herself to Medoro conforms to the syndrome of jealousy and shame we have charted among Angelica's other lovers. Awash in self-pity and jealousy, Rinaldo heads eastward; in the forest of the Ardennes, amidst a sudden deep gloom, the distraught warrior sees emerge from a dark cave a female monster, with a thousand lidless eyes and as many ears, who attacks Rinaldo with a great poisonous serpent that serves as a tail: "*di qua di là* gli vien sopra a gran salto [it lunged at him from one side and the other]" (OF 42.49.5, emphasis added; W 502). He flees but cannot escape her, in a fast-forward version of a knight wandering in the labyrinthine forest of desire or a recapitulation of Angelica's terrified flight from the rapacious intentions of her suitors:

Vada al traverso, al dritto, ove si voglia,
sempre ha con lui la maladetta peste;
né sa modo trovar, che se ne scioglia,
ben che 'l destrier di calcitrar non reste.
Triema a Rinaldo il cor come una foglia:
non ch'altrimente il serpe lo moleste;
ma tanto orror ne sente e tanto schivo,
che stride e geme, a duolsi ch'egli è vivo.

Nel più tristo sentier, nel peggior calle
scorrendo va, nel più *intricato* bosco,
ove ha più asprezza il balzo, ove la valle
è più spinosa, ov'è l'aer più fosco,
così sperando tôrsi de la spalle
quel brutto, abominoso, orrido tòsco;
e ne saria mal capitato forse,
se tosto non giungea chi lo soccorse.

(Wherever he went, lunging and wheeling, the cursed monster stuck to him, However much his steed bucked, Rinaldo could find no way to be rid of her. His heart trembled like a leaf, not so much lest the serpent molest him further as because it inspired in him such horror and revulsion. He cried out, he groaned, he wished he were dead. He sped through the worst paths, where the going was hardest, the woods thickest, the slopes steepest, the valleys thorniest, the gloom deepest, in the hope of shaking off the horrible, poisonous monster—hideous, loathsome thing. And he would perhaps have met a sorry end were it not that help soon arrived.)

(*OF* 42.51–52, emphasis added; W 502–3)

Suddenly—and as if he were indeed Angelica, or another woman threatened with ravishment in the forest—"un cavalliero / di bello armato e lucido metallo" (literally, a knight in shining armor) appears, his blazon a "giogo rotto" (broken yoke), who, using as his weapon a perpetually flaming club, beats the monster back into her cave, "ove rode se stesso e si manuca, / e da mille occhi versa il pianto eterno [there to gnaw at herself and weep eternally with her thousand eyes]" (*OF* 42.58.3–4), while advising Rinaldo to escape "per quella via che s'alza verso il monte [taking the road which climbed uphill]" (42.57.4), which he does, "ben che molto aspro era a salir quel colle [though the hill was a steep one to climb]" (42.57.8"). The savior knight follows, accompanying Rinaldo to the mountain top, "per trarlo fuor de' luoghi oscuri e bui [to deliver him from that place of deep gloom]" (42.58.8; all W 503), and leads him thence to a nearby spring; "Signor," the courtier-narrator explains to Cardinal Ippolito, "queste eran quelle gelide acque, / quelle che spengon l'amoroso caldo [These, my Lord, were the ice-cold waters which dowse Love's flames]" (42.61.1–2; W 504)—the infamous fountain that led Rinaldo to despise Angelica and later, after he had drunk from the fountain of enamorment, led her to reject his advances. Only after Rinaldo has drunk, and freed himself from his desire, does the knight who has saved him identify himself: "Sappi, Rinaldo, il nome mio è lo Sdegno, / venuto sol per sciorti il giogo indegno [Rinaldo, my name is Wrath. I am here only to free you from your shameful yoke]" (42.64.7–8; W 504). He then vanishes.

The obvious meaning of this melodramatic, hyper-Dantesque episode is psychological: Rinaldo, tormented by poisonous jealousy issuing from the depths of his shame and grief at losing Angelica to Medoro, is only saved from mental self-destruction—the madness we have already seen in Orlando—by a salutary, compensatory "attack" of angry disdain for Angelica, now reconstructed in his mind (defensively, but not, we would say, fairly) as an object of scorn, one unworthy of his attention:

Gli fu nel primier odio ritornata
Angelica; e gli parve troppo indegna
d'esser, non che sì lungi seguitata,
ma che per lei pur mezza lega vegna.

(He reverted to his original hatred for Angelica; now she did not seem worth pursuing a mile, let alone for so long a journey. [Cf. *OF* 29.1.4, where the narrator speaks of "amoroso sdegno" as a cause of the "instabil mente [inconstant minds]" of men.]) (*OF* 42.67.1–4; W 504)

To conquer his self-destructive jealousy, Rinaldo must let go of his desire by submitting it to the wrath of (sour) grapes. Ariosto's resort to allegory may seem moral (the escape from the dark wood by climbing the difficult path, à la *Inferno* 1) but a moment's reflection reveals it to be psychological instead. According to *OF*, the crisis caused Angelica's myriad suitors by their possessive, shame-driven desire can have only two outcomes: the destructive (and self-destructive) madness of Orlando, or Rinaldo's recovery of self-esteem by repressing jealousy via an attitude (achieved with difficulty) of self-righteous disdain for the object of desire, relegated to a position of unworthiness of the affection—indeed, the attention—of a noble warrior. The poem's obvious judgment is that neither recourse deserves much admiration, but, as I've suggested, if the end result is Rinaldo's prudence when presented with a test of his wife's virtue that could eventuate in his renewed subjection to corrosive jealousy, then this may be about the best that can be expected of fallible mortals seeking to find their way through the labyrinthine forest of desire within a culture that embraces a double standard with respect to male and female chastity.

The *Furioso*'s clearest critique of this double standard comes in canto 28, where an innkeeper relates a cynical novella exemplifying the time-honored, misogynistic discourse of female sexual voracity. A version of the framing tale of *The Thousand and One Nights*, it relates the search of the two handsomest men in the world, both of whom have been cuckolded by their wives with less worthy men—cf. Angelica's union with Medoro, in the eyes of Orlando, Rinaldo, et al.—first, to discover if all wives are as ready as their own to cuckold their respective husbands—"Se beltà non varrà né giovanezza, / varranne almen l'aver con noi danari [If neither good looks nor youth will serve us, at least our riches will help]" (*OF* 28.46.5–6; W 344)—and later, when they tire of the danger involved in so much cuckolding, to find a woman whom they can share, hoping thereby to satisfy her sexual appetite while keeping her what we might call bi-faithful. When the woman they choose for this relationship cuckolds them with a servant, in their very bed, the disenchanted protagonists decide to accept the reality of limitless female desire and return, resigned, to their wives.[40] Their resignation is the other side of the coin to Rinaldo's deliberate, prudent refusal to drink from the cup that will test his wife's "virtue"; in both cases, the alternative to becoming *furioso* over the trials and tribulations of desire is acceptance of its less-than-perfect reality.

The novella's ideological portrayal of women is immediately contested by a guest at the inn, who attacks not only its premise—as jaundiced, stereotyping opinion, induced by momentary anger rather than careful deliberation—but also the double standard that underlies (and sponsors) such portrayals:

Quivi era un uom d'età, ch'avea più retta
opiniön degli altri, e ingegno e ardire;
e non potendo ormai, che sì negletta
ogni femina fosse, più patire,
si volse a quel ch'avea l'istoria detta,
e gli disse: "Assai cose udimo dire,
che veritade in sé non hanno alcuna:
e ben di queste è la tua favola una.

A chi te la narrò non do credenza,
s'evangelista ben fosse nel resto;
ch'opiniöne, più ch'esperïenza
ch'abbia di donne, lo facea dir questo.
L'avere ad una o due malivolenza,
fa ch'odia e biasma l'altre oltre all'onesto;
ma se gli passa l'ira, io vo' tu l'oda,
più ch'ora biasmo, anco dar lor gran loda.
. . . .
Ditemi un poco: è di voi forse alcuno
ch'abbia servato alla sua moglie fede?
che nieghi andar, quando gli sia opportuno,
all'altrui donna, a darle ancor mercede?
credete in tutto 'l mondo trovarne uno? . . .

Conoscete alcun voi, che non lasciasse
la moglie sola, ancor che fosse bella,
per seguire altra donna, se sperasse
in breve e facilmente ottener quella? . . .

Quelle che i lor mariti hanno lasciati,
le più volte cagione avuta n'hanno.
Del suo di casa li veggon svogliati,

e che fuor, de l'altrui bramosi, vanno.
Dovriano amar, volendo essere amati,
E tor con la misura ch'allor dànno.

(Now there was present an old man—a man of shrewdness and courage, and more right-minded than the others. He would not allow that all womankind should be thus ill-considered, so he turned to the story-teller and told him: We hear scores of things which don't hold a grain of truth—your tale is one of them. I don't believe the man who told it to you, even if he spoke Gospel truth in all else: opinion, not his own experience of women, made him speak this way. He may have borne a grudge against one or two women which made him excessively hostile and captious about all the rest; but let his anger subside and I warrant you would hear him heaping far more praise on them now than blame earlier. . . . Now tell me: is there one among you who has kept faith with his wife, or denies ever going after another man's wife, given the opportunity, and even giving her presents? Do you believe you'll find one such man in all the world? . . . Do you know any man who would not leave his wife, however beautiful she was, to follow another woman, if he had hopes of a quick and easy conquest? . . . The women who have left their husbands, more often than not they've had good cause; they find their men tired of them at home and gone out eager for other men's wives. But men, when they love, ought to wish their love returned, to receive in measure as they give.)   (OF 28.76–77, 79.1–5, 80.1–4, 81.1–6; W 348)

To cap his rebuttal, the wise old man proposes a law, an obvious (though un-acknowledged) revision of the *aspra legge di Scozia* that nearly doomed Ginevra at the hands of Polinesso, himself a perfect example of the hypocrisy just castigated:

Io farei (se a me stesse il darla e tôrre)
tal legge, ch'uom non vi potrebbe opporre.

Saria la legge, ch'ogni donna colta
in adulterio, fosse messa a morte,
se provar non potesse ch'una volta
avesse adulterato il suo consorte:
se provar lo potesse, andrebbe asciolta,
né temeria il marito né la corte.

(If it fell to me to make and suspend laws, I would enact a law to which no man could object: every woman caught in adultery would be put to death unless she could prove that her husband had once done so too. If she could prove it, she would be absolved—she would need fear neither her husband nor the court.)   (*OF* 28.81.7–8, 82.1–6; W 348–49)

Even this ringing defense of women (a well-attested Renaissance rhetorical tradition, incidentally, and the other half—along with the misogynistic story to which it responds—of an exercise, on Ariosto's part, of a *disputatio ad utramque partem* [debate on both sides of an issue]) subscribes to the culture's conventional wisdom that chastity is the female virtue par excellence—"la incontinenza è quanto mal si puote / imputar lor [unchastity is the worst vice that can be imputed to women]" (*OF* 28.83.1–2; W 349)—but this does little to diminish the force of its implied critique of the subjection of so many of the *Furioso*'s Christian and Saracen heroes, married or betrothed, to their lust- (and honor-) driven pursuit of Angelica's virginity, irrespective of her desires in the matter.

In a further implied dissent to the novella's *opinïone*—but also a further endorsement of chastity as the crucial female virtue—the very next canto contains an episode in which Isabella, faithful beloved of Zerbino, kills herself rather than give in to the brutal advances of the Saracen bully, Rodomonte. As is so frequently the case, the *Orlando Furioso* shows itself in this episode to be a chronicle of the deleterious effects of male desire on men and women alike.

Throughout its great length, the *Furioso* raises the issue of authority in ways that are rarely supportive of that concept. To begin with us, the poem's readers: that our memories cannot encompass the warp and woof of what the narrator at one point (see the epigraph to this chapter) calls his tapestry of many threads—but what we might call his crazy quilt—is the clear implication of narratorial asides ostensibly designed to help, but actually to taunt us.[41] Alluding, tongue in cheek, to the difficulties of keeping his mammoth cast of characters and phalanx of stories in one's head, he comments, as he reintroduces Angelica into his tale in canto 19, finding the near-dead Medoro in the forest and feeling an unwonted pity for him, "Tanto è ch'io non ne dissi più novella, / ch'a pena riconoscer la dovreste [It is so long now since I last spoke of her, you may scarcely be able to recognize her]" (*OF* 19.17.5–6; W 218).

At another point, when returning, after only one intervening canto, to the narrative track belonging to the cruel pagan king, Rodomonte, the narrator addresses his patron thus: "Non so, Signor, se più vi ricordiate / di questo Saracin tanto sicuro [I do not know, My Lord, whether you still remember this Saracen of boundless temerity]" (OF 16.20.1–2; W 168). We have not forgotten Rodomonte, thanks to the cruelty and extreme violence that characterizes his activity in the battle for Paris, but we probably don't remember exactly what he was doing when the narrator took him away from us.

Or take this comment about a bracelet that Angelica, having scorned the love (read: lust) of a half dozen kings, princes, and counts, gives to Medoro:

Se lo serbò ne l'Isola del pianto
non so già dirvi con che privilegio,
là dove esposta al marin mostro [the Orca] nuda
fu da la gente inospitale e cruda.

(I cannot explain to you by what privilege she was able to keep it [the bracelet] on the isle of Ebuda, when she was exposed naked to the sea monster by the cruel, barbarous islanders.)   (OF 19.39.5–8; W 221)

This supposed admission of ignorance, about a sensational episode narrated nine cantos ago, reminds us how easily the poem could have slipped the inconsistency in question by us, and makes us wonder how many more we may have missed while trying to keep up with its cornucopia of characters and story lines.

My point is that we are not supposed to remember, and by remembering to domesticate, the world of the *Furioso*; the poem exists to remind us that we can no more achieve authority over it by acts of recollection than we, or the poem's characters, can exert meaningful authority over life, in all its complexity, by the application to it of will or force. Faced with the fact of our inability to contain such variety in a memorial frame, we sigh and submit to the pleasures of being swept along in the narrative tide. This is, I believe, the first and the dominant lesson, or meaning, that emerges from our experience of Ariosto's poem simply as a sequence (a very long sequence) of words received over time: just as in life, there's more in this text than you can ever hope to control, comprehend, or keep straight; wisdom lies in accepting your limitations (in this case, your limitations as an audience), as madness lies in seeking to exceed them.

As with our pretended, or desired, authority as readers of the *Furioso*, poetic and political authority, as well as the stature of Ariosto's patrons, Ippolito and Alfonso d'Este, all come in for some hard (and amusing) knocks in the course of the poem. As we've seen at its very beginning, Ariosto, assuming the narratorial voice of the obsequious court poet, offers his poem and its story of Ruggiero, the Este progenitor, to Ippolito, with a fanfare of flattery, in payment of an unnamed (and presumably metaphorical) debt: "Quel ch'io vi debbo, posso di parole / pagare in parte, e d'opera d'inchiostro . . . quanto io posso dar, tutto vi dono [My debt to you I can partly repay with words, with an outlay of ink . . . all I have to give, I give you]" (*OF* 1.3.5–6; W 1). But there's an Ovidian send-up hidden in the narrator's declaration that as "umil servo vostro [your humble servant]" (*OF* 1.3.4; W 1), he will pay his debt in words and ink: in the *Ars amatoria*, as I've noted earlier, Ovid, claiming that poets are too poor to give lavish gifts, says that in wooing a girl, "cum dare non possem munera, verba dabam [since I could not give gifts, I gave words]" (*Ars* 2.165–66), using an idiom (*dare verba*, to give words) that means *to lie*; given Ariosto's documented Ovidianism, I believe he is saying obliquely that what he will write about the Este family's glorious forebears will be what a tutor of mine at Oxford once called "a tissue of twaddle."

Support for this conjecture lies in a famously audacious passage in canto 35 of the *Furioso*, a conversation on the moon—that repository of everything lost on earth through imprudence and folly, according to Ariosto's Dantesque parody—between Astolfo, who, we recall, will eventually find Orlando's love-banished sanity there, preserved in a large jar, and the apostle and evangelist John, his guide through the lunar landscape.[42] The two men observe an allegorical pageant representing how people are remembered or forgotten after they die: an old man (Time) throws plaques, inscribed with the names of all those who have lived, into a fast running river (oblivion) from which only a few are rescued by beautiful swans, who fly with them to a temple of immortality where they are enshrined for all time. Using the language of simile, John explains to Astolfo:

Ma come i cigni che cantando lieti
rendeno salve le medaglie al tempio,
così gli uomini degni da' poeti
son tolti da l'oblio, più che morte empio.

(As the swans with their glad song convey the plaques safely to the shrine, so it is that men of worth are rescued from oblivion—crueller than death—by poets.)   (*OF* 35.22.1–4; W 424)

Hence, the evangelist continues—drawing a conclusion as commonplace in Renaissance poetry as it was self-serving—it's a wise prince who, following Caesar's example, makes poets [Vergil? *Ovid?*] his friends, thereby overcoming fear of being victims of Lethe's waters of forgetfulness:

> Oh bene accorti principi e discreti,
> che seguite di Cesare l'esempio,
> e gli scrittor vi fate amici, donde
> non avete a temer di Lete l'onde!"

(O shrewd and sagacious princes, if you follow Caesar's example and make writers your friends you need have no fear of Lethe's waters!)

(OF 35.22.5–8; W 424)

Still following a well-worn topical path, the evangelist condemns stingy lords who refuse to patronize the poets who would immortalize them:

> Credi che Dio questi ignoranti ha privi
> de lo 'ntelletto, e loro offusca i lumi;
> che de la poesia gli ha fatto schivi,
> acciò che morte il tutto ne consumi.

(Believe me, God has robbed these simpletons of their wits and clouded their judgment, making them shun Poetry so that death should consume them whole and entire.)   (OF 35.24.1–4; W 424)

Suddenly, however, as John warms to his explicatory task, his tone changes: if princes befriended poets, they would live in good fame despite their awful deeds—"ancor ch'avesser tutti i rei costumi"—for

> non si pietoso Enea, né forte Achille
> Fu, come è fama, né si fiero Ettorre; . . .
> ma i donati palazzi e le gran ville
> dai decendenti lor, gli ha fatto porre
> in questi senza fin sublimi onori
> da l'onorate man degli scrittori.

(Aeneas was not as devoted, nor Achilles as strong, nor Hector as ferocious as their reputations suggest. . . . What has brought them their sublime

renown have been the writers honored with gifts of palaces and great
estates donated by these heroes' descendants.)

(*OF* 35.25.1–2, 5–8; W 425)

In other words, if you want a pedigree of exemplary ancestors—such as
the *Furioso* more than once supplies for Ferrara's Este dynasty—just bribe
a poet; he'll do the job. The apostle rumbles on, picking up speed as he goes:

Non fu sì santo né benigno Augusto
come la tuba di Virgilio suona.
L'aver avuto in poesia buon gusto
la proscrizion iniqua gli perdona. . . .

Omero Agamennòn vittorioso,
e fe' i Troian parer vili et inerti;
e che Penelopea fida al suo sposo
dai Prochi mille oltraggi avea sofferti.
E se tu vuoi che 'l ver non ti sia ascoso,
tutta al contrario l'istoria converti:
che i Greci rotti, e che Troia vittrice,
e che Penelopea fu meretrice.

(Augustus was not as august and beneficent as Vergil makes him out in
clarion tones—but his good taste in poetry compensates for the evil of
his proscriptions. . . . Homer made Agamemnon appear the victor and
the Trojans mere poltroons; he made Penelope faithful to her husband, and victim of a thousand slights from her suitors. But if you
want to know what really happened, invert the story: Greece was vanquished, Troy triumphant, and Penelope a whore.)

(*OF* 35.26.1–4, 27; W 425)

So much for the truth value of Ariosto's many *ottave* devoted to praising
Cardinal Ippolito d'Este—including a few uttered by the evangelist to Astolfo at the beginning of this same thirty-fifth canto. But, the poem suggests,
why should skepticism about the poetry of praise—a skepticism that clearly
parallels the attitude toward literary traditions that runs through Chaucer's
House of Fame—stop there? Not when John, in seeming apology for his blunt-
ness, tells his guest,

Non ti maravigliar ch'io n'abbia ambascia,
e si di ciò diffusamente io dico.
Gli scrittori amo, e fo il debito mio;
ch'al vostro mondo fui scrittore anch'io.

E sopra tutti gli altri io feci acquisto
che non mi può levar tempo né morte:
e ben convenne al mio lodato Cristo
rendermi guidardòn di si gran sorte.

(Don't be surprised if this embitters me and if I talk about it at some
length—I like writers and am doing my duty by them, for in your world I
was a writer too. And I, above all others, acquired something which neither Time nor Death can take from me: I praised Christ and merited
from Him the reward of so great a good fortune.)

                                    (*OF* 35.28.5–8, 29.1–4; W 425)

What these words imply about scriptural verity (and therefore about the dubi-
ousness of both textual and institutional authority) makes them among the
most subversive of the entire poem.[43]

Quite apart from the Evangelist's cautionary *laus poetriae*, the many narratorial personae of the *Furioso* undermine their own authority in a variety of ways:
for example, at one point the narrator nearly loses his way within the forest of
his multiple narratives: he confesses,

Ma d'un parlar ne l'altro, ove sono ito
sì lungi dal camin ch'io faceva ora?
Non lo credo però si aver smarrito
ch'io non lo sappia ritrovare ancora.

(But with one thing and another we seems to have strayed right off
ourpath; where was I? No, wait, I don't believe I've lost it beyond recall.)[44]   (*OF* 17.80.1–4; W 186)

Nor is the chronicling narrator omniscient: I've already mentioned, in another context, his admission (*OF* 19.39.5–8) that he cannot explain how Angelica was able to keep, when stripped naked on the island of Ebuda to be
Orca's prey, the bracelet she later gives to Medoro; in addition, following a

precedent established by Boccaccio in *The Decameron*, he offers multiple possible explanations for all sorts of things, e.g., why Cimosco's gun doesn't hit and kill Orlando (9.76) or the fate of a monk thrown into the sea by a Rodomonte made *furioso* by his desire for Isabella:

> Che n'avenisse, né dico né sollo:
> varia fama è di lui, né si raguaglia.
> Dice alcun che sì rotto a un sasso resta,
> Che 'l piè non si discerne da la testa;
>
> et altri, ch'a cadere andò nel mare,
> ch'era più di tre miglia indi lontano,
> e che morì per non saper notare,
> fatti assai prieghi e orazioni invano;
> altri, ch'un santo lo venne aiutare,
> lo trasse al lito con visibil mano.
> Di queste, qual si vuol, la vera sia:
> di lui non parla più l'istoria mia.

(What became of the monk I cannot tell—I do not know. Various and conflicting stories exist: one claims that he was so shattered against a rock that there was no telling his head from his foot; another, that he landed in the sea, three miles away, and died for not being able to swim, having vainly offered up many a prayer and supplication; another, that a saint came to his aid, carrying him ashore with visible hand. One of these may be the truth—at any rate my story says no more about him.)   (OF 29.6.5–8, 7; W 352)

He's also not reliable, giving us misinformation, for example, about Angelica's supposed virginity, the possibility of which he mocks (1.58, referred to above), though it turns out to be genuine (cf. OF 19.33).

Particularly egregious is the amatory narrator's contradictory attitudes toward women. His observation about others at the beginning of canto 29 applies to himself as well:

> O degli uomini inferma e instabil mente!
> come siàn presti a variar disegno!
> Tutti i pensier mutamo facilmente,
> più quei che nascon d'amoroso sdegno.

(Oh the weak, inconstant minds of men! How ready we are to vacillate, how ready to change our ideas, especially those born of lovers' spite.)

(OF 29.1.1–4; W 351)

He blames Rodomonte, whose blanket condemnation of all women's infidelity has occurred in the preceding canto, the result of his loss of Doralice to Mandricado:

Donne gentil, per quel ch'a biasmo vostro
parlò contra il dover, sì offeso sono,
che sin che col suo mal non gli dimostro
quanto abbia fatto error, non gli perdono.

(Gentle ladies, I am so offended by what he said against you without cause that until I have shown him, to his chagrin, just how wrong he has been I shall not forgive him.)

(OF 29.2.1–4; W 351)

Yet at the end of this same canto, after recounting how Angelica saved herself from the mindless rage of the mad Orlando by means of the magic ring that renders her invisible, the narrator fulminates:

Deh maledetto sia l'annello et anco
il cavallier che dato le l'avea!
che se non era, avrebbe Orlando fatto
di sé vendetta e di mill'altri a un tratto.

Né questa sola, ma fosser pur state
in man d'Orlando quante oggi ne sono;
ch'ad ogni modo tutte son ingrate,
né si trova tra loro oncia di buono.

(A curse upon the ring and upon the knight who gave it to her—were it not for that, Orlando would at a stroke have been avenged on his own and on many another's account! Would that not she alone but the whole surviving sex had fallen into Orlando's hands: they're a nasty tribe and not one ounce of good is to be found in any of them!)

(OF 29.73.5–8, 74.1–4; W 359)

And then, at the beginning of canto 30, he apologizes to women for such an outburst. (Earlier, at the beginning of canto 20, he has heaped abundant praise on women, both ancient and modern, for their many virtues, blaming widespread ignorance of the former on [perhaps] "l'invidia o il non saper degli scrittori [envy or the ignorance of those who wrote about them]" [OF 20.2.8; my translation]—such as himself?—and hoping that the latter will find chroniclers—such as himself?—who can counter the "eterna infamia" of "odiose lingue [the calumnies of evil tongues]"—such as his? [OF 20.3.6; W 230]).

Perhaps the single moment that most challenges narratorial authority comes at OF 4.17–20, which proffers a description of the hippogryph ridden by the sorcerer Atlante, with whom Bradamante is duelling in order to free her beloved Ruggiero from the *mago*'s enchanted mountain-top castle:

> Non è finto il destrier, ma naturale,
> ch'una giumenta generò d'un grifo:
> simile ad padre avea la piuma e l'ale,
> li piedi anteriori, il capo e il grifo;
> in tutte l'altre membra parea quale
> era la madre, e chiamasi ippogrifo;
> che nei monti Rifei vengon, ma rari,
> molto di là dagli aghiacciati mari. . . .
>
> Non finzion d'incanto, come il resto,
> ma vero e natural si vedea questo.
>
> Del mago ogn'altro cosa era figmento.
>
> (The horse was no figment—he was real, begotten by a gryphon out of
> a mare. He had his father's wings and feathers, his forefeet, his head
> and beak; in all else he took after his mother. He was known as a
> hippogryph—they are indigenous to the Rifean hills (though rare), way
> beyond the frozen seas. . . . No magical figment, this horse: unlike the
> rest, this was as real as could be. Everything else about the magician was
> sheer trickery.)   (OF 4.18, 19.7–8, 20.1; W 32, translation modified)

Of course, this implicit indictment of the narrator's reliability here coincides with, indeed constitutes, one of the summits of Ariostan comedy; in particular, the careful qualification of 4.19.7—"nei monti Rifei vengon, *ma rari*"—is the signature moment of a peculiarly Italian comic genius.[45]

The barbs Ariosto aims at court poets (including himself) through John the Evangelist's ostensible praise of them in canto 35 can also be understood, *mutatis mutandis*, as directed (or indirected) toward idealized representations, by poets and humanists, of life at the courts of princes such as the Este and other northern Italian despots of the age. In canto 42 both sycophantic praise of the mighty and the tradition of poetic celebration of women are spoofed via a marble fountain in a luxurious palace, adorned with eight larger-than-lifesize statues of notable noblewomen, each of whom stands astride

> due belle imagini più basse,
> che con la bocca aperta facean segni
> che 'l canto e l'armonia lor dilettasse;
> e quell'atto in che son, par che disegni
> che l'opra e studio lor tutto lodasse
> le belle donne che sugli omeri hanno.

(A pair of beautifully carved figures depicted open-mouthed, as though happily indulging in melodious song. Their appearance, as they sang, seemed to convey a total dedication to their task of praising the fair ladies poised upon their shoulders.) (*OF* 42.81.2–8; W 506)

Scrolls identify the ladies and their dedicated, one might almost say domesticated, poets, all of whom are Ariosto's contemporaries; the language that describes the latter appears to suggest, by its conditionals and subjunctives, some doubts about the sincerity of this tableau of slavish poetic dedication. (Cf. the poets who similarly support on their shoulders the fame of nations in book 3 of Chaucer's *House of Fame*; see chapter 2, pages 116–17.)

The most celebrated, apparently idealized representation of court life is Castiglione's *Libro del cortegiano*, which offers a "portrait" of the court of Urbino under its invalid duke, Guidobaldo di Montefeltro, in the form of a series of after-dinner conversations among the duke's courtiers, presided over by the duchess, Elisabetta Gonzaga, and her confidante, the lady Maria Pia (the duke being absent, forced by his illness to retire early). Presented as a game having as its goal "formar con parole un perfetto cortegiano [the formation in words of a perfect courtier]"—and in the third (though written last) of four books, the formation of the perfect court lady, or *donna di palazzo*—the resultant dialogue seems at first reading a brilliant evocation of a golden moment in the history of the court, as the witty interlocutors recapitulate many of the favorite topics and debates of high-Renaissance humanism, alluding to but avoiding embroilment in the age's social and political crises. Although closer study of Castiglione's masterpiece reveals the near-constant presence of darker themes and, ultimately, a tragic sense of life beneath the dialogue's smooth surface of elegant discourse, that surface, apparently depicting court life as an idyll of leisure and privilege, can serve as an exemplary target for the distinctly disenchanted allusions to courtiership scattered throughout the *OF*, many of them focused on the career of Ruggiero, made progenitor of the Este dynasty in a flagrant adaptation (originally by Boiardo) of Vergilian dynastic mythology to the needs of Este propaganda.

At several points in the *Furioso*, Ruggiero's waverings between loyalty to Bradamante, his betrothed, and surrender to transgessive desire enacts the choice of Hercules, a popular high-Renaissance moral and artistic subject, represented iconographically as Hercules at the crossroads, choosing between the hard path to virtue and the easy road to pleasure and thence ruin.[46] Inflecting this Renaissance concern through the classical stories of Circe and Odysseus or Dido and Aeneas, *OF* depicts Ruggiero taken by the hippogryph to a magic island where he must choose between the two warring half-sister fairies, the wicked Alcina and the virtuous Logistilla. Warned by the warrior turned into a tree, Astolfo (an amalgam of analogous figures in Vergil and Dante), Ruggiero sets out on the rugged road to Logistilla's mountaintop fortress, where he is set upon by a semi-allegorical band of brigands and rescued by two beautiful, elegant women

> ch'ai gesti et al vestire
> non eran da stimar nate umilmente,
> né da pastor nutrite con disagi,
> ma fra delizie di real palagi.
>   . . . e tal saria
> Beltà, s'avesse corpo, e Leggiadria.

(To judge by their bearing and apparel, they were clearly not of mean birth, brought up in poverty by shepherds, but reared amid the opulence of a royal palace. . . . They could have passed for Beauty [had she a body] and Grace.)   (*OF* 6.68.5–8; 69.7–8; W 58)

Seduced by such beauty and elegance, Ruggiero is led by these maidens to the entrance portal to Alcina's domain, the extensive, sensuous description of which (*OF* 6.71–75) parallels the amorous *paysage ideal* entitled "Andrians," described by Philostratus in his third-century C.E. book of descriptions of imaginary paintings, the *Imagines*—a copy of which was in Alfonso d'Este's library—and painted by Titian on commission from Alfonso. Soon Alcina welcomes Ruggiero to her palace and retinue of perfect courtiers:

> Non tanto il bel palazzo era escellente
> perché vincesse ogn'altro di ricchezza,
> quanto ch'avea la più piacevol gente
> che fosse al mondo e di più gentilezza.

(What was remarkable about the splendid palace was not its opulence [unrivalled though it was] so much as its inhabitants—the most attractive, courteous people in the world.)   (*OF* 7.10.1–4; W 61)

In short order the knight is enthralled in errant desire for Alcina herself, thereby forgetting both Astolfo's warnings about Alcina (6.50–52) and his love for Bradamante:

> Quel che di lei già avea dal mirto inteso,
> com'è perfida e ria, poco gli giova;
> ch'inganno o tradimento non gli è aviso
> che possa star con sì soave riso.
>
> Anzi pur creder vuol che da costei
> fosse converso Astolfo in su l'arena
> per li suoi portamenti ingrati e rei,
> e sia degno di questa e di più pena:
> e tutto quel ch'udito avea di lei,
> stima esser falso; e che vendetta mena,
> e mena astio et invidia quel dolente
> a lei biasmare, e che del tutto mente.
>
> La bella donna che cotanto amava,
> Novellamente gli è dal cor partita.

(Little did it profit him [Ruggiero] to have been warned by the myrtle of her evil, treacherous nature—it did not seem to him possible for deceit and perfidy to keep company with so charming a smile. On the contrary, he preferred to believe that if she had changed Astolfo into a myrtle by the sandy shore, it was because he had treated her with stark ingratitude, and so deserved his fate and worse. Everything he had been told about her he dismissed as false, deeming rather that the wretch was moved by spite and envy and was a shameless liar. Intensely though he loved fair Bradamant, she was here and now wrested from his heart.)

(*OF* 7.16.5–8; 17; 18.1–2; W 62)

This episode appears to offer a paradigm of human freedom to choose (and choose badly) between virtue and folly: "ecco il giudizio uman come spesso erra!" But Ariosto complicates and confuses the paradigm in more than one way.[47] There is, first of all, the involvement of two inimical guardian figures, the sorcerers Atlante and Melissa: the former, Ruggiero's protector, attempting to keep him from his Este destiny, the latter, Bradamante's, making sure he fulfills it by marrying her. From this perspective, Ruggiero is no free-agent avatar of Hercules but a pawn in their battle: a tug-of-war that perforce reduces Alcina's seduction of Ruggiero to a mere trick played by Atlante, and her exposure as an ancient, surpassingly ugly crone—by means of the ring that Melissa (disguised as Atlante!) gives to Ruggiero to free him from enchantment (*OF* 7.65ff)—to an epiphanic enactment of destiny's irresistible claim on the young warrior, despite the lure of pleasurable avoidance.

A further complication arises from Ariosto's imposing on the Herculean paradigm another famous one, that of Achilles, whose destiny was to be either fame and early death or a long but uncelebrated life. Seen from this perspective, Atlante's enclosure of Ruggiero in a succession of courtly prisons is designed to ensure his survival, while Melissa's counter-schemes become attempts to make him a ritual sacrifice on the altar of Este despotism. A succession of octaves in canto 7, contrasting the perspectives of the two magicians, suggests the full complexity of the scrutiny under which Ariosto places the cultural authority of that despotism and of its courtly ideology:

Di Ruggier liberato e poi perduto,
e dove in India andò, tutto ha saputo. . . .

[E] ben sapea che stava in giuoco e in ballo
e in cibo e in ozio [cf. Latin *otium*] molle e delicato,
né più memoria avea del suo signore,
né de la donna sua, né del suo onore.

E così il fior de li begli anni suoi
in lunga inerzia aver potria consunto

si gentil cavallier, per dover poi
perdere il corpo e l'anima in un punto; . . .

Ma quella gentil maga, che più cura
n'avea ch'egli medesmo di se stesso,
pensò di trarlo per via alpestre e dura
alla vera virtù, *mal grado d'esso.* . . .

Ella non gli era facile, e talmente
fattane cieca di superchio amore,
che, come facea Atlante, solamente
a darli vita avesse posto il core.
Quel più tosto volea che lungamente
Vivesse e senza fama e senza onore,
Che, con tutta la laude che sia al mondo,
Mancasse un anno al suo viver giocondo.

L'avea mandato all'isola d'Alcina,
perché oblïasse l'arme in quella corte;
e come mago di somma dottrina, . . .
avea il cor stretto di quella regina
ne l'amor d'esso d'un laccio sì forte,
che non se ne era mai per poter sciorre,
s'invechiasse Ruggier più dei Nestorre.

(Ruggiero's delivery from Atlas [= Atlante], his abduction, where now he
was in India, all this was known to her [Melissa]. . . . Full well she knew
how he was passing his time now in amusements, in dancing and feasting,
in soft, pampered indolence [in Alcina's embrace], forgetful of his Liege,
of his beloved, of his own renown. And it might therefore have been the
lot of so goodly a knight to pass the best years of his life in sustained idleness, only to lose his soul and body all at once. . . . But the kind sorceress,
who took more care of him than he did of himself, thought how to bring
him back to true virtue, despite himself, by a hard and rugged way. . . .
She showed him no indulgence; a transcendant love made her so blind to
all else that she had, like Atlas, set her heart upon restoring his life to him.
Atlas, however, would have him enjoy long life bereft of honour and renown rather than forego one year of his carefree existence for all the praise
the world could accord him. He had sent Ruggiero to Alcina's island to

make him, at her court, forget about arms. And, being a magician of consummate art . . . he had bound that queen's heart to his in so strong a
bond that there was no question of her breaking free, though Ruggiero
were to grow as old as Nestor.)

(*OF* 7.39.7–8, 40.5–8, 41.1–4, 42.1–4, 43, 44.1–3, 5–8; W 65)

When taken together with the text's repeated testimony that both magicians
are aided in their campaigns by spirits of clearly diabolical origins, this set of
agendas, besides functioning as Ariosto's updating of Ovid's play with the
otium/negotium binary, makes Ruggiero's career seem suspiciously like a seriocomic allegory of the price to be paid in liberty and perhaps life by anyone
destined for service to a despotic court. Is Ruggiero's hypothetical freedom to
choose his destiny, denied in fact by the demands of Este history, also a wry
comment on Ariosto's lack of freedom as an Este servant?

The narrator's claim that Atlante has bound Alcina's heart to Ruggiero
beyond her power to change in turn undercuts the poem's suggestion (via Astolfo's warning to Ruggiero) that the sorceress is a personification of Fortune
who decides to make a paladin her lover, thus raising him to new heights of
luxury and bliss only to discard him abruptly a few months later; such is her
changeable nature. Astolfo's prediction combines the promise of Circean and
Ovidian metamorphosis with a recall of medieval depictions of kings raised
up on Fortune's wheel only to be subsequently thrown off it:

[A]vrai d'Alcina scettro e signoria,
e sarai lieto sopra ogni mortale:
ma certo sii di giunger tosto al passo
d'entrar o in fiera o in fonte o in legno o in sasso.

(A sceptre shall be yours, from Alcina's hand, and you shall reign, and
you shall be the happiest of mortal men: but make no mistake—your
time will soon come to be changed into a beast or a fountain, into wood
or rock.)   (*OF* 6.52.5–8; W 56)

In any case, it seems that Ruggiero's freedom is illusory: Atlante and Melissa in effect control him, dragging him back and forth (cf. *di qua, di la*), in and
out of temptation and imprisonment, and his adventures, far from enacting the
choice of Hercules, seem to call into radical question his status as a person able
to make choices—*especially* bad ones—at all. But (to compound complexity)

cannot Ruggiero's sudden perception of Alcina as an object of disgust, thanks to the magic ring given him by Melissa, be construed instead psychologically and morally, as a dramatization of his guilty realization that his infatuation with Alcina (the seductive, older woman) constitutes a betrayal of his fiancee?[48] In which case, the figures of Alante and Melissa become externalizations of a psychomachia raging within Ruggiero between duty and pleasure, rather like the female figures contending to turn an elegant young courtier in different directions in Veronese's version of the choice of Hercules. It would then follow that Ruggiero's emasculation at Alcina's court (OF 7.53–55; borrowed from *Aeneid* 4) is to be read as an emblem of the lure of court life as an alternative to moral autonomy—a longstanding theme in European court literature, especially satire.

We see an earlier instance of this danger in the narrator's comment when Bradamante captures Atlante and frees not only Ruggiero but also many other prisoners from the enchanted castle the old sorcerer has created to keep Ruggiero from his Este destiny and early death. As Bradamante breaks the spell and the castle disappears, many of the prisoners, far from welcoming freedom, lament the loss of the pleasure that marked their incarceration:

> Le donne e i cavallier si trovâr fuora
> de le superbe stanze alla campagna:
> e furon di lor molte a chi ne dolse;
> che tal franchezza un gran piacer lor tolse.

(The knights and ladies found themselves outside, delivered from the majestic halls, and not a few of them were displeased to recover their liberty at the price of so much pleasure.)   (OF 4.39.5–8; W 34)

Yet when Bradamante captures the aged magician, he defends his construction of this pleasure dome as the work of a parent protecting a beloved child:

> "Né per maligna intenzïone, ahi lasso!"
> (disse piangendo il vecchio incantatore)
> "feci la bella ròcca in cima al sasso,
> né per avidità son rubatore;
> ma per ritrar sol dall'estremo passo
> un cavallier gentil, mi mosse amore,
> che, come il ciel mi mostra, in tempo breve
> morir cristiano a tradimento deve.

Non vede il sol tra questo e il polo austrino
Un giovene sì bello e sì prestante:
Ruggiero ha nome, il qual da piccolino
Da me nutrito fu, ch'io sono Atlante.
Disio d'onore e suo fiero destino
L'han tratto in Francia dietro al re Agramante;
Et io, che l'amai sempre più che figlio,
Lo cerco trar di Francia e di periglio."

('Alas, I had no wicked intention,' explained the old enchanter, weeping,
'when I built the handsome castle on the crag's top. And it is not avarice
that has made me a robber: Love it was that moved me to rescue a gentle
knight from extreme peril—for Heaven revealed to me that he is shortly
to die a Christian, treacherously slain. Between here and the Southern
pole, nowhere does the sun behold a youth more excellent nor more fair
than he; Ruggiero he is called and I, whose name is Atlas, have brought
him up from his tenderest years. Thirst for honour and his own hard destiny have brought him to France in the following of Agramant the King;
and I, who have ever loved him more than I would a son, I would withdraw him from France, and from danger.)   (*OF* 4.29.30; W 33)

From this perspective, Atlante and Melissa complement each other as un-
compromising metaphors for harsh alternatives: loss of freedom or of life in
court service, the seductive lure of which obscures the fact that it requires
subordinating one's freedom of choice to the priorities of one's princely master. Atlante's castle in canto 4 embodies imprisonment by court pleasures
that cater to the desire for ease and advancement at the cost of independence,
judgment, honesty; Melissa's counter-strategies represent the sacrifice of
comfort and life to the imperatives of a despotic lineage's policies, aimed at
self-aggrandizement. Neither sorcerer makes a compelling case for the exaltation of Este authority.

Perhaps the *Furioso*'s most frontal assault on political authority involves
the "quadro di stupefazione" that confronts the Saracen monarch
Agramante in cantos 26 and 27. I have borrowed this wonderful phrase—the
tamer English equivalent is "ensemble of perplexity"— from the lexicon of
opera, in which it denotes a musical moment, shared by several or all of the
main characters of a music drama, that is designed, in the words of *The New*

Grove Dictionary of Music and Musicians, "to maximize confusion and bring matters to a peak." The consummate deployment of such ensembles for comic purposes in operas by Gioachino Rossini justifies my preference for the Italian terminology; by the conclusion of the first act of *Il barbiere di Siviglia, L'Italiana in Algeri,* or *La Cenerentola,* the schemes and counter-schemes driving the plot have achieved a level of complexity and cross-purposes that generates a moment of sublime comic frenzy, expressed by the principals in words of nonsensical desperation, sung to the accompaniment of what can best be described as orchestral mayhem: a mounting crescendo of hyperactive strings, shrieking piccolos, blaring trumpets, and eruptive percussion.[49]

Noting that Rossini and Ariosto were in some sense kindred comic spirits who enjoyed portraying confusion and bewilderment (which may be another way of saying that both were Italians) does not by itself constitute a profound critical insight. But in the case of the *Furioso,* it contributes to our understanding of how easily and totally authority can be undermined by events—especially events issuing from unregulated desires and the imprudent actions they generate. The reappearance of that labyrinthine term, "*intricato,*" within the script of the Ariostan *opera buffa* reminds us of this fact.

The *Cambridge Italian Dictionary* defines "*stupefazione*" as "surprise, astonishment, stupefaction, insensibility," to which I think it reasonable to add the category "terminal confusion." The most obvious, literal examples of *stupefazione* in the *Furioso,* serving as emblems or quintessences of its more indirect manifestations, result from exposure to three magical weapons that deprive their victims of self-control and the capacity for rational action: there is a magic lance, the mere touch of which in a joust violently unhorses even the most skilled opponent; a horn that when blown provokes all who hear it to flee in a state of uncontrollable panic; and an enchanted shield, the direct sight of which induces immediate loss of consciousness. Taken together, these weapons not only decisively tilt the playing field in favor of their bearers but also serve as stark symbols of how irresistible forces and unforeseen surprises can suddenly abort our plans, subvert our intentions, and reduce us to states of automatic rather than considered response, in short, to reflexive action that, by its nature, trumps more reasoned responses to other priorities, including subordination to authority, rational or political.

One of the most amazing, and amusing, passages in *OF* brilliantly juxtaposes the two main themes of this chapter, in a tableau of irresistible desire subverting political authority.[50] The occasion is a sequence of disputes among some of Agramante's premier supporters on the eve of another climactic confrontation outside Paris between Christians and Saracens. Cantos 26 and 27 depict quarrels over the proprietorship of women, horses, swords, shields, and heraldic emblems that have circulated among Christian and pagan warriors through reward, loss, and defeat[51]—or via theft by Brunello, a particularly odious Saracen famous, among other things, for stealing a horse out from under its rider, when the latter's attention was distracted:

> '[L]sottil ladrone,
> ch'in un alto pensier l'aveva colto,
> la sella su quattro aste gli suffolse,
> e di sotto il destrier nudo gli tolse.'

> (The subtle thief, catching him in a reverie, had propped the saddle on four stakes and walked the horse out naked from under them.)[52]
>
> (OF 27.84.5–8; W 332)

Like Brunello's dubious achievement, almost all these individual disputes originate in the *Orlando Innamorato*, but Ariosto's genius is to combine them into a single comic stew, which, by the time it comes to the boil in Agramante's camp, threatens by its complexity the authority of Agramante, who must try to adjudicate all the competing claims without offending anyone's honor, including his own—honor, itself a prime object of desire, being the reason why each of the Saracen warriors insists that his quarrel must be settled by the king before any of the others.[53]

The gigantic African monarch Rodomonte and Mandricardo, king of Tartary, are at violent odds over who wins Doralice, a Spanish princess promised to the former but abducted by the latter; Ruggiero and Rodomonte contend over the great steed, Frontino, snatched in the woods by the latter from a messenger who, dispatched by Bradamante, was bringing the animal to the former; Mandricardo and Marfisa—another female knight—prepare to come to blows over the former's proposal to offer the latter to Rodomonte as a substitute for Doralice; and Mandricardo and Ruggiero square off over who has the right to the heraldic emblem of a white eagle that both bear on their shields. As a consequence of this tangle of conflicting claims,

> Moltiplicavan l'ire e le parole
> *quando da questo e quando da quel lato*:
> con Rodomonte e con Ruggier la vuole
> tutto in un tempo Mandricardo irato;

Ruggier, ch'oltraggio sopportar non suole,
non vuol più accordo, anzi litigio e piato.

(Tempers rose, insults volleyed from side to side. Mandricardo, fuming,
wanted to settle scores with Rodomonte and Ruggiero both at once, while
Ruggiero, who was not accustomed to swallowing insults, would tolerate
no truce; brawl and broil is what he wanted. [W 320])

(OF 26.110.1–6, emphasis added; W 320)

And again,

Così, mentre Ruggiero e Mandricardo
e Rodomonte son tutti *sozzopra*,
ch'ognun vuol dimostrarsi più gagliardo
et ai compagni rimaner di sopra,
Marfisa ad acchetarli have riguardo,
e s'affatica, e perde il tempo e l'opra;
che come ne spicca uno e lo ritira,
gli altri duo risalir vede con ira.

(Thus, while Ruggiero, Mandricardo, and Rodomonte were all at sixes
and sevens, each one intent upon proving himself the toughest and overreaching his companions, Marfisa tried to calm them—for this she
strove, spending her time and effort in vain: she would take one of them
and pull him away only to see the other two flare up angrily.)

(OF 26.112, emphasis added; W 320)

It's not hard to imagine how Rossini would have set this scene to music. In fact,
the term "*sozzopra*" appears repeatedly in the *quadro di stupefazione* that ends
act I of *L'Italiana in Algeri*: "va sossopra il mio cervello [My brain is being fried]."

But the stew (and the plot) is to thicken further: a temporary truce brings
all these worthies to the camp of King Agramante, who attempts to establish
a sequence for settling their several quarrels without much cooperation from
them: Marfisa

dice che la pugna vuol finire,
che cominciò col Tartaro; perch'ella
provocata da lui vi fu a venire;
né, per dar loco all'altre, volea quella

un'ora, non che un giorno, differire;
ma d'esser prima fa l'instanzia grande,
ch'alla battaglia il Tartaro domande.

Non men vuol Rodomonte il primo campo
da terminar col suo rival l'impresa. . . .
Mette Ruggier le sue parole a campo,
e dice che patir troppo gli pesa
che Rodomonte il suo destrier gli tenga,
e ch'a pugna con lui prima non venga.

Per più *intricarla* il Tartaro viene anche,
e niega che Ruggiero ad alcun patto
debba l'aquila aver da l'ale bianche;
e d'ira e di furore è così matto,
che vuol, quando dagli altri tre non manche,
combatter tutte le querele a un tratto.

([Marfisa] wanted to finish the duel already started with the Tartar, Mandricardo . . . for she had been provoked into it by him. She refused to give
way to the others or to defer the battle by so much as an hour, let alone a
day; her battle with the Tartar must come first, she insisted. Rodomonte
was no less determined to have the field first to settle matters with his
rival. . . . Ruggiero put in his own claim, saying that Rodomonte's holding onto his steed was more than he could stomach: the first combat must
be his with Rodomonte. To make matters worse, Mandricardo stepped
in: on no account was Ruggiero to keep the eagle with the white wings.
He was so beside himself with rage that he wanted to settle all three quarrels at once.)
(OF 27.41.2–8; 42.1–2, 5–8; 43.1–6, emphasis added; W 327–28)

Agramante's attempted solution, the drawing of lots, only results in further
complications: as Mandricardo and Rodomonte, assigned the first joust, prepare for battle, Gradasso, an Asian monarch helping Mandricardo arm, notices
that the Tartar's sword is the famous Durindana, long possessed by Orlando,
long coveted by Gradasso, and only recently appropriated by Mandricardo from
among the armor that Orlando discarded in the process of becoming, through
thwarted desire for Angelica, a naked madman. Inevitably, Gradasso insists on

fighting Mandricardo for the sword before the latter settles his feud with
Rodomonte over Doralice; Mandricardo enthusiastically agrees, provided that
Rodomonte is willing to defer in this way. But Ruggiero, present for this exchange, and scheduled to fight Mandricardo as the second in the series of bat-
tles, refuses to allow any change in the order established by lot: if Rodomonte
agrees to a postponement, then Gradasso must first fight Ruggiero for the
right to bear the eagle-adorned shield. "Se turbarete voi l'ordine in parte," he
tells Mandricardo angrily,

> "io totalmente turbarollo ancora.
> Io non intendo il mio scudo lasciarte,
> se contra me non lo combatti or ora."

(If you upset the order in part, I shall upset it completely—I do not in-
tend to leave you my escutcheon unless you fight me for it here and now.)
(OF 27.62.1–4; W 330)

Gradasso modestly offers to fight both his challengers,

> "e vengane pel terzo Rodomonte,
> Africa e Spagna e tutto l'uman seme;
> ch'io son per sempremai volger la fronte."

(and Rodomonte too, and Africa, and Spain, and the whole human
race—I'm ready for the lot of you!)   (OF 27.65.2–4; W 330)

In response, Gradasso and Ruggiero now violently disagree who will attack
Mandricardo first, shouting like angry children; "'Va indietro tu!' 'Vavvi pur tu!'
né passo / però tornando, gridan tuttavia ['You get back! No, you get away!' they
kept shouting without moving]" (OF 27.66.5–6; my translation).

Simultaneously a new quarrel flares between Rodomonte and Sacripante,
king of Circassia, who while helping Rodomonte arm notices that the African is
mounted on Frontino, whom Ruggiero considers his but who had formerly (under another name, Frontalatte) been Sacripante's until the notorious thief
Brunello stole it to bestow on Ruggiero. At once declaring his ownership of the
steed, Sacripante says he will allow Rodomonte to ride it in his upcoming duel,
but only on condition that he recognizes that Frontino/Frontalatte is, as we
might say, a loaner horse and rightfully Sacripante's. Of course, Rodomonte

scorns the offer and the claim, and "venner da le parole alle contese, / ai gridi, alle minaccie, alla battaglia [from words they passed to growls, to shouts, to threats, to blows]" (*OF* 27.78.1–2; W 332).

Agramante, "confuso di discordie tante [thoroughly nonplussed by all these discords]" (*OF* 27.81.5; W 332), tries to extinguish the brush fires of contestation fed by blasts of anger, pride, and honor, only to have to deal with yet another outbreak, when Marfisa, having learned that the same Brunello who stole Sacripante's horse had stolen her sword, seizes the miscreant from his place among the spectators and drags him before Agramante, to whom she announces her intention to hang the thief three days hence. The narrator sums up what has clearly become a first-class *quadro di stupefazione*:

> Resta Agramante in tal confusïone
> di questi *intrichi*, che non vede come
> poterli sciorre. . . .
>
> Son cinque cavallier c'han fisso il chiodo
> d'essere i primi a terminar sua lite,
> l'una ne l'altra *aviluppata* in modo,
> che non l'avrebbe Apolline espedite.
>
> (These complications [knots] left Agramante so bewildered, he did not see how he could [untie] resolve them. . . . Now there were five knights all bent upon obtaining precedence for their own quarrel; and each quarrel was so involved with the next that Apollo himself would never have sorted them out.)
>   (*OF* 27.94.5–7, 27.102.1–4, emphasis added; W 333–34)

The narrator records the Saracen king's attempt to make some sense out of the *quadro di stupefazione* in language that assimilates his activity to a paladin's wanderings through the labyrinthine forest and to Ruggiero's earlier, desire-addled attempt to shed his armor so that he can rape Angelica:

> Commincia il re Agramante a *sciorre il nodo*
> de le prime tenzon ch'aveva udite. . . .
>
> Il re Agramante andò per porre accordo
> *di qua di là* più volte *a questo e a quello*,

e *a questo e a quel* più volte diè ricordo
da signor giusto e da fidel fratello.

(Agramant started to untie the knot of the first quarrel explained to
him. . . . The monarch went several times from the one to the other in
order to settle their difference; he appealed several times to each as a just
sovereign and faithful brother.)

(*OF* 27.102.5–6, 103.1–4, emphasis added; W 334–35)

Rather than coming to an orderly conclusion that would reestablish Agramante's authority over his litigious crew, the episode (as is so often the case in the
Furioso) dissolves into new adventures, new wanderings, new frustrations
within the forest of desire.

I mentioned earlier that Orlando's descent into madness comes midway
through the *Furioso*'s 46 cantos; immediately afterward, the narrator, in his
persona of frustrated lover, pulls together in a few lines the main strands of
metaphor that have expressed the poem's view of desire:

[N]on è in somma amor, se non insania,
a giudizio de' savi universale:
e se ben come Orlando ognun non smania,
suo furor mostra a qualch'altro segnale.
E quale è di pazzia segno più espresso
che, per altri voler, *perder se stesso?*

Varii gli effetti son, ma la pazzia
è tutt'una però, che li fa uscire.
Gli è come *una gran selva*, ove la via
conviene a forza, a chi vi va, fallire:
chi su, chi giù, chi qua, chi là travia.

(In sum, love is nothing but madness, according to the universal judgment
of wise men. And even if not everyone goes crazy like Orlando, its fury manifests itself in some other way. And what's a clearer sign of madness than to
lose yourself by desiring someone else? Yes, the effects vary, but the madness that generates them is still the same. It's like a great forest, and all who

enter it are doomed to lose their way, going astray this way and that, hither and yon.)   (*OF* 24.1.3–8, 2.1–5, emphasis added; my translation)

But since, as we know, "il giudizio uman come spesso erra," how can we be sure that this narrator, a self-confessed, near witless victim of desire himself, knows what he's talking about? Indeed, in the octave immediately following, the narrator imagines just such a skeptical, almost Biblical response to his dicta:

Ben mi si potria dir: "Frate, tu vai
l'altrui mostrando, e non vedi il tuo fallo."
Io vi rispondo che comprendo assai,
or che di mente ho lucido intervallo.

("You my friend are preaching to others," someone will tell me, "but you overlook your own failing." The answer is that now, in an interval of lucidity, I understand a great deal.)   (*OF* 24.3.1–4; W 283)

The reader's experience of *OF* can hardly be defined as a lucid interval. Rather, one can argue with some conviction that the confusion and lost sense of direction that define the labyrinthine experience of many of the poem's characters connects it (and them) to the poem's reader, who often feels equally lost in the labyrinthine intricacies of its plots. Indeed, the text's greatest challenge—a challenge we cannot possibly meet—is to keep straight the trajectories and situations of the myriad characters who appear and disappear at the narrator's whim: to remember who they are, where we last heard of them, and what they were doing then.

Even as we confess our inability to control the *Furioso*'s geography, narrative, or dramatis personae, we can perhaps recognize that such a confession with respect to a poem also provides a paradigm for dealing more effectively with experience, indeed with life itself. To admit that we are lost may turn out to be the first, salutary step toward finding, if not a way completely out of the woods, at least some satisfaction (even pleasure) from the denizens and events we encounter along the forest's labyrinthine ways.

NOTES

All Italian quotations of Ariosto are from Segre's edition; English translations are Waldman's (indicated W), with occasional modifications or exceptions, as indicated.

1. Cf. Donato, "'Per selve e boscherecci labirinti,'" 33: "Practically every incident in the vast construct of the *Orlando Furioso* consists of a tale of characters pursuing, with more or less success, the usually elusive object of their desire. The nature of the object matters little; it can be a woman, a helmet, a sword, a horse, or simply glory and renown."

2. "Ariosto is . . . a weaver of echoes from other texts and . . . the very multiplicity of these echoes undermines the priority of a single literary authority or source. . . . If echoes of Virgil point up Ariosto's deliberate deviation from him, other echoes in the poem reveal an awareness of such 'error' as the dynamic of literary history, the way in which poems could be said to challenge the authority, or priority, of earlier poetic models" (Parker, *Inescapable Romance*, 39, 41). See further note 43.

3. An implicit parallel within *OF* to contemporaneous events is the formation, rupture, and re-formation of temporary alliances among the knights and ladies who wander through the great Ariostan forest seeking separated loved ones, embattled allies, or elusive rivals. These constantly shifting arrangements (already a feature of Boiardo's *Orlando Innamorato*—on which see this chapter, page 186—but greatly expanded by Ariosto) suggest the political situation in Italy, where the arrival of foreign powers only exacerbated the notorious transience of alliances among the mutually suspicious peninsular powers; indeed, during the period that saw the composition of the *Furioso*, Ferrara had to change sides nimbly to retain any kind of independence when threatened by Venice, the papacy, or Milan. As Hale writes of the period between 1494 and 1515, "the significance of these 21 years lies in the number of countries that were sucked into the struggle over the dismemberment of Italy, the size of the alliances which were formed for this purpose, and the speed with which they broke up and were reconstituted. . . . While large-scale alliances were by no means novel . . . they had never before been constructed or reconstructed so rapidly" (*Renaissance Europe*, 58–59). The only thing more difficult to summarize than the plot of the *Orlando Furioso* is the record of these shifting real-world alliances. According to Ross in his edition of Boiardo's *Orlando Innamorato*, "There was something headstrong, almost Boiardan, about the way Pope Sixtus IV broke his alliance with Venice during the Ferrara war [of 1482–84] (one thinks of the knights who whimsically switch sides at the siege of Albraca)" (introduction, 16). Cf. Wiggins, *Figures*, 20–21, speaking of Rinaldo's temporary alliance with the Saracen Ferraù to find Angelica in canto 1: "Ariosto's audience among the ruling class of Ferrara must have seen many such alliances come and go in a period when Italy was in the throes of invasion and every petty state was out to protect its interests at any cost. . . . One is reminded of the Machiavellian dictum that princes should enter alliances and maintain them solely as circumstances demand."

   On travel and maps see, e.g., Hale, *Renaissance Europe*, 47–54. In a passage that captures the thrill of exploration (*OF* 10.69–70), Ruggiero, leaving the kingdom of the good enchantress, Logistilla, mounted on the winged steed, the hippogryph, takes a circuitous route in returning to France and his beloved: "Ben che di Ruggier fosse ogni desire / di ritornare a Bradamante presto; / pur, gustato il piacer ch'avea di gire / cercando il mondo, non restò per questo, / ch'alli Pollaccchi, agli Ungari venire / non volesse anco, alli Germani, e al resto / di quella boreale orrida terra.... // ... E spese giorni e mesi in questa via, / sì di veder la terra e il mar gli cale [For all his pressing desire to return to Bradamant, Ruggiero was unwilling to forgo the pleasure of discovering the world, but had perforce to pass by way of the Poles, Hungarians, and Germans and the rest of those bleak northern lands.... Days and months went by as he pursued his way, so eager was he to visit lands and seas]" (*OF* 10.72.1–7, 73.5–6; W 101).

   Cf. William Finnegan, "A Theft in the Libraries: The Case of the Missing Maps," *The New Yorker*, 17 October 2005, 74: "How do new things become imaginable? Looking at Old World maps you can see it happen. Around the turn of the sixteenth century, dragons start to withdraw from the seas west of Europe, and landmasses appear. Continents slowly take on more precise shapes. California is discovered, but remains an island, in the European mind, for two hundred years. Mapmaking, both science and art, is defined by imaginative leaps—some inspired, some ill-advised."

4. Ady, "The Invasions of Italy," 348.
5. Ferrara's university was chartered by Pope Boniface IX in 1391; it had achieved distinction within Italy by Ariosto's day.
6. Singleton, in his translation of Castiglione, *The Book of the Courtier*, 14.
7. Wiggins, *Figures*, 5, calls *OF* "one of the most intricately plotted works in the history of Western literature." Cf. Ross: "Mimicking the form of the *Innamorato* and borrowing the characters Boiardo invented, Ariosto's *Orlando Furioso* privileges Boiardo's text the way Vergil's *Aeneid* subsumes Homer's epics" (Boiardo, *OI*, introduction, 5). For a more provocative, because adversarial, statement of the relationship between *Furioso* and *Innamorato*, see Quint, "The Figure of Atlante," whose thesis is that "the difference between the two poems constitutes Ariosto's subject matter. A set of ironic variations on a theme by Boiardo, the *Furioso* derives a large part of its meaning from a critical reading of the *Innamorato*" (77)—a reading that opposes to the earlier poem's embrace of multitudinous, nonsequential romance adventures that indefinitely defer closure and death Ariosto's increasingly focused movement toward an epic conclusion, entailing the actual or promised deaths of many of the *Furioso*'s protagonists. "Ariosto, by putting an end to both the *Furioso and the Innamorato*, affirms the reality of death. The affirmation is cheerless enough but genuine: mortality is one unassailable fact in a poetic world where everything else human is illusion and madness" (84). Parker dissents from such an understanding of Ariosto's dependence upon epic (*Inescapable Romance*, 44–

53): although *OF* seems to turn away from romance's diversity, "wandering," and deferral of closure in order to move toward an ending dependent upon classical epic—Charlemagne's forces triumph over the pagan armies; Ruggiero kills Rodomonte in a final duel, thus assuring the eventual triumph of the Este lineage—"other, more submerged elements of [Ariosto's] poem tend in a more subversive direction, towards the deconstruction of the very idea of a fiction without 'error,' of an authoritative or privileged literary genre" (*Inescapable Romance*, 38–39).

   See further notes 20 and 43. Carne-Ross, "The One and the Many, Part 2," 203–8, takes a position more starkly opposed to Quint's, arguing forcefully that the last third of *OF* constitutes a betrayal of what has gone before: "The *Orlando Innamorato*, however, is unfinished, hence for his conclusion Ariosto went to the poem that his society honored beyond all others, the *Aeneid*, and began to lead the *Furioso* to a weighty Virgilian full-stop. . . . The mistake, which is radical and disastrous, is to graft on to an open-structured poem a closed-structure ending" (205). He even goes so far as to say that Ariosto "botched the ending" of *OF* (211).

8. Boiardo graphically describes the lightning-flash origin of this desire in *OI* I.i.29–30, where Orlando first lays eyes on Angelica, suddenly arrived at Charlemagne's Pentecost court (cf. French Arthurian romance's use of Pentecost as a time to begin adventures). The paladin gazes at her—"Col cor tremante e con vista cangiata [his heart was trembling, his face reddened]" (I.i.29.5)—and in his thoughts prophetically chastises himself: "Ahi paccio Orlando! . . . Come te lasci a voglia trasportare [Oh, mad Orlando! Look how you're letting your desire run away with you]" (I.i.30.1–2). According to Ross, "Ariosto, indeed, only develops what Boiardo's genius first envisaged, the fun of making Orlando a fool for love" (*OI*, introduction, 7). Ariosto's reimagining of the *Innamorato* seems to me more radical than is suggested by this comment.

9. The parody of Dante's trip to Paradise, guided by Beatrice, to regain the way he had lost in the dark forest of *Inferno* 1, would have been obvious to Ariosto's first readers. See note 42.

10. The frustrated, pleading voice of the narrator, common to medieval love lyrics, is first introduced into chivalric romance in late-twelfth-century French texts such as *Partonopeu de Blois* and *Libeaus desconnus* (The fair unknown one). See Grigsby, "The Narrator in *Partonopeu*"; Haidu, "Realism, Convention," 47–51.

11. At II.xxxi.22 of *OI*, Boiardo refers to Orlando as "il conte furioso," the reference is simply to his fury in battle, parallel to Ariosto's description of Agramante.

12. On this battle, see *OI* II.xxxi, where it is described in detail, though some of those details were ignored by Ariosto in picking up the story. At II.xxxi.42, Boiardo says of the battle, "Ben vi so dir che Carlo oggi tramaza, / E fia sconfitta la corte di Francia [I tell you, this day Charles will founder, / and the French court will be defeated]." He returns to the battle, as promised, describing the

rout of the Christian forces (III.iv.31–37) and their arrival, in disarray, at Paris (III. iv.46–49).

13. Cf. Donato, "'Per selve e boscherecci labirinti,'" 34: "The 'selva oscura' [*OF* 2.68], the 'scuri boschi' [*OF* 43.91], and the 'selve oscure' [*OF* 1.22] are mapped by a 'torta via de l'intricata selva' [*OF* 19.5], a 'strano sentiero' [*OF* 20.104], or 'calli obliqui' [*OF* 1.22] forming a 'labirinto ... di stretti calli' [*OF* 18.192] or 'boscherecci labirinti' [*OF* 13.42] that force the travelers into 'strani viaggi' [*OF* 1.33]." On the image of the labyrinth, see this chapter, pages 198–201.

14. In another example, Sacripante leaves Agramante's camp to overtake Rodomonte to settle a score, but he gets distracted by a drowning woman, whom he rescues. Then his horse won't let him remount but runs away with Sacripante following, and he then can't find the path he was originally on: "Ducento miglia *errò tra piano e monte*, prima che ritrovasse Rodomonte [Two hundred miles he wandered over hill and dale before he came up with Rodomont]" (*OF* 27.115.7–8; W 336).

15. Carne-Ross, "The One and the Many, Part 1," 204, refers to "the heart of the poem, which will show so many people searching through a world governed by a power one may agree to call Fortune for something they will not attain, or not fully, or not in the way they expect."

16. Cf. Ross in his edition of *OI*, introduction, 20, on the similar status of the forest in that work: "The image of Orlando, Ranaldo, and Feraguto chasing an illusion through a dark forest is typical of Boiardo's ellipticality and his lyrical project, which turns Arden Wood into a psychological landscape of desire."

17. Carne-Ross, "The One and the Many, Part 1," 200, 203; "The One and the Many, Part 2," 153, 153n, 161–62, 185–87.

18. According to Ady, "The Invasions of Italy," 366, during Ariosto's lifetime, "Alfonso d'Este had made the Ferrarese guns superior to all others."

19. See especially Carne-Ross, "The One and the Many, Part 1," 199–200; "The One and the Many, Part 2," 187, on "the Wood of Error."

20. Parker, *Inescapable Romance*, chapter 1, "Ariosto," building on the insights of Carne-Ross ("The One and the Many"), explores in brilliant and exhaustive detail not only this connection between physical wandering and moral errancy but also the many ways in which "error" in *OF* points outward to Ariosto's insights in "deliberately exposing the fictional principle of romance, uncovering the anatomy of potentially endless error" (29) and in recognizing "the fact that all fictions 'stray'" (48)—even the epic, championed by Renaissance Aristotelian critics for its "noble" verisimilitude against romance's "vulgar" fantasies. The analyses of Carne-Ross and Parker have repeatedly guided and enlightened me in my thoughts about and appreciation of *OF*; this chapter owes more to them than to any other of the many fine interpreters of the poem from whose works I have profited.

21. This passage has attracted much comment., especially because of the tissue of
Vergilian echoes it contains. See, e.g., Carne-Ross, "The One and the Many,
Part 1," 222–29; Wiggins, *Figures*, 113; Finucci, *The Lady Vanishes*, 130; and Javitch, "The Grafting of Virgilian Epic," 57–58 (who sees Boiardo [*OI* I.ii.22–28]
as well as Vergil [*Aeneid* 8.22–25] underlying the imagery of *OF* 8.71).

22. Carne-Ross, "The One and the Many, Part 1," 199–200: "Intensify the image of
the forest and it becomes, either literally or metaphorically, a labyrinth. . . . [T]
he forest, down whose 'boscherecci labirinti' [*OF* 13.42] so many figures in the
poem are sent wandering is itself a more comprehensive labyrinth image."

23. Ariosto's model is the pathetic tale of the youthful lovers Nisus and Euryalus in
Aeneid 9, imitated also by Statius in the *Thebaid*. On Ariosto's modifications of
Vergil here, see Javitch, "The Grafting of Virgilian Epic," 68–69.

24. Carne-Ross, "The One and the Many, Part 1," 200: "The palace is nowhere explicitly called a labyrinth, but that is undoubtedly what it is." Also see "The One
and the Many, Part 2," 160–63.

25. Luca Ronconi's 1970s piazza spectacle of *OF* ends with all the protagonists trapped
within this castle of illusion, represented by Ronconi as a network of nets and
ropes that drops down from above to entrap each one, while the audience is invited to wander through this labyrinth itself, observing the prisoners as each
pronounces aloud, as a soliloquy, his or her angry lament of loss and frustration.
Donato's discussion of Atlante's palace of illusion ("'Per selve e boscherecci labirinti,'" 45–47) notes that "the particular originality of this place is the incessant circular movement to which the characters are submitted in pursuing in
vain the image of what they take to be the object of their desire" (47; a point also
made by Carne-Ross, "The One and the Many, Part 2," 162). Donato contrasts
the stasis of Ruggiero under Alcina's spell in her palace with this incessant motion, proposing that the two locales and the responses to them "represent two
opposite extremes within desire's problematic" (47).

26. Carne-Ross, "The One and the Many, Part 1," 198, says of this line, "It gives neat,
rememberable expression to something that applies to scene after scene—the
recurrent failure of expectation, the sense that things always turn out in the way
one least expects."

27. Wiggins, *Figures*, 169, notes that *OF* 1.11 is based on both *Inferno* 15.122–23 and
Aeneid 2.379–82.

28. On Angelica see Wiggins, *Figures*, 166–82; Finucci, *The Lady Vanishes*, 107–44.
The last three words of 1.32 are quintessentially defining: "Angelica che fugge,"
Angelica who flees. See Carne-Ross, "The One and the Many, Part 1," 205; Finucci, *The Lady Vanishes*, 111: "Running away in fright from erotic and erratic
pursuits is, after all, Angelica's most recurrent activity." Parker, *Inescapable Romance*, 21, refers to Angelica as Ariosto's "symbol of the erotics of scarcity," while
for Shemek, "That Elusive Object," 118, Angelica's "signature in the poem" is

"withdrawal in flight." Shemek's Lacanian reading of Angelica as the unobtainable, because fantasized, object of desire, accords with and deepens my reading.

29. Cf. Finucci, *The Lady Vanishes*, 112–13: "It is almost axiomatic that whenever Angelica appears, male failure follows. . . . From Rinaldo to Orlando and from Ruggiero to Sacripante, Angelica consistently causes forgetfulness of proper civic and military duties." Here again, Ariosto follows Boiardo's lead, albeit with somewhat darker overtones; cf. Ross, in his edition of *OI*, introduction, 21: "Angelica's presence transforms the world of Charlemagne's crusaders, for everyone falls in love with her—married men; old men with white beards; the most hardened warriors; even Orlando." But cf. Finucci's caveat, *The Lady Vanishes*, 110.

30. Finucci, *The Lady Vanishes*, 113–14, 140–44, sees Angelica's choice and her exit from the romance's plot at its precise midpoint as narratively and ethically determined. Ariosto banishes her "in order to facilitate the narrative movement toward the providentially dynastic, and therefore normal and normative, plot woven around the emblematic figures of Bradamante and Ruggiero" (113), and as an expression of his disapproval. He "reconducts his heroine to the order of his world and takes care narratively to isolate and condemn her independence from codes and rules" (142). Cf. Carne-Ross, "The One and the Many, Part 2," 205.

31. See Carne-Ross, "The One and the Many, Part 1," 206–14, for a sensitive analysis of the poetry and passions of this scene.

32. Based on Catullus, *Poems*, 72–73.

33. Carne-Ross, "The One and the Many, Part 1," 212, refers to this narratorial intervention as "the indulgent amusement of the *homme moyen sensuel* who responds to these high-flown sentiments with a broad guffaw."

34. Wiggins, *Figures*, 130: "Since [Orlando] was never in possession of himself in the first place, his overt madness can amount to nothing more than an intensification of the state he has been in all along. . . . The image of Orlando writhing in that bed, surrounded by walls, windowsills, and door frames inscribed with the intertwined initials of Angelica and Medoro, is one of the most powerful in the *Furioso*. It is the image of someone who has crossed over to the other side of words and who is viewing them from the inside, from the perspective of the experience that produced them, and not with the detached omnipotence of the interpreter." Cf. Carne-Ross's memorable explanation of Orlando's madness: "He is the supreme exponent of single vision in a world where only multiple vision will serve. His mistake, which is not ignoble or ludicrous but disastrous, is to try to confine within the over-simplified terms of his own heroic loyalty a creature [i.e., Angelica] as inconstant as the play of reflected light" ("The One and the Many, Part 2," 192). And again, "The story of Orlando's love for Angelica . . . makes a statement about the mind's desire to impose a false unity on the incorrigible plurality of existence" (201).

35. Donato, "'Per selve e boscherecci labirinti,'" 37, speaks of "a desire [e.g., for Angelica's virginity] whose real quest is the establishing of a difference from one's rivals."

36. On this episode and Polinesso's central role within it, see Wiggins, *Figures*, 21–30, and Hanning, "Sources of Illusion."

37. "Whenever the Courtier chances to be engaged in a skirmish or an action or a battle in the field, or the like, he should discreetly withdraw from the crowd, and do the outstanding and daring things that he has to do in as small a company as possible and in the sight of all the noblest and most respected men in the army, and especially in the presence of and, if possible, before the very eyes of his king or the prince he is serving" (Castiglione, *The Book of the Courtier*, 99).

38. Cf. Wiggins, *Figures*, 27: "In a sense, Rinaldo learns from Dalinda that he was as much off course in his disquisition to the monks as he was in the first place when the storm blew him to Scotland."

39. Wiggins, 33–36, on this episode, interprets Rinaldo's "prudence" as "cynical indifference." His words "should be considered subject to the corrosive irony that we expect of Ariosto." For an excellent discussion that links Rinaldo's movements and behavior in this part of *OF* to the wanderings of Homer's Odysseus and Dante's Ulysses, see Martinez, "Two Odysseys," esp. 25–32.

40. Finucci, "The Masquerade," argues that the novella is really about "men . . . represented as masquerading masculinity, even when they aggressively test its most praised attribute, virility," thereby confirming that "gender is, in the Lacanian sense, a masquerade" (241–42).

41. Parker, *Inescapable Romance*, 30, evokes "a series of episodes so varied that few readers can be expected to remember the plot"; in my understanding of *OF*, those "few readers" are themselves a fable.

42. From my perspective, the best discussion of the lunar episode, its parodic allegories, and other undercuttings of Dante's *Commedia* remains Quint, "Astolfo's Voyage." See, e.g.,: "St. John is meant to recall Dante's Virgil, and the lunar episode caps the extended Dantesque parody of Canto XXXIV. But Ariosto has, in fact, reversed the allegorical principles which structure the *Commedia*. . . . The play of reference, where earthly sign A points to lunar sign B, which merely points back to A, is a closed circle which never opens onto significance beyond itself" (400). See further Parker, *Inescapable Romance*, 44–53, an analysis of this episode largely congruent with Quint's but linking it to the larger question of how to interpret Ariosto's elaborate citations of earlier poetic *auctoritates*, especially Vergil's *Aeneid* and Dante's *Commedia*. As she puts it, "The little allegory of Time and the Poets witnessed by Astolfo on his journey to the Moon . . . is . . . the place where the poem's challenges to the authority of both Dante and Virgil converge. . . . [W]hen the poem does finally take on an epic single-mindedness—with all its appropriate echoes of

Homer and of Virgil—it is only *after* the lunar revelations of the mendacity of these models" (44, 53).

43. Cf. Quint, "Astolfo's Voyage," 403–7, who argues that "Ariosto dismisses the Logos [the initial characterization of Christ in John's Gospel] with a joke, wittily reducing the status of the scriptural Word to the level of the words of his poem' (407). As a context to St. John's explanation to Astolfo about the lies of poets in order to please their patrons, cf. Castiglione, book 4, where it is discussed whether a courtier can tell the truth to his prince, or must instead flatter and lie to gain the prince's confidence in order to lead him to virtue or advance the courtier's own career. Wiggins, *Figures*, 156–57, sees an Ariostan parallel between poets' fictions as described by St. John and the fictions we make of our lives, following false ideals and mistaken goals.

44. Perhaps Ariosto drew inspiration from the *Orlando Innamorato*, whose narrator, in a moment of comic honesty, says to his audience about a particular violent encounter recorded earlier: "Scordato a voi debbe esser de legiero, / Ché io che lo scrissi, lo ramento apena [You've probably forgotten it, since I, who wrote it, almost have]" (*OI* III.v.48.3–4).

45. Cf. Donato, "'Per selve e boscherecci labirinti,'" 58: "I suggest that this animal . . . might be a fitting emblem for Ariosto's narrative enterprise."

46. Cf. Paolo Veronese, "Allegory of Virtue and Vice, or the Choice of Hercules," in the Frick Collection, New York City; Seminal references to this theme are in Cicero, *De officiis*, I.xxxii.118 and III.v.25. On the theme of Hercules' choice, or Hercules at the crossroads, the classic study is Panofsky, *Hercules am Scheidewege*, which has not been translated. See, more briefly, Panofsky, *Renaissance and Renascences in Western Art*, 177–78.

47. I think Wiggins, *Figures*, 73–74, has it right when he avers, "The allegorical contraption erected in cantos 6 and 7 is perhaps the greatest red herring in the *Furioso*. . . . One senses that the allegorical rigamarole of the Alcina episode is an elaborate joke played at the expense of allegory itself."

48. Wiggins, *Figures*, 72–86, offers a psychological, anti-allegorical reading of the episode as a whole.

49. No mere transcription of the text of these finales, with fragments scattered among the many singers on stage, can do justice to their magnificent chaos. Readers unfamiliar with them are strongly counseled to make their acquaintance at least with recorded versions.

50. Donato, "'Per selve e boscherecci labirinti,'" 40, sees this extended episode as the prime "illustration" of the "mechanism" in *OF* whereby "almost anything . . . can be an effective pretext to bring about a relationship of rivalry between any two knights. This rivalry is itself resolved only by the establishment of a difference generated between them through the unleashing of violence controlled in the form of ritualized combat." His lively analysis (40–41) differs from mine in

omitting any notice of the effect of all these rivalries in undermining the authority of the King Agramante.

51. Many of the artifacts over which these Saracen warriors quarrel have their origin, also in *OI*, in the marvelous armor that an Asian king, Galafrone, provides for his son, Argalia, sending him to Charles's court with Argalia's sister, Angelica (*that* Angelica); the latter will seduce Charles's warriors into fighting with her brother, who will magically defeat them and bring them back, prisoners, to Galafrone's fantastic gulag. For a catalog of Argalia's spell-created arms, see *OI* I.xxxviii.

52. This gambit is described in *OI* II.v.39–40.

53. Hoffman, "'Un così valoroso cavalliero,'" 189–92, argues that the episode demonstrates how "Ruggiero and his companions have jettisoned all pretense that their honor consists in helping others and are simply fighting for their own personal prestige. The more they isolate their individual honor as a purely personal quality, the more it contradicts itself: it becomes a moral imperative which can only be fulfilled by physical force and by lucky chance" (192).

REFERENCES

Editions of Primary Sources

Ariosto, Ludovico. *Orlando Furioso*. Trans. Guido Waldman. Oxford: Oxford University Press, 1974.

——. *Orlando Furioso*. A cura di Cesare Segre. Milan: Mondadori, 1976.

Boiardo, Matteo Maria. *Orlando Innamorato*. Trans. Charles Stanley Ross. Berkeley: University of California Press, 1989.

Castiglione, Baldesar. *The Book of the Courtier*. Trans. Charles Singleton. Garden City, N.Y.: Doubleday Anchor, 1959.

Catullus. *Poems*. Ed. and trans. Guy Lee. Oxford: Clarendon, 1990.

Cicero. *De officiis*. With a translation by Walter Miller. 1913. Loeb Classical Library. Reprint, Cambridge, Mass.: Harvard University Press, 2001.

Dante. *The Divine Comedy*. Trans. Charles Singleton. 3 vols. Princeton, N.J.: Princeton University Press, 1970–1975.

Ovid. *The Art of Love and other Poems*. With a translation by J. H. Mozley. 2d ed. Rev. G. P. Goold. Loeb Classical Library. Cambridge, Mass.: Harvard University Press; London: Heinemann, 1985.

——. *Heroides, Amores*. With a translation by Grant Showerman. Rev. G. P. Goold. Loeb Classical Library. Cambridge, Mass.: Harvard University Press, 1977.

——. *Metamorphoses*. With a translation by Frank Justus Miller. 2 vols. Loeb Classical Library. Cambridge, Mass.: Harvard University Press; London: Heinemann, 1968, 1971.

Vergil, *Aeneid*. With a translation by H. Rushton Fairclough. Rev. ed. 2 vols. Loeb Classical Library. Cambridge, Mass.: Harvard University Press; London: Heinemann, 1934.

Secondary Sources

Ady, Cecilia M. "The Invasions of Italy." In *New Cambridge Modern History*, ed. G. R. Potter, 343–67. 1957. Rev. ed. Cambridge: Cambridge University Press, 1961.

Carne-Ross, Donald S. "The One and the Many: A Reading of *Orlando Furioso*, Cantos 1 and 8, Parts 1 and 2." *Arion* 5 (1966): 195–234; *Arion* n.s. 3 (1976): 146–219.

Donato, Eugenio. "'Per selve e boscherecci labirinti': Desire and Narrative Structure in Ariosto's *Orlando Furioso*." In *Literary Theory/Renaissance Texts*, ed. Patricia Parker and David Quint, 33–63. Baltimore, Md.: Johns Hopkins University Press, 1986.

Finucci, Valeria. *The Lady Vanishes: Subjectivity and Representation in Castiglione and Ariosto*. Stanford, Calif.: Stanford University Press, 1992.

——. "The Masquerade of Masculinity: Astolfo and Jocondo in *Orlando Furioso*, Canto 28." In *Renaissance Transactions: Ariosto and Tasso*, ed. Valeria Finucci, 215–44. Durham, N.C.: Duke University Press, 1999.

——. ed., *Renaissance Transactions: Ariosto and Tasso*. Durham, N.C.: Duke University Press, 1999.

Grigsby, J. L. "The Narrator in *Partonopeu de Blois*, *Le Bel Inconnu*, and *Joufroi de Poitiers*." *Romance Philology* 21 (1967–68): 536–43.

Haidu, Peter. "Realism, Convention, Fictionality, and the Theory of Genres in *Le bel inconnu*." *L'Esprit Créatur* 12 (1972): 37–60.

Hale, J. R. *Renaissance Europe, 1490–1520*. The Fontana History of Europe. London: Collins, 1971.

Hanning, Robert W. "Ariosto, Ovid, and the Painters: Mythological *Paragone* in *Orlando Furioso* X and XI." In *Ariosto 1974 in America. Atti del Congresso Ariostesco— Dicembre 1974*, ed. Aldo Scaglione, 99–116. Ravenna: Longo, 1976.

——. "Sources of Illusion: Plot Elements and Their Thematic Uses in Ariosto's Ginevra Episode." *Forum Italicum* 5 (1971): 514–35.

Hoffman, Katherine. "'Un così valoroso cavalliero': Knightly Honor and Artistic Representation in *Orlando Furioso*, Canto 26." In *Renaissance Transactions: Ariosto and Tasso*, ed. Valeria Finucci, 178–212. Durham, N.C.: Duke University Press, 1999.

Javitch, Daniel. "The Grafting of Virgilian Epic in *Orlando Furioso*." In *Renaissance Transactions: Ariosto and Tasso*, ed. Valeria Finucci, 56–76. Durham, N.C.: Duke University Press, 1999.

Martinez, Ronald L. "Two Odysseys: Rinaldo's Po Journey and the Poet's Homecoming in *Orlando Furioso*." In *Renaissance Transactions: Ariosto and Tasso*, ed. Valeria Finucci, 17–55. Durham, N.C.: Duke University Press, 1999.

Panofsky, Erwin. *Hercules am Scheidewege und andere antike Bildstoffe in der neueren Kunst.* Leipzig: Teubner, 1930.

——. *Renaissance and Renascences in Western Art.* New York: Harper, 1960.

Parker, Patricia A. *Inescapable Romance: Studies in the Poetics of a Mode.* Princeton, N.J.: Princeton University Press, 1979.

Quint, David. "Astolfo's Voyage to the Moon." *Yale Italian Studies* 1 (1977): 398–408.

——. "The Figure of Atlante: Ariosto and Boiardo's Poem." *Modern Language Notes* 94 (1979): 77–91.

Shemek, Deanna. "That Elusive Object of Desire: Angelica in the *Orlando Furioso*." *Annali d'Italianistica* 7 (1989): 116–41.

Wiggins, Peter de Sa. *Figures in Ariosto's Tapestry.* Baltimore, Md.: Johns Hopkins University Press, 1986.

IN CONCLUSION
(OR INCONCLUSION)

Perhaps the Ariostan narrator's wonderful, terrifying phrase, "lucido inter-vallo," is the best way to describe the position of comic poets who make fun of those caught in desire's net: they do not claim to be above or outside that complex, troublesome part of the human experience, but through their adherence to a comic vision they are able to shed a little salutary light on it. Perhaps, also, this is the true significance of the outrageous passage in canto 4 of the *Orlando Furioso* asserting the reality of the hippogryph. There is truth, Ariosto may be suggesting, in the outrageous flights of fancy of comic writers—the distorted but revealing truth of the comic mirror, which Ovid holds up to Augustan Rome in the personae of hopeless lover and bogus professor of desire while confessing, in his lucid interval in *Amores* 1.4, that he's fully aware that his elaborate strategies for fooling a husband won't work or, at the conclusion of *Ars amatoria* book 1, that a thousand women require a thousand different ways of wooing. We find such comic truth also in Chaucer, who maps the relationship between social status and experience of desire in *The Parlement of Foules* but has his narrator admit in the lucid interval of the prologue to book 2 of *Troilus and Criseyde* (before that poem turns tragic) that everyone's experience of love is seemingly, if not actually, unique, creating an immense challenge to the love poet—especially one whose understanding of love is literary rather than experiential. To make people laugh about matters as serious and as potentially heart-breaking as crises of desire and authority is no mean feat. The three poets for whom I've attempted in these pages to offer an adequate appreciation deserve our thanks (and applause) for the comic mirrors and monuments to serious play that they have left us.

EPILOGUE

In the course of the introduction, I had occasion to quote some journalistic comments on contemporary comedy. The reader of this book may well be stimulated to ponder parallels between the comic themes, characters, and strategies examined here and the practices of comedy ubiquitous in today's entertainment media: on television (including situation comedies, political satire and parody, stand-up routines as part of late-night revues); in the movies and the theater; at improv and comedy clubs, casino nightclubs, and other venues; and on the Internet (in e-mail chains, on Youtube, and so on).

It's certainly true that with respect to the particular subjects under scrutiny in the following pages, there is abundant continuity between the perspective of an Ovid, a Chaucer, or an Ariosto and the present moment: the foibles and complexities of desire continue to amuse and (perhaps) chasten, as do the overstuffed egos and underdeveloped intelligence or judgment of authority at all levels, domestic, corporate and institutional, or governmental. But the way in which comedy is *produced, consumed,* and *evaluated*—and thus rewarded or (as it were) punished—has completely changed (at least in the United States) from what obtained in premodern (including ancient) Europe, for three reasons: technology, democracy, and capitalism.

Accordingly, although I will not attempt a comparative analysis of premodern and contemporary comic substance and styles—such a task lies outside my competence and, truth to tell, my interests—I will conclude this book by outlining some of the aspects of the production, consumption, and evaluation of comedy in twenty-first-century America that distinguish it from the circumstances in which Ovid, Chaucer, and Ariosto composed and, we assume, performed their comic poetry. My comments will focus on television, since that is the medium, thanks to technology, through which most Americans experience comedy (not only in formats expressly designed for television but also in transmissions of solo acts performed at comedy clubs and casinos).

PRODUCTION

Capitalism has made the production of comedy a business; in response, those who actually produce comedy have become unionized members of a profession. (The exception to this generalization would be comic novelists, writers of short fiction, or satirists and parodists in print; however, their works account for only a tiny minority of comedy produced in the United States today.) For the most part—again, with exceptions—the profession is characterized by a division of labor between performers and writers of comedy, who work together in order to earn a living. (This dichotomy has obtained in the European theater at least since the early modern period; Ariosto wrote plays for the Este court that were acted, of course, by others. But the Elizabethan/Jacobean theater in London seems to have been characterized by a much greater overlap between the two professions, as Shakespeare's acting career testifies.)

The professional comic writer for television is usually part of a staff that writes what has been commissioned by its employer: jokey dialogue as well as comic plots that frequently revolve around desire and authority. (In movies, another technology-based medium, usually only one or two people are given writing credit for a film, but multiple rewrites are nonetheless common, with many people paid but not credited for their work, in accord with arrangements between union and production company.) In addition to skill, versatility—not commitment to a particular social, political, or philosophical perspective—is the hallmark of today's professional comic writer, who can produce what is required of him or her, usually within a very restricted time frame, to fit the needs of performers within a contractually defined situation. The frequent borrowing and recycling of earlier material, as well as the references to contemporaneous events and people, may appear to parallel the appropriation and adaptation of antecedent poetry by the poets discussed in this book (as well as their topical allusions), but the ephemeral nature of the material (especially if the TV show fails) makes such borrowings an incidental, and not quite respectable, part of the overall comic effect, not authorial comments on poetic continuity or responses to political authority.

CONSUMPTION

The sheer multiplicity of venues and media—the technological added to the traditional (i.e., ensemble and solo performance to live audiences)—has a major effect on how comedy is received because it enables the presentation of a broad spectrum of comic productions, aimed at and deemed suitable for divergent target groups. There are, to be sure, a few cases of comic entertainment tailored for inclusiveness, to attract and amuse people of many ages, classes, professions, occupations, religions, ethnicities, and levels of education. More usually, a particular kind of comedy is aimed at "niche groups," often in connection with a specific medium—television, movies, theater, nightclubs—with the result that the potential audience for comedy in America today is in fact a multiplicity of overlapping or mutually exclusive audiences, catered to on the assumption that, in a democracy, every group expects to be entertained in a way aimed at its sensibilities and experience: children, teenagers, men and women (especially in the age cohort twenty-five to fifty), seniors, African Americans, sexual sophisticates, evangelicals, and so forth. Neither Ovid, nor Chaucer, nor Ariosto had to deal with this range of (real or commercially constructed) audiences, although Chaucer, according to a recent critical orthodoxy to which I've alluded, aimed some of his poetry at the royal court of King Richard II of England and some at a circle (or "coterie," in modish parlance) comprising literate, officially connected fellow Londoners. The audiences of all three poets were small and culturally elite; Ariosto, writing after the printing press revolutionized the production and consumption of literature, saw the *Orlando Furioso* through three editions, but even his audience was, by today's publishing standards, small and exclusive.

EVALUATION

Responses to comedy, approving or disapproving, and how they are determined provide the greatest contrast between premodern and contemporary comic writing. For a considerable period, spanning the mid-twentieth century, there was a consensual system of evaluation imposed on the subject matter of radio and television programs and motion pictures. Sponsored by church groups (especially the Catholic Church) and conservative business groups, it sharply limited, among other things, sexual content and reference, thereby denying comedy access to a major component of its dealings with desire. By the late 1960s, however, this system was in the process of breaking down; the creation of a rating system for films and television programs and the rise of cable television, with its self-selected, paying audience, liberated comedy from what must be called puritanical constraints.

Comic production today operates in a fairly complex cultural environment. From one perspective, democracy in action means that in matters of morals and taste there is no one powerful person or group that has the last word. Instead, what various interest groups (be they religious, ethnic, or political in nature) want is in dialectic with what they don't want, what offends them. From yet another perspective, producing comedy in a pluralistic society comes down to what you can get away with—how far you can push the envelope—before running afoul of a group or groups that finds its sensibilities being violated or its beliefs insulted. Interestingly enough, the arbiter in such matters of permissiveness and limitation is not a religious or political body, but an advertiser (in the case of electronic media) or an employer or investor (in the case of theatrical and individual performance, i.e., plays and nightclub routines).

This is because, thanks to capitalism, most forms of comedy appear under not patronage but sponsorship; comic writers and performers are employed and paid in order to make money for others. In such a system, evaluation proceeds along financial, as opposed to moral or political, lines. As long as comedy is profitable, it can be offensive to some; when it ceases to be profitable, it fails (and disappears from view), no matter how praised or popular it may be in certain quarters. Nor is negative evaluation simply a matter of numbers: of course, if no one is watching a TV show, going to see a movie, or coming to a nightclub to see a comedy act, this will mean the end of a program or a career. But since network television, for example, depends on advertising revenue to enable the production of comedy shows, if members of a particular group find a program (or an actor in the cast of a program) offensive, and those members galvanize others in the group (even if they have not seen the program) to boycott the products of the advertising sponsors, and if the boycott begins to affect sales of goods or services, then the sponsors may exert pressure on the network to cancel the show, under threat of withdrawing sponsorship and thus costing the network a good deal of money. In such a case, the fact that, say, three-quarters of the audience enjoys and approves of the show will be outweighed by the sponsor's concerns.

Given the large sums of money involved in these considerations, it is not surprising that (in the case of television and movies, at least) a good deal of time and money is invested by networks, sponsors, and studios in attempting to guess in advance what will make comedy financially successful and to tailor the production of comedy to accord with what are thought to be the tastes of particularly valuable (because wealthy and free-spending) audiences (or, in Hollywoodspeak, "demographics"). This is what I meant by my earlier reference to "commercially constructed" audiences. (One amusing byproduct of shaping comedy to attract a particular audience is the use of the code term "mature audience" to refer to material—bathroom humor, raunchy sex comedy—in fact likely to be most attractive to male adolescents.)

The use of "focus groups"—carefully selected mini-audiences who view programs still in development and offer their opinions on what has amused, bored, or offended them—is a mechanism of what one might call preemptive evaluation, designed to maximize the chances of profit and head off financial disasters. Other ex post facto evaluative techniques adopt a more indirect, and to the uninitiated perhaps more wishful (not to say more bizarre), approach. In an August 2009 article in the *New York Times*, Bill Carter reports on a scheme designed by a network to extract ever-larger payments from advertisers.[1] In a "'multi-engagement study' conducted by Harris Interactive Research," commissioned by the cable television channel, Comedy Central on behalf of "the politically charged versions of late-night humor that [it] offers"—*The Daily Show* with Jon Stewart and *The Colbert Report* with Stephen Colbert—viewers of other late-night talk shows with strong comedy components (including political satire) are offered a checklist of complimentary terms to describe, not Stewart and Colbert but their cohort of fans. By documenting that "more than sixty percent of people answering the survey" described frequent viewers of *The Daily Show* and *The Colbert Report* as "'enthusiastic,' 'friendly,' 'fun,' 'more informed,' 'more intelligent,' 'trustworthy,' 'warm,' and 'witty,'" the study supposedly provides Comedy Central with evidence sufficient to "prove that its late-night viewers are so impassioned about their hosts that their shows offer special value to beleaguered television advertisers looking to ensure that their messages reach truly engaged viewers."

Such engagement (the channel's reasoning apparently goes) will extend not just to the hosts but to the products advertised on their programs. As the executive vice president for advertising sales for MTV Entertainment Networks (Comedy Central's parent company), puts it, "The quality of the viewers is a big determinant in getting advertisers to spend money, especially in tough economic times." That, at least, is the hope: as the article reports, "Comedy Central is trying to use the Harris research to persuade advertisers that its late-night shows deserve a premium price." What really matters, in other words, is not how good the comedy provided for Stewart or Colbert by their writers may be, nor even how devoted their audience may be. Instead, the crucial, game-changing criterion is whether still other television viewers admire that audience and, by confessing their admiration in a multiple-choice survey, provide an advantage to the two comedians' employers in their financial tug-of-war with the sponsors.

Ovid, Chaucer, and Ariosto would doubtless find this situation perplexing, perhaps maddening, but certainly amusing. Whatever else, it clearly epitomizes the distance—cultural even more than chronological—between their comic universe and ours.

NOTE

1. Bill Carter, "Comedy Central Tries to Gauge Passions of Its Viewers," *New York Times*, 26 August 2009.

INDEX

Achilles, 25, 76, 242

Acteon, 63

Actium, battle of, 4, 5

adultery laws, 3, 21–22

advertising, 272

Ady, Cecilia M., 258n18

Aeneid (Vergil), 8, 13, 15, 45, 96n32, 110, 111;
Ariosto's adaptation, 245, 256–57n7,
259nn21, 23, 261n42; Chaucer's
adaptation, 109–15, 125, 171n38

Affrican (*Scipio Africanus*) (*The
Parlement of Foules*), 119

Africa, Thomas, 5, 6, 8

Agamemnon, 76–77

aging process, 43–44

Agramante (*Orlando Furioso*), 187, 189,
190, 246, 247–48; authority of,
threatened, 248–53, 262–63n50

agricultural imagery, *cultus* and, 38–40,
43–44, 84–85, 96n30

Ajax, 44

Alan of Lille, 120–21

Alceste (*Legend of Good Women*), 126,
129–31, 134–38, 140; as adviser,
148–49; antecedent in French
poetry, 146–47; as intercessor,
147–48; multiple significances,
144–50, 173n43; as voice of poet,
149–50

Alcina (*Orlando Furioso*), 208, 240–44

Alcyone (*Book of the Duchess*), 103

allegory, 119–21, 128

Amores (Ovid), xiv, xv, 12–23, 69, 110,
267; Augustus, references to, 15,
22–23; cultural climate, commentary
on, 14–15; Cupid's entourage, 182;
diminution in, 12; *Epigrama ipsius*,
12; generic decorum violated, 15–16;
hopelessness, comic effect of, 17–19;
impotence as theme, 18, 50; jealousy,
19, 30; lost control, images of, 16–17;
narrator-lover, xvi, 12–15; negative
allusion in, 22–23; poetic traditions,
commentary on, 12–14; *recusatio*,
10–11, 15–16, 44, 62, 94n16; shift in
perspective, 20–21

Andromache, 44

Andromeda, 48